Praise for *America's Revolutionary Mind*

"*America's Revolutionary Mind* is a tour de force that vastly expands our understanding of the ideas that launched the American Revolution. Thompson goes beyond the groundbreaking intellectual histories by Bernard Bailyn and Gordon Wood by explaining how Americans came to embrace Enlightenment ideas about human nature, reason, and moral principles in the years preceding 1776. For legal and constitutional scholars, this monograph will become an essential source on the original meaning of fundamental political and legal concepts in the founding era, especially when combined with his forthcoming companion book on the Constitution."

—Adam Mossoff, Professor of Law,
Antonin Scalia Law School, George Mason University

"Thompson's stunning new interpretation of the American Revolution restores the Declaration of Independence as the clearest window into Americans' thoughts regarding their rightful relationship with Great Britain—as well as with each other. Cogent and compelling, his careful analysis of the ideas and events leading to independence amounts to the best intellectual history of the Revolution in years."
—Robert M. S. McDonald, United States Military Academy, author of
Confounding Father: Thomas Jefferson's Image in His Own Time

"*America's Revolutionary Mind* says new things about and takes new approaches to the world of ideas in the era of the American Revolution. Since his *John Adams and the Spirit of Liberty*, C. Bradley Thompson has continued to enlighten us and to challenge conventional wisdom. By using moral philosophy as his book's foundation, Thompson changes our angle of vision on the subject: the Revolution looks different when we adopt his perspective. Beautifully written and formidably documented, his book confronts such predecessors as Bernard Bailyn, Gordon Wood, Henry Steele Commager, and Douglass Adair. Readers who disagree with his argument in whole or in part, particularly with his account of the relationship between the Revolution's intellectual world and the history

of American thought up to our time, must read him nonetheless. This is an essential book."
—R. B. Bernstein, City College of New York, author of *The Education of John Adams* and *Are We to Be a Nation?: The Making of the Constitution*

"Those who believe there is nothing new to say about the American Revolution are in for a great surprise. C. Bradley Thompson shows that an unprecedented change in the method of thinking in the decade preceding Lexington and Concord was the deepest cause of the 'shot heard round the world.' Before it unfolded on the battlefield, the real Revolution was born first in the minds of America's leaders and the public. Thompson's unerring mastery of this period provides us with an education, as important today as it was 250 years ago, into this nation's fundamental principles."
—James Ceaser, Professor of Politics, University of Virginia

"With *America's Revolutionary Mind*, C. Bradley Thompson launches a 'new moral history,' an approach to understanding our past and ourselves that puts front and center the American founders' claim to have grasped and to have acted on the basis of an objective moral reality. Thompson's book, at its heart, challenges us to see the American Revolution as rooted in a moral choice for freedom over slavery, a choice that faces each generation, and, indeed, each one of us."
—Bradford P. Wilson, Executive Director of the James Madison Program and Lecturer in Politics, Princeton University

AMERICA'S
REVOLUTIONARY
MIND

AMERICA'S REVOLUTIONARY MIND

A Moral History of
the American Revolution
and the Declaration
That Defined It

C. BRADLEY THOMPSON

Encounter
BOOKS

New York • London

First American edition published in 2019 by Encounter Books, an activity of Encounter for Culture and Education, Inc., a nonprofit, tax exempt corporation. Encounter Books website address: www.encounterbooks.com

Manufactured in the United States and printed on acid-free paper. The paper used in this publication meets the minimum requirements of ANSI/NISO Z39.48–1992 (R 1997) (*Permanence of Paper*).

FIRST AMERICAN EDITION

LIBRARY OF CONGRESS CATALOGING-IN-PUBLICATION DATA

Names: Thompson, C. Bradley, author.
Title: America's revolutionary mind : a moral history of the American Revolution and the Declaration that defined it / by C. Bradley Thompson.
Description: New York : Encounter Books, 2019. |
Includes bibliographica references and index.
Identifiers: LCCN 2019014130 (print) | LCCN 2019981311 (ebook) | ISBN 9781641770668 (hardcover : alk. paper) | ISBN 9781641770675 (ebook)
Subjects: LCSH: Political science—United States—History—18th century. |
United States. Declaration of Independence. |
United States—History—Revolution, 1775–1783—Moral and ethical aspects.
Classification: LCC JA84.U5 T478 2019 (print) | LCC JA84.U5 (ebook) |
DDC 973.3/1—dc23
LC record available at https://lccn.loc.gov/2019014130
LC ebook record available at https://lccn.loc.gov/2019981311

To all future students of the American Revolution

CONTENTS

PREFACE

This is the first of what—I hope—will be a two-volume study of the moral, political, and constitutional principles of America's Revolutionary and founding periods. The natural sequel to *America's Revolutionary Mind* would be *America's Constitutional Mind.* The relationship between the current and the proposed volume is virtually identical to the connection that Abraham Lincoln saw between the Declaration of Independence and the Constitution.

In January 1861, Lincoln wrote in an unpublished fragment that the American experiment in self-government had a "philosophical cause." The prosperity of the United States (the effect) was due in no small part to the Constitution and the Union, but the Constitution and the Union were just the political and constitutional expressions of a deeper moral principle—"the principle of 'Liberty to all,'" which in turn was housed in the Declaration of Independence. For Lincoln, there was an intimate and necessary connection between the Declaration and the Constitution. Paraphrasing Proverbs (25:11), Lincoln asserted that the Declaration's liberty principle "was *the* word, '*fitly spoken*' which has proved an 'apple of gold' to us." The Constitution was the "*picture* of *silver*" that "framed" the Declaration.[1] America's two great founding documents are each incomplete without the other. The present volume and its sequel will form a similar kind of relationship.

Although it forms a part of a larger whole, the present work stands on its own two feet. It has its own unity of purpose and a unique history. Readers of *America's Revolutionary Mind* may appreciate the story of its genesis. In June 2016, I was actually close to finishing *America's Constitutional Mind*, with no idea or intention of writing a prequel. The story I was then telling required a chapter on the natural-rights foundation of American constitutionalism. As I began the research on this particular chapter, I read a recently published and much-acclaimed book on the Declaration of Independence. Not only did I find that book's interpretation seriously flawed, but I also found its tone toward the Declaration and its readers condescending and insulting. I thought the Declaration deserved better. Then and there, I decided to write my own book on the subject.

Over the course of the year in which I wrote this book, my original idea expanded significantly from a narrowly focused and relatively short monograph on the Declaration to something much more ambitious and capacious. Almost from the beginning, I came to see that there was a much bigger and more important story to be told not just about the Declaration but about the nature and meaning of the Revolution itself. In something of an epiphany, I came to realize how little is actually known about the Revolution's deepest causes and consequences.

This may strike readers as odd given that probably more books and articles have been written on the American Revolution than any other topic in American history. There are countless intellectual, political, economic, social, military, and diplomatic histories of the Revolutionary era, just as there are innumerable biographies of the leading revolutionaries. What is surprising, however, is that there has not been a major reinterpretation of the Revolution's intellectual causes and consequences since the publication of Bernard Bailyn's *The Ideological Origins of the American Revolution* (1967) and Gordon S. Wood's *The Creation of the American Republic, 1776–1787* (1969). For five decades, these two books, noted for their originality and explanatory power, have cast a long shadow over scholarship on the American Revolution, profoundly shaping its nature and direction. As a result, original scholarship on the Revolution, the kind that fundamentally reorients the way we think about the causes of this transformative event, has not advanced very much in that time. Surely, though, it should not remain the case that the most influential books on the American Revolution were written in the 1960s.

What is most needed today is a book that challenges us to rethink the deepest causes and consequences of the American Revolution, one that will allow us to see this world-changing event in a new light. I have attempted to do that with *America's Revolutionary Mind*.

On a more personal level, I have been motivated to write this book for a second reason: to complete and go beyond the narrative first told by my former teachers, Bailyn and Wood. During my days in graduate school, I had the good fortune to attend classes given by these two great historians of the American Revolution, who inspired me to search for the underlying causes and hitherto unseen patterns of thought and action in that seminal event. It was once said of John Adams that he "saw large subjects largely." The story I tell here is different from those of Bailyn and Wood, but it is informed by their ambition to see large subjects largely. Following in their footsteps, I have attempted to write a book that is original, comprehensive, and transformative. *America's Revolutionary Mind* provides both a narrative history and a theoretical analysis of the principal ideas and modes of reasoning that shaped the contours of the American mind during the Revolutionary period.

✷ ✷ ✷

Writing the acknowledgments for a book is the best part of the authoring experience because it means you're done and because you get to thank all of the people who have assisted and supported your work.

When I was a young boy living in Ontario, Canada, I read a children's book that changed my life. It was *The How and Why Wonder Book of the American Revolution* by Felix Sutton, and when I read it I knew that I was an American born in the wrong country. That was the moment, some fifty years ago now, when I fell in love with the story of the American Revolution and the principles of the Declaration of Independence. In many ways, *America's Revolutionary Mind* is the fulfillment of a lifelong love affair with this country and its history. My first thanks go to Mr. Felix Sutton, a man whom I never met, and who died in 1977.

Needless to say, I have incurred many other debts along the way.

My agent, Don Fehr, pushed me hard and never gave up on the project. For that, I am thankful and appreciative. Roger Kimball, the legendary publisher of Encounter Books, took a chance on this project and inspired me with his very high standards of scholarly and popular writing.

I am grateful to Colin Pearce, Kimberly Hurd Hale, Josh King, Lori

Molinari, and Michael Zuckert for reading individual chapters of this book. I am particularly thankful for the superb editing of the manuscript by Ron Pisaturo and Robert Bidinotto. Each improved the manuscript in significant ways. I also owe a special note of thanks to Erin Luckett of Readex for giving me access to the online version of Early American Newspapers.

I am especially indebted and grateful to my friends Carl Barney and John Allison, who have supported my work for many years. I am also thankful for the longstanding friendship of Brendan McConville, who has never supported my work other than to be brutally honest with me and to share his encyclopedic knowledge of early American history.

It is with particular pleasure and much pride that I thank the students of my Political Thought of the American Founding class at Clemson University, who seemingly tolerated the fact that I could never end class on time. The ideas presented in this book were first tried out on my Clemson students over the course of several years.

I have dedicated this book to all future students of the American Revolution. I wrote it with them always in the back of my mind and with the hope that I might leave them something useful.

Per usual, I owe the most to my wife, Sidney, not only for her editorial acumen but for letting me chase my dreams. She told me several years ago that if I did not soon finish the long-awaited book on constitutionalism, I should pack my bags. A few weeks later, I decided to take a year-long detour and write a book on the philosophy of the Declaration of Independence. I hope she doesn't notice! Now it's back to the constitutionalism book.

INTRODUCTION

"By what means, this great and important Alteration
in the religious, Moral, political and Social Character of
the People of thirteen Colonies, all distinct, unconnected
and independent of each other, was begun, pursued and
accomplished, it is surely interesting to Humanity to
investigate, and perpetuate to Posterity."

—JOHN ADAMS, 1818

*T*he American Revolution is the most important event in American history. It announced the birth of a new nation, defined the noblest ideals and aspirations of the American people, created written constitutions and republican governments, and reformed laws and remodeled institutions. According to James Madison, America's revolutionary leaders "accomplished a revolution which has no parallel in the annals of human society: They reared the fabrics of governments which have no model on the face of the globe."[1]

This transformative event created a new kind of society unlike any other that had ever existed. Our present-day beliefs in equality, freedom, rights, justice, the rule of law, and constitutionalism were born during the Revolutionary era and expressed in its noblest symbol, the Declaration of Independence. In countless ways, the world in which we live was shaped by the ideas and actions of 1776.

This is why Americans are endlessly fascinated by the history of their Revolution. To meet popular demand, successive generations of scholars going back to the event itself have been inspired to research and write on this momentous event, which raises the obvious question: is there anything original left to say about the American Revolution and its causes? The answer is, in my view, unequivocally yes. Historians have only scratched the surface, I now believe, in their understanding of its nature and meaning. As a longtime scholar of the American Revolution, I only recently came to this startling—if not controversial—conclusion after reading and reflecting on four remarkable statements about the Revolution and its causes by four of its most articulate spokesmen: John Adams, Thomas Paine, Joel Barlow, and Thomas Jefferson.

During his retirement years, John Adams thought a good deal about the origin and meaning of the American Revolution. In a fascinating letter written to Thomas Jefferson in 1815, he asked a simple question: "What do we mean by the Revolution?" Surely not the war, he answered rhetorically. "That was no part of the Revolution," he declared. Rather, the war "was only an *Effect* and *Consequence*" of the Revolution. The true Revolution, he continued, "*was in the Minds of the People*, and this was effected…in the course of fifteen years before a drop of blood was shed at Lexington." Three years later, Adams suggested again that the "*real* American Revolution" was represented by a "radical change in the principles, opinions, sentiments, and affections" of the American people. The former president was suggesting in these letters that the root cause of the American Revolution was to be found in a radical change in the colonists' moral reasoning and political principles. For Adams, something important and transformative happened in the inner lives of people's minds, beliefs, and sensibilities in the years just before and just after the passage of the Stamp Act. Adams's comments raise obvious questions: how and why was the American mind revolutionized in the years before 1776, and, more particularly, what new moral ideas defined America's emerging revolutionary consciousness? Adams considered these questions "surely interesting to humanity to investigate, and perpetuate to posterity."[2]

Like Adams, Thomas Paine also understood that a revolutionary transformation had taken place in the American consciousness in the years leading up to 1776. As Paine put it so strikingly in *Common Sense*, "a new æra for politics is struck; a *new method of thinking* hath arisen."[3] He described this "new method of thinking" in an extraordinary letter to the French *philosophe* the Abbé Raynal. Paine told the French cleric that the American "style and manner of thinking ha[d] undergone a revolution, more extraordinary than the political revolution of the country." "We see with other eyes," he explained, "we hear with other ears; and think with other thoughts, than those we formerly used." This revolution of the mind transformed the colonists into "another people."[4] Paine identified the precise meaning of that revolution when he wrote in *Rights of Man*: "the Independence of

America" was "accompanied by a revolution in the principles and practice of governments." The Americans had done something, he continued, that no other people in history had ever achieved: they founded their new governments "on a *moral theory...on the indefeasible, hereditary rights of man*."[5] The discovery, development, and adoption of that "moral theory" by the American people in the years before 1776 is the embodiment of the "real" revolution described by Adams.

But what exactly was this "new method of thinking" and the new "moral theory" associated with the American Revolution? How and why did colonial Americans develop a "moral theory" about the "indefeasible, hereditary rights of man"?

In 1792, Joel Barlow, the American poet, diplomat, and politician, announced in his *Advice to the Privileged Orders, in the Several States of Europe, Resulting from the Necessity and Propriety of a General Revolution in the Principle of Government*, one of the first American books on the French Revolution, that the greatest difference between free and unfree peoples had nothing to do with an "original capacity of the mind" but was instead connected to a certain "*habit of thinking*." Man's "second nature" as shaped by ideas and experience, he continued, was "the *only* foundation" on which to build a free and just society. Men will become free and equal when they think themselves so, and they will likewise obey rulers if they think them genuinely superior in some way. Men accept what they believe, said Barlow, which means that by focusing on the "astonishing effects that are wrought in the world by the *habit of thinking*"[6] it might be possible to change a whole political system by changing the way men think.

This is precisely what happened in Britain's American colonies in the years after 1761. Under the pressure of events first precipitated by the Stamp Act, the colonists developed certain moral and political principles during the years of the imperial crisis that became a "habit of thinking" by the mid-1770s. In the New World, Barlow claimed, "the science of liberty is universally understood, felt and practiced," which means the Americans' "deep-rooted and inveterate habit of thinking is, that *all men are equal in their rights*."[7] The habit of thinking developed by the colonists after the end of the Seven Years' War was rooted in that "science of liberty," a notion that sums up perfectly both the method of reasoning and the substance of the American mind as it came to exist in 1776.

Finally, on May 8, 1825, Thomas Jefferson wrote a now well-known letter to Henry Lee in which he described the Declaration of Independence as "an expression of the American mind."[8] These are the most important words ever written about the Declaration, and they provide an important key to unlocking its deepest meaning. Through this felicitous phrase, the Declaration can now be seen as the fulfillment and symbol of Adams's "real" revolution, the revolution that occurred in the minds of the American people. The Declaration brought together ideas and assumptions that had hitherto been incomplete, unclear, or discordant during the years of the imperial crisis. Understanding how and why Jefferson and his fellow revolutionaries discovered, developed, and understood the Declaration's self-evident truths opens a new pathway to understanding the American Revolution itself.

After thinking about these extraordinary statements by Adams, Paine, Barlow, and Jefferson, I was struck by how little is actually known about the most salient causes of the American Revolution. Previous generations of scholars have neglected almost entirely what many leading eighteenth-century Americans considered the generative mainspring of the Revolution, namely, its *moral* causes. When we stitch together Adams's claim that the "*real*" American Revolution was in the "minds of the People," Paine's argument that the Revolution was based on a new "*moral theory*," Barlow's announcement that the moral principle of equal rights had become a "*habit of thinking*" in the American colonies, and Jefferson's description of the Declaration as an "expression of the American mind," we have important clues to help us uncover the Revolution's deepest causes and consequences and hence its ultimate meaning.

✴   ✴   ✴

The purpose of *America's Revolutionary Mind* is twofold: first, to elucidate the logic, principles, and significance of the Declaration of Independence as the embodiment of the American mind; and, second, to shed light on what John Adams called the *real* American Revolution—that is, the *moral* revolution that occurred in the minds of the people in the fifteen years before what Ralph Waldo Emerson, in his "Concord Hymn" (1837), famously called the "shot heard round the world."

The Declaration of Independence is used here as an ideological road map by which to chart the intellectual and moral terrain traveled by

American revolutionaries as they searched for new moral principles to deal with the changed political circumstances of the 1760s and early 1770s. This volume identifies and analyzes the modes of reasoning, the habits of thinking, the patterns of thought, and the new moral and political principles that served American revolutionaries, first in their intellectual battle with Great Britain *before* 1776, and then in their attempt to create new revolutionary societies *after* 1776.

In pursuing this project, I have reconstructed what amounts to a near-unified system of thought—what Jefferson called an American mind, or what I call America's revolutionary mind. To speak of an American mind suggests that certain ideas and modes of reasoning were representative of a distinct intellectual culture. Broadly defined, it refers to the modes of reasoning and the unique system of moral and political principles discovered, developed, and then implemented by American revolutionaries in the fifteen years on each side of 1776. This book traces the fundamental shift in ideas and values that occurred during the Revolutionary era that culminated in the development of and fealty to a common philosophy that was expressed in the Declaration and launched with the words, "We hold these truths to be self-evident."

There has probably never been another time in our history when the life of the American mind was so alive, so penetrating, and so innovative as it was during the Revolutionary period. While the formation of the American mind occurred with remarkable speed, it did not happen instantaneously. Enlightenment and Radical Whig moral and political ideas had been seeping into the American consciousness for several decades prior to the 1760s, but they became living concerns to the colonists only during the years of the imperial crisis. The American mind was forged when events precipitated first a political crisis and then a crisis of conscience among American colonists, which in turn forced them to reevaluate their deepest moral, political, and constitutional principles. The passage of the Sugar, Stamp, and Declaratory Acts in 1764, 1765, and 1766 challenged these New World provincials not only to rethink the extent of Parliament's authority in America and the nature of the British constitution but also to launch a searching investigation into the nature, source, and meaning of certain basic moral principles (e.g., equality, liberty, rights, virtue, happiness, justice, consent, and sovereignty).

The colonists took their traditionally English moral, political, and constitutional assumptions into new territories of moral thought and practice where they developed new ways of thinking about a just and free society. Through this process they confronted and worked out the ambiguities and inconsistencies of their inherited thought, thereby forging distinctly American-style ideas and institutions. These new moral and political principles led the Americans eventually toward self-rule and the creation of a new nation unlike anything known before.

✷   ✷   ✷

This book, however, is not simply a work of political theory or an old-fashioned intellectual history of the Revolution. It also attempts to reconcile theory and practice by examining how and why American revolutionaries guided their actions via moral principles. It is therefore concerned with *motives* as the mediating force between ideas and actions. To that end, I have developed a new approach to history writing that I call the new moral history.[9]

Broadly speaking, the new moral history employed in this book is concerned with the nature of causation and agency in the course of human events. It attempts to explain behavior in given historical contexts by showing the relationship between *principles* and *practice* in the day-to-day actions and interactions of men and women in a social context. This approach is not simply a history of the development of certain moral theories, although it can be that in part. Its primary goal is to examine the intersection between moral thought and moral action, between what people say and what they do (or don't do). The new moral history studies the what, why, how, and when of moral reasoning, and then it looks for the connections with the what, why, how, and when of moral action. It studies the modes of reasoning and ideas used by individual men and women as they evaluated, judged, and dealt with their social reality, and it examines the alternatives confronted by individuals and groups of individuals as they made decisions about what to do or how to act. It emphasizes thinking, judging, choosing, and acting individuals over large-scale social processes moved by unseen forces.

The new moral history begins with certain assumptions about human nature: first, that individuals are the primary unit of moral value; second, that human nature is knowable and sometimes predictable; third, that man's faculty of reason can know cause-and-effect relationships in nature and human nature; fourth, that individuals are confronted every day with choices, and that they have the free will to choose between alternatives; fifth, that freely thinking (rationally and irrationally) and freely acting (morally and immorally) individuals are capable of making decisions and acting on them; sixth, that purposive human agents cause events to happen; and finally, that human thought and action can have intended and unintended consequences. This view of human nature suggests that individuals are morally responsible for their decisions and actions and the consequences that follow therefrom. Thus the new moral history puts the thinking back into ideas, the judgment back into intentions, and the volition back into actions.

Doing history in this way has the benefit of being compatible with how eighteenth-century Americans saw the nature of reality, truth, causality, human nature, and the processes of historical change. All American revolutionaries believed that there are moral and political truths—truths absolute, certain, universal, permanent, and immutable—that can be known by reason and acted on. Such was the purpose of the Declaration of Independence—to declare certain self-evident truths thought to be accessible to all men everywhere. In *Federalist* No. 31, Alexander Hamilton appealed to "certain primary truths, or first principles, upon which all subsequent reasoning must depend." Hamilton and his fellow Americans assumed that human reason was fallible, but they also assumed that the discovery of truth about the most important matters was possible and that the grounding of principles on axiomatic truths "commands the assent of the mind."[10] These truths, because they transcended their immediate historical situation, not only could be assented to by other Americans but could be understood by all men everywhere. The revolutionary generation viewed these truths as objectively true and not simply as historically conditioned. It is not possible to understand the moral and political thought of America's revolutionary generation without knowing and respecting this fact.

Eighteenth-century Americans also assumed that society is made up of autonomous moral agents who define the course of events. Understanding men's moral principles, their modes of reasoning, their motives, their options, their choices, and their actions was the key to understanding the role of causation in human action and history. They believed that motives explain actions, that moral principles explain motives, and that moral reasoning explains moral principles. And if events are the direct consequence of individual (and group) moral principles, decisions, intentions, and actions, then it is imperative for historians to study those principles, decisions, intentions, and actions, which, if shared by many or most of the individuals in a society, shape that society's general character. In this way, then, a culture with its unique manners and mores reflects the moral character of individuals writ large, and historians should be able to discern patterns of moral belief and action that may reveal the existence of a common moral order.[11] Hence the history of human events is, for better or worse, the history of men and women acting according to a conception of what they think is good, right, just, and true.

*   *   *

In the America of the late-colonial and early-Revolutionary period, scholars can observe the genesis, development, and architecture of America's revolutionary mind. It was a time and place relatively isolated geographically, relatively simple socially, and relatively homogeneous philosophically. The thirty-year period between 1760 and 1790 supplies an ideal setting in which to observe how an imported and abstract system of ideas was adapted to unique local circumstances and then revolutionized during a period of political crisis. This testing ground offers a rare opportunity to extract certain generalizations about the relation of thought to experience and vice versa. The Declaration's universe of ideas—comprehensive, consistent, and didactic—stood, without serious modification, for the remainder of the eighteenth century and well into the nineteenth.

In order to access the deepest recesses of America's revolutionary mind, I have followed the advice of John Adams and Thomas Jefferson. Over two hundred years ago, Adams recommended that all future scholars of the American Revolution "undertake the laborious...task, of searching and collecting all the records, pamphlets, newspapers, and even handbills, which in any way contributed to change the temper and views of the people, and compose them into an independent nation."[12] Likewise, Jefferson advised that "the true history of the revoln, it's secret springs private passions, their influence and effect on the public transactions can never be truly known" unless historians have access to the "hoards of private correspdnce" of the revolutionary generation.[13]

Following Jefferson's advice, I have read and used virtually all of the official documents of the Revolutionary period (i.e., laws, legislative debates, petitions, resolutions, declarations, remonstrances, circular letters, and constitutions) as well as the major and minor treatises, pamphlets, essays, sermons, speeches, diaries, and newspaper articles, some of which have never been seen or used by scholars before. I have also read hundreds of private letters penned by the Revolution's leading thinkers and statesmen. Finally, the lens through which I examine both the Declaration and the Revolution is broadened to include not only the best-known and most influential revolutionaries, such as Benjamin Franklin, George Washington, John Adams, Thomas Jefferson, James Madison, and Alexander Hamilton, but also somewhat forgotten or neglected figures, such as James Otis, Patrick Henry, John Dickinson, and Samuel Adams, as well as scores of anonymous or unknown revolutionaries from New Hampshire to Georgia and from the Atlantic seaboard to the Appalachian Mountains. This book therefore represents an extended archeological excavation of America's revolutionary mind.

CHAPTER 1

The Enlightenment and the Declaration of Independence

"He that would seriously set upon the search of truth,
ought in the first place to prepare his mind with a love of
it....There is nobody in the commonwealth of learning, who
does not profess himself a lover of truth; and there is
not a rational creature that would not take it amiss
to be thought otherwise of."

—JOHN LOCKE, *An Essay Concerning
Human Understanding* (IV.xix.1)

On June 24, 1826, ten days before he died, Thomas Jefferson penned a letter in which he established the context and significance of the Declaration of Independence. "May it be to the world," he wrote to Roger C. Weightman, "what I believe it will be, (to some parts sooner, to others later, but finally to all,) the signal of arousing men to burst the chains under which monkish ignorance and superstition had persuaded them to bind themselves, and to assume the blessings and security of self-government."[1]

The American Revolution and the Declaration that expressed it were the existential embodiment of the Enlightenment's highest ideals. They restored to mankind, Jefferson implied, "the free right to the unbounded exercise of reason and freedom of opinion." And with the "general spread of the light of science" in the eighteenth century, the veil of ignorance that had covered men's eyes was lifted. The light of reason opened men's eyes to the "rights of man" and revealed the "palpable truth, that the mass of mankind has not been born with saddles on their backs, nor a favored few booted and spurred, ready to ride them legitimately, by the grace of God."[2] Understanding the Enlightenment's core tenets is therefore a precondition for understanding the principles of the Declaration and the American Revolution.

The Enlightenment represented an era of philosophic and scientific thinking that provided a new way to see the world and man's place in it. It stood for the ability of the reasoning mind to unlock nature's secrets, and it inspired men to sweep aside superstition, mysticism, prejudice, and the brutalities of the past. The Enlightenment represented, in the words of the eighteenth-century Scottish philosopher Thomas Reid, the "dawn of light"; it "opened the way to future discoveries"; and it "removed an infinite deal of rust and rubbish, collected in the ages of scholastic sophistry, which had obstructed the way."[3] The new learning generated by the Enlightenment was potentially available to all men—not just to philosophers, priests, and kings—if only each would use the proper method of acquiring and using knowledge: the method of right reason. As a result, there was an explosion of new knowledge with discoveries in physics, astronomy, mathematics, biology, geology, botany, medicine, navigation, mechanics, architecture, morality, and politics.[4] With the light of reason illuminating the world, nature's secrets could be revealed to man, and then mastered and conquered in order to eliminate prejudice, poverty, sickness, and oppression.

The Age of Enlightenment produced several generations of world-class scientists and philosophers, but in a well-known 1789 letter Thomas Jefferson identified the "three greatest men that have ever lived, without any exception" as Francis Bacon, Isaac Newton, and John Locke. These three intellectual giants were, in Jefferson's mind, the embodiment of the Enlightenment. Bacon was best known for his *Novum Organum* (1620), Newton for his *Philosophiæ Naturalis Principia Mathematica* (1687), and Locke for two philosophic treatises, the *Essay Concerning Human Understanding* (1689) and the *Second Treatise of Government* (1689). Jefferson credited this philosophic holy trinity with "having laid the foundation of those superstructures which have been raised in the Physical and Moral sciences."[5]

John Adams similarly identified Bacon, Newton, and Locke as the three thinkers most important to his intellectual development. Their importance lay in providing him with a proper method for thinking. During his undergraduate days at Harvard, the young man was introduced to the new philosophic rationalism associated with the modern revolution in the natural sciences by John Winthrop, the Hollis Professor of Mathematics and Natural Philosophy. Winthrop's lectures in "Experimental Phylosophy" explained the law-like regularity of the Newtonian conception of nature. On April 9, 1754, Adams recorded in his diary that "Sir Isaac Newtons three laws of nature" and their application to planetary motion were "proved and illustrated" in Winthrop's lecture. Years later, he would say that his training in the sciences gave him a "degree of Patience of Investigation, which I might not otherwise have obtained."[6] Adams soon realized that he could apply the new scientific method to the study of man and society. The concrete and detailed observations of human nature, the sharp and vivid descriptions of those around him, the acute dissection of motives and actions, and the painstaking accumulation and cataloguing of historical actors that fill the diary attest to the importance of Winthrop's method for Adams's intellectual development.

In at least four places in his early diary and in one important letter from 1760, Adams copied or paraphrased long passages from Locke's *Essay Concerning Human Understanding*.[7] These passages and others of the period show him embracing a Baconian-Newtonian conception of nature as understood by Lockean epistemology. "In Metaphysics," he wrote, "Mr. Locke, directed by my Lord Bacon, has steered his Course into the unenlightened Regions of the human Mind." Dramatically, Adams compared Locke to Columbus: he had discovered a "new World." This newfound epistemological continent was full of dangers and possibilities: it had "unwholsome Weeds," "unprofitable Brambles," and "motly Savages," but it also had "wholsome fruits and flowers," "useful Trees," and "civilized Inhabitants." Locke, Adams wrote, taught mankind how to excise the weeds and to cultivate the fruits of the human mind. And just as Locke cleared man's field of vision, so too had discoveries by natural philosophers such as Bacon and Newton "done Honour to the human Understanding."[8] Thus the modern world had advanced far beyond the high culture of the classical world in fields such as philosophy, mathematics, and astronomy.

James Wilson, a signer of the Declaration of Independence and the United States Constitution, likewise rated Bacon, Newton, and Locke as the three great minds who ushered in the Age of Enlightenment. In his

Lectures on Law, which he delivered while serving as an associate justice of the United States Supreme Court, Wilson identified the substance of the great discoveries made by Bacon and Newton:

> Till within these two hundred years, natural philosophy was in the same fluctuating state with the other sciences. Every new system pulled up the old one by the roots. The great Lord Bacon first marked out the only foundation, on which natural philosophy could be built. His celebrated successour, Sir Isaac Newton, gave the first and noblest examples of that chaste induction, of which his guide in the principles of science could only delineate the theory. He reduced the principles of Lord Bacon into a few axioms, which he calls "regulæ philosophandi,"—rules of philosophising. From these, together with the phenomena observed by the senses, which he likewise assumes as first principles, he deduces, by strict reasoning, the propositions of his philosophy; and, in this manner, has erected an edifice, which stands immovable upon the basis of first and self-evident principles. This edifice has been enlarged by the accession of new discoveries, made since his time; but it has not been subjected to alterations in the plan.

Wilson wrote no less enthusiastically about Locke and his connection to Newton, which means to Bacon as well: "The doctrines of Mr. Locke have been received, not only in England, but in many other parts of Europe, with unbounded applause; and to his theory of the human understanding the same kind of respect and deference has been paid, as to the discoveries of Sir Isaac Newton in the natural world."[9]

Jefferson's, Adams's, and Wilson's ranking of the world's greatest minds is our entry point into the Age of Enlightenment. The core ideas that grew out of the Enlightenment launched by Bacon, Newton, and Locke can be summed up in three words: nature, reason, and rights. These three concepts provide a systemic philosophic framework (i.e., a metaphysics, an epistemology, and an ethics) by which to examine the Enlightenment and its relationship to the formation of the American revolutionary mind. These organizing concepts also map directly onto the structure of the Declaration.

ENLIGHTENMENT METAPHYSICS: NATURE

Enlightenment philosophers and scientists reconceptualized the way modern man thought about nature.[10] They discarded the traditional Platonic-medieval viewpoint that treated nature as a shadowy, imperfect reflection of a transcendent dimension, which was said to reflect true reality. They also rejected the Aristotelian-Christian view that saw nature *teleologically*—that is, as guided by a divine purpose and naturally striving to achieve a hierarchy of preordained ends. By contrast, the new science launched by Copernicus, Tycho Brahe, Kepler, Leonardo da Vinci, and Galileo in the sixteenth and seventeenth centuries viewed nature as an autonomous realm defined by the laws of identity, noncontradiction, and causality. All inanimate entities and animate beings were subject to the same mechanical laws of nature—laws that could be understood and expressed mathematically. Nature was seen less and less as a realm open to miracles caused by an omniscient deity. Instead, nature follows scientific laws that are universal, eternal, and absolute.

Sir Isaac Newton's genius showed mankind, scientifically and mathematically, how to unlock nature's laws. His discovery of gravity and the uniform laws of planetary motion demonstrated scientifically how the laws of identity and causality work. Nature's laws display themselves by the way in which each *effect* follows a particular *cause*. Newton expressed this fundamental principle in one of his famous rules of reasoning: "to the same natural effects we must, as far as possible, assign the same causes."[11] Following Newton, enlightened thinkers now saw the universe as an essentially ordered machine (something like a well-tuned clock) that could be understood rationally.

Newton's discoveries brought light where there had been only darkness. To extend the metaphor, Newton and the other Enlightenment philosophers and scientists represent the dawning of a new age, in which the truth of nature could now be known to man. The universality and timelessness of nature's laws could be discovered through the application of a proper method of reasoning. That method, Locke wrote in the *Essay Concerning Human Understanding*, challenged men as "rational creatures, to employ those faculties we have about what they are most adapted to, and follow the direction of nature where it seems to point us out the way."[12] This was also the intellectual process by which the *moral* laws and rights of nature were revealed to man.

ENLIGHTENMENT EPISTEMOLOGY: REASON

The Enlightenment was the Age of Reason. Now, with unaided reason, man could gain knowledge of the world. If Enlightenment philosophers referred to nature metaphorically as a book, then the obvious question was this: How shall the Book of Nature be read?

One thing was certain during the Enlightenment: faith, revelation, mystic insight, innate ideas, and a priori speculation were rejected. The Newtonian cosmos had to be discovered, and in order to discover it Enlightenment thinkers needed a new way to study and access nature. The search for a method that would give objective and certain knowledge was the paramount philosophic problem of the seventeenth and eighteenth centuries. The two great treatises advocating the "new method" of reasoning were Bacon's *Novum Organum* and Locke's *Essay Concerning Human Understanding*.

In *Novum Organum*, Bacon developed a new method for discovering the truth about nature's secrets. He rejected the Scholastics' syllogistic reasoning that began from abstract, a priori first principles and then deduced conclusions that bore little relationship to concrete reality. Bacon's method proceeded by examining experience, collecting and organizing data, experimenting on nature's operations, inducing causes from effects, and then discerning patterns and law-like principles. Nothing could be accounted as real in nature that was not an observed fact or relation among facts. Experience and experiment for Bacon represented the only road to truth. The Scottish philosopher Thomas Reid, considered by some to have been a primary influence on Jefferson's philosophic development, said this of Bacon: "The rules of inductive reasoning, or of a just interpretation of nature," were "delineated by the great genius of Lord Bacon," whose "*Novum Organum* may justly be called *a grammar of the language of nature*."[13] The book's rules of inductive reasoning were, according to Reid, subsequently developed and perfected by Newton in his *Principia*.

Virtually all Enlightenment thinkers supported the idea that reason was efficacious and that it was man's only means of acquiring knowledge. By confidently promoting the unaided reason of each and every man,

Bacon, Newton, and Locke were saying that knowledge and objective truth were open to all men and not the preserve of a special few. Enlightenment reason was a social solvent that encouraged a deep-seated suspicion of authority. Men would no longer submit docilely to those whom Locke referred to as the "dictator[s] of principles."[14]

In the same way that Newton discovered and charted nature's physical laws and attempted to explain the way the universe works, Locke attempted to grasp human nature and the operations of the mind.[15] The general purpose of his 1689 *Essay Concerning Human Understanding* was to explain the "original, certainty, and extent of *human knowledge*, together with the grounds and degrees of *belief, opinion*, and *assent*." His particular purpose was to ascertain what it is possible for men to know and not know with regard to their conduct. Locke assumed there are *moral* laws of nature to be discovered and revealed. "Our business here," he wrote, "is not to know all things, but those which concern our conduct." The goal of such knowledge was to guide man in determining what he "ought to do, as a rational and voluntary agent, for the attainment of any end, especially happiness." The *Essay*, then, is primarily an epistemological analysis of the "skill of right applying our own powers and actions, for the attainment of things good and useful," particularly as they seek out "those rules and measures of human actions which lead to happiness, and the means to practice them."[16]

It was critically important, Locke wrote, that men use the right method of thinking in the pursuit of moral knowledge, by which he meant the use of evidence-based reason. Locke's goal was to determine whether "we can find out those measures whereby a rational creature, put in that state in which man is in this world, may or ought to govern his opinions and actions depending thereon." Despite its complex discussion of the workings of human reason and the acquisition of knowledge, the *Essay* was a treatise with a practical purpose: to help men guide their moral actions. Interestingly, Locke regarded his philosophically abstract book to be not one of "bare speculation and the knowledge of truth" but one concerned primarily with the truth about "right" and the "conduct suitable to it."[17]

Locke began the *Essay Concerning Human Understanding* by rejecting the doctrine of innate ideas—that is, the idea that certain propositions or principles are inscribed on the mind from birth—held by René Descartes and the Cambridge Platonists.[18] The doctrine of innate ideas discouraged men from using their own mental faculties, and it also encouraged them to blindly follow those who claimed to have accessed their innate ideas. By contrast, for Locke the acquisition of true knowledge started with two premises: first, that man is born with a cognitive *tabula rasa*, a blank slate; and, second, that knowledge begins with "experience, and the observation of things." Lockean man begins in ignorance and builds up his knowledge through the experience that comes to him through the sense data imprinted on the mind, which is the basis of, and the building block for, all human knowledge. More *complex* ideas—for example, ideas of morality and law—are put together from simple ones by the faculty of reason, that is, by the mental functions of repetition, comparison, combination, and abstraction. Locke called his method the "historical, plain method," which is a nod to the Baconian method of experiment and observation. Locke also declared himself to be an "under-laborer" for the "incomparable Mr. *Newton*." As he saw it, his job was to clear out the Scholastic "rubbish" from man's mind.[19]

Ultimately, though, Locke's epistemological goal was moral: in a world inundated with religious mysticism, his intention was to show that man's rational faculties were in fact capable of discovering and knowing objective moral laws for the purpose of guiding human conduct. This goal was achievable for Locke because the world in which man lives is knowable by reason. The natural world for Locke was a rationally ordered and therefore comprehensible place where everything has its purpose and function.[20]

Despite certain flaws and contradictions in his epistemology, Locke was nevertheless one of the Enlightenment's great advocates of reason and its role in guiding human affairs. He believed that reason is the faculty that collates, organizes, ranks, and judges the evidence of the senses. As he put it in his *First Treatise of Government*, "Reason" is man's "only Star and compass."[21] And in the *Essay*, the Englishman emphasized that "*Reason* must be our last judge and guide in everything."[22] Underlying this exhortation is Locke's conviction that men can govern their actions according to reason, which means they are capable of discovering true and certain knowledge of moral principles to guide their conduct and relations with others. By the last quarter of the eighteenth century, virtually all of America's revolutionary founders accepted this view of reason.

Bacon's scientific method, Newton's laws of nature, and Locke's attempt to demonstrate the relationship between nature and the human mind ushered in a new age confident that reality was ordered and hence capable of being understood by rational human minds. Inspired by Bacon, Newton, and Locke, eighteenth-century thinkers felt assured that the meticulous charting of the lawful operations of the cosmic clockwork would inevitably lead to knowledge of moral virtue and happiness. Enlightenment thinkers believed that the accumulation of knowledge was compounding and that human progress—moral, social, political, technological, and economic— was virtually unlimited. As Locke put it in the *Essay*, reason "penetrates into the depths of the sea and earth, elevates our thoughts as high as the stars, and leads us through the vast spaces and large rooms of this mighty fabric." The general purpose of the *Essay*, then, is to explore and discover those horizons, which set "the bounds between the enlightened and dark parts of things."[23]

ENLIGHTENMENT ETHICS: RIGHTS

Just as Enlightenment philosophers revolutionized man's understanding of nature and human nature, so they sought to transform man's understanding of moral action. Human action and human relations would no longer be defined and constrained by the doctrines of original sin (i.e., the view that man is naturally depraved) and predestination (i.e., the view that only some are divinely preordained at birth to achieve salvation). Instead of looking to the church for morality, the great ambition of Enlightenment philosophers was to establish a demonstrative and secular science of ethics. And even though most Enlightenment philosophers were practicing Christians, several attempted to establish a moral code that would be true, even if, as Grotius and Montesquieu suggested, there were no God.[24]

Enlightenment thinkers believed that just as there were *physical* laws of nature, so there were *moral* laws of nature waiting to be discovered. These moral laws of nature were to be uncovered by the very same methods used by the Baconian-Newtonian science—an inductive method based on experience and observation. The search for moral and political truths grounded in nature was really an attempt to establish morality on an objective foundation. Knowledge of the laws and rights of nature could furnish men with a firm and unalterable foundation for moral goodness, natural justice, and political order.

John Locke's moral theory was simultaneously the most influential and elusive of the Enlightenment. His ethical teaching is difficult to piece together, but it was presented primarily in his two most famous works—the *Essay Concerning Human Understanding* and the *Second Treatise of Government*, both published in 1689. The *Essay*, which at first blush seems to be a work on epistemology—the "original, certainty, and extent of human knowledge"—is really concerned with "our conduct."[25]

The most remarkable element of Locke's moral theory is his extraordinary claim in the *Essay* that an objective system of ethics can be discovered and constructed scientifically, and that this moral code is as *certain* and *absolute* as mathematics and the Newtonian laws of nature. Locke believed that there are *moral* laws and rights of nature discernible to unaided human reason that do and should govern human affairs. The idea or possibility of a demonstrative science of ethics was the Holy Grail of Enlightenment thinking.

Locke's attempt to establish a demonstrative science of ethics can be reduced to three questions. First, how is certain and absolute moral knowledge capable of discovery and demonstration? Second, what are the moral laws and rights of nature? Third, what are the rewards and punishments associated with the moral laws and rights of nature?

QUESTION ONE: *How is certain and absolute moral knowledge capable of discovery and demonstration?*

When Locke suggests that a demonstrative science of ethics and politics is possible to man, what he means is that an objective moral code grounded in truth can be developed from an examination of human nature in the same way that scientific laws of nature can be known from the observation of physical reality. In his *On the Reasonableness of Christianity* (1695), Locke argues that the moral laws of nature can be known through either reason or revelation. Any man, Locke says, who would pretend to "have his rules pass for authentic directions, must show that either he builds his doctrine upon principles of reason, self-evident in themselves, and that he deduces all the parts of it from thence, by clear and evident demonstration, or must show his commission from heaven, that he comes with authority from God to deliver his will and commands to the world."[26] The whole purpose of the *Essay* is to show men how they might discover moral laws of nature through the application of reason.

Locke did not think that knowledge of the moral laws of nature was innate or imprinted on man's mind. Instead, such knowledge must be acquired "by the use and due application of our natural faculties." Locke made it very clear that he disagrees with those who "deny that there is a law knowable by the light of nature, i.e. without the help of positive revelation." He envisaged the construction of a moral science that would determine the "measures of right and wrong." The veracity of these moral principles, Locke declared, must be ultimately grounded on "men's own unprejudiced *experience* and observation."[27]

Locke thought it possible to discover rules of moral action that are both true and can be known with certainty, such that "*morality is capable of demonstration*, as well as mathematicks."[28] By "demonstration," Locke meant deriving specific moral rules from first principles, that is, from either a metaphysical axiom (e.g., all men are created equal) or a self-evident maxim (e.g., whatever is, is). By mathematics, Locke was mostly thinking about geometry as a model for his new science of ethics. He believed that "rational beings" could build the "foundations of our duty and rules of action" in a way that morality might be placed "*amongst the sciences capable of demonstration*." The key to the discovery of a true moral science, Locke argued, one that establishes absolute moral rules known with certainty, is the development and use of a "right *method*." Although his discussion of this method is less than one might hope for, he does leave a couple of clues as to its general principles: first, "the precise real essence of the things moral words stand for may be perfectly known" and thus the "congruity and incongruity of the things themselves" can be "discovered," and, second, from "self-evident propositions" can be deduced "*necessary consequences*," which lead to moral truths "as incontestable as those in mathematics." By Locke's account, these moral truths would be self-evidently true.[29]

From these general statements, it can be seen that Locke's "right method" follows a three-step process: first, it begins with certain clearly defined ideas or propositions; second, it examines the relationship between certain clearly formed moral concepts parallel to the way geometers define and measure the relationships and boundaries between shaped objects so that they may order and control them; and third, it deduces certain necessary relationships between or consequences from these ideas in a causal chain of reasoning. With the proper method of reason, Locke says, "it will become us, as rational creatures, to employ those faculties we have about what they are most adapted to, and follow the direction of nature where it seems to point us out the way." The end result is the discovery of principles that determine proper human relationships. Such moral rules are discovered and can be deemed universal, certain, and self-evident because they are based on the laws of identity and causation and the settled definitions of terms. Thus, Locke concludes "that *morality* is *the proper science and business of mankind in general* (who are both concerned and fitted to search out their *summum bonum*)."[30]

Locke applies this method to discovering and constructing a demonstrative science of ethics. As an example of this kind of reasoning from geometry to morality, Locke notes that by understanding the definition of a triangle, it can be demonstrated that the sum of its angles is equal to two right angles. Likewise, the same method of definition and deduction can be used with regard to morality and politics. He gives two examples—and only two—of how this kind of reasoning can be applied to moral-political issues:

PROPOSITION ONE: *"Where there is no property, there is no injustice."*

PROPOSITION TWO: *"No government allows absolute liberty."*[31]

Both propositions, Locke says, are as *certain* as any demonstration in Euclid! On what grounds can Locke make this claim?

These propositions are logically necessary based on the relationship of the definitions of the key terms one to another. Take the first proposition: it is necessarily true given that the definition of property (i.e., "the *idea* of *property* being a right to anything") cannot be squared with the definition of injustice (i.e., "the invasion or violation of that right"). Or consider the second proposition: *if* the "*idea* of government" is defined as "the establishment of society upon certain rules or laws which require conformity to them" and *if* the "*idea* of absolute liberty" is defined as doing whatever you want, then it logically follows that "no government allows absolute liberty." Locke believes that moral and political knowledge gained by this method of reasoning can be considered permanent, universal, absolute, and self-evident.

QUESTION TWO: *What are the moral laws and rights of nature?*
The idea that there are moral laws and rights of nature was the touchstone of John Locke's political philosophy. The notion of natural justice extends back to Scholastic philosophers—the Christian fathers, Roman lawyers of the Middle Ages—and had its birth with the Stoics and Greek

philosophers. According to Locke, the law of nature provided a system of ethical principles to guide human conduct, including the conduct of political rulers and magistrates. As Locke put it in the *Second Treatise*: "The law of nature stands as an eternal rule to all men, legislators as well as others. The rules that they make for other men's actions, must…be conformable to the laws of nature."[32]

Locke's teaching on the moral laws and rights of nature begins with a radically new first principle—the principle of self-ownership. Moral sovereignty for Locke begins with the self, which is inseparable from his notion of the "state of nature"—that place or condition where there is no government. The idea of a state of nature provides Locke with a kind of philosophic laboratory where he can isolate, observe, and identify the essential elements of man's nature. Man's natural condition is defined by two primary qualities. In the natural state, man's condition is first described as one of "*perfect freedom* to order [his] actions, and dispose of [his] possessions and persons, as [he] think[s] fit, within the bounds of the law of nature, without asking leave, or depending upon the will of any other man." The second fundamental quality of man's natural condition is that of *equality*, "wherein all the power and jurisdiction is reciprocal, no one having more than another: there being nothing more evident, than that creatures of the same species and rank, promiscuously born to all the same advantages of nature, and the use of the same faculties, should also be equal one amongst another without subordination or subjection, unless the lord and master of them all should, by any manifest declaration of all his will, set one above another."[33] Locke describes these qualities not as moral principles but as facts of human nature that indicate or point toward certain moral principles.

These immutable facts of nature (i.e., freedom and equality) provide Locke with a foundation on which to build a new moral teaching that is announced in an important passage from chapter 5 of the *Second Treatise*, where he writes: "every Man has a *Property* in his own *Person*. This no Body has a Right to but himself."[34] Locke builds his entire moral theory from this moral first principle. Locke has transitioned from what *is* (freedom and equality) to what *ought* to be (self-ownership). He is stating both a fact and a moral principle. Property is natural for Locke, which means that property is naturally just. His meaning here is twofold: first, that each and every individual is fully sovereign over his own life; and, second, that moral good begins with the individual and his relationship to reality.

Locke reinforced his case for self-ownership in at least two other places in the *Second Treatise*. In chapter 9, Locke claims unequivocally, "Man is absolute lord of his own person and possessions, equal to the greatest, and subject to nobody." And again in chapter 15: "He that is master of himself, and his own life, has a right too, to the means of preserving it." Self-ownership is the fundamental right for Locke. It is a right that excludes and overrides all other claims against a man. From the moral right of self-ownership, other rights follow deductively, which he sums up as "that *equal right* that every man hath *to his natural freedom*."[35] Self-ownership and the requirements of human life mean that it is *right*—indeed, necessary—that men have freedom in order to pursue the values necessary for them to live and to live well.

Locke opened a new moral vista for the Western world with this radical first premise. In Locke's moral universe, men are morally self-owning, which means that they are sovereign—fully sovereign—over their own lives. Self-ownership for Locke means self-governance. And at the heart of self-governance is the *self*. Locke is the first political philosopher in history to make the individual the primary unit of moral and political value. For Locke, the identity of the *self* is in part fixed by nature and in part self-made. The "I," or the self, is forged out of the operations of the sensations, reflection, judgment, and man's free will. It is only the individual who experiences sensations, who reasons, who judges, who values, who wills, who acts, and who pursues, achieves, and experiences happiness or misery.[36] In all cases of human action, it is only the individual who determines "the general power of directing" the mind and body toward chosen values.[37]

With Locke's new first principle, the *Essay Concerning Human Understanding* provides the method that Locke will use in the *Second Treatise* to construct a new secular ethics. From this first premise—the idea that individuals are sovereign and self-governing by moral right—Locke attempts to construct a science of ethics that is objective, demonstrable, and certain. Locke famously defines what he means by the law of nature in the second chapter of the *Second Treatise of Government*: "The state of nature has a law of nature to govern it, which obliges every one: and reason, which is that law, teaches all mankind, who will but consult it, that being all equal and independent, no one ought to harm another in his life, health, liberty, or possessions."[38] The first thing to note about Locke's moral teaching is that the law of nature is consonant with reason. The moral law of nature is discovered and promulgated through what he calls in the *Essay* the "light of reason."[39] We may attain knowledge of it, he says, "by the use and due application of our natural faculties" *without* the assistance "of positive revelation." To know and follow the law of nature in our conduct is to be guided by the faculty of reason, which teaches, based on the facts of nature, that "no one ought to harm another in his life, health, liberty, or possessions."[40]

Reason may teach right and wrong, but that is no guarantee that individuals will act on such knowledge. For Locke, moral knowledge is not the same as moral action. Those moral principles "derived from nature," he says, "are there for operation, and must produce conformity to action, not barely speculative assent to their truth." Morality consists of first knowing and then acting in accordance with true moral principles. As a corollary to his defense of reason, Locke also argues that men have free will to order their lives morally. To be a moral, rule-following person, man must be a free agent. Acting and acting freely are one and the same for Locke. Thought is a prerequisite for freedom and action. Consider, for instance, how Locke presents the relationship between reason and man's free will:

> The mind, having...a power to *suspend* the execution and satisfaction of...its desires...is at liberty to consider the objects of them, examine them on all sides, and weigh them with others. In this lies the liberty man has; and from the not using of it right comes all...mistakes, errors, and faults...in the conduct of our lives and our endeavours after happiness....To prevent this, we have a power to suspend the prosecution of this or that desire, as everyone daily may experiment in himself. This seems to me the source of all liberty.[41]

Self-government for Locke is grounded in reason and free will, both of which are necessarily interrelated. Reason requires freedom and freedom requires reason. As Locke said: "The *freedom* then of man and liberty of acting according to his own will, is *grounded* on his having *reason*, which is able to instruct him in that law he is to govern himself by, and make him know how far he is left to the freedom of his own will."[42] For him, using one's rational faculty to guide one's liberty in the right way is what constitutes morality.

Having come this far, Locke is now able to formulate his greatest contribution to political thought and practice: the concept of "rights." Rights for Locke serve as a moral principle that defines the means by which men pursue their fundamental values in relation to other men. The concept "rights" is a deduction from the fundamental fact of self-ownership. The claim to property in one's own person is a moral claim to noninterference and exclusivity. No person has a claim on any other person's life (i.e., their body, mind, and actions). That which is yours is not mine and vice versa. Because all human beings are fully sovereign over themselves as individuals, it is imperative that the same right of sovereignty be recognized in each and every person. Locke's concept of rights therefore designates the boundaries of a man's freedom of action. For Locke, rights define and create a sphere of action in which the individual is free—free from the initiation of physical force by others. Rights are moral principles and juridical barriers against the initiation of force. Rights for Locke are also natural, by which he means they are deduced from the requirements of man's nature (i.e., reason and free will) and from the first principle of self-ownership.

Readers may well wonder at this point what the difference is between a law and a right of nature. The rights of nature recognize certain facts and requirements of human nature, and the laws of nature are moral principles discovered by reason that help us to achieve our most fundamental values. For Locke, rights imply laws and obligations. The moral laws of nature are rationally induced principles emanating from the nature of the human condition and its most urgent needs and wants. The purpose of these laws is to protect the rights of individuals, from which the laws of nature are deduced. The "*fundamental law of nature*," Locke says in the *Second Treatise*, teaches that man is "*to be preserved*." Issuing from the fundamental law are corollary laws that promote the rational self-interest of all individuals. The secular law of nature, Locke says, insists "not so much the limitation, as the direction of a free and intelligent agent to his proper interest." To that end, the secular law of nature, Locke says, does not abolish or restrain a man's freedom but preserves and enlarges it. The law of nature draws boundaries preventing men from walking into "bogs" and over "precipices."[43]

Ultimately, Locke's secular law of nature provided an outline of ethical principles to guide human conduct, including the conduct of political rulers and magistrates.

From the fundamental right to preserve one's self, which is formulated as the right to life (and with it the corollary rights of liberty and property), Locke then deduces certain moral laws of nature, the purpose of which is to serve man's rights. Locke's fundamental law of nature (i.e., to follow right reason) issues two commands: first, each and every man should pursue his rational, long-term self-interest; and, second, "No one ought to harm another in his life, health, liberty, or possessions."[44] In other words, men are implored by the law of nature to do no harm. From these primary laws of nature, Locke then deduces other rules, such as *"One should do as he would be done unto,"* "men should keep their compacts," "it is unreasonable for men to be judges in their own cases," "every man has a *property* in his own *person,*" "Whatsoever [a man] removes out of the state that nature hath provided, and left it in, he hath mixed his *labour* with and joined to it something that is his own, and thereby makes it his property," and *"Parents, preserve and cherish your Children."*[45]

From the moral laws of nature, one can further deduce political laws of nature, such as "no taxation without representation." Man knows these moral laws of nature by the "right rule of reason"; they are "intelligible and plain to a rational creature, and a studier of that law."[46] Locke's moral laws of nature provide the foundation on which he will construct a just civil society and government.

QUESTION THREE: *What are the rewards and punishments associated with the moral laws of nature?*

In addition to identifying the content of the moral law of nature and the method by which it is known, Locke was faced with another challenge: to ascertain its rewards and punishments. Moral laws without rewards and punishments would be toothless. The truth is that some men obey and some violate the law of nature. The law of nature must have sanctions because, as it turns out, all men are "biased by their interest" and not all men are students or followers of the law of nature.[47] Men must therefore have a *motive* and be given an incentive to follow the moral law of nature. It would be "utterly in vain," Locke writes, "to suppose a rule set to the free actions of man without annexing to it some enforcement of good and evil" through "some reward or punishment annexed to that law." For a law to be a law it must have known rewards and punishments, and "all men must have a certain and unavoidable knowledge that certain and unavoidable punishment will attend the breach of it." Locke's clearest statement defending natural morality (with rewards and punishments) is presented as follows:

> Good and evil as hath been shown…are nothing but pleasure or
> pain, or that which occasions or procures pleasure or pain to us.
> *Morally good and evil*, then, is only the conformity or disagree-
> ment of our voluntary actions to some law, whereby good or evil is
> drawn on us from the will and power of the law-maker; which good
> and evil, pleasure or pain, attending our observance or breach of
> the law by the decree of the law-maker, is that we call *reward* and
> *punishment*.[48]

The rewards and punishments associated with Locke's secular law of nature come in three forms: *natural*, *social*, and *civil*. Natural rewards and punishments are legislated and enforced voluntarily by each individual; social rewards and punishments are legislated and enforced by society through social approbation and disapprobation; and civil rewards and punishments are legislated and enforced by government authorities through coercive power.

The *natural* rewards and punishments associated with Locke's law of nature are pleasure, well-being, and happiness if the law is obeyed, and pain, misery, penury, and even death if it is violated. "Nature," Locke confessed, "has put into man a desire of happiness and an aversion to misery: these indeed are innate practical principles which…do continue constantly to operate and influence all our actions without ceasing; these may be observed in all persons and all ages, steady and universal." The good and right for Locke is determined by whatever tends to increase human happiness and to diminish misery. Thus for Locke there is a natural and necessary connection between "*Virtue* and *public Happiness*." In fact, he says that it is in the interest of the "virtuous man" to "not only allow, but recommend and magnify those rules to others, from whose observance of them he is sure to reap advantage to himself." According to Locke, "self-interest and the conveniences of *this* life make many men own an outward profession and approbation" of the moral laws of nature. The actions of rational and virtuous men "sufficiently prove that they very little consider the Law-giver that prescribed these rules, nor the hell he has ordained for the punishment of those that transgress them."[49]

The problem with a purely naturalistic law of nature, however, is that a simple *knowledge* of such a law is not a sufficient *motive* for men to obey or disobey it. Their passions, opinions, and short-term interests often overwhelm their knowledge of right and wrong. Nor is the "natural convenience or inconvenience" that comes from obeying or disobeying right reason a sufficient sanction for the moral laws of nature, particularly relative to the rewards and punishments that most men believe issue from God's law.[50] Moreover, in addition to human fallibility and errors of reason, far too many men have an irrational and corrupt understanding of what is in their self-interest. Some men even take pleasure in lying, cheating, and stealing, or worse. Those who live their lives by the laws of reason are often left defenseless against those who are guided by their corrupted passions. Unlike God's law, with its clearly known rewards and punishments, a purely naturalistic law of nature seems to lack obligatory force. The ultimate question that Locke must solve is, from whence does obligation arise?

Part of the problem is that, even though the moral law of nature is "plain and intelligible to all rational creatures," most men are "biased by their interest, as well as ignorant for want of study of it."[51] Man is neither omniscient nor infallible. Even the wisest man makes mistakes in his knowledge and application of the moral law of nature. In other words, not all men follow the law of nature all the time and some men live in violation of it most of the time. Why, then, should the perfectly just man follow a law that not everyone else follows? If one gets ahead in life by violating the law of nature (e.g., through stealing), what then is the incentive to follow that law? Moreover, those who do follow the law of nature often do not experience its rewards in a timely way, and those who do not follow the law of nature often go unpunished. The problem with the law of nature, therefore, is that it lacks an adequate enforcement mechanism. Unfortunately, the natural rewards and punishments of the law of nature are both insufficient as a motivating force and not always immediately felt or even known. In other words, they are too tepid and weak.

The rewards and punishments of the moral laws of nature therefore require additional supports. Something else is needed, and that something else comes in two forms: first, there are social sanctions, or what Locke calls "the *law of opinion or reputation*"; and, second, there are civil sanctions that Locke designates as "*civil* law."[52]

The social law of opinion and reputation is for Locke synonymous with the law of virtue and vice as understood by the ancient Greek and Roman philosophers. There are virtues and vices that are objectively good or bad, which "are names pretended and supposed everywhere to stand for actions in their own nature right and wrong; and as far as they really are so applied." These moral virtues and vices (which are corollaries of the law of nature), Locke continues, "are constantly attributed only to such actions as in each country and society are in reputation or discredit."[53] What is virtue and vice in eighteenth-century Persia will be different from that in England. In fact, what constitutes virtue and vice in Dorset may very well be different from that in Northumberland.

The social or conventional rewards and punishments associated with these virtues and vices will likewise vary from place to place. Nevertheless, these moral laws of convention come with rewards and punishments. The law of opinion and reputation comes in the form of social praise and blame for our actions, "which by a secret and tacit consent establishes itself in the several societies, tribes, and clubs of men in the world...according to the judgment, maxims, or fashions of that place." Despite the multiculturalism of virtue and vice, every community everywhere attaches praise to virtue and blame to vice. It is a universal feature of human societies despite place and time that "*Virtue* is everywhere that which is thought praiseworthy; and nothing else but that which has the allowance of public esteem is called *virtue*." The law of opinion and reputation is for Locke genuine law with meaningful rewards and punishments.

> I think I may say that he who imagines commendation and dis-
> grace not to be strong motives on men to accommodate themselves
> to the opinions and rules of those with whom they converse seems
> little skilled in the nature or history of mankind, the greatest part
> whereof he shall find to govern themselves chiefly, if not solely, by
> this law of fashion.[54]

The praise or blame of those we respect is a powerful force in human affairs. Most men are concerned with their honor, dignity, and reputation. They desire and seek the approbation of others and are pleased—and sometimes even proud—when they get it, and they likewise fear and loathe the disapprobation of others and are ashamed if others judge them negatively. The informal manners and mores of a just and moral society will therefore reflect and reinforce the moral laws of nature.

Locke's law of opinion or reputation is both natural and conventional. It is a naturally occurring, sociopsychological phenomenon that manifests itself through tacit or explicit social agreement. It provides the transition from the purely natural rewards and punishments of the law of nature to those that are purely conventional.

The rewards and punishments that issue from human nature and social convention are powerful forces in human life, but they are still incomplete and insufficient. They do not quite finish the job; they do not bring all men under the purview of the law of nature. Most moral and law-abiding men (those who follow the "right rule of reason") are motivated to follow the moral laws of nature through either natural or social rewards and punishments. And yet there is still a class of men (those who are "not under the ties of the common law of reason") who "live by another rule" and regularly transgress the law of nature and live by the rule of "force and violence."[55] For those who violate the laws of nature and infringe on the rights of others, punishments with greater force than shame or guilt are needed.

Enter civil *government*, the purpose of which is to make, adjudicate, and execute laws that mirror the moral laws of nature. The law of nature provides the standard by which to judge all properly made civil law: it "stands as an eternal rule to all men, legislators as well as others."[56] The law of nature, which is the law of reason, is that set of rules that elucidate the means by which man's rights are to be secured by government. In his writings on education, Locke categorized this particular form of moral-political knowledge under the rubric of knowledge of the "original of societies and the rise and extent of political power."[57]

Positive law for Locke should reinforce the moral law of nature. The civil law provides its own sanctions for those who violate the moral laws of nature. The art of legislation, according to Locke, must therefore begin with knowledge of the principles of political right and power followed by a knowledge of the art of governing and the "civil law," which is "grounded upon principles of reason."[58] In the *Second Treatise*, Locke makes clear that the "municipal laws of countries," to the extent that they are "right," should be "founded on the law of nature, by which they are to be regulated and interpreted." The "great art of government" is to promulgate "established laws of liberty to secure protection and encouragement to the honest industry of mankind against the oppression of power."[59]

The purpose of the law of nature translated into civil law is to secure the natural rights of individuals. Civil government therefore complements and serves the law of nature. Generally speaking, *political power*," Locke says, is "*a right* of making laws with penalties of death and consequently all less penalties, for the regulating and preserving of property, and of employing the force of the community, in the execution of such laws, and in the defence of the commonwealth from foreign injury; and all this only for the public good." To that end, civil government, rightly understood, does three things: first, it creates an "*established*, settled, known *law*" that mirrors the law of nature and serves as the "standard of right and wrong"; second, it establishes "a known and indifferent judge, with authority to determine all differences according to the established law"; and finally, it creates "*power* to back and support the sentence when right, and to *give* it due *execution*."[60]

Civil law recreates, adjudicates, and executes the law of nature. Good civil law embodies the law of nature and thus fulfills the requirements of genuine law: it has a lawgiver, it is promulgated, it inspires obligation, and it comes with sanctions. This is precisely how American revolutionaries saw the purpose of civil law.

LOCKE AND THE AMERICAN MIND

America's revolutionary mind is virtually synonymous with John Locke's mind. The moral modes of reasoning used in Locke's *Essay* and the political principles contained in his *Second Treatise* profoundly shaped the worldview of eighteenth-century Americans.[61] Locke's ideas deeply influenced American Whigs of all ranks and descriptions—from uneducated farmers and mechanics to college-educated clergymen and statesmen in the years before 1776.[62]

As early as 1725, in one of the first colonial publications to explicitly examine Locke's political thought, the Connecticut minister John Bulkley wrote of the "Great Man Mr. Lock," who, he argued, "well understood the true Origine of all Lawful Authority, and what Powers over themselves or others, Persons by the Law of Nature & Antecedent to their Entering into

Society are Vested with." It was not uncommon for the colonists to refer to Locke as "the finest reasoner, and best writer on government, that this or any other age has produced," as a "great Philosopher and Statesman," as a "great and generous friend to the rights of human nature"; or to speak of the "great authority, of the clearest luminary England ever produced, Mr. Locke"; or to address him as the "great and judicious Mr. Locke."[63]

Locke's influence on the American mind was ably expressed in a 1773 advertisement published in *The Boston Gazette* for the first-ever American edition of Locke's *An Essay Concerning the True Original, Extent, and End of Civil Government*, which was the full title of his first and second treatises of government combined:

> This Essay alone, well studied and attended to, will give to every
> intelligent Reader a better View of the Rights of Men and of
> Englishmen, and a clearer Insight into the Principles of the British
> Constitution, than all the Discourses on Government—The Essays
> in Politicks and Books of Law in our Language.—It should be
> early and carefully explained by every Father to his Son, by every
> Preceptor in our public and private Schools to his Pupils, and by
> every Mother to her Daughter.[64]

The influence of the "great Mr. Locke" or, as he also was often called, the "incomparable Mr. Locke," can also be found in the writings of major revolutionaries such as James Otis, John and Samuel Adams, Richard Bland, Thomas Jefferson, and James Wilson, and so too can it be found in the writings of many New England ministers and in the petitions of hard-scrabble and largely uneducated farmers living on the western frontier.[65] In fact, it was rare for a newspaper article or pamphlet written on the debates over the imperial crisis between 1764 and 1776 not to mention, quote, or paraphrase Locke. In 1774, Nathaniel Ames III, inheritor of his famous father's almanac business, wrote: "As it is unpardonable for a Navigator to be without his charts, so it is for a *Senator* to be without his, which is Lock's 'Essay on Government.'"[66]

Locke's influence in America was so extensive that even the Loyalists and opponents of the Declaration of Independence recognized the central importance of the Englishman's thought in the coming of the Revolution. In *A View of the Causes and Consequences of the American Revolution* (1797), the Tory and Anglican clergyman Jonathan Boucher identified Locke as the Revolution's philosophic godfather. According to Boucher: "Mr. Locke had the good fortune to enjoy a pre-eminent reputation for political wisdom longer than most men who have degraded great abilities by employing them to promote the temporary purposes of a party. Till the American war, he was looked up to as an oracle; and the whole nation implicitly pinned their faith, in politics, on his dogmas."[67]

John Locke's Enlightenment philosophy provides a bright light by which to better understand the substance and meaning of the Declaration of Independence and the modes of reasoning employed by its authors, signers, and supporters. As shown throughout this book, an exhaustive examination of the pamphlet and newspaper literature of the period demonstrates that American revolutionaries were unadulterated Lockeans. Their position can be summed up with the following syllogism:

> *Major premise*: The Declaration of Independence is an expression of the American mind.
> *Minor premise*: America's revolutionary mind was an expression of Locke's political philosophy.
> *Conclusion*: The Declaration of Independence was an expression of Locke's mind.

Locke's reasoning and intellectual hegemony over the American revolutionary mind was as thoroughgoing as Karl Marx's was over the minds of the Russian revolutionaries—indeed, possibly even more so. By 1776, the American revolutionaries might very well have said, "We are all Lockeans now."

CHAPTER 2

Declaring the Laws of Nature

"When in the Course of human events, it becomes
necessary for one people to dissolve the political bands
which have connected them with another, and to assume
among the powers of the earth, the separate and equal station
to which the Laws of Nature and of Nature's God entitle
them, a decent respect to the opinions of mankind requires
that they should declare the causes which
impel them to the separation."

*T*he Declaration of Independence is a précis of the Enlightenment's fundamental principles, which can be summed up in four words, each connected to one of the four branches of philosophy: in metaphysics—*nature*; in epistemology—*reason*; in ethics—*rights*; and in politics—*constitutionalism*.[1] The Declaration's underlying philosophic structure and logic mirrors the Enlightenment project: it has a *metaphysics* and an *epistemology* that are presented in the first paragraph, and it has an *ethics* and a *politics* that are presented in the second paragraph. The Declaration captures the spirit of the philosophic revolution launched by the Enlightenment's two greatest thinkers: Isaac Newton and John Locke. Its metaphysics and epistemology are drawn from Newton's *Philosophiae Naturalis Principia Mathematica* and Locke's *Essay Concerning Human Understanding*, and its ethical and political teachings are drawn from Locke's *Second Treatise of Government*. It was Newton who taught the colonists about the physical laws of nature, and it was Locke who most influenced their views on the nature of reason and the moral laws and rights of nature.[2]

In 1787, the Reverend Nathanael Emmons captured the importance of Newton and Locke to the revolutionary generation in these terms:

"Newton, by his discoveries in the material, and Locke, by his discoveries in the intellectual world, have enlarged the boundaries of human knowledge, and of human happiness." Three years earlier, the Reverend Samuel McClintock delivered a sermon to the New Hampshire legislature in which he lauded America as the home of the Enlightenment, a place where the "Locks and Newtons making new discoveries in the laws of nature, and the latent powers of the human mind" could inspire a new society "rising to a degree of perfection hitherto unknown."[3]

The Declaration's first paragraph is rarely read with the care it deserves. Readers should ponder its words carefully:

> When in the Course of human events, it becomes necessary for
> one people to dissolve the political bands which have connected
> them with another, and to assume among the powers of the earth,
> the separate and equal station to which the Laws of Nature and
> of Nature's God entitle them, a decent respect to the opinions of
> mankind requires that they should declare the causes which impel
> them to the separation.

The first paragraph introduces in an abstract form the Declaration's *purpose*, its *principles*, and the *actions* that follow therefrom. Its *purpose* is to "declare" to the world the "causes which impel" the colonists to separate from Great Britain. Its *principle* is defined by the "Laws of Nature and of Nature's God," against which the colonists have judged the actions of their oppressors and to which they now appeal in order to refound their political institutions. And its *action* is defined by the necessity to dissolve their connection to Great Britain.

Implicit in this opening paragraph are certain metaphysical and epistemological assumptions that are respectively Newtonian and Lockean in character, and which can be summed up in two words: *nature* and *reason*. By nature and reason, Newton, Locke, and America's founders meant something like this: first, that nature is fixed (which means that all entities have a fixed identity) and is governed by universal laws of cause and effect; second, that nature is knowable (which means the efficacy of human reason); and third, that nature and reason therefore provide the standard of human action. In sum, the first paragraph says this: reason is the means and nature is the standard by which men must distinguish between freedom and slavery. Let us now unpack this highly essential-ized summary.

REASON, OR "A DECENT RESPECT TO THE OPINIONS OF MANKIND"

The first paragraph of the Declaration announces to the world the intention of the colonists to declare their independence from Great Britain. Out of a "decent respect to the opinions of mankind," the Americans will demonstrate to "a candid world" the "causes which impel them to the separation." By showing respect to the "opinions of mankind" and by appealing to the "Laws of Nature," the Declaration says that the American Revolution is to be guided by reasoned philosophic analysis. In effect, it says this: We, the assembled representatives of the United States, shall identify and define our fundamental principles and then announce them to the world as demonstrably true. The objective of the Declaration is to elucidate the conditions of slavery and freedom that justify the Americans in their separation.

Jefferson and his fellow Americans are thus appealing to nature and to man's reason as the standard of moral and political right. According to the Declaration's first paragraph, reason is capable of apprehending three important things: first, the evidentiary facts that prove a design on the part of British imperial officials to enslave them; second, the moral standard against which these unjust acts are to be judged (and on which new political institutions are to be built); and third, the necessity of separation. Jefferson and his revolutionary compatriots believed that their indictment of wrongs committed by George III and the self-evident truths on which they would construct a new political society could be known and understood by all men everywhere.

Jefferson's affirmation of the important role played by reason was common among the revolutionary generation. In his *Notes on the State of Virginia*, Jefferson advanced one of the clearest Enlightenment statements on the efficacy of reason: "Reason and free inquiry are the only effectual agents against error....They are the natural enemies of error, and of error only....Reason and experiment have been indulged, and error has fled before them. Truth can stand by itself."[4] Unassisted human reason was for Jefferson the only means by which to discern the laws of nature. In a 1787 letter to his nephew, Peter Carr, Jefferson advised the young man to "fix reason firmly in her seat and call to her tribunal every fact, every opinion. Question with boldness even the existence of God; because, if there is one, he must more approve of the homage of reason, than that of blindfolded fear."[5] This is the same principle that Jefferson, Adams, Washington, and the other revolutionaries applied to their dispute with Great Britain. The overarching principle of the Declaration's first paragraph is that reason can distinguish between just and unjust, good and bad, freedom and tyranny. The American case will rest on facts submitted to a candid world, with reason as the judge.

✷ ✷ ✷

The main burden of the Declaration was to demonstrate that the actions of King George III and the British Parliament necessarily amounted to despotism, thus impelling the Americans to declare their independence from Great Britain. In the middle of the Declaration's second paragraph, Jefferson presents an informal indictment against George III, the purpose of which was to define the conditions of tyranny. Recent events (a long train of abuses by the king and Parliament) demonstrated, according to Jefferson, nothing less than a "design to reduce" the Americans "under absolute despotism." This is a stunning claim. What could it possibly mean?

From the beginning of the imperial crisis, the most impressive American minds charged British authorities with a "design" to enslave them.[6] As early as 1765, John Adams raised the alarm in his "Dissertation on the Canon and Feudal Law," in response to the Stamp Act: "Nothing less than this seems to have been meditated for us, by somebody or other in Great Britain. There seems to be a direct and formal design on foot, to enslave all America."[7] A few years later, in response to the Townshend Acts, John Dickinson of Pennsylvania pursued the revolutionary logic in his *Letters from a Farmer in Pennsylvania* (1766–67):

> Some person may think this act of no consequence, because the duties are so *small*. A fatal error. *That* is the very circumstance most alarming to me. For I am convinced, that the authors of this law would never have obtained an act to raise so trifling a sum as it must do, had they not intended by *it* to establish a *precedent* for

future use....In short, if they have a right *to* levy a tax of *one penny* upon us, they have a right to levy a *million* upon us.[8]

And Jefferson himself warned in his 1774 *Summary View of the Rights of British-America* that "single acts of tyranny may be ascribed to the accidental opinion of a day; but a series of oppressions begun at a distinguished period, and pursued, unalterably through every change of ministers, too plainly prove a deliberate and systematical plan of reducing us to slavery."[9]

What are twenty-first-century readers to make of these charges? Proving their veracity is the Declaration's central political task. The Declaration presents inductively its case against the king in order to justify its claim that there was a "design to reduce" the American colonists "under absolute Despotism." From the Declaration's list of grievances emerges the general charge that these Anglo-American provincials' natural right to freedom and self-government has been violated. How so? The Declaration says: "The history of the present King of Great Britain is a history of repeated injuries and usurpations, all having in direct object the establishment of an absolute Tyranny over these States." Consider the nature and meaning of this remarkable charge: Great Britain, the freest nation in the Old World, stands accused of tyranny and despotism! How is this possible?

The plot thickens, given that these charges are all brought against George III. This may strike readers as odd. Why is the bill of indictment brought against George III and not against Parliament? Prior to 1776, virtually all of the American petitions and remonstrances were directed against the actions of Parliament. Why the change? The answer is to be found in the evolving logic, substance, and strategy of the American argument against British usurpations in the years between 1764 and 1776, which underwent a profound transformation after 1774. Until that year, the great villain for the Americans was Parliament, which had, after all, passed the Sugar, Stamp, Declaratory, Townshend, Tea, and Intolerable Acts.

During the 1760s, the central constitutional disagreement between British imperial officials and their American colonists concerned the question of political sovereignty—whether it lay in Parliament or in the colonial legislatures. This issue had been brought to the forefront of the imperial debates by the passage of the Declaratory Act in 1766, which said that the American colonies were subject to the laws of Parliament "in all cases whatsoever." The British position was clear: the constitutional authority of Parliament did and must extend to the colonies because "two supreme or independent authorities cannot exist in the same state." The idea of an *imperium in imperio* (i.e., a state within a state) was an absurdity. Accordingly, there could be "no possible medium between absolute independence" on one hand, and "subjection to the authority of Parliament" on the other.[10] Logically, this was a tough nut for the colonists to crack. It was not until 1773 and 1774 that America's best constitutional theorists—men such as John Adams and James Wilson—developed a powerful counter-argument to the British case for parliamentary sovereignty.

In sum, the Americans challenged the claim that the colonies were members of the British state and therefore subject to Parliament. Most colonies, they argued, were founded in the seventeenth century, before Parliament became the sovereign political authority in the British state. Instead, they argued, their only political connection with Great Britain was through their legally chartered allegiance to the *person* of the king. In return for the colonists' homage and fealty, the king would provide his colonies with protection. From the beginning, so the argument went, the provincials were independent of Parliament. And now in 1776, having been denied the king's protection through the Prohibitory Act of 1775, it became necessary to dissolve their connection and allegiance to the British Crown.

To "prove" to a "candid world" the charge that there was a design to impose a tyranny over the American colonies, the Declaration enumerates twenty-seven injuries and usurpations allegedly committed by the king. Each of the charges refers to a specific action taken or not taken by the king. Read closely, the list of injuries and usurpations can be divided into three main sections.[11] The first section, counts one through twelve, enumerates the king's abuse of his executive powers. His offenses include disallowing or suspending colonial legislation, dissolving colonial legislatures, obstructing the colonial system of justice, corrupting the separation of powers by making judges dependent on his will, and keeping standing armies. The second section, counts thirteen through twenty-two, details the king's collusion with Parliament to subject the colonies "to a jurisdiction foreign to our constitution, and unacknowledged by our laws." His offense here was not having vetoed Parliament's abuses, such as: quartering British troops in America and putting them above criminal law, restricting American trade, restricting trial by jury and other common law rights, imposing taxes without the consent of the governed, and destroying the colonists' right to self-government. Of special significance is the charge that Parliament has declared its power to be arbitrary in America through the passage of the Declaratory Act of 1766. The third section, counts twenty-three through twenty-seven, identifies those abuses that amount to an undeclared state of war. The king's abuses include what one scholar has referred to as "*war atrocities*": he has initiated the use of physical force by turning his navy and army against the lives and property of the colonists.[12]

The Declaration's indictment provided a summary of all the injuries and usurpations committed by king and Parliament, from the Stamp Act of 1765 to the so-called Intolerable or Coercive Acts of 1774 (which effectively destroyed the self-governing political institutions of Massachusetts). The king had violated the British constitution, the colonial charters, common law rights and liberties, and, most importantly, the colonists' natural rights to life, liberty, and property. He had, in other words, destroyed the provincials' ability to govern themselves. Taken separately, these injuries and usurpations did not amount to despotism, but taken all together, this "long train of abuses" could reasonably be seen as nothing less than "a design to reduce" the colonists "under absolute despotism." The revolutionary generation saw in Parliament's actions, taken as a whole, a pattern leading to tyranny and slavery.

The Declaratory Act of 1766 was the theoretical embodiment of non-objective, despotic rule, and the Intolerable Acts of 1774 were its existential result. The colonists' revolutionary logic worked inductively. Their observation and experience of repeated actions (the effects) inspired them to integrate separate and discrete events into a pattern in order to identify the ultimate motive (the cause). Jefferson's logic went something like this: "When we see two facts accompanying one another for a long time, we are apt to suppose them related as cause and effect."[13] The Declaration's moral and political charge—that is, "the establishment of an absolute Tyranny over these States"—is "proved" by presenting, integrating, and evaluating the facts of the case.

To know what injustice and despotism are, one must also know what justice and freedom are. The Americans, according to the Declaration's first paragraph, are "to assume among the powers of the earth, the separate and equal station to which the Laws of Nature and of Nature's God entitle them." These "Laws of Nature and of Nature's God" (discussed in the next section) provide some kind of standard against which the actions of king and Parliament, indeed, all government, are to be judged. Or, as Jefferson writes close to the end of the Declaration, the standard against which these actions are to be judged is what he calls natural "right."

In sum, the Americans were not concrete-bound pragmatists. They did not take Britain's various depredations as separate and distinct events. They kept a tally and then added it all up. The Americans studied, weighed, and measured the separate actions of king and Parliament (i.e., the evidence of the crime); they integrated the totality of British actions and drew the evaluative conclusion that king and Parliament had a "design" (i.e., the motive) to reduce them under absolute despotism (i.e., the ultimate crime itself); and then they contrasted the actions of British imperial officials with their own moral principles (i.e., the standards of justice). In 1768, John Dickinson in his famous *Letters from a Farmer* described perfectly the Americans' mode of thinking: "Ought not the PEOPLE therefore to watch? to observe facts? to search into causes? to investigate designs? And have they not a right of JUDGING from the evidence before them, on no slighter points than their *liberty* and *happiness*?"[14] The revolutionaries' Enlightenment moral principles provided the touchstone by which to judge the actions of king and Parliament, and their principles necessitated the nature of their response. In July 1775, in its Declaration of the Causes and Necessity of Taking Up Arms, the Continental Congress declared that the American colonies had been enslaved "by violence," and the colonists "have thereby rendered it necessary" to "close with their last appeal from Reason to Arms."[15]

Jefferson and his fellow revolutionaries understood that there are two basic ways to deal with men in political society: either by faith and force or by reason and freedom. According to Jefferson, once man has surrendered his reason, he "has no remaining guard against absurdities the most monstrous, and like a ship without rudder, is the sport of every wind." In such cases, "gullibility, which they call *faith*, takes the helm from the hand of reason, and the mind becomes a wreck." Or, as the Virginia statesman Richard Bland understood this distinction: "Right and Power have very different Meanings, and convey very different Ideas."[16]

Jefferson and the Declaration's co-signers understood that reason and freedom are inseparably one; that liberty "takes root and growth in the progress of reason"; that "truth is certainly a branch of morality"; that "reason and persuasion" are the only practical means to deal with other individuals in a free society; that "honesty is the first chapter in the book of wisdom"; that individuals must be free to act on their judgment if they are to pursue the values necessary to sustain and advance their lives (e.g., justice, freedom, wealth, and happiness); that freedom from force is an objective requirement of human life; that moral and political right exist "independent of force"; that "force cannot change right"; that a "government of reason is better than one of force"; that the mind must not be forced by physical compulsion; that the initiation of physical force stops individuals from thinking and acting on their judgment, which therefore leads to slavery; and that force is the handmaiden of despotism. "In a republican nation whose citizens are to be led by reason and persuasion and not by force," Jefferson wrote in an 1824 letter, "the art of reasoning becomes of first importance." By contrast, "force," he noted in his first inaugural address, is "the vital principle and immediate parent of despotism."[17]

The essence of force for American revolutionaries was the dominion of some men over others. They considered the *initiation* of physical force to be a direct violation of the moral law. Ultimately, force meant the use of physical compulsion and coercion by some men against others, all of which they saw inherent in the Stamp, Townshend, and ultimately in the aptly named Coercive Acts. Eighteenth-century Americans saw offensive power and force as grasping, aggressive, malignant, corrupting, and morally imperialistic.

Quite possibly the greatest achievement of the American Revolution was to free men to follow the dictates of their own minds, guided by unencumbered reason. "We believed," Jefferson wrote, reflecting on what had been accomplished in 1776, "that men, enjoying in ease and security the full fruits of their own industry, enlisted by all their interests on the side of law and order, habituated to think for themselves and to follow their reason as their guide, would be more easily and safely governed than with minds nourished in error and vitiated and debased…by ignorance, indigence and oppression." The American experiment in self-government would ultimately result, Jefferson hoped, "in establishing the fact, that man may be governed by reason and truth." In a free, republican society, "every man's own reason must be his oracle" or "his own rightful umpire." In fact, there was for Jefferson a direct and reciprocal connection between self-government and reason. In a truly free and self-governing society, each and every man must freely "act according to the dictates of his own reason" and he "must form his judgment on the evidence accessible to himself."[18] Political self-government depends on moral *self*-government, which in turns depends on an individual's ability and willingness to follow the "standard of reason." Jefferson was confident that the American people were capable of political self-government precisely "because they are under the unrestrained and unperverted operation of their own understandings." This is precisely why Enos Hitchcock of Rhode Island could say of the American Revolution that it did something achieved by no other nation in history: "a revolution by reasoning."[19]

For Thomas Paine, the American Revolution was about more than just independence from Great Britain. It was, first and foremost, an intellectual and a moral revolution that swept away the "tyranny and the antiquity of habit" that had "established itself over the mind." The real revolution was to free the minds of men to pursue the truth in the light of day. Men were now no longer "afraid to think." The Revolution changed everything—it forever changed the way men viewed the world. The "present age will hereafter merit to be called the Age of Reason." Henceforth, Paine announced: "Mankind are not now to be told they shall not think, or they shall not read; and publications that go no farther than to investigate principles of government, to invite men to reason and to reflect, and to show the errors and excellences of different systems, have a right to appear." One extraordinary thing about the Declaration of Independence is that it took what many of the most enlightened Europeans of the time considered to be the best constitution, the best form of government, and the best laws in the world, held them up to the tribunal of reason—and found them wanting. By liberating and elevating reason to discover the "errors" and "defects" of every constitution and government, the Declaration provided both the means and the standard by which to judge all governments everywhere. Hence, from July 4, 1776, "despotism felt a shock, and man began to contemplate redress."[20]

But of course the Declaration did more than justify the use of reason in combating injustice and tyranny. The revolution that occurred in the minds of men was followed, according to Paine, by a "revolution in the principles and practice of governments." Reason would now be the means by which men discovered the moral laws and rights of nature on which their new constitutions and governments would rest. With the Declaration of Independence and the American Revolution, there is, Paine wrote hopefully, "a morning of reason rising upon man, on the subject of government, that has not appeared before."[21]

The Declaration of Independence and America's revolutionary generation elevated the sovereignty of reason to a place of prominence in man's moral and political affairs. The titles of Ethan Allen's best-known work, *Reason the Only Oracle of Man* (1784), and Elihu Palmer's newspaper, *The Temple of Reason*, summed up the epistemological self-confidence of America's revolutionary mind. Unlike their Puritan forebears, American revolutionaries claimed that reason can discover and know with certainty the moral laws and rights of nature that undergird the political institutions of a free society. In his *Principles of Nature; or, A Development of the Moral Causes of Happiness among the Human Species* (1801), Palmer declared that "reason, which is the glory of our nature, is destined eventually, in the progress of future ages, to overturn the empire of superstition." Along with most enlightened revolutionaries, Palmer believed that the "strength of the human understanding is incalculable, its keenness of discernment would ultimately penetrate into every part of nature," including human nature, "were it permitted to operate with uncontrolled and unqualified freedom." Most importantly, though, Palmer believed that for man to be morally good, he must be given full scope to use the "operation" of his "intellectual powers," and he "must feel an unqualified confidence in his own energies." With epistemological self-confidence came moral and political self-confidence. By exploring the "empire of reason" and by using the "unlimited power of human reason," the revolutionary generation believed that man could discover objectively true moral laws of nature just as Newton had discovered the physical laws of nature. In fact, "Reason, or the intellectual powers of man, must eventually become both the deposit and the guardian of the rights and happiness of human existence."[22]

NATURE, OR "THE LAWS OF NATURE AND OF NATURE'S GOD"

By dissolving the political bands that had connected them to Great Britain, American provincials were reclaiming the right of self-government to which the "Laws of Nature and of Nature's God" entitled them. But what exactly did Jefferson and the other revolutionaries mean when they spoke of the "Laws of Nature and of Nature's God"? What was their understanding of a moral law of nature (including its attributes and sanctions), its source, how it is known and promulgated, how it differs from a right of nature, and how it should be used in a political, legal, and constitutional context?

Following the philosophic trends of the European Enlightenment, eighteenth-century Americans believed that just as there are physical laws of nature, so there are *moral* laws of nature. The "Laws of Nature and of Nature's God," they argued, apply to man's ethical, social, and political relations in ways similar to how these laws apply to the inanimate objects of nature. As we saw in chapter 1, the great hope of Enlightenment moral theory was summed up in the words of John Locke, who famously claimed in his *Essay Concerning Human Understanding* that morality can and should be placed "amongst the sciences capable of demonstration."[23] As Newton's laws of nature describe the nature of reality, Locke's moral laws of nature describe the reality of human nature: what human nature is, how it operates, and the requirements needed for human life and flourishing. More importantly, Locke's moral laws of nature also direct individuals to act in a certain way; they tell them how they *ought* to behave.[24]

In the *Second Treatise*, Locke famously identified the laws of nature with reason, which means that unassisted reason provides the means by which man discovers principles of human action and interaction that serve his life. Eighteenth-century Americans learned from Locke that the laws of nature are rationally discoverable principles, the applications of which promote human flourishing, social order, and peaceful relations among individuals in a social context. The founding fathers believed that these laws of nature should also be the basis for civil laws. Because the laws of nature (whether divine or secular) do not specify adequate or complete natural sanctions—that is, punishments for those who violate them—societies of men must give their collective sanction to a neutral arbiter—that is, to government, with the power to punish criminals.

This is the intellectual universe that American revolutionaries were drawn toward and relied on when they announced to the world their moral claim to assume a "separate and equal station." Throughout much of the eighteenth century, and certainly in the period between 1765 and 1800, Americans regularly invoked the "law of nature" as the guiding principle of their moral and political thought.

In reaction to the British Parliament's passage of the Stamp Act in 1765, John Adams encouraged his fellow colonial Americans to "study the law of nature" and to search for the foundation of all just government "in the frame of human nature, in the constitution of the intellectual and moral world."[25] A decade later, an eighteen-year-old Alexander Hamilton, then a student at King's College in New York, advised his American compatriots to apply themselves "without delay, to the study of the law of nature." He recommended they read the great seventeenth- and eighteenth-century "law of nature" theorists, such as "Grotius, Puffendorf, Locke, Montesquieu, and Burlemaqui."[26] To Hamilton's impressive list, John Adams, Thomas Jefferson, and James Wilson added Richard Cumberland, Emmerich de Vattel, and Jean Barbeyrac.

For Enlightenment philosophers and America's revolutionary generation, the laws of nature were not created by human will, but were, rather, discovered, defined, institutionalized, and enforced by man. The laws of nature transcend the commands made by legislatures, and they apply regardless of whether they are recognized and enforced by any political institution. According to James Otis, the "law of nature was not of man's making, nor is it in his power to mend it or alter its course." Instead, man's relationship to the law of nature, he continued, can follow only one of two paths: "He can only perform and keep or disobey and break it."[27] The Americans learned from their philosophic tutors that the moral laws of nature were discoverable by reason and that such laws should guide man's individual ethical and social behavior.

✱　✱　✱

Over the course of the eighteenth century, colonial Americans developed and used a rather sophisticated understanding of the moral concept "law of nature." Following Locke and other Enlightenment philosophers, colonial and revolutionary Americans typically defined the law of nature as synonymous with reason or as a dictate of "right reason."

As early as 1717, John Wise, in his *A Vindication of the Government of New England Churches*, argued that right reason provides the rule for each man "in all their Actions; obliging each one to the performance of that which is Right" relative to justice and "to all other Moral Vertues." The law of nature is, according to Wise, synonymous with "Mans Reason." It is a "dictate of Right Reason," which means that "the Understanding of Man is Endowed with such a power, as to be able, from the Contemplation of humane Condition to *discover* a necessity of Living agreeably with this Law: And likewise to find out some Principle, by which the Precepts of it may be clearly and solidly Demonstrated." Man can discover the law of nature and the principles of human association, according to Wise, by "a narrow Watch, and accurate Contemplation of our Natural Condition."[28]

Forty-five years later, on the eve of the imperial crisis, the Reverend Abraham Williams in a 1762 election sermon argued that the laws of nature are "founded in Reason and Equity."[29] As the American Enlightenment reached its peak starting in the 1760s and 1770s, the best colonial thinkers saw the philosophic relationship between right reason and the moral law of nature. Revolutionary-era pamphlets, sermons, and official declarations and petitions are replete with similar attempts to associate the moral laws of nature with reason or "right reason."[30] It was critically important to American colonials that they ground their moral, political, and constitutional "Principles upon the solid Basis of Truth," and "Reason points out to us the Method" for determining the truth relative to the moral laws of nature. The Americans were "bound by the sacred law of reason and nature," wrote "An American" in the *Massachusetts Spy*, to oppose the Sugar, Stamp, and Townshend Acts as "tyranny," and they were to view the money taken from them by these laws as "downright robbery."[31]

How did the American colonists understand the relationship between reason and the moral laws of nature?

The revolutionary generation most often said that the laws of nature were known and promulgated through a *discovery* process—that is, by the application of right or proper reasoning to the study of nature and human nature. One anonymous writer from Hampshire County in Massachusetts summed up in 1775 the emerging American understanding of how the laws of nature are known and promulgated when he indicated that the purpose of man's "principle of intelligence" is to "discover truth from falsehood, good from evil, to investigate the nature and tendency of actions, their qualities, causes and effects, the connection and relation of things and the duty resulting therefrom." And in the context of the imperial crisis, the Americans' happiness, he continued, "depends upon carefully distinguishing between propositions deduced from the fine spun hypothesis framed by designing men, and self-evident principles; between plausible representations, and plain stubborn facts." Later that year, a New Yorker writing under the pseudonym "The Monitor" declared that the law of nature is synonymous with the law of reason, which in turn is little more than the "dictates of common sense" applied to "unalterable relations of right and wrong, justice and injustice." Such laws, he continued, "retain their force" in spite of the "arbitrary constructions," "perverted conceptions, or contaminated principles" of kings and ministers.[32]

John Adams probably thought more seriously about the relationship between human reason and the moral laws of nature than did any other American revolutionary. As early as 1756, a twenty-one-year-old Adams was writing in his *Diary* that reason is man's only tool for determining what is morally right. Man has been given "reason," he argued, "to find out the Truth, and the real Design and true End of our Existence." For Adams, the moral law of nature was synonymous with reason: "Law is human Reason," he asserted; it governs "all the Inhabitants of the Earth; the political and civil laws of each Nation should be only the particular Cases, in which human Reason is applied." In fact, "Nature and Truth or rather Truth and right are invariably the same in all Times and in all Places. And Reason, pure unbiassed Reason perceives them alike in all Times and in all Places."[33]

As a young man, Adams took seriously the possibility that there are principles of natural justice grounded in an objective moral order that can be known through reason. Reason itself, however, is not a law of nature. It is a means by which to discover the laws of nature. The moral laws of nature denote a relationship between existence broadly speaking and man's consciousness, that is, between nature and human nature. Moral principles are *necessary* and must be discovered because man, given his particular nature as a volitional and rational being, bears a certain relationship to the world in which he lives, including his relationship to other men. As Adams put it in 1765: "Tis impossible to judge with much Præcision of the true Motives and Qualities of human Actions, or of the Propriety of Rules contrived to govern them, without considering with like Attention, all the Passions, Appetites, Affections in Nature from which they flow. *An intimate Knowledge therefore of the intellectual and moral World is the sole foundation on which a stable structure of Knowledge can be erected*."[34] Untutored reason was not, however, enough for Adams. "Right" reason was a method—the proper method—for thinking and acquiring knowledge. And it was principally that "method," Adams mused, that allowed Isaac Newton to discover and demonstrate "the true system of the World." Newton rose above other

English scientists of the time because he had "employed Experiment and [Geometry?]"—that is, induction and deduction—in scientific inquiry. "It [is] the Method then," concluded Adams, that discovers nature's secrets and potentially reveals the moral laws of nature.[35]

Advocating something like the "historical plain method" advanced by Locke in the *Essay Concerning Human Understanding*, Adams defined "Natural Phylosophy" as "the Art of deducing the generall laws and properties of material substances, from a series of *analogous* observations."

> The manner of reasoning in this art is not strictly demonstrative, and by Consequence the knowledge hence acquired, not absolutely Scientifical, because the facts that we reason upon, are perceived by Sence and not by the internal Action of the mind Contemplating its Ideas. But these Facts being presumed true in the form of Axioms, subsequent reasonings about them may be in the strictest sence, scientifical. This Art informs us, in what manner bodies will influence us and each other in given Circumstances, and so teaches us, to avoid the noxious and imbrace the beneficial qualities of matter.[36]

The Lockean method of "right reason" applied as much to the study of man and society as it did to the study of nature. Adams and the thinking revolutionaries who joined him assumed that moral and political philosophers must devote themselves to observing and experiencing the world around them, to examining their own ideas and passions introspectively, and to studying the history of mankind. The primary mode of reasoning applied by revolutionary Americans to discovering the moral laws of nature was therefore inductive. The very same method they would have used to investigate the physical laws of nature—that is, an empirical, a posteriori, inductive mode of reasoning—was also used to reveal the moral laws of nature.[37]

No founding father *before* the Revolution thought longer and harder about the method of reason by which to discover and reveal the moral laws of nature than John Adams. By observing empirically the nature of "terrestrial enjoyments" and sufferings—that is, the rewards and punishments consonant with the moral law of nature—Adams thought it possible to reason backward from effects to causes and then forward again to the principles that might guide human action. The most important and fruitful field of study for Adams was that of human nature, or what he often referred to as the "Constitution of our Minds and Bodies."[38] From an early age, he drove himself to understand and give an account of his own mental operations and those of others. "Let me search for the Clue, which Led great Shakespeare into the Labyrinth of mental Nature! Let me examine how men think," he demanded of himself. Adams always began with himself, turning inward and observing his passions and the operation of his own mental processes: "Here I should moderate my Passions, regulate my Desires, increase my Veneration of Virtue, and Resolution to pursue it, here I should range the whole material and Intellectual World, as far as human Powers can comprehend it, in silent Contemplation."[39] Adams's mode of reasoning was perfectly consistent with Locke's "historical plain method."

In the years *after* the Revolution, Ethan Allen of the Green Mountain Boys was one of America's leading thinkers in search of the moral laws of nature. In *Reason the Only Oracle of Man* (1785), Allen identified the process by which the laws of nature are known. Nature is like a book and the Book of Nature can be read, he reasoned analogously, but it must be opened first before it can be read. And how is the Book of Nature opened? Allen insisted that it must be opened and then read inductively. Nature's laws are discovered through our experience of cause-and-effect relationships. He argued that experience teaches man that all consequences have causes, that the events of the world we experience are causally dependent on preceding ones. The Book of Nature says that all entities in nature are interconnected and that nature's order and harmony are not the result of "blind chance." To change the metaphor, the universe—that vast system of cause and effect—is run like a perfectly calibrated watch by God the Watchmaker and the promulgation of its laws "is co-extensive and co-existent with, and binding on all intelligent beings in the universe."[40]

Following Locke and his Enlightenment students, eighteenth-century Americans saw a direct relationship between the physical laws of nature and the moral laws of nature as they apply to human action.

Many colonists echoed Montesquieu's description of the laws of nature in the *Persian Letters* (1721), wherein the Frenchman defined such laws as the relations between things. "Justice," or the moral law, he wrote, "is a relation of suitability, which actually exists between two things."[41] The laws of nature describe the *forces* of, *regular actions* by, and *relations* among entities of various kinds, both in nature and in society. Nature's laws describe the way nature and human nature are related, and they prescribe moral rules of behavior.

As early as 1725, Benjamin Franklin, a coeditor of Jefferson's draft declaration and the quintessentially enlightened thinker, identified how eighteenth-century Americans typically saw the relationship between the scientific and moral laws of nature: "How exact and regular is every Thing in the *natural* world! How wisely in every Part contriv'd!...All the heavenly Bodies, the Stars and Planets, are regulated with the utmost wisdom! And can we suppose less care to be taken in the order of the *Moral* than in the *Natural* System."[42] Forty-nine years later, another "Philadelphian" declared "To the Freeman of America" that the "laws of mechanics apply in politics, as well as philosophy." In fact, he implied that the Americans were following the moral law of nature while the British were following the law of armed force.[43]

In 1766, in the wake of the Stamp Act crisis, Richard Bland, a writer, planter, and long-standing member of the Virginia House of Burgesses, mocked the common British viewpoint that the Britannic empire was a vast physical system revolving around the dictates of Whitehall. Bland noted that there were Newtonian "Laws of Attraction in natural as well as political Philosophy," and "that Bodies in Contact, and cemented by mutual Interests, cohere more strongly than those which are at a Distance, and have no common Interests to preserve." Bland charged the British with violating this law of nature in order to destroy the colonies "whose real Interests are the same, and therefore ought to be united in the closest Communication, are to be disjoined, and all intercommunication between them prevented." In trying to resolve the debate between colonies and mother country, Bland argued, "we can receive no Light from the Laws of Kingdom, or from ancient History, to direct us in our Inquiry." Instead, he urged his fellow Americans to have "Recourse to the Law of Nature, and those Rights of Mankind which flow from it."[44]

A generation later, Elihu Palmer, one of America's leading Deists in the quarter century after the end of the War of Independence, presented the Enlightenment view quite clearly in his treatise on the *Principles of Nature* (1801), stating that there are laws of nature that define man's "physical relation...to all existence" (i.e., descriptive scientific laws), and there are laws of nature that define man's moral relationship "to his own species and to all other inferior animals" (i.e., prescriptive moral laws).[45] Both forms of the law of nature are instances of, and are necessitated by, the law of causality as they apply to man and his relationship to nature and human nature. The careful, painstaking observation of nature, sometimes enhanced through social experimentation and trial and error, leads man from the facts of nature or human nature to a mechanical law or a moral principle, from change or indeterminacy to a fixed, law-like pattern in nature or a certain moral principle for man.

We can better grasp how the revolutionary generation understood and applied the idea of a moral law of nature by seeing it in the form of an "*if-given-then*" conditional imperative. Their reasoning about the moral laws of nature went something like this: *If* you want to achieve the following outcome X, *given* certain facts of nature and human nature Y, *then* you must recognize and respect the following principles or rules Z.[46] These principles or rules are the moral laws of nature. They are laws of nature because they partake of necessity—a necessity that describes what *is* (i.e., the constitution of human nature), what *ought* to be (i.e., living a free and flourishing life), and what is necessary to link what *is* with what ought to be (i.e., moral rules of action and the institutions necessary for their fulfillment). "It is *Necessity, Necessity alone,*" intoned Jonas Clark, the pastor of a congregational church in Lexington, Massachusetts, in 1781, "which combines men in society, and gives rise to civil government."[47]

A simple example will illustrate the founders' moral reasoning. Assume that you are a liberty-loving American colonist and the year is 1776. *If* you want to continue living in a free and just society (i.e., one that respects the rights of individuals), *given* the legislation passed by the British Parliament and supported by the Crown during the preceding eleven years (e.g., the Sugar, Stamp, Declaratory, Townshend, Tea, Coercive, and Prohibitory Acts, which not only taxed the colonists without their consent but also denied them long-established common law rights), *then* you must take the appropriate actions necessary to secure your freedom (i.e., to declare your independence from Great Britain and to defend your freedom with arms if required). The moral laws of nature are those rules that can be first induced and then deduced from man's metaphysical condition as it applies to both his relationship with nature and his relationship with other men.

American revolutionaries understood the law of nature as it applied to man and his relations with others to be a code of moral principles defining and regulating man's relationship to himself and to others. In 1762, during that period when the American mind was in the process of being revolutionized and constitutionalized, the Reverend Abraham Williams described the laws of nature as "those Rules of Behaviour...[describing] the Relation [men] bear to one another." A decade later, an anonymous writer in Boston declared that nature's "laws are the measure of right and wrong: We refer to them in all cases as citizens, and on that reference is founded the security of our properties, our persons, and our rights." The following year another Bostonian, the pseudonymous "Massachusettensis," announced that a free and flourishing society was one where every individual was guided by a "sure and righteous rule of action in every occurrence in life." This rule of action secured, to all men who obeyed it, freedom "from the molestation and disturbance of all men." In a free and just society, this rule of action was the municipal law, "which is no more than the law of nature applied to man in society, having for its principal objects, the freedom of the person, conscience, and security of the subject in his property." In 1778, as Massachusetts was entering its fourth year without a legally functioning government, William Whiting told a group of radical libertarians in western Massachusetts that, "in a state of nature, each individual has a right...to dispose of, order, and direct, his property, his person, and all his own actions, within the bounds of the law of nature."[48] The ultimate goal of the moral laws of nature was to expand man's freedom and to protect and promote his well-being and happiness in a social context.

Revolutionary Americans considered the moral laws of nature to have the following attributes: they must be necessary (i.e., governed by the law of cause and effect), absolute, fixed, universal, eternal, uniform, orderly, harmonious, binding, demonstrable, and unalienable. The moral laws of nature as understood by the Americans begin with the law of identity; they begin with the fact that all entities, including men, have a fixed nature or specific identity made of particular, unchanging attributes. The law of identity for the revolutionary generation implied the law of causality, which meant that cause-and-effect relationships could only be understood in the light of identity. "Human nature is every where the same," asserted a writer in the *Boston Gazette*, which means that "similar effects will always flow from the same cause." James Otis likewise characterized the qualities of the moral laws of nature in this pithy statement: "The laws of nature are uniform and invariable. The same causes will produce the same effects from generation to generation." The laws of nature are "always binding," declared the anonymous Boston author of "A Dialogue Between a Ruler and a Subject" in 1772, and two years later Richard Wells declared the "laws of right and wrong" to be "eternally and invariably the same." According to an anonymous writer in the *Massachusetts Spy*, the moral law of nature is known by studying the "nature of man" and the "constitution of things"; it is "discoverable by reason"; it provides all of the "principles and springs of action"; it is "discharged by conforming to the laws of eternal justice, and the practice of every social virtue"; it is "binding all over the globe, in all countries, at all times, same at Rome, at Athens, in Britain and America"; no "senate, no parliament, no assembly, can dispense with it, retrench or alter it"; and "no law, no transaction repugnant to this law is of any validity."[49]

In his pamphlet *The Farmer Refuted* of 1775, Alexander Hamilton attributed to the law of nature the following characteristics: it is an "eternal and immutable law"; it is "indispensibly, obligatory upon all mankind, prior to any human institution whatever"; and it is "binding over all the globe, in all countries, and at all times." According to Hamilton, the general commands of the law of nature are as follows:

> Upon this law, depend the natural rights of mankind, the supreme
> being gave existence to man, together with the means of preserv-
> ing and beatifying that existence. He endowed him with rational
> faculties, by the help of which, to discern and pursue such things, as
> were consistent with his duty and interest, and invested him with
> an inviolable right to personal liberty, and personal safety.
>
> Hence, in a state of nature, no man had any *moral power* to
> deprive another of his life, limbs, property or liberty; nor the least
> authority to command, or exact obedience from him; except that
> which arose from the ties of consanguinity.

Given human nature, the moral law commands two things: first, that man must identify and pursue those values "consistent with his duty and interest," and he has a moral right to his life, liberty, and property; and, second, that he may not deprive others of their natural rights. It was on the basis of this "criterion," Hamilton claimed, that the Americans detected "injustice" in Parliament's legislation of the 1760s and 1770s.[50]

In 1787, Elizur Goodrich delivered an election-day sermon on "The Principles of Civil Union and Happiness Considered and Recommended" to the Connecticut legislature, in which he described some of the principal characteristics of the moral laws of nature. Goodrich's statement is important for shedding light on what the revolutionary generation meant by a moral law of nature, and for demonstrating unequivocally Locke's influence on the development of America's revolutionary mind. "The principles of society are the laws," he wrote,

> which Almighty God has established in the moral world, and made *necessary* to be observed by mankind; in order to promote their true happiness, in their transactions and intercourse. These laws may be considered as principles, in respect of their fixedness and operation; and as maxims, since by the knowledge of them, we discover those rules of conduct, which direct mankind to the highest perfection, and supreme happiness of their nature. They are as fixed and unchangeable as the laws which operate in the natural world. Human art in order to produce certain effects, must conform to the principles and laws, which the Almighty Creator has established in the natural world."[51]

Goodrich's reasoning is one of the best examples of how the revolutionary generation understood the Declaration's call to the "Laws of Nature and of Nature's God." According to Goodrich, there are laws of the moral world—prescriptive moral laws that are as "fixed and unchangeable" as the laws governing the physical universe—that can be discovered and should be applied as rules of conduct to human life. These laws, principles, rules, and maxims, if understood and followed, will help men to perfect their lives as individuals and to improve their relations with others. Based on what man *is*, these moral laws instruct men in how they *ought* to act and live if they are to achieve their highest values.

Such moral laws of nature also have consequences—consequences certain and absolute—for those who follow and do not follow them, and so wise legislators, according to Goodrich, should base their laws on them:

> Moral connections and causes in different circumstances produce harmony or discord, peace or war, happiness or woe among

mankind, with the same certainty, as physical causes produce their
effect. To institute these causes and connexions belongs not to men,
to nations or to human laws, but to build upon them. It is no more
in the power of the greatest earthly potentate to hinder their operation, than it is to govern the flowing and ebbing of the ocean.

This is why "Human art in order to produce certain effects, must conform
to the principles and laws, which the Almighty Creator has established
in the natural world." Reality is the standard from which man must make
certain choices and take certain actions that will result in consequences that
either diminish or further his life and happiness. To deny these principles
is to deny reality: "For he, who attempts these things, on other principles,
than those of nature, attempts to make a new world; and his aim will
prove absurd and his labour lost."[52] These makers of new worlds who deny
or do not follow the laws of nature are utopians, who deny the reality of
this world; they are fantasists, who always resort to force to make people
accept their untrue ideas. In the context of the time, they become Jacobins.
The moral laws of nature, by contrast, provide men with true principles of
action by which to guide their conduct in the pursuit of certain ends (e.g.,
their "true happiness").

American revolutionaries continued to use the language of the moral
law of nature well into the 1790s. Other than John Adams, no member of
the revolutionary generation thought longer and harder about the moral
laws of nature than James Wilson. In fact, he devoted an entire chapter
to it in his *Lectures on Law*. Wilson considered the moral law of nature to
be immanent in human nature. The fundamental characteristics of the law
of nature are, he argued, immutability and universality: the "law of nature
is *immutable*, not by the effect of an arbitrary disposition, but because it
has its foundation in the nature, constitution, and mutual relations of men
and things"; and the "law of nature is *universal*...having its foundation in
the constitution and state of man, has an essential fitness for all mankind,
and binds them without distinction." Drawing on the authority of Cicero,
his description of the moral law of nature sums up the view of an entire
generation:

This law, or right reason, as Cicero calls it, is thus beautifully
described by that eloquent philosopher. "It is, indeed," says he, "a

true law, conformable to nature, diffused among all men, unchangeable, eternal. By its commands, it calls men to their duty: by its pro-
hibitions, it deters them from vice. To diminish, to alter, much more
to abolish this law, is a vain attempt. Neither by the senate, nor by
the people, can its powerful obligation be dissolved. It requires no
interpreter or commentator. It is not one law at Rome, another at
Athens; one law now, another hereafter: it is the same eternal and
immutable law, given at all times and to all nations: for God, who is
its author and promulgator, is always the sole master and sovereign
of mankind."[53]

For Wilson and America's revolutionary statesmen, the moral laws of
nature provided them first with a universal moral standard by which to
judge the actions of the British Parliament during the 1760s and 1770s
and then with a moral base on which to design and build their new constitutions and governments. The law of nature stands above man's law.
Governments hitherto owed their origin to accident and force, but the
Americans could now design and build governments on the basis of rationally discernible and true moral principles.

The law of nature should guide all law, including the international law
of nations. When he was Secretary of State in the Washington administration, Thomas Jefferson argued that America's foreign policy should be
guided by "the moral law of our nature." This higher moral law, Jefferson
argued, creates "moral duties which exist between individual and individual
in a state of nature," and such a law accompanies men when they enter
"into a state of society." In fact, the "aggregate of the duties of all individuals composing the society constitutes the duties of that society towards
any other." The result is that "between society and society the same moral
duties exist as did between the individuals composing them, while in an
unassociated state, and their maker not having released them from those
duties on their forming themselves into a nation."[54]

And what is the source of the moral laws of nature? The Declaration of
Independence speaks of the "Laws of Nature and of Nature's God," a phrase
that captures rather nicely the revolutionary generation's ambiguity or being
of two minds about the nature, source, and sanctions associated with the laws
of nature. Jefferson's equivocation in that phrase, however, leaves open the
question whether nature simply, or nature's God, is the source of these laws.

Do the moral laws of nature depend on the existence of a divine creator? This much can be said with confidence: when Jefferson wrote of "Nature's God" he almost certainly meant the impersonal, far-removed, deist God that set the world in motion according to laws that were meant to govern in his absence. The Declaration's God is not the God of the Old Testament (nor is it even the God of the New Testament) but is Nature's God. Jefferson's God is posited but not known. What can be established, however, and what is immediately relevant to the Declaration, is nature and its laws.[55] Thus Jefferson could tell his nephew Peter Carr, "those facts in the Bible which contradict the laws of nature, must be examined with more care, and under a variety of faces."[56]

The claim that the laws of nature are God's laws appeared frequently in the literature of the American Revolution. The revolutionary generation, almost to a man, considered God the source or first cause of nature's laws. In *The Farmer Refuted*, Alexander Hamilton summed up—while quoting, ironically enough, Blackstone—what was probably the common sense of the subject among most Americans. "Good and wise men, in all ages," according to Hamilton, have

> supposed that the Deity, from the relations we stand in to himself
> and to each other, has constituted an eternal and immutable law,
> which is indispensably obligatory upon all mankind, prior to any
> human institution whatever.
>   This is what is called the law of nature, "which, being coeval
> with mankind, and dictated by God himself, is, of course, superior
> in obligations to any other....No human laws are of any validity,
> if contrary to this; and such of them as are valid derive all their
> authority, mediately or immediately, from this original."[57]

The purest Christian form of this teaching can be seen in a 1770 sermon delivered by the Reverend Samuel Cooke, who argued that faith, not reason, was the foundation of man's moral duties. Cooke argued:

> without a true fear of God, justice will be found to be but an empty
> name. Though reason may in some degree investigate the rela-
> tion and fitness of things, yet I think it evident that moral obliga-
> tions are founded wholly in a *belief* of God and his superintending

providence. This belief, deeply impressed on the mind, brings the most convincing evidence that men are moral agents, obliged to act according to the natural and evident relation of things, and the rank they bear in God's creation; that the divine will, however made known to them, is the law by which all their actions must be regulated, and their state finally determined.[58]

In contrast to Cooke, most revolutionary Americans argued that the moral law of nature is known by right reason and not through revelation. In fact, a few attempted to pick up where John Locke left off—that is, to establish a demonstrative science of ethics that did not necessarily rely on the existence of God to be knowable or operational. This latter group might include Thomas Jefferson, John Adams, Ethan Allen, and Elihu Palmer. It is important to note that all four were believers, but they also attempted to ground the law of nature on what might be called metaphysical law or what Jefferson variously referred to as the "laws of our being," the "order of nature," the "moral law of our nature," and "universal law."[59] They followed a tradition extending from Grotius, Locke, and Montesquieu down to the founders, which said that the moral law of nature would still be valid and operational even if, in the words of Grotius, "there is no God, or that he has no Care of human affairs."[60]

Several revolutionary thinkers came very close to adopting a similar position. Ethan Allen, for instance, echoing Montesquieu in the *Persian Letters*, wrote that the moral laws of nature are derived not from sacred texts or books of philosophy but from the Book of Nature—that is, from "the fitness of things."[61] Moral science, according to Allen, is known by reason and derived from experience. The moral laws of nature can therefore be known without knowing or proving the existence of God. Likewise, Elihu Palmer, seemingly combining Grotius and Montesquieu, stated the fundamental issue in unmistakable terms:

> If a thousand Gods existed, *or if nature existed independent of any,* the *moral relation* between man and man would remain exactly the same in either case. *Moral principle is the result of this relation*, it is founded in the properties of our nature and it is as indestructible as the basis on which it rests. If we could abandon for a moment every theistical idea, it would nevertheless remain substantially true, that

the happiness of society must depend upon the exercise of equal
and reciprocal justice.

Palmer's statement represents the intellectual revolution toward which
the American mind was slowly moving—toward a view of natural justice
grounded in a potentially godless metaphysical law. The challenge of this
law was to discover the naturally proper "moral relation between man and
man" that would promote a flourishing human life and serve as the basis for
a new legal and political order. Such a law would exist, to repeat Palmer's
felicitous expression, whether "a thousand Gods existed, or if nature existed
independent of any."[62]

America's revolutionary thinkers typically identified the particular content of the laws of nature and their sanctions based on where they located
the source of those laws. Not surprisingly, they viewed the substance of the
laws of nature in one of two ways: as either God-centered and duty-based
on one hand, or as man-centered and rights-based on the other. Those who
saw God as the first cause of the laws of nature (e.g., James Wilson, John
Witherspoon, and the colonies' religious leaders) typically established two
laws as fundamental: first, the law to obey God's commands; and, second,
the Golden Rule to "do unto others as you would have them do unto you."
The sanctions associated with God's laws of nature were dependent on
the immortality of souls and the promise of eternal bliss or suffering in
the afterlife.[63]

Contrariwise, those who turned to nature and to what John Adams
referred to as the "constitution of the human mind" as the first cause
of the laws of nature (e.g., Adams, Jefferson, Ethan Allen, and Elihu
Palmer) typically established two laws as fundamental: first, the law of
self-preservation; and, second, the law to respect the rights of others.
The punishments associated with violating the secular first law of nature
were penury, misery, and death, and the rewards for obeying it were life,
health, and happiness. The punishments for violating the secular second
law of nature were social neglect and contempt, and the rewards for
obeying it were social esteem and admiration.[64] Whereas God-centered
laws were synonymous with man's duties, man-centered laws issued from
man's rights.

American revolutionaries studied the moral laws of nature with a practical purpose in mind: to translate these laws into the civil or municipal laws

that govern society. America's founding statesmen and jurists viewed proper conventional, customary, and statutory law as the existential embodiment of the law of nature. A free and just society was, they argued, grounded on such laws. The distinction between the law of nature and man-made law was admirably summed up by one long-forgotten writer in Boston as the difference between unwritten and written law. The unwritten law "dictates the doing of justice to individuals, and the injuring no one." This law of nature "is not peculiar to any nation or people"; instead, it is "put in every breast universally."[65] An intermediary form of law between the law of nature and statutory law is described by our author as customary law, which arises spontaneously and informally in particular societies over the course of decades, centuries, and millennia. The authority of customary law is found both in its ancientness and the voluntary assent of people to live by certain folkways over long periods of time.[66] Written or statutory law—or at least the best kind, the kind that protects the rights of individuals—is an instantiation of the law of nature and the customary law. The purpose of written law is to put the laws of nature and custom into written and legal form and ultimately "into force, by executing tribunals, and annexing penalties." For many eighteenth-century Americans, the laws or principles associated with Magna Carta, the English common law, and the English constitution were conventional expressions of the laws of nature. "These principles of right, called the Unwritten Law," when combined with customary and statutory laws such as those represented in the pre-1688 English constitution, were adopted in America "not as receiving authority from Britain, but as being founded in the nature and fitness of things."[67] For American colonials, the original Saxon constitution was the embodiment of the moral law of nature, which is why they fought so hard to defend their ancient constitution during the early years of the imperial crisis.

The great theoretical and practical problem confronted by America's Lockean statesmen was in translating the unwritten into written law. As noted in chapter 1, in the state of nature, the law of nature was seen as toothless. It had no enforcement mechanism to deal with those who violated its rules. Samuel Cooke, the Pastor of the Second Church in Cambridge, Massachusetts, illuminated the problem in his 1770 sermon on "The True Principles of Civil Government." As men form larger and more complex societies, the "temptations to injustice and violence increase," noted Cooke, "and the occasions of them multiply in proportion to the increase and opulence of the society." The problem is that the moral laws of nature only influence, guide, and "bind the conscience of the upright," which means such laws are "insufficient to restrain the sons of violence." Hence arises the need for men to escape the state of nature and to form governments in order to provide an enforcement mechanism for the moral laws of nature. The role of government in a free and just society is to establish "rules or laws" that mirror the moral laws of nature, "with proper penalties to enforce them, to which individuals shall be subjected." Or, as the Reverend John Tucker of Newbury preached in his election sermon to the governor and legislature of Massachusetts in 1771, the purpose of government is to establish "certain laws, as the general measures of right and wrong." Political rulers in a free and just government serve as "watchmen and guardians over the state, whose special business it is" to "curb and restrain the unrighteous and factious, from acts of fraud, rapine and violence, and to protect others in the peaceable enjoyment of their rights."[68]

A decade after Tucker addressed the Massachusetts governor and legislature, the Reverend Jonas Clark, speaking to the same body, compared a duly established civil government to "a Shield, as it is instituted for the defence and protection of the subjects of the state." He reminded the Massachusetts rulers that "they are intrusted with several powers of government, that individuals may be protected and defended in their life, liberty, property and rights—that the internal peace and order of society might be preserved; and that the external defence, of the whole, against the encroachments, violence, assaults, or invasions of enemies, or oppressors, might effectually be provided for." When government is viewed as a "shield," its role is to protect individuals in their rights. The protection of the rights of individuals requires a government to make statutory laws that "flow from the constitution, as the streams from a fountain, and even grow out of it, as the tree from the root, or the branches from the stock."[69] The constitution—a written constitution—is built in turn on the unwritten, moral laws of nature.

In 1775, John Joachim Zubly from Georgia defined a law as a "rule of behavior, made under proper authority, and with penalties annexed, suitable to deter the transgressions." This definition applied to both the unwritten and the written law. The problem with the unwritten law or the law of nature, however, is that it lacked the necessary punishments and enforcement mechanisms to make it salutary. If the moral law of nature is God's law, then its ultimate punishments were not delivered until after death, which meant they were useless in terms of providing satisfaction in the context of life here and now. If the moral law of nature is a reflection of man's natural constitution and the requirements of human life, then its ultimate sanctions and punishments could only be executed by those who were the victims of such transgressions, which of course would lead naturally to the war of all against all. This is why, Zubly argued, men create governments. They cannot exist without just laws enforced equally. He described the problem this way: "The will, minds, tempers, dispositions, views and interests of men are so very different, and sometimes so opposite, that without law, which cements and binds all, every thing would be in endless disorder and confusion." The unwritten law must be therefore translated into written law with the force of a neutral, third party to back up its commandments. The challenge of course is for government to make laws that actually reflect the moral law of nature and thereby expand the boundaries of freedom. The connection between law and liberty was crucial. The "well regulated liberty of individuals is the natural offspring of laws," Zubly insisted, "which prudently regulate the rights of whole communities." In fact, Zubly assumed that law and liberty are "perfectly consistent." Liberty that is not regulated by law, he continued, "is a delusive phantom, and unworthy of the glorious name."[70] Thus the single greatest theoretical and practical task of revolutionary statesmanship was in translating the unwritten law into written law and in designing laws consistent with liberty.

Writing in Boston's *Continental Journal*, the pseudonymous "Benevolus" identified the precise relationship between the moral laws of nature and the coercive laws of government. According to Benevolus, the most common crime in civil society—the most common violation of the laws of nature—is the theft of property, which is the result of stealing either by individuals or governments, including democratic majorities. The "wisdom of philosophy," noted Benevolus, has offered to statesmen certain "remedies" and "policies" for dealing with violations of the laws of nature in civil society. They include:

1. A constitution of government derived from the law of nature and right reason, the real original of all positive laws.

2. A government founded upon the fundamental principles of justice and equity; wherein power is restrained from tyranny, and liberty from licentiousness.

3. A code of laws, so digested with such clearness and precision, as to exclude cavil and chicanerie from the shifting scales of justice, poised equally to ALL, by an impartial administration of it.

4. A government, in which, every member of the legislative is so far subjected in his person and property, as immediately and effectually to feel, *equally*, with his fellow citizens, every mischief and inconvenience resulting from all and every act of legislation: A government, in short, wherein the exercise of the moral virtues is impressed upon the governed, not only by precept, but by the uniform example of those who govern.[71]

Benevolus's statement is the clearest expression of how the revolutionary generation understood the four-step connection between the laws of nature, constitutions, governments, and laws statutory and municipal.

In contrast to their Loyalist brethren, many revolutionary statesmen of the founding era believed that any positive law that violated the laws of nature was necessarily null and void. In 1764, James Otis declared that any statutory law that violated "*natural* equity" and "*his* natural laws" should be declared "void" by the king's "executive courts." In 1772, Samuel Adams, writing for the Committee of Correspondence of the Boston Town Meeting, declared: "All positive and civil laws should conform, as far as possible, to the law of natural reason and equity." Two years later, James Wilson announced, quoting the Swiss legal and political theorist Jean-Jacques Burlamaqui, that the law of nature "must regulate the legislature itself." That same year, the First Continental Congress in its Declaration and Resolves invoked "the immutable laws of nature" against Parliament's recently passed Coercive Acts.[72] A year later, in 1775, Alexander Hamilton followed Wilson's lead and defended the actions of the Continental Congress with a direct appeal to the laws of nature:

When the first principles of civil society are violated, and the rights of a whole people are invaded, the common forms of municipal law

are not to be regarded. Men may then betake themselves to the law
of nature; and, if they but conform their actions to that standard,
all cavils against them betray either ignorance or dishonesty. There
are some events in society, to which human laws cannot extend,
but when applied to them, lose all their force and efficacy. In short,
when human laws contradict or discountenance the means which
are necessary to preserve the essential rights of any society, they
defeat the proper end of all laws, and so become null and void.[73]

From the American perspective, the clearest example of an unjust
law that violated the law of nature was the Stamp Act, which taxed the
Americans without their consent. In 1772, Joseph Warren captured the relationship between natural and conventional justice in an oration delivered
to commemorate the Boston Massacre. Warren reminded his audience
"that the greatest and most important right of a British subject is, that he
shall be governed by no laws but those to which he either in person or by
his representative hath given his consent." He continued: "And this I will
venture to assert, is the grand basis of British freedom; it is interwoven
with the constitution; and whenever this is lost, the constitution must be
destroyed."[74] The rule of consent is grounded on the right of property,
which in turn is grounded on the natural law of self-ownership. Or consider the view of an anonymous writer in New York, who declared, "That
representation should accompany taxation is an eternal law of nature, and
inseparable from the very idea of property, so that no property can exist
without it: whatever is a man's own, no other person can have a right to
take from him, without his consent, expressed by himself, or his representative." Correctly parsed, the law of nature says, "whatever is a man's own, no
other person can have a right to take from him, without his consent." The
municipal or statutory expression of this law of nature says that consent
in the context of civil society is best expressed through the principal of
political representation. Therefore, whoever attempts to tax an individual
without his direct or indirect consent "attempts an injury" and "whoever
does it, commits a robbery."[75] The philosophic concept "law of nature" was
at the heart of the American revolutionaries' case against the actions of
the British Parliament.

In sum, there was a consensus across a broad spectrum of American
opinion in 1776 that the political laws of a free and just society should

reflect the fundamental moral laws of nature. When Jefferson wrote in the Declaration of Independence that the Americans were now prepared to break their familial ties with Great Britain and to establish new political societies on the basis of the "Laws of Nature and of Nature's God," he was expressing what he referred to as the common sentiments of the "American mind." Virtually all Americans during the Revolutionary period believed that there are moral laws of nature, that they transcend the laws of men, that such laws must be discovered through reason and by studying the Book of Nature, that they describe cause-and-effect relationships between man and nature and between man and man, that they prescribe principles of action and moral rules of behavior, and that such laws are fixed, absolute, universal, and eternal. Not all Americans agreed on the exact content of those laws or whether their ultimate source was to be found in "Nature" or in "Nature's God," but Jefferson's felicitous ambiguity was also an expression of both the Enlightenment mind and the American mind.

CHAPTER 3

Self-Evident Truths

"We hold these truths to be self-evident..."

On July 4, 1776, the American people proclaimed a revolutionary credo to the world. Through their representatives in the Continental Congress, they openly declared why it was "necessary" to "dissolve the political bands" that had connected them to Great Britain and why it was their *right* to assume that "separate and equal station" to which they were entitled by "the Laws of Nature and of Nature's God."

The fundamental laws to which the Americans appealed were not local laws derived from custom or history, nor were they derived from holy scripture or declared by saintly prophets. "Our Revolution commenced on more favorable ground," Thomas Jefferson told the English radical Whig John Cartwright in 1824. Rather than searching into "musty records," hunting up "royal parchments," or investigating "the laws and institutions of a semi-barbarous ancestry," the Americans appealed to the great principles "of nature, and found them engraved on our hearts." The Revolution, according to Jefferson, presented the Americans with "an album on which we were free to write what we pleased."[1] Unlike the lawgivers of classical antiquity, American constitution makers did not claim, as John Adams noted, to have interviewed "with the gods," nor were they "in any degree under the inspiration of Heaven." Instead, these New World Solons and Lycurguses built their new governments on "the simple principles of nature" as determined "by the use of reason and the senses."[2]

After dissolving the political bands connecting them to king and country, American revolutionaries then established a new nation based on certain philosophical ideas. As Alexander Hamilton noted in the first essay of *The Federalist*, the United States of America was the first nation in history founded not on accident or force but on reflection and choice, and thus on reason and free will. In contrast to the monarchical and aristocratic societies of Europe, the founding fathers established governments, according to John Taylor of Caroline, "rooted in moral or intellectual principles" rather than in "orders, clans or [castes]."[3] This much is clear: American revolutionaries appealed to moral principles they considered *true*—absolutely, permanently, and universally true—in order to justify the extraordinary course of action they were about to embark on. These truths, they argued, are potentially knowable to all men because they are grounded in an objective moral reality that can be known by unassisted human reason. In the words of Enos Hitchcock, chaplain of the Continental Army in 1779 and 1780 and later pastor of the First Congregational Church in Providence, Rhode Island, "Justly may it be said, 'The present is an age of philosophy, and America the empire of reason.'"[4]

The moral philosophy of the American Revolution was stated most eloquently in the second paragraph of the Declaration, which begins with a few simple words: "We hold these truths to be self-evident." These seven words are probably the best known if not the most beloved words of the Declaration. They are also the document's most important words. They are a proem for everything that follows, and they provide a metaphysical and epistemological foundation for the four moral and political truths the Declaration sets out.[5] The four self-evident truths are

1. "that all men are created equal";
2. "that they are endowed by their Creator with certain unalienable Rights, that among these are Life, Liberty and the pursuit of Happiness";
3. "that to secure these rights, Governments are instituted among Men, deriving their just powers from the consent of the governed"; and
4. "that whenever any Form of Government becomes destructive of these ends, it is the Right of the People to alter or to abolish it; and to institute new Government, laying its foundation on such principles and organizing its powers in such form, as to them shall seem most likely to effect their Safety and Happiness."

The Declaration's truths can be reduced to just four words: equality, rights, consent, and revolution. The identification and listing of these self-evident truths serves a twofold function: first, to establish a moral standard against which the actions of king and Parliament will be judged, and, second, to establish the axiomatic principles on which the Americans will design and build new republican governments. Taken together, the Declaration's four truths form a concise synthesis of a new, American-style republicanism.

The Declaration's "truths" were more than mere propositions—they were self-evident *truths*. Truth—not opinion or convention—would now be the standard of moral, political, and constitutional decision making. American revolutionaries viewed truth as a necessary condition for human flourishing. But what exactly is a *self-evident* truth? How are such truths known? More precisely, to what in reality were Jefferson and the signers of the Declaration referring when they declared that that all men are created equal, that they are endowed with unalienable rights, that governments derive their just powers from the consent of the governed, and that it is the right of the people to alter or abolish their government when it becomes destructive of its proper ends?

The Declaration's use and meaning of the concept "self-evident truth" is best seen in three contexts: first, in the broader philosophic context of the seventeenth and eighteenth centuries; second, in the light of what Jefferson and the revolutionary generation thought about the nature of truth and self-evidence; and, third, in the context of its use in the Declaration itself.

THE ENLIGHTENMENT AND SELF-EVIDENT TRUTHS

The most influential statement on the nature of self-evident truths in the seventeenth and eighteenth centuries can be found in John Locke's *An Essay Concerning Human Understanding* (1689). In the *Essay*, Locke initially defined a self-evident truth as a proposition whose subject and predicate necessarily relate to one another without contradiction: "The mind cannot but assent to such a proposition as infallibly true as soon as it understands the terms, without…need of proof."[6] In other words, a self-evident truth is an idea or proposition that strikes the mind as immediately and perceptually true given the correspondence of the terms invoked. Locke, who was reacting against the doctrine of innate knowledge, filled out the meaning of what a self-evident truth is in this way:

For if we will reflect on our own ways of thinking, we shall find that sometimes the mind perceives the agreement or disagreement of two *ideas* immediately by themselves, without the intervention of any other; and this I think we may call *intuitive knowledge*. For in this the mind is at no pains of proving or examining but perceives the truth, as the eye doth light, only by being directed toward it. Thus the mind perceives that *white* is not *black*, that a *circle* is not a *triangle*, that *three* are more than *two* and equal to *one* and *two*. Such kind of truths the mind perceives at the first sight of the *ideas* together, by bare *intuition*, without the intervention of any other *idea*; and this kind of knowledge is the clearest and most certain that human frailty is capable of. This part of knowledge is irresistible and, like bright sunshine, forces itself immediately to be perceived, as soon as ever the mind turns its view that way; and leaves no room for hesitation, doubt, or examination, but the mind is presently filled with the clear light of it. It is on this *intuition* that depends all the certainty and evidence of all our knowledge, which certainty every one finds to be so great that he cannot imagine, and therefore not require, a greater.[7]

For Locke, a self-evident truth is one in which the evidence for an idea or proposition is contained within the definition, syntax, and grammar of the words that make up the idea or proposition. Its truth is known immediately by direct *perception*, or what Locke imprecisely calls intuition. Self-evident truths carry their own evidence such that one's reason or understanding must assent to them as soon as their terms are comprehended. The principle or proposition itself is self-evident if one understands the terms or propositions involved and their relationship to one another. Simple examples of self-evidence include the following kinds of propositions: "black is not white," "up is not down," a "triangle is not a circle." This kind of self-evident truth is open to all human beings, regardless of intelligence or education. All men are equal in their ability to comprehend these kinds of self-evident truths. Slightly more advanced self-evident truths might include: "$1 + 1 = 2$." Self-evident truths of this sort are likewise accessible to virtually all individuals.

In addition to reading Locke's *Essay* directly, Anglo-American provincials learned of the Englishman's views on self-evidence through the writings of William Duncan, an eighteenth-century Scottish philosopher and classicist. Duncan was the teacher of William Small, who in turn was Jefferson's teacher at the College of William and Mary. It was Duncan who made Locke's understanding of self-evidence popular in the eighteenth century through his influential text, *Elements of Logick* (1748).[8] A professor of natural philosophy at Marischal College in Aberdeen, Duncan clarified Locke's definition by arguing that self-evident truths consist of two elements: first, such truths must be basic axioms that are grounded in no prior or anterior idea or proposition, and, second, their constituent parts must be in a noncontradictory relationship with each other. As Duncan put it:

> When any Proposition is offered to the View of the Mind, if the Terms in which it is expressed are understood; upon comparing the Ideas together, the Agreement or Disagreement asserted is either immediately perceived, or found to be beyond the present Reach of the Understanding. In the first Case the Proposition is said to be *self-evident*, and admits not of any Proof, because a bare Attention to the Ideas themselves, produces full Conviction and Certainty; nor is it possible to call in any thing more evident, by way of Confirmation.[9]

Duncan's definition of a self-evident truth is virtually identical to Locke's. The simplest self-evident truths for Locke and Duncan do not require proof. They are perceptually and immediately known to the mind, including to the mind of a child. Even a relatively small child knows that up is not down, that white is not black, and that bitter is not sweet. This kind of truth for Locke and Duncan also yields the highest degree of certainty. A self-evident truth is infallibly certain.[10]

At first blush, however, there is an insurmountable problem in applying either Locke's or Duncan's definition of a self-evident truth to the Declaration of Independence. Most obviously, the Declaration's four self-evident truths do not meet the baseline criteria for self-evidence established by Locke and Duncan. Such criteria (i.e., that self-evident truths be irreducible and noncontradictory) might plausibly apply to the metaphysical claim that "all men are created equal" (and even that claim is and was contested), but surely Locke's and Duncan's strict or technical definitions do not apply to the second, third, and fourth self-evident truths.

How, then, can the Declaration's truths be self-evident if they do not fit the most commonly used eighteenth-century definition of "self-evident"? It turns out that both Locke in the *Essay* and Duncan in the *Elements* used the concept "self-evident" in a more capacious sense than scholars of the Declaration have realized.[11] They both begin with the standard definition of "self-evident" as their baseline, but they also go beyond it to develop a more complex concept defined by "different degrees and ways of evidence and certainty."[12]

In various places in the *Essay*, Locke subtly advances a more nuanced and sophisticated view of self-evidence. He recognizes degrees or a hierarchy of self-evident truths that move from simple to complex. The simplest self-evident truths are known perceptually, that is, one can see that black is not white, that up is not down, and that the whole is bigger than the part. The recognition of these baseline truths is, as Locke says, "irresistible," but perceptually evident truths are not the only kind for Locke. Higher-level, more abstract truths can be metaphysically and logically self-evident (without being perceptually self-evident) because they "carry their own evidence with them," such as "*What is, is*" or "*It is impossible for the same thing to be and not to be.*"[13] Logically, such truths cannot be anything other than what they are. A slightly more abstract self-evident truth might be, "nutrition is necessary to growth and health." Some self-evident truths might even require a simple deduction, such as the famous syllogism: "All men are mortal; Socrates is a man; therefore Socrates is mortal." Self-evidence of this sort is accessible to almost all people.

As one ascends Locke's ladder of truth, perceptual awareness and internal consistency are not enough or not necessary. Higher-level self-evident truths require varying degrees or steps of reasoning beyond perceptual awareness or simple deduction. Two plus three equals five is self-evident only *after* one understands not only the meaning of numbers but also the definitions of "plus" and "equals" and the reasoning associated with addition. At an even higher level of abstraction, the self-evidence of the truth "the three angles of a triangle are equal to two right ones" requires a foreknowledge of the properties and relationships among different geometric points, lines, shapes, surfaces, spaces, and their measurements. What Locke calls "intervening" or "intermediate" ideas that "serve to show the agreement of any two others are called *proofs*; and where the agreement or disagreement is by this means plainly and clearly perceived, it is called *demonstration*: it being *shown* to the understanding, and the mind made to see that it is so."[14] In other words, connecting ideas can extend the self-evidence to higher and more abstract levels of knowledge and truth.

More complex truths can achieve a degree of certainty and even self-evidence if they are grounded on a perceptually self-evident axiom. Moral truths can be discovered that are as certain as mathematical truths, but they require "thought and attention, and the mind must apply itself to a regular deduction of it from some part of our intuitive [i.e., self-evident] knowledge." Locke's meaning can be seen in the following extended passage from the *Essay*:

> We must therefore, if we will proceed as reason advises, *adapt our methods of inquiry to the nature of the ideas we examine*, and the truth we search after. General and certain truths are only founded in the habitudes and relations of abstract *ideas*. A sagacious and methodical application of our thoughts, for the finding out these relations, is the only way to discover all that can be put with truth and certainty concerning them into general propositions. *By what steps we are to proceed in these is to be learned in the schools of the mathematicians who, from very plain and easy beginnings, by gentle degrees, and a continued chain of reasonings, proceed to the discovery and demonstration of truths, that appear at first sight beyond human capacity.* The art of finding proofs, and the admirable methods they have invented for the singling out, and laying in order those intermediate *ideas* that demonstratively show the equality or inequality of unapplicable quantities, is that which has carried them so far and produced such wonderful and unexpected discoveries.[15]

As man moves to the "next degree of *knowledge*," which Locke calls "*demonstrative*" knowledge, he must carry forward with him a perceptually self-evident axiom "in all the connexions of the intermediate *ideas*, without which we cannot attain knowledge and certainty." These intermediate ideas or truths provide what Locke calls "*proofs*" that "serve to show the agreement of any two" other ideas that are not self-evidently connected in the simple sense. Where proofs are "plainly and clearly perceived," it is, Locke says, "called *demonstration*." Demonstrative knowledge must follow a "steady application and pursuit" toward the discovery of a new truth, "and there must be a progression by steps and degrees, before the mind can in this way arrive at certainty and come to perceive the agreement or repugnancy between two *ideas* that need proofs and the use of reason to show it."[16] Knowledge or truths acquired in this way are, or can be, self-evident in that the logic carrying the agreement of one idea to another follows a necessary path.

At the top of Locke's ladder of self-evident truths are "moral principles," which are the most difficult to discover and understand. Such truths do not necessarily carry their own evidence with them. The ascent to moral truths requires, Locke argues, a higher level of "reasoning and discourse, and some exercise of the mind, to discover the certainty of their truth."[17] Moral truths can be self-evident, but only after they are discovered through a process of demonstration, which means a process of reasoning.

Consider, for instance, proposing to a person who has never before heard the "most unshaken rule of morality and the foundation of all social virtue, that *One should do as he would be done unto*." At this point it would be entirely appropriate to ask *why* or *how* the Golden Rule is true or self-evidently true. Locke insists that "*there cannot any one moral rule be proposed whereof a man may not justly demand a reason*." He concedes that the Golden Rule is neither innate nor self-evidently true in the perceptual sense. The author or proposer of the Golden Rule, he argues, is "bound to make out the truth and reasonableness of it." This means that the truth of the Golden Rule and all other "moral rules plainly depends upon some other, antecedent to them and from which they must be deduced," a step that would not be necessary if they were self-evident in the narrow sense.[18]

How, then, can moral rules (simple and complex) be self-evident? It turns out that Locke's initial understanding of self-evident truths (i.e., where the agreement or disagreement of ideas "is perceived immediately by itself, without the intervention or help of any other") is expanded in the *Essay* beyond this first and simple understanding. Locke concedes that there are "several other truths"—indeed, there is "an infinite number of other propositions"—that qualify as self-evident but that go beyond the narrow conception.[19] Locke considers some propositions rationally and objectively deduced from a self-evident axiom to be self-evident, but in a higher, more abstract sense. For example, the existence of God is a self-evident truth for Locke, but only after a series of complex deductions from an axiomatic principle grounded in certain facts of human nature that are known through and confirmed by "experience and observation."[20] Some abstract truths come to some men only as "discoveries made and verities introduced and brought into the mind" by the use and application of the right method of reason. The self-evidence of these truths is seen only *after* the use of reason and demonstration through a series of logically necessary arguments.[21] Such truths are what might be called *conceptually* self-evident rather than *perceptually* self-evident.

William Duncan, the Scottish logician, likewise presented an expanded definition of "self-evident" beyond the simple understanding. Directly following the passage from Duncan's *Elements of Logick* quoted above, the Scot expanded his definition of "self-evident" to include truths arrived at from a process of deductive reasoning. In the very next sentence, after he promotes the standard eighteenth-century definition of "self-evident," Duncan offers this expanded understanding.

> But where the Connection or Repugnance comes not so readily under the Inspection of the Mind, there we must have Recourse to Reasoning; and if by a clear Series of Proofs we can make out the Truth proposed, insomuch that Self-evidence shall accompany every Step of the Procedure, we are then able to demonstrate what we assert, and the Proposition itself is said to be *demonstrable*. . . .
>
> From what has been said it appears, that Reasoning is employed only about demonstrable Propositions and that our intuitive and self-evident Perceptions, are the ultimate Foundation on which it rests.

Duncan is saying that self-evident truths can issue from a "Recourse to Reasoning" and from a "clear Series of Proofs" that "accompany every Step of the Procedure." Such truths are "demonstrable," but they rest on a "Foundation" of "self-evident perceptions." Self-evidence can, in other words, be derived reasoning. Truths conceptually understood through a series of proofs that are self-evident, one to the other, and which are built on a self-evident axiom can therefore be viewed as self-evident truths, according to Duncan.[22]

Interestingly, the well-known and influential Scottish philosopher Thomas Reid also shared the more advanced notion of self-evidence held by Locke and Duncan. Reid, who held the prestigious Professorship of

Moral Philosophy at the University of Glasgow, indicated in his widely read *An Inquiry into the Human Mind, on the Principles of Common Sense* (1764) and in *Essays on the Intellectual Powers of Man* (1785) that truths rationally deduced from axioms can still be self-evident. In a chapter in the *Essays* on "Whether Morality Be Capable of Demonstration," Reid argues that "Moral truths...may be divided into two classes, to wit, such as are self-evident to every man whose understanding and moral faculty are ripe, and such as are deduced by reasoning from those that are self-evident." All moral reasoning, according to Reid, begins with and is drawn from self-evident propositions that he calls the "axioms of morals." But it is also the case, according to Reid, that the "application" of moral first principles "to particular actions is often no less evident." In sum, there can be self-evident moral truths that are not perceptually evident but are rather deduced from perceptually evident axioms.[23]

The expanded understanding of "self-evident" offered by Locke, Duncan, and Reid makes it possible for us to view how American revolutionaries understood the nature of a self-evident truth and how it might have been used by Jefferson in the Declaration.

THE MEANING OF TRUTH

What exactly did Jefferson and the signers of the Declaration of Independence mean when they announced, "We hold these truths to be self-evident"? Most scholars have answered this question by focusing on the meaning of the adjective "self-evident." The more interesting question is this: what did the revolutionary generation mean by the noun "truth"? In many ways, the power and relevance of the Declaration's four self-evident truths rest on whether or not the concept "truth" is valid. Then and only then can it be determined whether the four moral-political "truths" of the Declaration are "self-evident" and whether they are actually true or not.

Virtually all English-speaking peoples in the eighteenth century understood the concept "truth" in the same way. Samuel Johnson's dictionary, the lexicographic bible of all colonial Americans, defined truth as that which is "contrary to falsehood; conformity of notions to things." Johnson further defined truth as synonymous with reality, as representing a "real state of things."[24] *The London Encyclopædia*, expanding on Johnson's dictionary, defined truth as "a term used in opposition to falsehood, and applied to propositions which answer or accord to nature and reality of the thing whereof something is affirmed or denied."[25] Noah Webster's eponymous first dictionary defined the noun "truth" as that which is in "conformity to fact or reality; exact accordance with that which is, or has been, or shall be," and it defined the adjective "true" in the following way: "Conformable to fact; being in accordance with the actual state of things; as a true relation or narration; a true history. A declaration is true, when it states the facts. In this sense, true is opposed to false."[26]

These dictionary definitions comport with Locke's understanding of the concept "truth" as presented in his *Essay Concerning Human Understanding*. In a chapter titled "Of Truth in General," Locke defined truth at the highest level of abstraction as signifying "nothing but *the joining or separating of signs* [i.e., words], *as the things signified by them do agree or disagree one with another.*" One arrives at "*real truth,*" according to Locke, "when these signs are joined as our *ideas* agree, and when our *ideas* are as such as we know are capable of having an existence in nature."[27] Truth, as expressed in ideas and words, must embody and represent the reality of nature, which is to say facts.

Consider one last eighteenth-century view of truth that maps directly onto the substance and ordering of the Declaration's four self-evident truths. In his *Essays on the Intellectual Powers of Man*, Reid argued that truth comes in two forms: "The truths that fall within the compass of human knowledge, whether they be self-evident, or deduced from those that are self-evident, may be reduced to two classes. They are either necessary and immutable truths, whose contrary is impossible, or they are contingent and mutable, depending upon some effect of will and power, which had a beginning, and may have an end."[28] The Declaration's first and second truths (i.e., equality and rights) are "necessary and immutable truths," which means absolute and certain, and the Declaration's third and fourth truths (i.e., consent/government and revolution) are "contingent and mutable," which means they are contextually absolute.

By "truth," Jefferson and the statesmen of the Declaration are referring to certain ideas or principles that share the following characteristics: they must be absolute, certain, universal, permanent, and immutable. A *true* moral principle does not rest on majority opinion or even universal acceptance. It must be *objectively* true, which means that the idea or principle must correspond to reality. It must be fact-based, and it must be capable of verification. The concept "truth" identifies a kind of relationship between an idea, a proposition, or a principle (e.g., all men are created equal, or all men are endowed with certain unalienable rights) and certain facts of reality or nature. The truth is identified by reference to a body of evidence (e.g., "facts submitted to a candid world") that can be integrated with other propositions or facts. For an idea, proposition, or principle to be true it must therefore be demonstrably true, that is, it must be validated with reality-based evidence and arguments arising from reason and rational judgment. By contrast, a self-evident lie is a false proposition that contradicts the evidence and/or some aspect of the wider context.

The clearest and fullest discussion of the nature of truth in the Revolutionary period is to be found in James Wilson's *Lectures on Law*, delivered in Philadelphia in 1790–91. According to Wilson, one of the primary concerns of law courts, and, more particularly, of the legal science of evidence, is the discovery of the truth. (Wilson devoted an entire chapter to the "Nature and Philosophy of Evidence.") In a law case, he declared, "facts are the objects of evidence." The role of a court in a lawsuit is to determine "the truth of facts." This task is the particular job of juries in British and American jurisprudence and legal practice. Juries are presented with evidence (sometimes competing or contradictory statements) from which the truth is to emerge. The role of juries is to "try the truth of facts, on which depend the property, the liberty, the reputation, and the lives of their fellow citizens." This is the primary reason why it is the case, Wilson noted, that "before the testimony of a witness can be received" in a court of common law, "he is obliged to swear, that it shall be the truth, the whole truth, and nothing but the truth." In determining the facts, "nature should always be consulted." In a court of law, according to Wilson, this is the "criterion of truth." Without connecting the truth to the facts of reality, we are led "to the destruction of all truth."[29]

Not surprisingly, the Americans conducted their debates with Great Britain during the years of the imperial crisis very much like a criminal or civil court case, where the primary task is to discover the truth based on evidence and facts. As John Adams indicated in his defense of British soldiers at the Boston Massacre trial, there is and must be a necessary relationship between facts and truth: "Facts are stubborn things; and whatever may be our wishes, our inclinations, or the dictates of our passion, they cannot alter the state of facts and evidence."[30] In this vein, the Declaration submits "facts" to a "candid world" to prove that the "history of the present King of Great Britain is a history of repeated injuries and usurpations, all having in direct object the establishment of an absolute Tyranny over these States." For the statesmen of the Declaration, the concept "truth" applies to questions of morality, law, and politics. Moral action, by this account, can and should be guided by facts and objective reality, which means *true* value judgments.

And how is the moral law known? The concepts "truth" and "self-evident" are used in the Declaration as claims about how man comes to know four particular moral-political truths. "Self-evident" is used as an adjective to the noun "truth." More specifically, truth is the end to which "self-evident" is the means. The truth is *known* because it is self-evident, but the Declaration's truths are self-evidently known only after they emerge from an analysis of facts. The idea of a self-evident truth begins with the assumption that truth—including moral truth—is possible, necessary, and desirable. The idea or possibility of truth—particularly the idea of a self-evident truth—rests on certain assumptions about nature and human nature. It assumes that there is a common human nature despite differences of culture and history; that truth is a recognition, an identification, and an acquisition; that man has or controls the means (i.e., the faculty of reason) necessary to acquire truth; that there is a correspondence between reality and the human mind; and, finally, that man's rational faculty is his only means of acquiring and holding truth. The Americans are saying in 1776 that in their pursuit of justice they are united by their adherence to a moral law that is true, which means to transcend time and place.

Readers of the Declaration's first paragraph will recall Jefferson's claim that when "it becomes necessary for one people to dissolve the political bands which have connected them with another"—that is, to foment revolution and declare their independence—"a decent respect to the opinions of mankind requires that they should declare the causes which impel them to the separation." They are appealing to the rational faculty of men around the world to see the truth of their claim. The Declaration is an act of public reason. The ultimate purpose of the second paragraph is to provide irrefutable evidence of "a design to reduce them under absolute Despotism" and to persuade mankind of the justice and rightness of their cause. To that end, American revolutionaries begin by proclaiming their fundamental moral and political principles, which they present as self-evident truths, and then they lay out the evidence of British tyranny for all to see.

The actions of king and Parliament are to be evaluated and judged against the Declaration's self-evident truths. In doing so, American revolutionaries are affirming to the world the power of reason to apprehend universal moral truths that can be used to judge existing governments or to build new ones. As Jefferson wrote in his *A Bill for Establishing Religious Freedom* (1779), "truth is great and will prevail if left to herself...she is the proper and sufficient antagonist to error, and has nothing to fear from the conflict unless by human interposition disarmed of her natural weapons, free argument and debate; errors ceasing to be dangerous when it is permitted freely to contradict them."[31] Reason, according to America's revolutionary generation, is the tool that distinguishes truth from error and just from unjust actions.

American revolutionaries believed there is a necessary connection between truth and freedom of the mind. The freedom to think is both an aspect and requirement of human flourishing. Freedom is to man's reason what oxygen is to his lungs. The freedom to think (e.g., to collect, weigh, and judge evidence) and to choose is the necessary precondition for the discovery of true principles of right action, both morally and politically. Human nature requires freedom—the freedom to think and act—in order to pursue the truths and to acquire the knowledge necessary to live and live well.

Freedom can, however, be corrupted, which is why it must be guided by reason and true moral principles. Likewise, reason can be corrupted, which is why it must exist in freedom, so that ideas can compete with one another in the search for truth. Errors of knowledge and logic are the testing ground for the ascent to truth. Because truth is not innate and because man is not determined to act one way or another, the human mind must be free to pursue and discover the truth.

The Declaration of Independence assumes what is affirmed in Jefferson's Bill for Establishing Religious Freedom, "that Almighty God hath created the mind free, and manifested his supreme will that free it shall remain by making it altogether insusceptible of restraint." It is the "irresistible nature of truth," Tom Paine wrote in *Rights of Man*, "that all it asks, and all it wants, is the liberty of appearing." Or, as Jefferson wrote in an 1824 letter to David Harding, "in a republican nation, whose citizens are to be led by reason and persuasion, and not by force, the art of reasoning becomes of first importance."[32] The revolutionary generation believed, to a man, that freedom and reason are the necessary preconditions of truth.

How, then, do men reason to truth, and what does it mean for truth to be self-evident?

ON SELF-EVIDENCE IN AMERICA

During the Revolutionary period, moral and political ideas such as "law of nature," "equality," "liberty," "rights," "consent," "power," "sovereignty," and "republic" were employed countless times. By contrast, the concept "self-evident truth" was rarely used. There are virtually no instances of its use in America in the decade before 1776. In fact, other than in the Declaration, there are just a few known instances of its use over the thirty-year period from 1760 to 1790, and those coming after the publication of the Declaration. These three instances, however, even though they occurred after Jefferson wrote the Declaration, shed some light on how Jefferson and his fellow revolutionaries may have understood and used the concept in the Declaration.

The first significant use of the concept "self-evident" occurred in a pamphlet printed in 1783 in New York and titled *Defensive Arms Vindicated and the Lawfulness of the American War Made Manifest*. Signed "A Moderate Whig," the pamphlet is thought to be the handiwork of Stephen Case, a veteran of the Revolutionary War.[33] The theme of the pamphlet is the "lawfulness of the use of defensive arms against tyrants and tyranny," which the author considered to be a self-evident truth scarcely in need of "demonstration." The right to "self-preservation and defense" is a truth, he continued, that should be known "for its self-evidencing clearness, being scarcely capable of any farther elucidation than what is offered to the rational understanding by its simple proposition." First principles such as the right to life and the corollary right to defend it do not need proof, according to A Moderate Whig, "because they need no probation, and cannot be made any clearer than they really are." In fact, it is "superfluous to make a doubt or a debate of this self-evident truth."[34] Case's self-evident truth has its analog in the Declaration's fourth self-evident truth.

The second major use of the idea of self-evident truths during the Revolutionary period can be found in three essays of *The Federalist* (Nos.

23, 31, 44). In *Federalist* No. 31, Alexander Hamilton announces, following Locke and Duncan, that there are "certain primary truths or first principles upon which all subsequent reasonings must depend." Although Hamilton does not use the term "self-evident," his definition of these primary truths is clearly Lockean: "These contain an internal evidence, which antecedent to all reflection or combination commands the assent of the mind." Hamilton then gives examples of these self-evident first truths drawn from the maxims of geometry: "'The whole is greater than its part; that things equal to the same are equal to one another; that two straight lines cannot inclose a space; and that all right angles are equal to each other.'" Likewise, following Locke, Hamilton notes that ethics and politics have their own truths that are analogs to geometric truths. Among the self-evident ethical and political truths, Hamilton includes the following: "that there cannot be an effect without a cause; that the means ought to be proportioned to the end; that every power ought to be commensurate with its object; that there ought to be no limitation of a power destined to effect a purpose, which is itself incapable of limitation." He immediately concedes, however, that there are ethical and political truths "which if they cannot pretend to rank in the class of axioms, are yet such direct *inferences* from them, and so obvious in themselves, and so agreeable to the natural and unsophisticated dictates of common sense, that they challenge the assent of a sound and unbiased mind, with a degree of force and conviction almost equally irresistible."[35] Hamilton accepts and uses Locke's broader definition of self-evident to include truths that are necessary deductions or inferences from simple axioms.

This kind of reasoning is obvious in the Declaration's movement from the first to the second, third, and fourth truths. As with the Declaration's third and fourth self-evident truths, Hamilton takes the axiomatic political truth that "every power ought to be commensurate with its object" and then deduces an intermediate but logically inferred, self-evident principle that a "government ought to contain in itself every power requisite to the full accomplishment of the objects committed to its care." He ends this chain of reasoning by drawing the following conclusion: the "necessity of a general power of taxation in the government of the union."[36] In *Federalist* No. 23, Hamilton likewise uses the same definition of a self-evident truth and applies it to the issue of national defense. Governments must, by definition, take care of the common defense, he argued, which includes "to raise armies—to build and equip fleets—to prescribe rules for the government of both—to direct their operations—to provide for their support." It is necessarily and logically inferred, therefore, that these "powers ought to exist without limitation: *Because it is impossible to foresee or define the extent and variety of national exigencies, or the correspondent extent & variety of the means which may be necessary to satisfy them.*" Like the Declaration's third and fourth self-evident truths, the political truth Hamilton describes here is not self-evident according to Locke's simple definition, but it certainly does rise to the level of Locke's more advanced formulation in that Hamilton's truth is arrived at through demonstrative reasoning from a simple axiom. In language almost identical to that shown in *Federalist* No. 31, Hamilton claims that it is "one of those truths, which to a correct and unprejudiced mind, carries its own evidence along with it."[37] The self-evidence of the axiom is carried along or through the process of reasoning to more advanced truths, thus making the more advanced truths self-evident, but in a form different from that of the axiom.[38]

James Wilson's four chapters in his law lectures—"Of the Law of Nature," "Of Man, as an Individual," "Of the Nature and Philosophy of Evidence," and "Of the Constituent Parts of Courts, of Juries"—present the founding era's most sophisticated discussion of the nature of self-evident truths. In the chapter "Of the Law of Nature," Wilson claims that there must be "first principles" in the moral sciences, "which derive not their evidence from antecedent principles, but which may be said to be intuitively discerned." These building blocks of the moral and political sciences may be divided, according to Wilson, "into two classes; such as are selfevident, and such as, from the selfevident ones, are deduced by reasoning." First-tier moral truths are directly self-evident, which means that they are known perceptually. Their truth is not known via demonstrable reasoning and proofs. The complexity of life, however, requires the acquisition of moral truths beyond those that are immediately self-evident on the perceptual level. This is why in the moral sciences "reason is usefully introduced, and performs many important services."[39]

What are those "many important services" played by reason in the discovery and development of moral truths? (This is the subject of Wilson's chapter "Of Man, as an Individual.") Reason, according to Wilson, "regulates our belief" and "conduct"; it "determines the proper means to any end"; it "decides the preference of one end over another"; it ascertains the "circumstances and determines[s] the motives to action"; it discerns the "comparative value of objects and gratifications"; and it judges "concerning subordinate ends." Reason also "considers the relations of actions, and traces them to the remotest consequences," which is the most important service played by the rational faculty in the development of higher-level moral truths.[40] But man cannot live by self-evident truths alone. Moral reasoning beyond basic axioms is required to navigate through the complexities of human life.

In the chapter "Of Man, as an Individual," Wilson argues that the ability of reason to establish the cause-and-effect relationship of moral actions is the catalyst that initiates a "chain of reasoning" wherein the "evidence must proceed regularly and without interruption from link to link: the evidence of the last conclusion can be no greater than that of the weakest link in the chain; because if even the weakest link fails, the whole chain is broken." In this chain of reasoning, the mind deduces one truth from another. And in his chapter "On Evidence," Wilson argues: "Reasoning is the process, by which we pass from one truth to another as a conclusion from it. In all reasoning, there must be a proposition inferred, and one or more, from which the inference is drawn. The proposition inferred is called the conclusion: the name of premises is given to the proposition or propositions, from which the conclusion is inferred."[41] This is precisely the kind of reasoning that connects the Declaration's four self-evident truths one to another.

Wilson goes on to note in his lecture on "Juries" that in the natural sciences "evidence depends on causes which are fixed and immovable, liable to no fluctuation or uncertainty arising from the characters or conduct of men." But what of the moral and political sciences? In the humane sciences, he says, "truths, if selfevident, are instantly known." But Wilson also recognizes that not all moral and political truths are immediately known axioms or first principles. The evidence of some moral and political truths depends "on their connexions with other truths," and these are "evinced by tracing and discovering those connexions."[42] The concept "self-evident" therefore applies to more abstract moral truths that are necessarily derived from perceptually evident first principles.

The self-evidence of these higher-level moral and political truths is thus made possible, according to Wilson, in two ways. First, the self-evidence of an axiomatic first principle can be carried forward to more abstract truths in such a way that they too become self-evident. These advanced moral truths contain within them trace elements of the axiomatic truth. Second, the movement of an axiomatic first principle to higher-level, derivative truths must follow a logical chain of reasoning. As one ascends the ladder of moral truth, the relationship between one truth and another must follow self-evidently (i.e., logically) from one to another. Following Locke's argument in the *Essay*, Wilson declares that "intermediate proofs" launch and connect this "chain of reasoning."[43]

When the concept of self-evident truths, particularly as they relate to moral and political truths, is seen in the context of this wider understanding, Jefferson's use of the term in the Declaration can be viewed in a new light. The Declaration's four truths need not be seen and dismissed as self-evident in the narrow sense. They can now be understood as self-evident in the more capacious sense used by Locke, Duncan, Reid, Hamilton, and Wilson.

INTERPRETING THE MEANING OF "SELF-EVIDENT TRUTHS" IN THE CONTEXT OF THE DECLARATION

The most direct way to recover the revolutionaries' meaning is to interrogate the Declaration with a few obvious and not-so-obvious questions. The most obvious is, how or in what way is each of the Declaration's truths self-evident? To answer this question, a series of corollary questions must be asked and answered: In the opening of the second paragraph, to whom does the "we" refer, what does it mean to "hold" these truths, and what are "these" truths that are said to be self-evident? Probing more deeply leads to several additional questions. Did the Declaration's signers think that its self-evident truths were known or could be known to all men? How did the members of the Continental Congress come to know the Declaration's four moral and political truths at one moment in time? Did the colonists know the Declaration's self-evident truths in 1765? Did American revolutionaries expect ordinary Americans to know these truths in the same way as those who wrote and signed the Declaration? Is there a difference between having the kind of mind capable of *discovering* the moral laws and rights of nature and the kind of mind capable of *grasping* or understanding them once identified and promulgated in written form?

To answer these questions, the first thing to note is that Thomas Jefferson was not speaking in his own name. As the principal author of the Declaration, he was speaking for "we" the members of the Continental Congress, who in turn were speaking on behalf of "we" the American people. The Declaration's "we" ultimately refers to the "one people" mentioned in the first paragraph. Still, that is a large number of people of varying intellectual capacities expected to grasp and "hold" the Declaration's four self-evident truths at one moment in time. Is that even possible? For "we" the people to hold these four truths simultaneously as self-evident in the narrow sense would suggest that these truths must be knowable to any person who simply opens his eyes or that the truths can be somehow intuited by all men. If that were true, however, presumably all people everywhere—including American Loyalists—would have immediately recognized the veracity of each self-evident truth; but that was not the case.

How is it, then, that the fifty-six signers of the Declaration of Independence and then "we" the American people—this "one nation"— all came to "hold" these four truths as self-evident at the same moment in time?[44] To understand Jefferson's meaning, it is necessary to determine *how* and *when* these truths became self-evident, first to the author and signers of the Declaration and then to the American people.

This much seems clear: the Declaration uses the concept "self-evident" in a different way from the most commonly accepted epistemological definition used in the eighteenth century. A self-evident truth for the signers of the Declaration was neither obvious nor meant to be known instantaneously, either by perceptual awareness or by the noncontradiction of the terms, propositions, or ideas themselves. American revolutionaries also could not have viewed the second, third, and fourth self-evident truths as axioms. Only the first self-evident truth ("All men are created equal") could be considered an axiom, but the others meet none of the standard criteria. If they had met the criteria, the Declaration might very well have been written to say "These truths *are* self-evident" rather than "We *hold* these truths to be self-evident." This is not a difference without a distinction. In fact, the difference goes to the heart of the Declaration's meaning. If three of the Declaration's four truths are not self-evident in the simple sense, how or in what way are they self-evident? How did the signers of the Declaration and "we" the people come to "hold" them as self-evident?

For "one people" to "hold" these self-evident truths suggests that they were *grasped* and *acquired* over a period of time (i.e., "in the course of human events") such that the authors and signers of the Declaration and then the American people *discovered* and came to *accept* these truths over the course of many years. The Declaration's self-evident truths were actually discovered, developed, formulated, and validated throughout a fifteen-year period from 1760 to 1775. This is why John Adams could write that the true Revolution "*was in the Minds of the People*, and this was effected…in the course of fifteen years before a drop of blood was shed at Lexington."[45]

As early as 1765, John Adams proposed in his "Dissertation on the Canon and Feudal Law" a research agenda and plan of study that would ultimately lead his countrymen to identify and know the truths that the Declaration would later announce as self-evident. Adams encouraged America's citizen-statesmen to engage in philosophical "researches into the grounds and nature and ends of government and the means of preserving the good and demolishing the evil."[46] At the very least, the Americans should study the history of liberty, "the nature of that power and the cruelty of that oppression which drove" their ancestors from their homes in England, and the "views and ends, of our own immediate forefathers, in exchanging their native country for a dreary, inhospitable wilderness." He also proposed that they "search into the spirit of the British constitution; read the histories of ancient ages; contemplate the great examples of Greece and Rome; [and] set before us the conduct of our own British ancestors who have defended for us the inherent rights of mankind against foreign and domestic tyrants…."[47]

For his more ambitious and philosophical students, however, Adams recommended that they go beyond history to study "the laws of nature" and to "search for the foundations of British laws and government in the frame of human nature, in the constitution of the intellectual and moral world." Equating English rights and liberties with the Lockean laws of nature, Adams reminded his readers that "British liberties are not the grants of princes or parliaments but original rights, conditions of original contracts, coequal with prerogative and coeval with government." Many of these rights, he insisted, "are inherent and essential, agreed on as maxims and established as preliminaries even before a parliament existed." In order to inspire his citizen-statesmen to seize the opportunity and to aspire to great thoughts and deeds, Adams drew a historical parallel between the colonists' present situation and that confronted by the English in the seventeenth century. In the very same way that the tyranny of the Stuarts encouraged the best minds in England to reflect on the nature and role of government, producing a generation of philosophers such as John Selden, James Harrington, Algernon Sidney, and John Locke, Adams hoped that the recent actions by Parliament would produce in America a new generation of statesmen dedicated to the principles of natural justice.[48] It was precisely this kind of research agenda pursued by Americans high and low over the course of the next eleven years that culminated in the Declaration's assertion that "We hold these truths to be self-evident."

In addition to reading and reasoning, the colonists were compelled by experience and the pressure of events to *search* for the truth in their contest with British parliamentarians. In his 1765 *Considerations on the Propriety of Imposing Taxes in the British Colonies*, one of the most important pamphlets published during the Stamp Act crisis, Daniel Dulany argued that the propriety of the act must stand or fall "as the principle is true, or false."[49] The intellectual and political battles they fought with English and American Tories over the Sugar, Stamp, Declaratory, Townshend, Tea, Coercive, and Prohibitory Acts challenged the colonists to think seriously about their fundamental moral principles and standards of justice. They sought to distinguish the just from the unjust in a particular historical context that consisted of the coming together of an intellectual context (Enlightenment philosophy) and a political context (their confrontation with British imperial officials). American revolutionaries saw close-up and in real time how the criteria established by Locke in his *Second Treatise of Government* for determining the conditions of tyranny and revolution mapped directly onto the different inflection points of the imperial crisis.

The revolutionaries' principles became self-evidently true to them only after a long process of reading and reasoning on the "facts" that had been "submitted to a candid world" and in the relationship of those "facts" to the "Laws of Nature and of Nature's God." The self-evidence of the Americans' truth claims came at the end of a *process* of reasoning and not at the beginning. It seems unlikely that the Declaration's four self-evident truths were explicitly self-evident to them (or at least to "we" the people) in 1764, although, as students of John Locke's *Essay Concerning Human Understanding* and the *Second Treatise of Government*, some Americans would have been familiar with Locke's general principles, and they would have almost certainly understood these truths implicitly when presented to them. Ultimately, the revolutionaries' "self-evident" truths had to be proven, demonstrated, and assented to, which means they were not self-evident in the technical or narrow sense of the term. But, as was seen with Locke and Duncan (as well as Hamilton and Wilson), the concept of a self-evident truth can be determined and established through other means.

Let us return now to our original question: How are the Declaration's four self-evident truths self-evident? It seems most likely that Jefferson and his colleagues identified these truths based on their reading, their experiences, and their thinking. They reasoned their way to these "self-evident" truths in the light of their experiences. But if three of the four self-evident truths are not self-evident in the narrow sense, in what way *are* they self-evident? It seems most likely that Jefferson understood and used the concept "self-evident" in the expanded sense indicated by Locke, Duncan, and Reid. The kinds of moral and political truths ultimately presented in the Declaration can be self-evident, but only *after* they are discovered and presented through a process of reasoning and demonstration. That is, Jefferson and his fellow revolutionaries started with an *axiomatic* self-evident truth (equality), and then they deduced three self-evident *corollary* truths.

The proposition that "all men are created equal," the Declaration's first self-evident truth, is the axiom from which the other self-evident truths (i.e., rights, consent, and revolution) are deduced. To say that all men are created equal is a truism that cannot be derived from an antecedent truth. Equality is both a fact (an *is*) and a standard (an *ought*). As an axiom, equality is, as Jefferson put it in a different context, "pregnant with salutary consequences."[50] Locke viewed equality in this way as well. As he wrote in the *Second Treatise*: "there being nothing more *evident*, than that creatures of the same species and rank, promiscuously born to all the same advantages of nature, and the use of the same faculties, should also be equal one amongst another without subordination or subjection, unless the lord and master of them all should, by any manifest declaration of his will, set one above another."[51]

By equality, Locke meant what might be called "species equality." The differences between men are differences of degree that do not justify one man's ruling another by nature, whereas the difference between a man and a dog is such that men can naturally rule dogs. Dogs are incapable of consent, which means they have no rights-claim to be ruled by consent. Species equality says that all men are of the same species and thus equal or have the same equal status relative to all nonhumans.[52] All men are therefore equal relative to donkeys and dogs. They are equal in that they all share the same qualities that define what it is to be a human. Such "equality of men by nature" is, according to Locke, "evident in itself, and beyond all question." Moreover, from this "foundation" of equality, men will "build" "the duties they owe one another, and from whence he derives the great maxims *of justice* and *charity*."[53] As an axiom, equality is induced from empirical observation. Knowledge of it is neither automatic nor innate. It is a truth that must be grasped and acquired by a process of observation and reasoning.

The Declaration's second self-evident truth—"unalienable Rights"—is not quite a self-evident or axiomatic truth, but it is what might be called a moral first principle that is virtually synonymous with the truth of equality and that serves as a linchpin (what Locke refers to in the *Essay* as an "intermediate" truth) connecting the axiomatic truth of equality with the contingent truths of consent and revolution. Equality and rights (see chapters 4–7) reflect realities grounded in human nature. The third and fourth self-evident truths are contingent and necessary truths based on deductions from the self-evident axiom and the moral first principle (see chapters 8–11). Whereas the first and second truths are presented as absolute and unalienable truths, the application of the third and fourth self-evident truths requires practical judgment of probable consequences in particular situations.

The Declaration's second, third, and fourth truths are not self-evident in the narrow sense, but they are self-evident when taken as a logical whole and as part of a demonstrative continuum. The Declaration provides a demonstration or a reasoned proof of the origin and consequences of man's rights in political communities. Its truths are self-evident in their necessary and deductive relationship to each other. Thus, if the Declaration's first self-evident truth is metaphysically true, the second, third, and fourth truths ought to follow as necessary and should be considered as certain as the conclusion of a mathematical proof.

The morally demonstrative argument of the Declaration's truths can be seen through the following chain of reasoning.

Step 1: All men are created with equal rights.
Step 2: Governments are instituted among men to secure rights.
Step 3: Governments that do not secure rights may be altered or abolished.

The first step in this chain of reasoning provides the axiom of the proof; the second step provides the link to the conclusion; and the conclusion justifies a logically necessary action. The Declaration therefore announces through reasoned argument what men's rights and responsibilities are, how they stand in relation to each other, how they form the basis of legitimate government, the conditions by which they are violated, and the grounds on which revolution is justified. Hence the Declaration's second, third, and fourth truths are self-evident in the broader sense indicated in Locke's *Essay Concerning Human Understanding*. This is precisely the sort of "plain and firm" reasoning that Jefferson said, in his 1825 letter to Henry Lee, would "command" the "assent" of the American people.[54]

The revolutionary generation understood and used the concept "self-evident" as requiring a positive or *proactive*—indeed, a demonstrable—action or form of reasoning. Epistemologically, three of the Declaration's self-evident truths were inferences and *conclusions* drawn from an axiom and a *process* of thought and experience. As Thomas Paine put it, the Americans' principles were drawn from "nothing more than simple facts, plain arguments, and common sense."[55] They were truths grasped, discovered, and validated over a period of time. They were principles validated inductively based on the revolutionaries' reading of and reasoning on certain philosophical and historical texts (e.g., Locke's *Second Treatise of Government*) as well as through their experiences of events (e.g., the contest with imperial officials over the Sugar, Stamp, Declaratory, Townshend, Tea, Coercive, and Prohibitory Acts). These self-evident truths were not revealed to them as self-evidently obvious the moment they turned their minds to them. Nor did the signers of the Declaration mean to assert the obvious untruth that these self-evident truths were self-evidently obvious to any person anywhere who simply looked at them in written form. They were not self-evident to the Declaration's statesmen as a form of intuitive knowledge or by virtue of the meaning and relations of the terms themselves. It was only over time that the Declaration's truths *became* self-evident to the leaders of the revolutionary movement, and then once identified they were promulgated in written form as self-evident conclusions to the Declaration's readers. From that point forward, they could be "held" by the American people as self-evidently true. In the words of the Reverend Samuel Cooper of Massachusetts: "We want not, indeed, a special revelation from heaven to teach us that men are born equal and free....These are the plain dictates of that reason and common sense with which the common parent of men has informed the human bosom."[56]

Still, it is almost certainly the case that not all Americans discovered or grasped these self-evident truths at the same moment in time. They were self-evident to Samuel Adams before they became self-evident to John Dickinson. They were self-evident to Thomas Jefferson and American Patriots in 1776, but they were never self-evident to Thomas Hutchinson and the Loyalists. Some came to these truths later than others, and some never viewed them as self-evident. The Declaration's truths only became self-evident to most Americans through the experience of the imperial crisis and after a long period of political education both theoretical and practical. Thus, when the Declaration states, "We hold these truths to be self-evident," it is saying this: "We" the authors and signers of the Declaration hold these truths to be self-evident, and we believe they will *become* self-evident to readers of the document once they see these truths stated in print and think about them. In the form in which the Declaration's truths are presented, the mind will naturally *assent* to them. These truths were not self-evident to all until they were stated clearly in written form and in the context of the historical evidence demonstrating that British actions had violated the laws of nature and Americans' natural rights. Temporally, there is a difference between the first-ever identification of the truth by a philosophic few and its *recognition* by the unphilosophic many after it is stated publicly in written form.

It is also important to recognize that all Americans could *hold* the Declaration's truths without necessarily knowing their full philosophic import. To "hold" (i.e., to accept or embrace) these truths is not the same as *knowing* their deepest meaning philosophically. After all, "For one man of science," Jefferson claimed, "there are thousands who are not."[57] Not all Americans in 1776 were Aristotles or Lockes, but neither were they the ignorant and brutish herd that had hitherto been representative of human civilization. Ordinary Americans could know and hold these truths when they were stated clearly and simply.[58]

In sum, the Declaration's four self-evident truths share three major qualities.

First, they present an integrated and hierarchically structured system of principles that proceed logically, one building on the other. The claim that "all men are created equal" is the foundation on which the next three self-evident truths follow as necessary corollaries. The Declaration's four self-evident truths form a unified whole.

Second, they also complete the Declaration's broader but implicit philosophical system. If, as was seen in chapter 2, the Declaration's first paragraph implies a metaphysics and an epistemology, the second paragraph's self-evident truths establish the next two branches—ethics and politics—needed to complete a systematic philosophy. The first two of these self-evident truths—"equality" and "rights"—represent the Declaration's metaethical teaching, and the last two—"consent" and "revolution"—its political-social teaching.

Third, the logical structure of the Declaration's moral-political teaching mirrors that of Locke's *Second Treatise of Government*. In fact, not only is the logical structure of the Declaration's theoretical argument a virtual précis of the *Second Treatise*, but particular phrases transcribed in the former were first written in the latter. This parallel suggests that Jefferson not only had read carefully Locke's little-big book but that he almost certainly had a copy with him at his desk when he wrote America's revolutionary manifesto.

CHAPTER 4

Equality

"We hold these truths to be self-evident,
that all men are created equal."

In 1859, Abraham Lincoln was invited to deliver a speech in Boston honoring Thomas Jefferson's birthday. Lincoln was unable to participate in the celebration, but he did send a letter to the event's sponsors that amounted to a testimonial for Jefferson: "All honor to Jefferson," he wrote, "to the man who, in the concrete pressure of a struggle for national independence by a single people, had the coolness, forecast, and capacity to introduce into a merely revolutionary document, an abstract truth, applicable to all men and all times, and so to embalm it there, that to-day, and in all coming days, it shall be a rebuke and a stumbling-block to the very harbingers of re-appearing tyranny and oppression." The universal and timeless "abstract truth" to which Lincoln referred was the Declaration's first self-evident truth, that "all men are created equal"—the claim that, throughout American history, has been the most contested principle associated with the Declaration of Independence. For Lincoln, the Declaration's self-evident truths "are the definitions and axioms of a free society."[1]

What could it mean to say "all men are created equal"? Lincoln's defense of Jefferson's equality principle was, in many ways, the defining feature of his 1858 run for a seat in the United States Senate. While on the campaign trail against his great nemesis, Senator Stephen A. Douglas, Lincoln asked his audience in Chicago two poignant questions: "I should like to know if taking this old Declaration of Independence, which declares that all men are equal upon principle, and making exceptions to it, where will it stop? If one man says it does not mean a negro, why may not another say it does not mean some other man?" Lincoln's answer to his own questions went to the heart of the matter: "If that Declaration is not the truth, let us get the Statute book in which we find it and tear it out!" Lincoln saw further and knew better than anyone what would happen if Americans allowed any exceptions to the equality principle. For him, not only was the equality principle a self-evident truth, it was the "father of all moral principle."[2] That Jefferson's principles were, as Lincoln said time and again, a free society's "definitions and axioms" meant that they must be recurred to periodically as the foundation of all political judgment.

America's national obsession with equality began in the 1760s, and it has stayed with us ever since. The doctrine of equality was at the heart of colonial Americans' protest against the imposition of British authority in America during the 1760s and 1770s; it served to dissolve many of the inherited aristocratic manners and mores of eighteenth-century Anglo-American culture; it provided the moral-legal foundation for the new governments created by the founding generation; its contested meaning led to a civil war; and it has provided Americans with a moral and legal benchmark by which to judge their national aspirations and political policies.[3]

While Jefferson's ringing declaration of human equality has meant different things to different people throughout the course of American history, it actually meant something specific to the people who aspired to it in 1776. "It is this principle of equality, this right," wrote the pseudonymous Virginian "Democritatus" in 1776, "which is inherent in every member of the community, to give his own consent to the laws by which he is to be bound, which alone can inspire and preserve the virtue of its members, by placing them in a relation to the publick and to their fellow-citizens, which has a tendency to engage the heart and affections to both."[4] And in his 1778 "Oration on the Advantages of American Independence," the Revolutionary historian David Ramsay announced that equality was the "life and soul" of America's new Revolutionary republicanism.[5]

The Declaration's equality principle can only be understood by first searching through several historical layers of philosophical and political context. These layers include the various ways in which equality was understood and applied by Americans in the decades before and after 1776. And then, of course, there is the actual meaning and use of the equality principle as a self-evident truth within the logical structure of the Declaration itself. This chapter peels back and examines these various layers in order to recover the revolutionary generation's original understanding of equality and the way in which the equality principle became a central component of the American mind.

EQUALITY IN THEORY:
THE DEVELOPMENT OF AN IDEA

The use and meaning of equality in the Declaration must first be seen in its broader philosophic context. That context begins, per usual, with John Locke at the end of the seventeenth century. The Englishman begins his *Second Treatise of Government* with the revolutionary claim that all men are by nature "equal and independent." Locke is here claiming equality as a metaphysical fact that can be seen through observation. In this sense, equality is not yet a moral or legal principle. It describes a characteristic of human nature. By describing all men as naturally "equal and independent," Locke is describing man's natural state, which he constructs through a metaphor that he calls a "state of nature." The state of nature is a kind of philosophic laboratory for Locke; it is that place where there is no government and where the philosopher can examine natural man stripped of the layers of conventional manners and mores that have built up over millennia.

Man's natural state as described by Locke is that condition that all men share everywhere and always until they create a social contract that brings them into civil society. To be independent is, for Locke, to be perfectly free from the commands or coercion of other men; it is to be self-owning, self-governing, and self-reliant; it is that "state of perfect freedom" in which men "order their actions and dispose of their possessions and persons, as they think fit, within the bounds of the law of nature; without asking leave, or depending upon the will of any other man." Man's natural condition is also, according to Locke, a state of equality, "wherein all the power and jurisdiction is reciprocal, no one having more than another; there being nothing more evident, than that creatures of the same species and rank, promiscuously born to all the same advantages of nature, and the use of the same faculties, should also be equal one amongst another without subordination or subjection."[6] In the state of nature, there are no artificial distinctions putting one man above or below another. Man's essential nature is determined, in part, by what he is not: he is neither beast nor God. Thus all men, sharing the essential features of a common nature, are equal in that no man is naturally dependent on or subordinate to other men.

For Locke, equality and independence are inextricably linked. Independence implies equality and vice versa; you cannot have one without the other. But when Locke says that all men are by nature equal, he does not mean to imply that all men are equal in all respects. For example, he says that

> *Age* or *virtue* may give men a just precedency: *Excellency of parts and merit* may place others above the common level: *Birth* may subject some, and *alliance* or *benefits* others, to pay an observance to those whom nature, gratitude, or other respects may have made it due; and yet all this consists with the *equality*, which all men are in respect of jurisdiction or dominion one over another, which was the *equality* I there spoke of, as proper to the business in hand, being that *equal right*, that every man hath, *to his natural freedom*, without being subjected to the will or authority of any other man.

Equality for Locke means that each and every man is or should be self-owning and self-governing, that is, no one man or group of men has a natural "jurisdiction or dominion" over any other man, whatever physical or moral inequalities may subsist between them. This means, then, that no man can or should be "subjected to the will or authority of any other man" without the former's consent.[7]

Locke's view of human nature was revolutionary, and it had wide-ranging consequences that would forever change the modern world. The Englishman rejected a near two-thousand-year-old, classical-Christian philosophical synthesis that identified human nature and natural right with *inequality, dependence,* and *duty.* This older view held that the just and good society would mirror the hierarchic order of man's natural constitution, that man was naturally and permanently suited to living in political communities, and that his primary moral duty was to perfect his nature by sacrificing for the common good. Locke completely upended and demolished this worldview.[8]

In its place, he announced that all men everywhere are naturally equal in terms of their moral claim to govern themselves and that all men are naturally independent and free of each other. For Locke, the individual is the primary unit of moral value and the starting point of the political world. Locke substituted the ancients' and the Christians' transcendent and intrinsic ethic of duty and self-sacrifice for a new ethic that emancipated men (particularly those whom Locke referred to as the "industrious and rational") to pursue their individual self-interest. This meant that Lockean man would be distinguished by a new moral ethos, one defined by individualism, rationality, productiveness, and wealth acquisition. Locke's moral revolution consequently revolutionized the social, political, and economic landscape of the modern world.

Locke's philosophic understanding of equality percolated throughout American culture beginning in the early eighteenth century. As early as 1717, the post-Puritan minister John Wise introduced a new idea of man and society into colonial American culture that would have been foreign to his ancestors and that points toward the revolutionary view of equality supported by the signers of the Declaration of Independence. In his 1717 essay "A Vindication of the Government of New England Churches," Wise constructed a secular theory of social and political organization similar to Locke's that was grounded exclusively on the ability to know the law of nature through reason rather than through biblical revelation. Wise, following Locke and Samuel von Pufendorf, argued that men in a state of nature were in a condition of equality and natural freedom. Equality, according to Wise, is a rationally demonstrable fact of human nature that has moral implications. Writing in language similar to both Locke's and the American revolutionaries', he said it would be an absurdity and a violation of the law of nature

> to believe, that Nature actually Invests the Wise with a Sovereignty over the weak; or with a Right of forcing them against their Will; for that no Sovereignty can be Established, unless some Humane Deed, or Covenant Precede: Nor does Natural fitness for Government make a Man presently Governour over another; for that as *Ulpian* says, *by a Natural Right all Men are born free*; and Nature having set all Men upon a Level and made them Equals, no Servitude or Subjection can be conceived without Equality; and this cannot be made without Usurpation or Force in others, or Voluntary Compliance in those who Resign their freedom, and give away their degree of Natural Being.[9]

Thus did John Wise initiate an intellectual revolution in the American colonies by importing Locke's idea into the New World, the culmination of which was Jefferson's declaration in 1776 that "all men are created equal."

Seven years after the publication of Wise's pamphlet, John Bulkley of Connecticut formally introduced Locke's political philosophy to America with a brief synopsis of the *Second Treatise of Government*. To quote Bulkley again, the "Great Man Mr. Lock well understood the true Origine of all Lawful Authority, and what Powers over themselves or others, Persons by the Law of Nature & Antecedent to their Entering into Society are Vested with." Bulkley affirmed Locke's view of equality: "I firmly Believe that *the Law of Nature* knows no difference or Subordination among Men." All men, he continued, "are otherwise *Equal, Free & Independent* & remain so till by Contracts, Provisions and Laws of their own they divest themselves of those *Prerogatives*."[10]

In 1728, Daniel Dulany Sr. (whose son in 1765 would write an important pamphlet against the Stamp Act) taught the Maryland colonists, in their battle with the proprietary government of Charles Calvert, 5th Baron Baltimore, that what the "Learned Mr. Locke, says of natural Equality" was applicable to their present discontents with the governor:

> A State of Equality, (says that great Man), wherein all Power and
> jurisdiction, is reciprocal; no one having more than another: There
> being nothing more evident, than that Creatures, of the same
> Species, and Rank, promiscuously born, to all the same Advantages
> of Nature, and the Use of the same Faculties, should also be Equal,
> One, amongst another, without Sub-ordination, or Subjection;
> unless, the Lord, and Master of them All should, by any manifest
> Declaration of his Will, set One above Another, and confer on
> Him by an evident and clear Appointment, an undoubted Right, to
> Dominion, and Sovereignty.

Dulany goes on to use Locke's logic of equality and applies it to the political rights of colonial Marylanders in the context of Britain's imperial constitution. Paraphrasing "that great Man" John Locke, Dulany asks:

> Can any Thing be more evident, than that All the Subjects, of
> the same Prince, living within his Dominions, adhering to their
> Allegiance and in a Word behaving themselves, as dutiful and loyal

Subjects ought, and promiscuously born under the same Obligation of Allegiance, Obedience, and Loyalty to their Prince, and to the same Right of Protection, should also be entitled to the same Rights, and Liberties, with the rest of the Subjects, of the same Prince, of their Degree, and Condition, Or can anything be more clear, than that Subjects, having an equal Right to Priviledges, must also have an equal Right to the Laws, made to create or preserve such Privileges? And without which, they cannot be preserved; unless the supreme Power, by any manifest Declaration, distinguish some Subject from Others, by depriving some, of their Privileges; and continuing them to Others.[11]

The elder Dulany's prescient argument is similar, if not nearly identical to, the arguments used forty years later by his son's fellow Patriots during their controversy with Parliament during the imperial crisis.

Nearly two decades later, Elisha Williams, a Congregational minister who served as a Connecticut legislator and jurist and rector of Yale College during the early to mid-eighteenth century, published one of the most profoundly Lockean pamphlets of the entire colonial period. *The Essential Rights and Liberties of Protestants* (1744) is remarkable for its unabashedly open use of Locke's account of human nature and his theory of "*the Origin and End of Civil Government.*" Williams's account of human equality follows directly from Locke's reasoning in the *Second Treatise*. Reason, claims Williams, "teaches us that all men are naturally equal in respect of jurisdiction or dominion one over another." This equality of self-rule is based on two elemental facts of human nature: first, each and every man has been given "an understanding to direct his actions," and, second, all men have a "freedom of will and liberty of acting" within the boundaries established by the law of nature. Thus all men, according to Williams, are born "naturally equal, i.e. with an equal right to their persons," which Williams describes as a right each man has to his "own actions and labour and to what he can honestly acquire by his labour." Williams then goes on to sum up and to give "a short sketch of what the celebrated Mr. Lock in his *Treatise of Government* has largely demonstrated" relative to the basic principles of a legitimate government.[12]

Locke's philosophic influence during the Revolutionary period, particularly on the question of equality, can be seen from the start of the imperial crisis. Consider the views of the Congregationalist minister

Abraham Williams, whose 1762 election sermon rehearsed all the Lockean themes but with a Calvinist twist. "All men," Williams announced, are "naturally equal." The evidence for this, he says, is that they are all "descended from a common Parent" and they all have "like Faculties and Propensities." As such, no man or group of men is, according to Williams, born with "any *difference, distinction, natural Preheminence, or Dominion* of one over another." In this way, all men are equal. (Such views would have been incomprehensible to his seventeenth-century Puritan forebears.) And yet, Williams did not mean to suggest that all men are "equally industrious and frugal," which means that society does and should recognize inequalities in "their Properties and Enjoyments." Williams is representative of the entire revolutionary generation in thinking that a "Society without different Orders and Offices, like a body without Eyes, Hands and other Members, would be incapable of acting, either to secure its internal Order and Well-being, or defend itself from external Injuries."[13] Properly understood, for the revolutionary generation equality and inequality went hand in hand.

During the years between 1764 and 1776, American Whigs used Locke's principles and reasoning on equality and rights so often that it was hard to know sometimes where Locke's argument ended and the Americans' began. It was common for colonial newspapers to quote long passages from the *Second Treatise* without attribution because everyone knew Locke's ideas were being quoted. The Englishman's ideas were the common currency of the age. In 1767, an anonymous writer in Boston claimed that "All Men are by Nature in a state of Equality, in respect of Jurisdiction or Dominion: This I take to be a Principle in itself so evident, that it stands in need of little Proof." He then goes on to quote extensively from the *Second Treatise of Government* on equality.[14] Seven years later, in 1774, Gad Hitchcock delivered the annual Massachusetts election sermon in which he applied Locke's political reasoning and teaching to the political crisis of the moment. Following Locke, Hitchcock invoked the state-of-nature metaphor and declared that all men were equal in that condition, which meant that all men were "exactly on a par in regard to authority; each one is a law to himself, having the law of God, the sole rule of conduct, written on his heart." Hitchcock summed up the American view of equality as it stood in 1774 in these terms:

No individual has any authority, or right to attempt to exercise any, over the rest of the human species, however he may be supposed to surpass them in wisdom and sagacity. The idea of superior wisdom giving a right to rule, can answer the purpose of power but to one; for on this plan the Wisest of all is Lord of all. Mental endowments, though excellent qualifications for rule, when men have entered into combination and erected government, and previous to government, bring the possessors under moral obligation, by advice, perswasion and argument, to do good proportionate to the degrees of them; yet do not give any antecedent right to the exercise of authority.[15]

We can see from this brief survey that Locke's philosophic understanding of equality was accepted and adopted almost in toto and virtually unchanged by colonial Americans in the five decades before independence. When the Sugar Act was passed in 1764 and the Stamp Act the following year, the American view of equality was cast in stone and ready to be used.

EQUALITY IN PRACTICE: THE IMPERIAL CRISIS

The meaning of equality in the Declaration of Independence will come to light if we can determine more precisely how the concept was understood and used during the 1760s and 1770s. Curiously, as recent scholarship has demonstrated, eighteenth-century American society was distinguished by a certain paradox. It is important to recall that colonial America was still, strictly speaking, a monarchical society. Anglo-Americans swore allegiance to the British Crown, and colonial society maintained, or at least aped, many of the aristocratic forms and formalities that defined life in the mother country.[16] Despite its relatively truncated social hierarchy, American society did nevertheless recognize meaningful differences in wealth, rank, and social pedigree. As colonial society matured throughout the eighteenth century, many Americans aspired to import their manners and mores from English high society and to regulate them in the colonies accordingly. Inequality for white Americans was largely a matter of Anglophile affectation as opposed to something created and enforced by law. There were—to be sure—laws supporting primogeniture and entail, but they were falling by the wayside and made ineffective by the wide availability of land in America.[17]

Despite these forms of inequality, eighteenth-century American society was the most egalitarian society in history. The New World lacked the glaring economic and social inequalities that defined life in the Old World. Because land was so much more available in America than it was in Europe, economic opportunity and wealth creation were open to virtually all people willing to be rational, industrious, and economical. Widespread land ownership and increasing wealth accumulation also meant that many more people in colonial America had the suffrage and were thus able to participate in local and provincial politics. Looking back on the early settlement and building years of the colonies, the Reverend Samuel Williams, in his history of Vermont, captured the uniquely egalitarian nature of Anglo-American society. What is most notable about Williams's description of American society is how closely it mirrors John Locke's description in his *Second Treatise* of a theoretical state of nature. For Williams, the social reality of seventeenth- and eighteenth-century America was the existential embodiment of that Lockean place where there is no government. The passage quoted here is long but it deserves to be read with some care:

> Equality.—The nearest equality that ever can take place among
> men, will also be found among the inhabitants of a new country.
> When a number of men are engaged in the same employments and
> pursuits, and have all of them to depend upon their own labour
> and industry for their support, their situation, views, and man-
> ners, will be nearly the same; the way to subsistence, to ease, and
> independence, being the same to all. In this stage of society the
> nearest equality will take place, that ever can subsist among men.
> But this equality will be nothing more than an equality of rights;
> and a similarity of employment, situation, pursuit, and interest.
> In a new country this similarity will be so great, as to form a near
> resemblance of manners and character; and to prevent any very
> great inequalities of privilege from taking place in society, either
> from rank, offices of government, or any other cause....The distinc-
> tions derived from birth, blood, hereditary titles and honours, and
> a difference of rights and privileges, are either unknown or resolve

themselves into nothing, among a people in such a situation; in every view, they cease to be of any use or importance to them. Their situation naturally leads them to discern the tendencies, and designs of nature. They all feel that nature has made them equal in respect to their rights; or rather that nature has given to them a common and an equal right to liberty, to property, and to safety; to justice, government, laws, religion, and freedom.[18]

Williams's America was similar to the world so elegantly captured by Alexis de Tocqueville several decades later in his classic portrait of American society, *Democracy in America*. As the Frenchman famously said of the Americans, their great advantage "is that they have arrived at democracy without having to suffer democratic revolutions, and to be born equal instead of becoming so."[19]

Colonial America was the place where equality and inequality lived together in the bosom of a stable colonial culture. All that changed in 1765, when the British Parliament passed the Stamp Act and introduced a new form of inequality into the colonies, thereby forcing the Americans to reexamine their relative standing within the empire. This new tax caused the colonists to think seriously and deeply about basic moral and political principles beyond even the constitutional issues directly related to the Stamp Act and various other parliamentary measures of the period. Thus the nature and meaning of equality and inequality took on a whole new meaning and importance to the colonists.[20]

Initially, the burning issue in the wake of the Stamp Act was the status of equality not *within* the colonies but *between* the subjects of the realm and those of the colonies. The conflict between Great Britain and her American colonies came down to a question of political and constitutional equality. Anglo-American provincials claimed rights inherited from their English ancestors that they believed were as fully protected in America by the British constitution as were those same rights claimed by their fellow subjects still living in the mother country. Virtually all eighteenth-century American colonists believed that their primary rights were first conceived and incubated in the womb of English life and then brought with them to the New World undiminished. Such rights had not been conferred on them by king or Parliament but were "inherent" in them by virtue of their English descent. In the legal language of the Anglo-American world, these provincials claimed an equal "inheritance."[21] They were, in other words, born equal in their rights with all other Britons.

The colonists viewed the passage of the Sugar and Stamp Acts in 1764 and 1765 as a direct assault on their fundamental right—their equal right—not to be taxed without their consent. In his *Rights of the British Colonies Asserted and Proved*, published in 1764, James Otis stated the American position clearly and directly: "The colonists, being men, have a right to be considered as equally entitled to all the rights of nature with the Europeans." The Americans would brook no constitutional inequality between their fellow subjects in England and themselves. According to the Virginia Resolves, published the following year by Virginia's House of Burgesses, the American colonists were entitled to "all the Liberties, Privileges, Franchises, and Immunities, that have at any Time been held, enjoyed, and possessed, by the people of *Great Britain*"—that is, "to all Liberties, Privileges, and Immunities of Denizens and natural Subjects, to all Intents and Purposes, as if they had been abiding and born within the Realm of *England*." A few months later the colonists' Stamp Act Congress declared "that his majesty's liege subjects in these colonies are entitled to all the inherent rights and privileges of his natural born subjects within the kingdom of Great Britain." The colonists expected no more and no less—in other words, they refused to accept an inferior status when it came to their rights and liberties, which meant they expected to be equal to their fellow subjects in the realm and in other parts of the empire. Silas Downer of Rhode Island reminded his fellow provincials in 1768 that when their ancestors came to America from England they did not forfeit "the privileges of Englishmen by removing themselves hither, but brought with them every right, which they could or ought to have enjoyed had they abided in England."[22] The colonists demanded equal treatment before the common law of England.

The Americans would not accept second-class status when it came to the most fundamental principles of English justice. Like their fellow British subjects, they refused to be taxed without their consent. Moreover, they refused to accept Parliament's new policy of enforcing British tax laws through admiralty courts, which proceeded without juries and according to civil law rather than local common-law courts.

Stephen Hopkins, the governor of Rhode Island, captured the standard pre-1776 view of equality that was at the heart of the imperial crisis:

"it will appear beyond a doubt that the British subjects in America have equal rights with those in Britain; that they do not hold those rights as a privilege granted them, nor enjoy them as a grace and favor bestowed, but possess them as an inherent, indefeasible right, as they and their ancestors were freeborn subjects, justly and naturally entitled to all the rights and advantages of the British constitution." Note that the Americans did not view their equal rights as privileges or favors granted to them by government. They viewed their rights as "inherent" and "indefeasible." That same year, Boston's "Britannus-Americanus" mocked "the folly and nonsense" of British ministers such as George Grenville, "who fancy that the American subjects are not entitled to all the rights of native Britons." A decade before Thomas Jefferson wrote the Declaration of Independence, John Adams declared in no uncertain terms, "all men are born equal."[23]

In his powerful and influential 1766 pamphlet, *An Inquiry into the Rights of the British Colonies*, the Virginian Richard Bland went even further than Otis and the other American critics of the Sugar and Stamp Acts in his analysis of American equality and rights. For Bland, not only were Parliament's recent revenue acts unjust, but so too were the Navigation Acts passed during the reign of Charles II in the seventeenth century, which, in his view, unjustly restricted American commerce relative to the subjects of the realm. Not until the mid-1770s were American Whigs such as Thomas Jefferson willing to suggest that the Navigation Acts were discriminatory, thus constituting "an unnatural Difference between Men under the same Allegiance, born equally free, and entitled to the same civil Rights." Bland summed up the American position with this powerful dictum: "*Rights* imply *Equality*."[24] Equality provides the necessary condition for the existence of rights. In this way, equality was often seen as synonymous with the legal concept "equity," which meant that common-law rights and liberties be applied impartially to all Englishmen no matter where they lived. In the years ahead, American Whigs applied Bland's standard—that rights imply equality—to the various provisions of the Townshend, Tea, and Coercive Acts.

In order to compare the rights of English subjects with those of Americans, a Pennsylvanian writing in 1775 under the pseudonym "Camillus" prepared a useful table demonstrating the disparity and inequality of rights that had developed between mother country and colonies over the course of the previous decade.[25] The differences were stark:

IN ENGLAND	IN AMERICA
1 A trial by a jury of his country, in all cases of life and property.	1 A trial by jury only in some cases; subjected in others, to a single Judge, or a Board of Commission.
2 A trial where the offence was committed.	2 A trial, if a Governour pleases, three thousand miles from the place where the offence was committed.
3 The Civil authority supreme over the Military, and no Standing Army in time of peace kept up, but by the consent of the people.	3 The Military superior to the Civil authority, and America obliged to contribute to the support of a Standing Army, kept up without and against its consent.
4 The Judges independent of the Crown and people.	4 The Judges made independent of the people, but dependent on the Crown for the support and tenure of their commissions.
5 No taxation or imposition laid, but by those who must partake of the burthen.	5 Taxes and impositions laid by those, who not only do not partake of the burthens, but who ease themselves by it.
6 A free trade to all the world, except the East-Indies.	6 A trade only to such places as Great Britain shall permit.
7 A free use and practice of all engines and other devices, for saving labour and promoting manufactures.	7 The use only such engines as Great Britain has not prohibited.
8 A right to petition the King, and all prosecutions and commitments therefore illegal.	8 Promoting and encouraging petitions to the King declared the highest presumption, and the Legislative Assemblies of America dissolved therefor in 1768.
9 Freedom of debate and proceedings in their legislative deliberations.	9 Assemblies dissolved, and their legislative power suspended, for the free exercise of their reason and judgment, in their legislative capacity.
10 For redress of grievances, amending, strengthening, and preserving the laws, Parliaments to be held frequently.	10 To prevent the redress of grievances, or representations tending thereto, Assemblies postponed for a great length of time, and prevented meeting in the most critical times.

By 1774, the logic of the revolutionaries' political understanding of equality was extended to the nature of the empire itself. Equality now meant that Americans and Englishmen not only were equally subject as individuals to the same king and possessed the same rights as all other Englishmen, but also that each colony was subject only to the internal laws of its own provincial legislature just as the subjects of the realm were subject to the laws of Parliament. The American people were equal to the British, which meant that their colonial legislatures were politically equal to that of Parliament. If, as James Wilson noted, "all men are, by nature, equal and free" and if "no one has a right to any authority over another without his consent," then by what right, he demanded to know, do the people of England claim "an absolute and unlimited power over us? By what title do they claim to be our masters?" Thus Wilson drew the inevitable conclusion: the "commons of Great Britain have no dominion over their equals and fellow subjects in America: they can confer no right to their delegates to bind those equal and fellow subjects by laws." Jefferson's *A Summary View of the Rights of British-America*, published in the same month as Wilson's pamphlet, drew a similar conclusion. In it he asked: "Can any one reason be assigned why 160,000 electors in the island of Great Britain should give law to four millions in the states of America, every individual of whom is equal to every individual of them, in virtue, in understanding, and in bodily strength?"[26]

On this level, and at this point in the debate, the colonists were asserting their basic juridical and political equality with the English people. Ultimately, though, the principle of equality was directed less at the Sugar, Stamp, Townshend, and Tea Acts and more at the Declaratory Act, with its claim that the colonies were subject to the authority of Parliament in "all cases whatsoever."[27] The Declaratory Act denigrated the colonial legislatures to second-class status and therefore reduced the colonists' legal rights to a second-class status as well.

By 1775, the Americans' understanding and use of the concept of equality had undergone a profound transformation. After the armed battles with imperial troops at Lexington and Concord in April of that year, the Americans began to think that their political understanding of equality was insufficient for the new context in which they found themselves. When it became clear to them that they could not peacefully achieve political and juridical equality within the empire, they announced their independence from Great Britain, and they declared that a more radical form of equality would provide the basis for their new societies. From 1776 onward, America would no longer be a monarchical society with its structural hierarchies, dependencies, pageantry, and trappings. Instead, America's various governments would be founded on a new understanding of equality—on the idea that *all* men should share equal rights by nature—an idea first imported to America in the early decades of the eighteenth century. American revolutionaries were about to establish a socially de facto egalitarian society unlike any other in history.

REVOLUTIONARY EQUALITY

When Thomas Jefferson announced to the world that "all men are created equal," a claim supported by virtually all American revolutionaries, what exactly did he and they mean by it? History, experience, and mere observation might suggest that Jefferson's claim is self-evidently false. In their day-to-day life experiences, most people (then and now) see nothing but inequality all around them. It is virtually a self-evident truth that not all persons are equal in all respects with regard to size, intelligence, virtue, beauty, strength, speed, and so on. Indeed, Jefferson believed that there is a "natural aristocracy among men. The grounds of this are virtue and talents." In fact, Jefferson believed the natural aristocracy to be "the most precious gift of nature for instruction, the trusts, and government of society."[28]

The meaning of equality as used in the Declaration can be understood, at least in part, if the term is viewed in the context of contemporary criticisms of the revolutionaries. In 1774, the Massachusetts Loyalist Daniel Leonard took on the colonial Whigs and their representatives at the First Continental Congress for inciting rebellion among ordinary Americans. The firebrands of the revolutionary movement "kindled" a "latent spark" into a "flame" by appealing to the people's democratic sentiments. Leonard chastised men such as John Adams for "reminding the people of the elevated rank they hold in the universe, as men; that all men by nature are equal; that kings are but the ministers of the people; that their authority is delegated to them by the people for their good, and they have a right to resume it, and place it in other hands, or keep it themselves, whenever it is made use of to oppress them." America's most thoughtful Loyalist, Thomas Hutchinson, who served as the last civilian governor of Massachusetts and by 1776 had permanently decamped to England, could make neither heads nor tails of the Declaration's claim that all men are created equal. It seemed to have no connection to reality. Besides, echoing Samuel Johnson's famous quip, Hutchinson assumed that the Americans must not know anything about equality given the fact that so many of them held a subject population in chattel slavery.[29]

Without question, though, Jonathan Boucher, an Anglican minister from Annapolis, Maryland, offered the most intellectually sophisticated analysis and critique of the American view of equality. Boucher attacked the notion that "the whole human race is born equal." He simply did not think it true; in fact, he thought it demonstrably false "that no man is naturally inferior, or, in any respect, subjected to another; and that he can be made subject to another only by his consent." Experience and world history, according to Boucher, teach us otherwise, and this point can be seen in two ways. First, natural aristocracy is wrought into the very essence of human nature itself, and this fact must lead ineluctably to "supremacy and subjection." Second, the artificial or man-made aristocracy is an inescapable element of any society because man is by nature social, and that sociality requires government in order to be satisfied. The simple truth is that government itself cannot exist "without some relative inferiority and superiority."[30] If men are naturally unequal, according to Boucher, the idea of government being founded on the consent of the governed was an absurdity. By definition, then, just government must mean the institutionalization of inequality.

Likewise several English pundits had a field day with the Declaration's first self-evident truths, which they treated with contempt. Writing in the influential *Scots Magazine*, "An Englishman" announced that the Americans' equality principle was not a self-evident truth but rather a self-evident lie. He challenged any "American rebel" to identify publicly "any two men throughout the whole world of whom it may with truth be said, that they are created equal." Further, he asked in what attribute it could be said that they are created equal: "Is it in size, strength, understanding, figure, moral or civil accomplishments, or situation of life?" The fact was, he said in answering his own question, that every "ploughman knows that they are not created equal in any of these." Perhaps the most damning English criticism of the Declaration and its doctrine of equality came from the pamphleteer John Lind in his stinging *Answer to the Declaration of the*

American Congress. Lind sneeringly characterized the political opinions of those he described as "modern Americans" as little different from the views of "their good ancestors on witchcraft." The Americans have advanced a "new discovery," Lind said in mockery, a new "self-evident truth" hitherto unknown to mankind: the idea that "*All men* are created equal," which means, he says, the idea "that a child, at the moment of his birth, has the same quantity of *natural* power as the parent, the same quantity of *political* power as the magistrate."[31] The American doctrine of equality was, he argued, a *reductio ad absurdum*.

In light of these kinds of criticisms, how might Jefferson and his fellow revolutionaries have responded? Is the claim that all men are created equal a descriptive or a prescriptive claim? How or in what way are all men created equal? What is it that all men share by nature? Did Jefferson mean to say that all men are the same by nature, that they share a common moral sense, that they are equal in their human dignity, or that they have equal rights?

The self-evident truth that "all men are created equal" is, first, a descriptive truth that identifies and states a fact about human nature. Jefferson's meaning becomes clearer if equality is examined in the light of his first draft of the Declaration, which adds "independent" to the equality clause so that it reads: "all men are created equal and independent." Jefferson's first pass at elucidating the equality truth actually comes closer to how the concept was used by John Locke and by American revolutionaries in 1776 and in the years shortly thereafter. Virginia's 1776 Bill of Rights, drafted by George Mason, states that "all men are by nature equally free and independent." Mason's language was replicated in slightly altered form three months later in the Pennsylvania Declaration of Rights, a year later in the Vermont constitution, and eight years later in the New Hampshire constitution, all three of which declare "that all men are born equally free and independent." The New York constitution copied the exact words of the Declaration of Independence. John Adams's 1780 Massachusetts Declaration of Rights used a slightly different but common formulation in claiming "all men are born free and equal." To suggest, as these state documents do, that all men are "created," "born," or "are by nature" equal is to suggest that human equality is a fact of human life that transcends the traditions of time and place.

Interestingly, the concept "equality" is applied by the Virginia, Pennsylvania, and New Hampshire constitutions using the adverb "equally" to modify the adjectives "free and independent," which in turn describe what man (the noun) is. The adverb describes man's natural condition. Locke, Jefferson, and Adams applied the concept using the adjective "equal," but conjoined with an additional and related adjective, either "independent" or "free." In either case, the adverb or the adjective help to describe man's original condition relative to what Locke would have called other "species and ranks." Locke's understanding of equality was described in chapter 3 as "species equality." All men share the fundamental characteristics of a common nature and are in that sense equal relative to all other species. All men are therefore equal relative to dogs and donkeys; they are equal or the same in some fundamental respect. The equality truth means that there is no natural subordination or natural claim to rule among men. Each and every man is free—equally free—to order his actions and possessions, as long as he does not violate the reciprocity rule, which guarantees the same freedom to all others. To claim that all men are naturally equal is to say that every man has an equal right to be independent and free of the dominion of others.[32]

In one of the best pieces of political writing penned during the Revolutionary era, Theophilus Parsons, writing on behalf of the towns of Essex County in Massachusetts in response to the proposed state constitution of 1778, declared: "All men are born equally free. The rights they possess at their births are equal, and of the same kind." Equality means rights—the equal right to be self-owning and self-governing. It was a core moral belief of the Revolutionary era that men are not naturally subject to the rule of others. As the town of Northampton declared during the debates over the ratification of the newly proposed Massachusetts constitution of 1780: "all men are naturally equal with respect to a right of dominion, government, and jurisdiction, over each other, that is to say, no one has any degree or spark of such right over another."[33] There was a clear consensus in America during the Revolutionary period that the people were largely capable of ruling themselves once the artificial weights of Old World hereditary privilege and legal restrictions were removed.

Following Locke, American revolutionaries understood equality to mean species equality. In his influential pamphlet, *The Rights of the British Colonies Asserted and Proved,* James Otis imported and used Locke's understanding of species equality to challenge the passage of the Sugar Act in 1764. "In order to form an idea of the natural rights of the colonists,"

Otis wrote, "I presume it will be granted that they are men, the common children of the same Creator with their brethren of Great Britain." Otis then draws a connection straight to Locke's view of equality as stated in the *Second Treatise*:

> There is nothing more evident, says Mr. Locke, than "that creatures
> of the same species and rank, promiscuously born to all the same
> advantages of nature and the use of the same faculties, should also
> be equal one among another without subordination and subjection,
> unless the master of them all should…set one above another and
> confer on him by an evident and clear appointment an undoubted
> right to dominion and sovereignty."

A decade later, John Dickinson, quoting the eighteenth-century Swiss student of Locke, Jean-Jacques Burlamaqui, announced: "Nature has made us all the same species, all equal, all free and independent of each other; and was willing that those, on whom she has bestowed the same faculties, should have all the same rights. It is therefore beyond doubt that in a primitive state of nature, no man has of himself an original right of commanding others, or any title to sovereignty." Lastly, John Adams was particularly clear in what he meant by equality when he wrote, "all men are of the same species and of one blood; there is neither a greater nor a lesser nobility."[34]

As presented in the final draft of the Declaration, Jefferson's claim that "all men are created equal" is saying that all men share a common nature or identity. As such, Jefferson and the revolutionary generation began with equality as the metaphysical precondition for the second self-evident truth (discussed in the next two chapters): that all men are "endowed by their Creator with certain unalienable rights." In other words, the *is* of the Declaration implies an *ought*. Equality implies rights. Or, as Thomas Paine put it in *Rights of Man*, all accounts of man's creation

> agree in establishing one point, the unity of man; by which I mean,
> that *men are all of one degree*, and consequently that all men are born
> equal, and with equal natural right….and consequently, every child
> born into the world must be considered as deriving its existence
> from God. The world is as new to him as it was to the first man
> that existed, and his natural right in it is of the same kind.[35]

What man *is* determines how he *should* act. The Declaration's *is* (i.e., the self-evident truth that "all men are created equal") implies the *ought* (i.e., the self-evident truth that all men are "endowed by their Creator with unalienable rights.") Individuals have rights by virtue of the fact that they are by nature equal in their independence and freedom. The unalienable rights of all men are *derived* from the fact of their equality.

The premise that all men share a common nature suggests that they are the *same* in *some* essential way, but it does not mean that they are equal or the same in *every* respect. Equality did not mean quantitative *sameness* for Jefferson and America's revolutionary thinkers. They knew that British critics of the Declaration were right in one respect, that not all men are equal with regard to size, strength, speed, intelligence, beauty, and so on. They also knew that there were acquired inequalities relative to moral action. The revolutionary generation certainly did not think that all men were equal with regard to moral virtues such as rationality, honesty, integrity, fortitude, courage, justice, and productiveness.[36]

But Jefferson and the other founders also knew that to speak of "men" is to speak of the distinguishing characteristics that *all* men share in common vis-à-vis other species (e.g., reason and free will), which means a capacity to govern oneself. All men have reason and many other things in common (e.g., some amount of strength, some amount of speed, some amount of intelligence), but the distinguishing measurements or quantities of these characteristics differ from man to man. In Jefferson's understanding of equality, the measurements have been omitted. Jefferson considers only the quantitative differences between men after the more fundamental understanding of equality is acknowledged. Following Locke's epistemological innovation that all men are born *tabula rasa*, Jefferson meant to suggest that all men are created equal in that, whatever their natural differences might be, they are not so great as to confer a natural title to rule over any individual by nature, that is, without that individual's consent.

Thomas Jefferson, John Adams, and virtually all of the other founders recognized that men, while being equal in their metaphysical independence and freedom, are not only *different* in their various natural abilities and circumstances but are fundamentally unequal in a myriad of ways not relevant to their political equality. The "right to equality," wrote "Democraticus" from Virginia in 1776, "is adverse to every species of subordination beside that which arises from the difference of capacity, disposition, and virtue."[37] Equality recognizes and is the foundation for inequality rightly understood.

James Wilson offered the most robust philosophical analysis by an American of the role played by inequality in human affairs and with it an answer to the challenges posed by Boucher and Lind.

> When we say, that all men are equal; we mean not to apply this equality to their virtues, their talents, their dispositions, or their acquirements. In all these respects, there is, and it is fit for the great purposes of society that there should be, great inequality among men. In the moral and political as well as in the natural world, diversity forms an important part of beauty; and as of beauty, so of utility likewise. That social happiness, which arises from the friendly intercourse of good offices, could not be enjoyed, unless men were so framed and so disposed, as mutually to afford and to stand in need of service and assistance. Hence the necessity not only of great variety, but even of great inequality in the talents of men, bodily as well as mental. Society supposes mutual dependence: mutual dependence supposes mutual wants: all the social exercises and enjoyments may be reduced to two heads—that of giving, and that of receiving: but these imply different aptitudes to give and to receive.

Inequality and diversity are responsible, according to Wilson, for promoting "social happiness." Even the "beauty" that comes with a division of labor in a society that recognizes and promotes "friendly intercourse" and "mutual dependence" can be traced to inequality in the species. Paradoxically, inequality—indeed, "great inequality"—in the "talents of men, bodily as well as mental," provides the material cause of social interaction, order, and harmony. Still, Wilson makes absolutely clear that such inequality is compatible with—indeed, it is grounded on—a more basic form of equality: "With regard to all, there is an equality in rights and in obligations; there is that 'jus aequum,' that equal law, in which the Romans placed true freedom." This equality of rights

> forms a part of that great system, whose greatest interest and happiness are intended by all the laws of God and nature. These laws

prohibit the wisest and the most powerful from inflicting misery on the meanest and most ignorant; and from depriving them of their rights or just acquisitions. By these laws, rights, natural or acquired, are confirmed, in the same manner, to all; to the weak and artless, their small acquisitions, as well as to the strong and artful, their large ones. If much labour employed entitles the active to great possessions, the indolent have a right, equally sacred, to the little possessions, which they occupy and improve.[38]

According to the revolutionary generation, it is a metaphysical fact that all men stand in relations of equality and inequality to each other at one and the same time. Thus equality and inequality are brought together in harmony in the philosophy of Locke and therefore also in the Declaration.

The Reverend Samuel Williams brilliantly captured the American view reconciling equality and inequality. After describing America's uniquely egalitarian society (quoted above), Williams also notes that the Americans understood the important and naturally occurring role played by inequality in a social order grounded on species equality. Men are equal, according to Williams, in a limited sense: "The whole race resemble one another in the make and form of their bodies; in their original appetites, passions, and inclinations; in reason, understanding, and the moral sense, &c. But in these respects it is similitude, not equality, which nature has produced." Equality means sharing a common nature with common attributes. It does not mean an equality of attributes.

Nothing ever did, or ever can produce an equality of power, capacity, and advantages, in the social, or in any other state of man. By making men very unequal in their powers and capacities, nature has effectually prevented this....To some, the Author of Nature has assigned superior powers of the mind, a strength of reason and discernment, a capacity of judging, and a genius for invention, which are not given to others. To others, the Deity has assigned a strength, vigour, and firmness of constitution, by which the bodily powers are more favoured in one, than in another.

From this natural inequality and arising from man's natural needs and wants, Williams notes, a free society will naturally experience a plethora of differences and natural inequalities that cannot and should not be altered:

> Causes thus natural and original, will be followed with their natural and proper effects. Superiour wisdom and abilities, will have superiour influence and effect in society. Superiour strength and activity of body, will also have advantages peculiar to themselves. In making these natural distinctions, nature evidently designed to qualify men for different attainments, and employments. And while she gave to all the nature and the rights of man, she assigned to some a capacity and a power, to make a much more useful improvement and exercise of that nature, and of those rights, than she has given to others.[39]

When true equality (i.e., equal rights) is protected and combined with freedom and the division of labor, the just society will naturally imitate nature's inequality.

While it is true that some individuals have greater reasoning abilities than others, it is no less true that all individuals are endowed with sufficient abilities such that each man naturally has the means and the right to self-government. In 1790, Jefferson put the same point this way: "Everyman, and every body of men on earth, possesses the right of self-government. They receive it being from the hand of nature."[40] In other words, all men are by nature morally sovereign, which means that each man is an end in himself and that all are equally free to govern themselves within the context of the rights of others. The differences between men are not so great that one man is by nature the master of another, and by the same token no man is by nature the slave of another.

Differences—measurable quantitative differences—between men do not mean that one man has a natural right to rule another. Following Locke, the revolutionary generation believed that no man was born with the right to rule over another. As Jefferson wrote to Henri Grégoire in 1809, "Because Sir Isaac Newton was superior to others in understanding, he was not therefore lord of the person or property of others."[41] The Virginian therefore recognized and celebrated differences of wisdom and virtue, and he could even accept differences of wealth, birth, and beauty so long as it was understood that they did not give one man the authority to rule over another.

What, then, is equality? How is it that all men are created equal? For Locke, as for Jefferson and the other American revolutionaries, equality means equal natural liberty and the equal right that all men have to self-government. Equality as fact and principle does not and did not mean equality of condition or equality of dignity. Such an interpretation would require the violation of someone else's rights. Jefferson and the founding generation did not recognize the right of one man to violate those of another. That would mean inequality. The Declaration's claim that all men are created equal served not only as the justification for breaking with Great Britain but also as the moral foundation of the new governments that were to be established once British authority came to an end.

We cannot leave the subject of equality, however, without recognizing and examining the obvious contradiction between the revolutionaries' avowed principle of equality and the brutal reality of slavery in the United States. In fact, it is only in the light of slavery that the Americans' understanding of equality can be fully understood.

CHAPTER 5

Equality and Slavery

"Convince me that one man may rightfully make
another man his slave, and I will no longer subscribe
to the Declaration of Independence."
—WILLIAM LLOYD GARRISON, 1854

*I*n 1856, Abraham Lincoln told a gathering of Chicago Republicans that the American system of government rested on public opinion, and public opinion "always has a 'central idea,' from which all its minor thoughts radiate." For Lincoln, America's central idea was, and always had been, the equality of mankind. Seven years later, at Gettysburg, he reminded those assembled that America's founding fathers had created a new nation "dedicated to the proposition that all men are created equal."[1]

Lincoln took his idea of equality from the Declaration of Independence. Like Jefferson, Lincoln meant something precise by it: that *all* men have equal rights—humans are not divided by nature into masters and servants—and that no man has a natural claim to rule others without their consent. As Jefferson put it late in his life, men are not born with saddles on their backs, nor are others born booted and spurred to ride them. Now, it is true that some men and women do saddle and ride horses (and sometimes with boots and spurs), but the differences between people and horses are differences of kind and not of degree. Likewise, that people leash and then walk dogs bespeaks the natural differences between people and dogs. Neither horses nor dogs suffer an injustice by virtue of being tamed and domesticated. America's revolutionary generation believed that the law of nature permits ruler–ruled relationships between different species, but it is forbidden among men.[2] This is why the Second Continental Congress affirmed unequivocally in its 1775 Declaration of the Causes and Necessity of Taking Up Arms that reason teaches the absurdity of the idea that some men could "hold an absolute property in, and an unbounded power over others." Expressing the spirit of American liberty, the Congress resolved "to die freemen rather than to live slaves."[3]

The revolutionaries' understanding of equality led them to adopt a particular view of government, the sole purpose of which was to protect the equal rights of all citizens in the community. But the revolutionary generation also knew that the protection of equal rights leads to unequal results. In the tenth essay of *The Federalist*, James Madison summed up the revolutionary generation's view of justice and government when he argued that the "rights of property originate" in the "diversity in the faculties of men" and that the "first object of government" is the *equal* protection of the *unequal* faculties of acquiring property.[4] To that end, American revolutionaries were proponents of the rule of law, which meant that laws must be applied equally to all individuals in society. An individual's unequal social status as determined by birth, wealth, intelligence, or even moral virtue provided no greater or lesser claim to the equal protection of the laws. The founders believed that the proper function of government was to ensure that the playing field was level and not artificially tilted to aid or hinder particular individuals or groups.

This was the central teaching of the American Revolution, but it is subject to an all-too-obvious question: How could a nation dedicated to the proposition that *all* men are created equal tolerate the existence of chattel slavery? The Declaration of Independence states clearly and unequivocally, "all men are created equal"; it does not say that some men are created equal, or that all white men, or all Englishmen, or all Americans, or all Christians are created equal.[5] And yet the author of the Declaration and more than half of its signers were slaveholders. What are the implications of that fact for the Declaration's simple words? Does the fact that Jefferson and so many of the founders held other human beings in bondage change or diminish the truth status of the Declaration's first self-evident truth?

AMERICAN SLAVERY, AMERICAN FREEDOM

The full meaning of equality in the Declaration of Independence is best seen by examining it relative to the long-standing existence of chattel slavery in America. Ideals must not be confused with reality, particularly given the fact that Jefferson and his revolutionary colleagues expected their principles to be put into practice. Slavery had of course existed in one form or another as a worldwide phenomenon for several millennia, and it was introduced to Britain's American colonies in the first half of the seventeenth century. Dutch traders brought the first shipment of African slaves (seized from a Spanish slave ship) to Jamestown, in the Virginia colony, in 1619. The practice was subsequently institutionalized in colonial American law, beginning in the 1640s through various court decisions that legalized ownership of persons. The great turning point in the history of slavery came in 1680 when the Virginia legislature passed the first slave code, which declared that slaves—and the children of slave women—would serve for life, as would their children and their children's children.[6]

American-style slavery denoted a legal and social relationship between a master and a slave wherein the master owned the body and labor of the slave as chattel property. According to the abolitionist and former slave Frederick Douglass, a "master is one…who claims and exercises a right of property in the person of a fellow man." Sanctioned by law, the institution of chattel slavery "gives the master absolute power over the slave." The master may, Douglass explained, "work him, flog him, hire him out, sell him, and, in certain contingencies, kill him, with perfect impunity." For all intents and purposes, the "slave is a human being, divested of all rights." As such, the slave

> has no wife, no children, no country, and no home. He can own nothing, possess nothing, acquire nothing, but what must belong to another.…He toils that another may reap the fruit; he is industrious that another may live in idleness; he eats unbolted meal, that another may eat the bread of fine flour; he labors in chains at home, under a burning sun and a biting lash, that another may ride in ease and splendor abroad; he lives in ignorance, that another may be educated; he is abused, that another may be exalted.[7]

With the possible exception of the Quakers, few Americans (or anyone anywhere else for that matter) before the 1760s seriously questioned the moral status of slavery. It was a worldwide institution almost as old as the family itself, and, though distasteful to many and immoral to some, was regarded by most as a necessary evil.

In order to understand the full context of slavery and its existence in the colonies, it is also important to note that chattel slavery was only the most brutal institution of a brutal age. Some of the inequalities and degradations of Old Europe's ancien régime were replicated in colonial America. Day-to-day life for ordinary people in seventeenth- and eighteenth-century Anglo-American society could be described as, to quote Thomas Hobbes, "solitary, poor, nasty, brutish, and short." In a monarchical society defined by inequality, statuses, and rank orders of dependency and unfreedom, slavery was distinguished by being only the most degraded status. Voluntary and involuntary servitude came in many forms and degrees in this unenlightened age. Though not enslaved as chattel, many eighteenth-century Anglo-American whites were hardly free, being kept in various states of dependency as indentured servants. The difference in social standing and quality of life between a white indentured servant and a black house slave in the northern colonies during the colonial period was one of degree rather than kind, although the moral and legal differences were differences of kind. Still, equality, rights, and freedom were *not*, in the centuries leading up to the Revolution, the norm. This is why so many colonial Americans unthinkingly took slavery for granted in the decades leading up to the 1760s and 1770s, or were not as repulsed by it as we are today.[8]

By the 1770s, the institution of slavery was well established in the British (and French, Spanish, Portuguese, and Dutch) Americas, where it had existed for more than a century and a half and had planted deep roots in the economy, social structure, and law. It was legally practiced in every Anglo-American colony; in the thirteen colonies there were approximately half a million slaves, one-fifth of the total American population. Plantation owners in the South held most of the enslaved population (Virginia alone held 200,000), but there were also substantial numbers of slaves held in northern states such as New York, New Jersey, and Rhode Island. The slave trade with Africa carried on unabated throughout the colonial period. Slavery was, whether or not all Americans were willing to admit it, a national institution woven into the social fabric of everyday life.[9] On a more personal level, many leading revolutionaries—including George Washington, Patrick Henry, Thomas Jefferson, George Mason, and James Madison—owned slaves. (It should also be noted that many American revolutionaries did not own slaves, including John Adams, Samuel Adams, James Wilson, and Alexander Hamilton.)

It is a tragic irony that American revolutionaries—including, if not most especially, those who owned slaves—understood as well as anyone that slavery was an ugly, degrading, and brutal institution wherever it had been practiced. They hated and condemned it as immoral and anathema to the principles and institutions of a free society. Not a single revolutionary leader ever publicly praised slavery as a positive good. Benjamin Franklin, speaking as president of the Pennsylvania Society of Promoting the Abolition of Slavery, described slavery as "an atrocious debasement of human nature." George Washington, a slaveholder, told a friend, "There is not a man living, who wishes more sincerely than I do to see a plan adopted for the abolition of [slavery]." At the Constitutional Convention in 1787, James Madison told his colleagues, "We have seen the mere distinction of color made in the most enlightened period of time, a ground of the most oppressive dominion ever exercised by man over man." And John Adams told a correspondent in 1819 that he had held "the practice of slavery in abhorrence" through his entire life.[10]

America's leading revolutionaries and founding fathers knew that American-style slavery was a vicious institution defined by arbitrary power and tyranny. It was clearly anathema to all of their declared moral principles, and yet more than half of the signers of the Declaration were slave owners. That the principal author of the Declaration held men, women, and children in bondage raises the charge of hypocrisy to the highest level. Should Jefferson's declaration to the world that *all* men are created equal and endowed with unalienable rights be taken seriously? More to the point, did the Declaration's equality principle apply only to whites?[11] And if the Declaration applied only to whites, then was it not, by definition, a racist document? How could American revolutionaries tolerate, sanction, or participate in such a noxious institution as chattel slavery? Was the American Revolution a revolution *for* slavery? Why was it not ended immediately? Finally, were American revolutionaries little more than rank hypocrites?

These are difficult, even painful, questions. To answer them honestly and accurately, however, we must resist our contemporary inclination to assume as fact that America's revolutionary founders were imprisoned by the biases of their own time even as we condemn them for holding those biases. Such an approach prevents us from truly understanding and accurately judging their ideas and actions. Those ideas and actions should first be understood and judged by the founders' own perspective and standards before we apply our own standards to past thought and action. Instead, the method employed here is simple without being simpleminded: to examine the ideas, decisions, and actions of America's revolutionary generation on the founders' own terms, as they understood themselves. Then and only then can the question of slavery in light of the Declaration be understood—and judged—in the proper historical and philosophical light.[12]

SLAVERY AND AMERICAN REVOLUTIONARIES

Given the fact of slavery in colonial America, what did America's revolutionary generation *think* about it? During the 1760s and 1770s, colonial Americans argued nonstop in their pamphlets, newspapers, and sermons that taxation without representation was a form of tyranny and slavery. It was the most rhetorically powerful argument in their intellectual arsenal. Almost immediately, some Americans understood—though some evaded it—that this argument with the British, and the moral principles it invoked, also applied to the institution of American chattel slavery. With time, more and more Americans confronted the contradiction between their ideals and their institutions. Some sought to change their institutions, and several decades later some sought to change their ideals. Consider the views of five American revolutionaries—James Otis, Benjamin Rush, Richard Wells, Patrick Henry, and Thomas Jefferson—on the question of slavery, which offer a representative range of American opinions.

James Otis was one of the first American colonists to connect the philosophic dots between their Lockean philosophy of equality and freedom and their inherited institutions. In his influential 1764 pamphlet on *The Rights of the British Colonies Asserted and Proved*, Otis argued that all American colonists "white or black" are freeborn "by the law of nature." There is no right by nature, according to Otis, "to enslave a man because he is black." Race, and all of the physiological features that go with it, provide no grounds or "logical inference in favor of slavery." Indeed, the slave trade and the practice of slavery represented "the most shocking violation of the law of nature." It therefore followed from the law of nature, he continued, that all men, "black and white, born here are freeborn British subjects"; that they are "entitled to all the essential civil rights of such is a truth not only manifest from the provincial charters, from the principles of the common law, and acts of Parliament, but from the British constitution, which was re-established at the Revolution [of 1688] with a professed design to secure the liberties of all the subjects to all generations." Otis then issued an ominous warning to his countrymen: it is a certain truth, he argued, "that those who every day barter away other men's liberty will soon care little for their own."[13] One might quibble with Otis's assessment of the legal status of enslaved blacks in the American colonies, but his moral principles were consistent and clear.

In his 1773 pamphlet *An Address to the Inhabitants of the British Settlements in America, on the Slavery of the Negroes in America*, Benjamin Rush denounced "Slave-keeping" as an unmitigated "evil." Addressing the claim that blacks were intellectually and morally inferior to whites, Rush described "all the vices which are charged upon the Negroes" as "the genuine offspring of slavery, and serve as an argument to prove that they were not intended for it." Slavery was "so foreign to the human mind," he continued, that the "moral faculties, as well as those of the understanding are debased, and rendered torpid by it." Rush called upon his fellow citizens in Philadelphia to end the slave trade as quickly as possible by "petitioning the king and parliament" through their legislatures and by shunning their countrymen who continued to "engage in the slave trade." Moreover, he favored gradual emancipation laws and extending to freed slaves "all the privileges of free-born British subjects." He also encouraged his fellow Pennsylvanians to support the education of both extant and freed slaves in "the principles of virtue and religion." He hoped they would be taught to "read, and write," and then instructed "in some business" so that they might "be able to maintain themselves." For him the prospect of abolition and emancipation was tied directly to the moral and social ideals unleashed by the revolution in thinking that was then occurring in America:

> Ye men of Sense and Virtue—Ye Advocates for American Liberty,
> rouse up and espouse the cause of Humanity and general Liberty.
> Bear a testimony against a vice which degrades human nature, and
> dissolves that universal tie of benevolence which should connect
> all the children of men together in one great Family.—The plant
> of liberty is of so tender a Nature, that it cannot thrive long in the
> nieghbourhood of slavery. Remember the eyes of all Europe are
> fixed upon you, to preserve an asylum for freedom in this country,

after the last pillars of it are fallen in every other quarter of the Globe.[14]

The following year Richard Wells, a Philadelphia Quaker, published a devastating critique of American slavery. In his 1774 pamphlet *A Few Political Reflections*, Wells excoriated his countrymen for their complicity in slavery and called on them to examine their "own conduct" relative to the peculiar institution. He asked the question that some were asking but too many were evading: "whether we can reconcile the *exercise* of SLAVERY with our *professions of freedom, 'founded on the law of God and nature, and the common rights of mankind.'*" The Americans could hardly object to British violations of their colonial rights, he declared, if "*every colony* on the continent is deeply involved in the inconsistent practice of *keeping their fellow creatures in perpetual bondage.*" Borrowing the logic and argument of Lord Mansfield's famous 1772 decision in the Somerset case in England, Wells declared that "ALL *the inhabitants of America* [including slaves] are entitled to the privileges of the inhabitants of Great-Britain." Wells supported this position by paraphrasing a famous line from Mansfield's judgment in which the British jurist said "the instant a slave sets his foot in England he claims the protection of the laws, and puts his master at defiance." By extension, given the fact that the Americans were claiming that British rights extend to America, the same principle relative to slaves in England must apply to slaves in America. By Mansfield's judgment in Somerset, the common law does not recognize chattel slavery. As a result, unless a slaveholder could provide a "personal contract" between him and his slave, no common-law court in America could in good conscience support the perpetuation of slavery in the colonies.[15] Again, as with Otis, Wells's invocation and understanding of English common law did not win the day in most American colonies.[16]

Many American revolutionaries such as Otis, Rush, and Wells were unalterably opposed to slavery and understood the hypocrisy of owning slaves while accusing their British opponents of attempting to enslave them. A particularly tortured and complicated view of American slavery can be seen in the opinions of Patrick Henry, who was one of America's most eloquent spokesmen for freedom and also a slave owner. It was Henry, after all, who ended his famous 1775 speech at Saint John's Church in Richmond, Virginia, with these memorably fiery words: "Is life so dear, or peace so sweet, as to be purchased at the price of chains and slavery? Forbid it, Almighty God! I know not what course others may take; but as for me, give me liberty, or give me death."[17] Slavery was a central trope for this freedom fighter in his battle against British imperial officials. Indeed, there was no greater evil for Henry, which is why he was tortured by his own collusion with the institution.

Two years before he delivered his Richmond speech, he sent a letter to his friend Robert Pleasants in which he bared his soul on the question of chattel slavery. Henry was perplexed that Christianity "should encourage a Practice so totally repugnant to the first Impression of right & wrong." He was even more stupefied that Europeans should have introduced this "Abominable Practice" into the Americas during the most enlightened period of human history, a time when the "Rights of Humanity are defined & understood with precision, in a Country above all others fond of Liberty." But Henry's moral principles did not match the reality of his life, and he knew it. In a moment of painful candor, he admitted to Pleasants that he owned other human beings and held them in perpetual bondage. The letter is brimming with regret and shame and guilt. Given his reputation as one of America's leading proponents of liberty, he knew that the charge of hypocrisy stuck to him like no other: "Would anyone believe," he exclaimed, "that I am Master of Slaves of my own purchase!" It was nothing but shameful weakness on his part, he admitted, that made giving up his slaves a "general inconvenience." He could not "justify" his conduct, which he described as "culpable." He lamented the fact that he could not conform his actions to the call of "Virtue" so as to "own the excellence & rectitude of her Precepts."[18]

Fourteen years later, Henry's shame and guilt had not abated. Indeed, it seems only to have intensified. Speaking at the Virginia Convention to ratify the proposed federal constitution, he told a room filled with many fellow slaveholders:

> Slavery is detested—we feel its fatal effects—we deplore it with all the pity of humanity....As much as I deplore slavery, I see that prudence forbids its abolition....I repeat it again, that it would rejoice my very soul, that every one of my fellow beings was emancipated. As we ought with gratitude to admire that decree of Heaven, which has numbered us among the free, we ought to lament and deplore

the necessity of holding our fellow-men in bondage. But is it prac-
ticable by any human means, to liberate them, without producing
the most dreadful and ruinous consequences?[19]

Henry's remarks are a symptom of a divided soul: on one hand, he seems
full of guilt, remorse, and self-loathing, and on the other, he seems to be a
steely-eyed pragmatist prepared to rationalize the existence of an institution that he hates but from which he benefited economically.

Finally, let us turn to Thomas Jefferson, to the man who wrote the
most famous words in American history: "We hold these truths to be
self-evident, that all men are created equal, that they are endowed by
their Creator with certain unalienable Rights, that among these are Life,
Liberty and the pursuit of Happiness." Jefferson's libertarian creed has
provided the highest moral ideal for Americans for over 225 years, but
he was also a lifelong slaveholder, who did not free the vast majority of
his slaves upon his death. When he declared to the world, "all men are
created equal," he owned over 150 slaves. How are Jefferson's views on
slavery to be understood and evaluated? Did he intend to include blacks
when he spoke of the self-evident truth of equality and rights? Was he
the ultimate hypocrite?[20]

Not surprisingly, the Virginian's views on slavery were complicated.
Jefferson's first public statement on slavery was published in 1774, in *A
Summary View of the Rights of British-America*, in which he denounced
George III for vetoing American legislation attempting to end the African
slave trade:

> For the most trifling reasons, and sometimes for no conceivable
> reason at all, his majesty has rejected laws of the most salutary ten-
> dency. The abolition of domestic slavery is the great object of desire
> in those colonies, where it was unhappily introduced in their infant
> state. But previous to the enfranchisement of the slaves we have, it
> is necessary to exclude all further importations from Africa; yet our
> repeated attempts to effect this by prohibitions, and by imposing
> duties which might amount to a prohibition, have been hitherto
> defeated by his majesty's negative: Thus preferring the immediate
> advantages of a few African corsairs to the lasting interests of the
> American states, and to the rights of human nature, deeply wound-
> ed by this infamous practice.[21]

Jefferson's position in the *Summary View* is notable in two respects: first, his ultimate goal in ending the slave trade was the "abolition of domestic slavery" in America; and, second, he believed that slavery violated the "rights of human nature." Two years later, Jefferson again attacked the king for his refusal to sanction the colonists' attempt to abolish the African slave trade. In his original first draft of the Declaration, Jefferson wrote a stirring denunciation of slavery. The king of Britain has, Jefferson declared,

> waged cruel war against human nature itself, violating its most
> sacred rights of life and liberty in the persons of a distant people
> who never offended him, captivating and carrying them into slavery
> in another hemisphere....Determined to keep open a market where
> MEN should be bought and sold, he has prostituted his negative for
> suppressing every legislative attempt to prohibit or to restrain this
> execrable commerce.[22]

Again, it is abundantly clear that Jefferson believed the slave trade and by extension slavery itself to be a "violation of human nature" and of "its most sacred rights of life and liberty." For Jefferson and the revolutionary generation, the rights of nature are grounded on the fact of human equality (i.e., species equality), which means that no man is either a natural slave or the natural ruler of another. In sum, the charge that Jefferson did not think that Africans were equal in their rights relative to whites is false.

There is no reason to think that Jefferson did not believe what he wrote or that he was simply a hypocrite. In fact, Jefferson was committed to the antislavery cause in more than just speech. In 1779, he authored a bill for the Virginia House of Burgesses that provided for gradual emancipation in Virginia. Five years later, he proposed (unsuccessfully) a law that would have banned slavery from the entire western territory of the United States. Jefferson's proposed law was later used as the basis of the Northwest Ordinance of 1787, which did in fact bar slavery from the newly formed territory between the Appalachians and the Mississippi. As president of the United States, he lent his public support in 1807 to ending the international slave trade. He implored Congress to "withdraw the citizens of the United States from all further participation in those violations of human rights which have been so long continued on the unoffending inhabitants of Africa, and which the morality, the reputation, and the best interests of our country, have long been eager to proscribe."[23]

Given his very real antislavery views, why then did Jefferson not more forcefully support the total abolition of slavery or free his own slaves? There can be little doubt that Jefferson struggled throughout his life (as did Patrick Henry) with what might be called the postemancipation problem. Late in life, he summed up the dilemma in this way: "We have the wolf by the ears, and we can neither hold him, nor safely let him go. Justice is in one scale, and self-preservation in the other." This was a real and meaningful issue for eighteenth-century Americans, and Jefferson meant self-preservation quite literally. He predicted that if the slaves were freed and lived in America, "deep-rooted prejudices entertained by the whites' ten thousand recollections, by the blacks, of the injuries they have sustained; new provocations; the real distinctions which nature has made; and many other circumstances, will divide us into parties, and produce convulsions which will probably never end but in the extermination of the one or the other race."[24] Jefferson and America's revolutionary slave-holders were stuck on the horns of a genuine dilemma: on one hand, they knew slavery was morally wrong and they wished to abolish it; but on the other hand, they assumed that slave emancipation would have devastating effects on both whites and blacks in particular and for American society in general. They were damned if they did and damned if they didn't. From Jefferson's perspective, neither personal financial nor civilizational suicide was a viable option.

Still, a nagging doubt remains about Jefferson's view of equality and whether he thought the principle applied to African Americans. His views on race were complex and sometimes contradictory. Jefferson thought there were meaningful physiological, moral, and cultural differences (as did virtually all eighteenth-century Americans) between whites and blacks that were "fixed in nature."[25] He also thought those very same differences applied *within* racial groups. But he did not think such differences affected the moral and political implications of the Declaration's equality principle. Slavery was a moral wrong, according to Jefferson, because it violated the equality principle and with it the corollary principle of individual rights. He viewed the relationship between "master and slave" as inherently immoral and corrupting. It promoted, he argued, "a perpetual exercise of the most boisterous passions, the most unremitting despotism on the one part, and degrading submissions on the other." He was certain that slavery debased everything it touched, including the moral character of those who owned

slaves. Possibly even referring to himself, Jefferson denounced those statesmen who, "permitting one half the citizens thus to trample on the rights of
the other, transform those into despots." Slavery, he continued, turns men
"into enemies" and it "destroys the morals of the one part, and the amor
patriae of the other." Jefferson's soul was filled with contempt for the institution of slavery—a contempt that he no doubt felt for himself on some
level. He clearly agonized over the glaring anomaly between his ideals and
his chosen reality. In the end, though, he knew right from wrong—and he
knew that he was wrong—and he knew that "God is just" and that "his
justice cannot sleep forever."[26]

America's revolutionary founders recognized a spectrum of natural and
conventional differences and inequalities among all men (white and black),
none of which, they argued, had any bearing on the natural equal rights
shared by all men. Racial differences and unequal intellectual or physical
abilities do not, according to Jefferson, have any bearing on the equal right
to freedom born to each individual by nature. He insisted that the natural
and sometimes unequal differences between men are therefore "no measure
of their rights." The only morally and politically relevant truth, Jefferson
declared in a pithy aphorism worth quoting again, is this: "Because Sir
Isaac Newton was superior to others in understanding, he was not therefore
lord of the person or property of others."[27] In the end, the revolutionaries' idea of natural or species equality renders politically irrelevant natural
inequalities and differences of intelligence, strength, speed, beauty, virtue,
personality, and ambition. Their view of equality meant that each and every
adult person, regardless of race, is naturally independent of all others and
has a right to self-government.

Still, the Revolution's ideals were too big for some of the men who held
and proclaimed them to actually practice them.

THE PARADOX OF AMERICAN FREEDOM:
CONTRADICTIONS, HYPOCRISY, AND GUILT

American revolutionaries understood better than modern scholars the
degree to which their moral ideals conflicted with their actions relative to
slavery. British Tories and American Loyalists savaged American Patriots
mercilessly for their hypocrisy and seemingly *faux* cries of "tyranny" and
"slavery" during the years of the imperial crisis. In his 1775 essay *Taxation*

No Tyranny, Samuel Johnson brutally mocked the Americans for their posturing and famously asked, "how is it that we hear the loudest yelps for liberty among the drivers of negroes?" Johnson's question left the Americans stammering for an answer. It haunted them for decades. It still does. A year later, Thomas Hutchinson, the self-exiled former governor of Massachusetts, taunted his fellow Americans from London for the mendacity and posturing of their Declaration of Independence, which announced to the world that all men are created equal at the same time, he wrote, that they deprived "more than an hundred thousand Africans of their rights to liberty, and *the pursuit of happiness*, and in some degree to their lives."[28] The charge of hypocrisy, particularly from the hated Hutchinson, stung the Americans like no other. Indeed, with every passing year after 1776, the weight of guilt tugged at the conscience of revolutionary Americans—particularly slaveholders such as George Washington, Patrick Henry, and Thomas Jefferson—with increasing pressure.

As the political crisis with Great Britain mounted in the late 1760s and early 1770s, the status of slavery in the colonies raised difficult, even painful questions for American Patriots. The principal American argument against British imperial legislation was that it represented a form of tyranny. To be taxed without representation, they argued, was just the first step on the road to their eventual enslavement. Alexander Hamilton in *A Full Vindication of the Measures of the Congress* claimed that British parliamentarians and their Loyalist supporters in America were "enemies to the natural rights of mankind" as evidenced by their attempt to "enslave" the colonists. The Declaratory Act and its claim of absolute parliamentary sovereignty over the Americans was akin to "absolute slavery." Hamilton went on to define the differences between freedom and slavery as they applied in the context of the imperial crisis.

> The only distinction between freedom and slavery consists in this: In the former state, a man is governed by the laws to which he has given his consent, either in person or by his representative: in the latter, he is governed by the will of another. In the one case, his life and property are his own, in the other they depend upon the pleasure of his master. It is easy to discern which of these two states is preferable. No man in his senses can hesitate in choosing to be free rather than a slave.[29]

It did not take some American Patriots very long to see the contradiction between their protestations against imperial British legislation and the existence of domestic slavery in the colonies. Benjamin Rush, for instance, told a French correspondent, "it would be useless for us to denounce the servitude to which the Parliament of Great Britain wishes to reduce us, while we continue to keep our fellow creatures in slavery just because their color is different from ours."[30]

In fact, the Revolution caused some Americans to launch a searching debate over the nature of slavery and freedom—a debate that lasted until the conclusion of the Civil War. Late colonial newspapers, pamphlets, and petitions launched the world's first antislavery campaign condemning slavery as anathema to the moral philosophy of the revolutionary movement. In 1768, a correspondent to a Philadelphia newspaper minced no words in asking rhetorically, "How suits it with the glorious cause of Liberty to keep your fellow men in bondage, men equally the work of your great Creator, men formed for freedom as yourselves."[31] In 1773, a letter published in a Boston newspaper highlighted the contradiction between the revolutionaries' antislavery rhetoric and the reality of slavery in the colonies: "It has long been a surprise to me and many others, that a people who profess to be so fond of freedom, and are taking every method to preserve the same themselves, and transmit it to their posterity, can see such numbers of their fellow men, made of the same blood, not only in bondage, but kept so even by them." This anonymous writer then moved in for the final blow by asking: "Can such a conduct be reconcilable with the love of freedom?"[32]

A year later, John Allen in Salem, Massachusetts, mocked and denounced his fellow Americans for perpetuating or tolerating slavery:

> Blush ye pretended votaries for freedom! ye trifling patriots! who
> are making a vain parade of being the advocates for the liberties of
> mankind, who are thus making a mockery of your profession, by
> trampling on the sacred natural rights and privileges of the *Africans*;
> for while you are fasting, praying, non-importing, non-exporting,
> remonstrating, resolving, and pleading for a restoration of your
> charter rights, you at the same time are continuing this lawless,
> cruel, inhuman, and abominable practice of enslaving your fellow-
> creatures,…a greater part of which I am sorry to say are dwellers in
> this *American* land of freedom![33]

In 1775, Levi Hart denounced the African slave trade as a *"flagrant violation of the law of nature, of the natural rights of mankind."* He further told his congregation in Farmington, Connecticut, that they must "wake up and put an effectual stop to the cruel business of stealing and selling our fellow men." Otherwise, they had no moral claim to suggest that they were being enslaved by British legislation when in fact they were the true "tyrants" engaged in "inconsistence and self contradiction." That same year, the residents of Darien, Georgia, in the heart of Georgia lowcountry slavery, declared their "disapprobation and abhorrence of the unnatural practice of Slavery in *America*,…a practice founded in injustice and cruelty, and highly dangerous to our liberties."They denounced slavery as "debasing part of our fellow-creatures below men, and corrupting the virtue and morals of the rest." Slavery, they continued, was "laying the basis of that liberty we content for…upon a very wrong foundation."They concluded by resolving "at all times to use our utmost endeavours for the manumission of our Slaves in this Colony, upon the most safe and equitable footing for the masters and themselves."The following year, in 1776, the Massachusetts state house of representatives formally resolved that chattel slavery is "utterly inconsistent with the avowed principles in which this and other states have carried on their struggle for liberty." Likewise, John Jay, both a New York slaveholder and an abolitionist, did not shy away from the central issue: "That men should pray and fight for their own freedom and yet keep others in slavery is certainly acting a very inconsistent as well as unjust and perhaps impious part."[34] And on and on it went.

The revolutionary logic of the Declaration's self-evident truths began to seep into American thinking as the Patriots began to apply their moral principles to a myriad of domestic institutions, including if not most especially the institution of slavery. In 1776, the influential New England theologian Samuel Hopkins published *A Dialogue Concerning the Slavery of Africans*, which he dedicated to the members of the Continental Congress. His argument was clear and direct: slavery, he argued, "is wrong" and a "very great public sin," and those who practice it are "worse than *Egyptian* taskmasters." It was therefore the "duty and interest of the American states," he wrote in the subtitle, "to emancipate all their African slaves." It was not uncommon in the context of 1776, Hopkins argued, for America's only true slaves to hear their masters talk about their "struggle for liberty" and the "aversion" they "have to slavery and how much liberty is prized."What were

America's black slaves to think when they heard their white masters declare that "slavery is more to be dreaded than death" and that they "are resolved to live free or die"? Not surprisingly, then, America's African slaves saw "themselves deprived of all liberty and property, and their children after them, to the latest posterity, subjected to the will of those who appear to have no feeling for their misery." And not without a hint of irony did America's enslaved "see the slavery the *Americans* dread as worse than death" to be actually "lighter than a feather," when compared with "their heavy doom" and "the most abject slavery, and unutterable wretchedness to which they are subjected." Hopkins captured the ultimate paradox of the Revolution when he claimed sarcastically that America's domestic slaves "behold the *sons of liberty*, oppressing and tyrannizing over many thousands of poor blacks, who have as good a claim to liberty as themselves." Not surprisingly, he continued, the slaves "are shocked with the glaring inconsistence," and they "wonder" why their white masters "do not see it."[35]

By the end of the Americans' war for independence, equality, and freedom, David Cooper from New Jersey delivered a remarkable address *To the Rulers of America on the Inconsistency of Their Conduct Respecting Slavery: Forming a Contrast Between the Encroachments of England on American Liberty, and American Injustice in Tolerating Slavery.* Cooper's strategy was as simple as it was effective: to remind American Patriots of the purposes and rhetoric of the Revolutionary cause. To that end, he quoted a series of passages from the most important documents of the Revolutionary era, including the Declaration of the Causes and Necessity of Taking Up Arms, the Declaration and Resolves on Colonial Rights of the First Continental Congress, the Declaration of Independence, the Pennsylvania Declaration of Rights, and the Massachusetts Declaration of Rights. Regarding each Patriot statement denouncing the actions of the British Parliament and defending the colonists' rights, Cooper reminded his audience that the same principles applied with equal—if not greater—force to the status of black slaves held in America.

Cooper's stinging rebuke to his fellow Americans' hypocrisy went directly to the heart of the issue. He implored them "to demonstrate to Europe, to the whole world, that America was in earnest, and meant what she said, when, with peculiar energy, and unanswerable reasoning, she plead the cause of human nature, and with undaunted firmness insisted, that all mankind came from the hand of their Creator *equally free*." It was imperative that America not give anyone "an opportunity to charge her conduct with a contradiction to her solemn and often repeated declarations; or to say that her sons are not real friends to freedom; that they have been actuated in this awful contest by no higher motive than selfishness and interest." The reasoning and principles of the Revolutionary cause must, by definition, he argued, "apply equally to Africans." This is why throwing the words of the Declaration of Independence back into the faces of the Americans stung like no other charge: "IF these solemn *truths*, uttered at such an awful crisis, are *self-evident*: unless we can shew that the African race are not *men*, words can hardly express the amazement which naturally arises on reflecting, that the very people who make these pompous declarations are slave-holders, and, by their legislative conduct, tell us, that these blessings were only meant to be the *rights* of *whitemen* not of all *men*." If the Declaration's self-evident truth that "*all* men are created equal" was actually true and not a fiction, then it was a moral imperative for American slaveholders to cease and desist immediately from holding their fellow men as they do their "cattle." The promise of the Declaration of Independence and the American Revolution, Cooper continued, was clear: "The disquisitions and reasonings of the present day on the rights of men, have opened the eyes of multitudes who clearly see, that, in advocating the rights of humanity, their slaves are equally included with themselves." The time had therefore come for America's Patriot leaders, Cooper concluded, to practice what they preached: "We expect, mankind expects, you to demonstrate your *faith* by your *works*; the *sincerity* of your *words* by your *actions*, in giving the *power*, with which you are *invested*, its utmost *energy* in promoting *equal* and *impartial* liberty to *all* whose lots are cast within the reach of its influence."[36]

The great achievement of the American Revolution was to launch forces that would lead over time to the reconciliation of moral theory and moral practice. Still, the story of slaveholders fighting for freedom and equal rights was the central anomaly of the American Revolution and the new society it created.

Three years after Cooper's broadside, the residents of Frederick and Hampshire counties in Virginia sent a petition to the Virginia legislature in which they reminded their elected officials of the meaning and implications of the Revolution: "That the Glorious and ever memorable Revolution can be Justified on no other Principles but what doth plead with greater

Force for the emancipation of our Slaves in proportion as the oppression exercised over them exceeds the oppression formerly exercised by Great Britain over these States."[37]

As the years passed, the psychic guilt brought on by the simultaneous existence of freedom and slavery in the same place intensified and would not go away—at least not for many individuals in the North. Indeed, the guilt only deepened and intensified. Benjamin Franklin, a man who rarely felt any guilt about his behavior, certainly felt it relative to slavery. In 1790, just before his death, Franklin authored a petition on behalf of the Pennsylvania Society for the Abolition of Slavery that called for "the Restoration of liberty to those unhappy Men, who alone, in this land of Freedom, are degraded into perpetual Bondage, and who, amidst the general Joy of surrounding Freemen, are groaning in Servile Subjection." The petition, written by a man who had once owned house slaves decades before, recognized that the moral principles of the Revolution, which provided a "just & accurate Conception of the true Principles of liberty," had "spread through the land" and awakened Americans to the injustice of slavery and its glaring contradiction with the Declaration's self-evident truths. The Pennsylvania Abolition Society sent its petition to the United States Congress, calling on the national government to "devise means for removing this Inconsistency from the Character of the American People." Because of the Revolution and the moral principles on which it was fought, Franklin now saw all too clearly the crime of slavery and the necessity of emancipation not only to correct a profound injustice but also to save "the Character of the American People." Franklin encouraged the federal government to use all powers necessary and proper at its disposal to "promote mercy and Justice towards this distressed Race," and to discourage "every Species of Traffick in the Persons of our fellow men."[38] Emancipation was first and foremost about correcting a moral wrong, but it was also about saving America.

In 1794, Theodore Dwight of Connecticut bore witness to the painful hypocrisy of those who loved freedom and yet kept men in chains:

> And if any thing can sound like a solecism in the ears of mankind, it will be this story—That in the United States of America, societies are formed for the promotion of freedom. Will not the enquiry instantly be made—"Are the United States of America not free? Possessed of the best country, the wisest government, and the

most virtuous inhabitants, on the face of the earth; are they still enslaved?" No—America is not enslaved; she is free. Her country is still excellent, her government wise, and her inhabitants virtuous. But this reply must be mixed with one base ingredient. The slavery of negroes is still suffered to exist.

The guilt did not abate as one moved southward. St. George Tucker, a professor of law at the College of William and Mary, in hindsight captured the moral dilemma and ultimate delinquency of the revolutionary generation's confrontation with slavery when he wrote in 1796:

> Whilst we adjured the God of Hosts to witness our resolution to live free, or die, and imprecated curses on their heads who refused to unite with us in establishing the empire of freedom; we were imposing upon our fellow men, who differ in complexion from us, a slavery, ten thousand times more cruel than the utmost extremity of those grievances and oppressions, of which we complained....Such [is] that partial system of morality which confines rights and injuries, to particular complexions; such the effect of that self-love which justifies, or condemns, not according to principle, but to the agent....Should we not have loosed their chains, and broken their fetters? Or if the difficulties and dangers of such an experiment prohibited the attempt during the convulsions of a revolution, is it not our duty to embrace the first moment of constitutional health and vigor, to effectuate so desirable an object, and to remove from us a stigma, with which our enemies will never fail to upbraid us, nor our consciences to reproach us?[39]

The ugly contradiction between the stated ideals of American revolutionaries and the brutal reality of slavery was, however, more easily denounced than overcome. A self-evident contradiction did not provide a self-evident solution to the problem.

THE CHALLENGE OF SLAVERY

Assuming for the moment that all of America's founding revolutionaries were opposed to slavery in theory, the great challenge is to determine why they did not abolish it in practice. It was certainly easy for them to denounce slavery, and it is even easier for twenty-first-century Americans to denounce the revolutionary generation for not abolishing it. But to determine *why* they did not do so is a much more interesting and difficult project. To that end, our task is threefold: first, to examine how various American revolutionaries dealt with the problem of slavery; second, to present the actual steps they took—if any—toward achieving that goal; and, third, to understand the forces that made abolition problematic.

When it came to actually doing something about slavery, there was a range of views and practices as to what could or should be done given the moral, social, political, and economic context of the time. In the best cases, many revolutionaries—including Samuel Adams, John Adams, Thomas Paine, and Alexander Hamilton—never owned slaves and were unalterably opposed to the institution throughout the entirety of their lives. In a few cases, revolutionaries such as Benjamin Franklin, John Jay, and Benjamin Rush owned and then freed house slaves while also being vocal public critics of slavery and leaders in a burgeoning antislavery movement. In some cases, leading southern revolutionaries such as George Washington owned large plantations worked by slaves, but they also vehemently opposed slavery in private and manumitted their slaves after they died. In the worst cases, some leading revolutionaries—including George Mason, Thomas Jefferson, and James Madison—were opposed to slavery in speech, embarrassed by the obvious contradiction between their professed ideals and their personal interests, and worked to end slavery in America by preventing its extension and supporting the colonization movement, but nevertheless enjoyed the convenience of having slaves, whom they did not free after they died, thereby giving their private moral sanction to slavery's perpetuation. Finally, it should be noted that there were *no* proponents of slavery as a positive good during the period of the Revolution and founding. The intellectual case *for* slavery did not arise in America until the late 1830s, when the institution came under direct attack from northern abolitionists.[40]

There were a host of reasons why the revolutionary generation did not immediately abolish slavery. The majority of American revolutionaries believed (naively) that slavery was not an economically viable institution and that it would die a natural death over time, particularly with the end of America's involvement with the slave trade in 1808. Speaking at the Constitutional Convention in August 1787, Connecticut's Oliver Ellsworth spoke for many when he declared, "As population increases poor laborers will be so plenty as to render slaves useless. Slavery in time will not be a speck in our Country."[41] In the context of the time, slavery's eventual demise seemed likely. No one during the Revolutionary era could have anticipated the invention of the cotton gin in 1793.

On a more somber note, some American revolutionaries chose not to manumit their slaves or to work to abolish slavery because they could not reconcile theory and practice in their private lives. They knew slavery was wrong, they wanted to abolish it, but for various personal reasons they chose to do nothing about it. Some felt a psychic attachment and loyalty to their slave-owning parents or to their parents' way of life, and some even felt a perverse attachment and loyalty to their slaves. More commonly, most could not bear the prospect of financial ruin either for themselves or for their progeny. The obvious truth is that most had been corrupted by the lifestyle slavery afforded them. Simply put, they were either morally weak or morally bankrupt. Thomas Jefferson is the classic example of someone whose private life, tragically, was intertwined with, profited from, and ulti-mately was corrupted by slavery. Jefferson's moral character was no match for his moral and political principles.[42]

In the end, however, one reason stands out above all others to explain why the revolutionary generation did not abolish slavery: the post-eman-cipation problem. Even the purest, nonslaveholding abolitionist stumbled over this hurdle. Many antislavery southerners such as James Madison were genuinely uncertain as to *how* they could abolish slavery without creating massive social dislocation or personal devastation for both blacks and whites. It is difficult for twenty-first-century students of the past to appreciate the enormous distance between the ideal of emancipation and the actual conditions required for its successful implementation. Various structural—moral, religious, social, economic, and political—impedi-ments to change enfeebled what might have been a robust movement for emancipation.

Several probing questions highlight the challenge of the post-eman-cipation problem. How were southern slaveholders to end an institution that was so deeply woven into local economies? How and when were America's slaves to be manumitted? Should slave owners be compensated, and by whom? What would emancipation mean in those areas of the Deep South where the slave population equaled or surpassed the free white population? Should freed slaves be integrated into white American society, or should they be repatriated to Africa or colonized in the trans-Appalachian West? Who would pay for colonization? And lurking behind all these questions was the prospect of a race war between freed slaves and the white population. These were serious questions for both slaveholders and nonslaveholders, and no one quite knew how to answer them. In light of these problems and challenges, what steps did American revolutionaries take to end slavery?

THE REVOLUTION TO END SLAVERY

The great story of the American Revolution is not that the founding generation failed to end slavery, but rather that it set in motion forces that would lead to the eventual abolition of America's "peculiar institution." The proper historical question to ask is, what effect did the logic of America's revolutionary ideals have on the institution of slavery? What did American revolutionaries actually do about slavery in the light of their ideas about freedom and justice?

Without question, the most important step in abolishing slavery was taken on July 4, 1776, when the American people declared to the world as a self-evident truth, "all men are created equal." America's revolutionary constitution-makers then built their new governments to reflect this fundamental truth. The 1776 Virginia Bill of Rights likewise declared, "*all* men are by nature equally free and independent." The declaration of rights attached to the 1776 Pennsylvania constitution announced, "*all* men are born free and equal." The Massachusetts constitution of 1780 likewise proclaimed, "*All* men are born free and equal." Identical language can be found in the revolutionary state constitutions of New York (1777), Vermont (1777), and New Hampshire (1784). That so many state constitutions and bills of rights would replicate the Declaration's language of "all men" seems to make clear that America's revolutionary founders meant the phrase literally and without qualification.

The Americans' public declaration that all men are created equal and that each and every man is entitled by right to freedom represented the moment of America's great moral awakening—the moment when the institution of slavery was put on notice and its abolition became a moral and political necessity. From this point forward, a new moral consciousness and conscience was born in Anglo-American culture. The Declaration's moral principles established for the first time in American history a benchmark by which to judge and condemn a long-practiced social evil. Those principles represented a profound transformation in moral thought and action, a transformation that led a growing number of Americans to see slavery as a moral abomination. For the first time, some Americans began to see the incompatibility between human liberty and bondage, that liberty for one must mean liberty for all.

The principles enunciated in the Declaration of Independence represented a direct challenge to chattel slavery, and they inspired the creation of America's first antislavery movement. In the thirty years after 1776, all of the northern states began the process of dismantling slavery.[43] Vermont's revolutionary state constitution of 1777 declared, "*all* men are born equally free and independent, and have certain natural, inherent and unalienable rights, amongst which are the enjoying and defending life and liberty; acquiring, possessing and protecting property, and pursuing and obtaining happiness and safety," and then proceeded to abolish slavery outright in these words:

> No male person, born in this country, or brought from over sea,
> ought to be holden by law, to serve any person, as a servant, slave
> or apprentice, after he arrives to the age of twenty-one Years, nor
> female, in like manner, after she arrives to the age of eighteen years,
> unless they are bound by their own consent, after they arrive to
> such age, or bound by law, for the payment of debts, damages, fines,
> costs, or the like.[44]

In 1779, Pennsylvania passed a law to gradually emancipate all slaves in the state. Five years later, Connecticut passed its Gradual Abolition Act, which emancipated all those born into slavery after that year and once they had reached the age of twenty-five. Slavery was abolished in Massachusetts and New Hampshire through a series of court decisions in the 1780s, which held that their respective state bills of rights affirming "all men are born free and equal" made slavery unconstitutional. Rhode Island and Connecticut passed gradual abolition laws in 1783 and 1784. New York and New Jersey did the same in 1799 and 1804. By 1798 every state in the Union had outlawed the African slave trade, and by 1804 every northern state had committed itself to emancipating its slaves in one form or another.

Interestingly, in the first few years after 1776, there was a particularly strong antislavery movement in the South, which, for a time, had more antislavery societies than in the North. Some places in the South were even moved by revolutionary ideals to start manumitting slaves. The number of free blacks in Virginia, for instance, increased from 3,000 in 1780 to 13,000 by 1790. South Carolina's Low Country slaveholders freed more slaves during the 1780s than they had during the previous three decades.[45] Overall, by 1810, more than 100,000 slaves had been emancipated in the United States, either through court decisions, legislation, or acts of individual manumission.[46] It was the largest emancipation of slaves in world history.

At the federal level, the Congress of the Confederation of the United States passed the Northwest Ordinance in 1787, which expressly forbade slavery in the newly organized territory between the western slope of the Appalachian Mountains and the Mississippi River (i.e., the future states of Ohio, Indiana, Michigan, Illinois, and Wisconsin). The following year, the newly ratified federal Constitution authorized Congress to end America's involvement in the international slave trade in 1808.

In virtually all cases, those who worked to abolish slavery in the states and at the federal level did so based on the revolutionary principles of the Declaration of Independence. In the preamble to its Act for the Gradual Abolition of Slavery, the Pennsylvania legislature declared, "it is our duty…to extend a portion of that freedom to others, which hath been extended to us, and release them from that thralldom, to which we ourselves were tyrannically doomed." In the best-known freedom case in Massachusetts, *Commonwealth v. Jennison* (1783), the state Supreme Judicial Court ruled in favor of freeing the slave Quock Walker. In his instructions to the jury, Chief Justice William Cushing held that the state constitution did, in fact, grant rights to all men that were incompatible with slavery:

> It is true, without investigating the right of christians to hold
> Africans in perpetual servitude, that they had been considered
> by some of the Province laws as actually existing among us; but
> nowhere do we find it expressly established. It was a usage,—a
> usage which took its origins from the practice of some of the
> European nations and the regulations for the benefit of trade of
> the British government respecting its then colonies. But whatever
> usages formerly prevailed or slid in upon us by the example of
> others on the subject, they can no longer exist. Sentiments more

favorable to the natural rights of mankind, and to that innate desire
for liberty which heaven, without regard to complexion or shape,
has planted in the human breast—have prevailed since the glorious
struggle for our rights began. And these sentiments led the framers of our constitution of government—by which the people of this
commonwealth have solemnly bound themselves to each other—to
declare—*that all men are born free and equal*; and that *every subject
is entitled to liberty*, and to have it guarded by the laws as well as
his life and property. In short, without resorting to implication in
constructing the constitution, slavery is in my judgment as effectively abolished as it can be by the granting of rights and privileges
wholly incompatible and repugnant to its existence. The court
are therefore fully of the opinion that perpetual servitude can no
longer be tolerated in our government, and that liberty can only
be forfeited by some criminal conduct or relinquished by personal
consent or contract.

Cushing's decision was explicitly based on the state constitution's proposi-
tion—similar to the Declaration's—that "*all* men are born free and equal."
Likewise, the Rhode Island law that abolished slavery, paraphrasing the
Declaration of Independence, states:

Whereas all men are entitled to life, liberty and the pursuit of
happiness, and the holding mankind in a state of slavery, as private
property, which has gradually obtained by unrestrained custom
and the permission of the laws, is repugnant to this principle, and
subversive of the happiness of mankind, the great end of all civil
governments: *Be it therefore enacted by this General Assembly*...that
no person or persons, whether Negroes, Mulattos or others, who
shall be born within the limits of this State, on or after the first day
of March, A.D. 1784, shall be deemed or considered as servants for
life, or Slaves.[47]

But all of this is to view the antislavery movement from the perspective of freed whites. Possibly the greatest impact of the Revolution on the
status of slavery in America was its effect on those who were actually held
in bondage. The ideas and actions of American Patriots inspired some

American slaves to fight for freedom and equality. The revolutionaries' principles and rhetoric motivated many slaves to escape from their masters and to flee to the British army, which had offered them freedom in exchange for service. Interestingly, some liberated slaves actually enlisted to fight alongside their fellow Americans in order to gain their freedom. Alexander Hamilton argued that any enlisted slave should be given his "freedom with their muskets."[48]

Public acceptance of slavery was also tarnished during the Revolutionary period whenever slaves petitioned state legislatures for their freedom, or used the legal system to launch lawsuits in state courts to secure their freedom.[49] One such petition from slaves in Massachusetts used the same arguments that some of their white masters were using against Great Britain: "We have in common with all other men a natural right to our freedoms without Being depriv'd of them by our fellow men as we are freeborn Pepel and have never forfeited this Blessing by aney compact or agreement whatever."[50] A group of black freemen in New Hampshire employed the principle of natural rights to demand the abolition of slavery:

> That the God of nature gave them life and freedom, upon the
> terms of the most perfect equality with other men; That freedom
> is an inherent right of the human species, not to be surrendered,
> but by consent, for the sake of social life; That private or public
> tyranny and slavery are alike detestable to minds conscious of the
> equal dignity of human nature;...they hold themselves in duty
> bound strenuously to exert every faculty of their minds to obtain
> that blessing of freedom, which they are justly entitled to from that
> donation of the beneficent Creator.[51]

Slaves did not suffer from false consciousness in thinking that the principles of the Declaration applied just as well to them as to white Americans.

The American Revolution was, from beginning to end, an antislavery revolution in the broadest sense—a revolution *for* equal rights and *against* arbitrary power. Slavery and arbitrary power come in many forms, and the principles of the Revolution, once unleashed, inspired Americans to ameliorate and abolish all forms of injustice, arbitrary power, tyranny, dependency, and slavery over time and wherever it existed in America. This was the promise of the Declaration of Independence.

The birth and growth of an American antislavery movement was not possible without a standard or benchmark by which to condemn a universal institution virtually as old as human civilization. That benchmark was the natural-rights philosophy articulated by the American Revolution and expressed in the Declaration of Independence. There could be no antislavery movement—then or now—without the universal principle of individual, natural rights. It was the lodestar of emancipation.

As the revolutionary movement proceeded in the years and then decades after 1764, as Americans talked with greater urgency of the natural rights of "man," the American people came to better see and understand the meaning and full implications of the ideas they were espousing. It dawned on some almost immediately and others only later that their arguments *for* equal rights and *against* tyranny applied to their slaves as well. The philosophy at the heart of the Revolution was identical to the philosophy that called for the end of chattel slavery. Not surprisingly, Anthony Benezet, colonial America's first great antislavery leader, identified the simple truth from which honest men could not escape: America's black slaves were, morally speaking, "as free as we are by nature."[52] What cannot go on forever will not, and the logic of the Americans' revolutionary principles led them inexorably to begin the process of ending chattel slavery in America. Many of the Americans who chose to recognize and live their lives by the moral principles that would one day be expressed in the Declaration of Independence were compelled to purge this monstrous inconsistency from their lives. They could no longer claim liberty for themselves and deny it to others. When in the course of their lives it became necessary to bridge the gulf between words and deed, they acted. This is why, starting in 1774, the Continental Congress called on the colonies to end their involvement in the international slave trade, which six northern states subsequently did. This was the first political act taken against slavery.[53] A year later, Philadelphia Quakers organized the world's first antislavery society, which was, interestingly, replicated in several southern states.

The revolution to end slavery in America was flawed from the outset because of various intractable problems, but we should never forget that it began with and was inspired by the logic of the Declaration's self-evident truths.

THE DECLARATION AND FREEDOM

In the end, how should American revolutionaries be evaluated on the slavery question? To judge and condemn them for having failed to abolish slavery is easy, but it is also to engage in historical anachronism and simple-minded presentism. Historical truth is far more complicated and requires a much more sophisticated analysis. America's revolutionary founders took seriously the moral and political ideals enunciated in the Declaration of Independence, and they started the process of applying those ideals to their own lives and to their domestic institutions—a process that would take decades to complete. They saw the gaping chasm between their rhetoric and reality, principles and practices, ideas and institutions, and they sought to reduce if not one day to eliminate the contradiction. In other words, adherence to their expressed moral principles caused them to rethink the institution of slavery and to begin the process of eliminating it. John Jay of New York, a onetime slaveholder and one of the leading abolitionists of the founding period, captured the moral state of mind that developed in America in the years before and after 1776:

> Prior to the great Revolution our people had been so long accus-
> tomed to the practice and convenience of having slaves, that very
> few among them even doubted the propriety and rectitude of it.
> Some liberal and conscientious men had indeed, by their conduct
> and writings, drawn the lawfulness of slavery into question....Their
> doctrines prevailed by almost sensible degrees, and was like the
> little lump of leaven which was put into three measures of meal.[54]

Jay's statement on the revolutionary affects and effects of the Revolution describes near perfectly the moment when the institution of slavery went from being seen as a necessary evil to simply evil. The road to emancipation was long and tortuous, but the journey began—symbolically at least—in 1776 and with the Declaration's proclamation "that all men are created equal."

The American Revolution did not and could not end slavery on its own, but the logic of its core moral principles did bring about its denoue-ment. Something fundamental happened in the minds of Americans during the Revolutionary era. The natural-rights philosophy at the core of the Revolution burst forth into American society with consequences both intended and unintended. Thomas Jefferson and the signers of the Declaration of Independence planted a seed that would later grow and bloom into something much bigger. That germination gave rise to forces that would break down all kinds of cultural, political, and economic barriers and eventually destroy slavery.

The expression, acceptance, and institutionalization of the Declaration's first two truths brought about a fundamental shift in American values. The Declaration's revolutionary philosophy was the first cause and accelerant promoting the equal freedom of all men everywhere, and it provided a direct challenge to the institution of slavery. The antislavery and abolitionist movements drew their inspiration directly from the Declaration's moral principles. A new nation dedicated to the proposition that all men are created equal now had the moral principles and vocabulary necessary to undermine chattel slavery over time.

The moral ideals unleashed by the revolutionary generation forever changed the content of the American mind and with it America's social reality. Jefferson in particular knew that the free society that was then being created in America would eventually spell the end of slavery.[55] The only question was when and how. The forces of history are not predetermined and nothing about the future is inevitable, but with the publication of the Declaration of Independence a slow-burning civil war between freedom and slavery was ignited.

Almost all of America's revolutionary leaders (including those who owned slaves) hated slavery, but they understood better than we can today the difficulties and challenges associated with ending it. The social, economic, and political obstacles to ending slavery were formidable. More importantly, we must remember that those who led the Revolution were men, not angels—men driven by a tangled maze of contradictory passions, opinions, and interests. Too many of them were unable to overcome the limitations of their own moral horizons, their financial interests, and their social habits. They saw the self-evident inconsistency between the Declaration's professions of equality and liberty and the reality of slavery—and it tormented them. Their struggle was one of finding a way to abolish slavery without destroying the very nation they were striving to build. Still, such men can and should be judged morally in the light of those among their contemporaries who did own slaves at one time but eventually freed them and became leading proponents of the burgeoning antislavery movement.

By placing the equality principle and the doctrine of individual, unalienable rights at the very heart of America's system of republican government, the revolutionary generation put slavery on notice. Abraham Lincoln, the greatest student of the Declaration, probably summed up most eloquently the relationship between the Declaration's principles and the role they would play in the process of ending slavery. In responding to the claims of Roger B. Taney, Chief Justice of the Supreme Court, and Senator Stephen A. Douglas that the language of the Declaration "did not intend to include negroes," Lincoln explained what he thought Jefferson and the signers of the Declaration meant when they declared all men to be created equal:

> I think the authors of that notable instrument intended to include all men, but they did not intend to declare all men equal *in all respects.* They did not mean to say all were equal in color, size, intellect, moral developments, or social capacity. They defined with tolerable distinctness, in what respects they did consider all men created equal—equal in "certain inalienable rights, among which are life, liberty, and the pursuit of happiness." This they said, and this meant. They did not mean to assert the obvious untruth, that all were then actually enjoying that equality, nor yet, that they were about to confer it immediately upon them. In fact they had no power to confer such a boon. They meant simply to declare the *right,* so that the *enforcement* of it might follow as fast as circumstances should permit. They meant to set up a standard maxim for free society, which should be familiar to all, and revered by all; constantly looked to, constantly labored for, and even though never perfectly attained, constantly approximated, and thereby constantly spreading and deepening its influence, and augmenting the happiness and value of life to all people of all colors everywhere.[56]

Many modern scholars reject Lincoln's understanding of the Declaration of Independence. Ironically, they unwittingly follow the lead of Taney and Douglas (and John C. Calhoun) in arguing that the birth of the American republic sanctioned and institutionalized racism and slavery. If this is true, then Lincoln was clearly mistaken if not dishonest in claiming at Gettysburg, on November 19, 1863, that America was "conceived in liberty, and dedicated to the proposition that all men are equal." But Lincoln was not wrong. He told the truth, and he was wise in ways unfamiliar to modern academics. He understood that the Declaration's noble ideals were true, but he also knew that they might take decades to percolate down and through American society. He understood that the battle for the soul of America was then being waged over the meaning and implementation of a few simple words—"that all men are created equal, that they are endowed by their Creator with certain unalienable Rights, that among these are Life, Liberty and the pursuit of Happiness." In other words, he understood the proper relationship between theory and practice and how it is mediated by prudence.

As he stood on the blood-soaked fields of Gettysburg, Lincoln knew that tens of thousands of brave men had fought and died in order to fulfill the noble ideals and promise of the American Revolution and to help launch a "new birth of freedom" in America. Like the men who died at Gettysburg, Lincoln challenged the living to dedicate their lives "to the great task remaining before us—that from these honored dead we take increased devotion to that cause for which they gave the last full measure of devotion." True equality—the equality of liberty—was and is a revolutionary ideal to which many Americans still aspire. If revolutionary Americans fell short in producing equal liberty for all, they left us with an ideal that still inspires and is still worth striving for.

CHAPTER 6

The Nature of Rights

"We hold these truths to be self-evident, that all men ...are
endowed by their Creator with certain unalienable Rights ..."

*I*n 1776, many colonial Americans were ambivalent about launching a
war for independence, and some were actively opposed to it, but on
one principle virtually all Americans were in agreement: "With respect to
our rights, the acts of the British government contravening those rights,
there was but one opinion on this side of the water; all American Whigs
thought alike on these subjects."[1] Under the pressure of events during the
1760s and 1770s, American Whigs developed and used a relatively new
understanding of rights—rights grounded not in history but in nature. They
variously referred to such rights as "natural rights," the "rights of nature,"
the "rights of human nature," the "rights of mankind," or, as the Declaration
describes them, as "unalienable rights." When John Adams wrote that the
real American Revolution was a revolution in the minds of the American
people (i.e., a revolution in their *"principles, opinions, sentiments, and affections"*), he was no doubt referring to the Americans' development and use
of this new conception of rights in the years between 1760 and 1776. At the
most fundamental level, the American Revolution was about rights—the
unalienable and natural rights of the individual.

American revolutionaries studied and used the principle of "unalienable rights"—just as they did the related principle of "equality"—for two
related purposes in the years between 1760 and 1790: first, as the standard
by which to measure and judge the actions of king and Parliament during
the years of the imperial crisis, and second, as the moral foundation on
which to build their constitutional structures and political institutions in
the years after 1776. The Declaration's natural-rights philosophy was used

to mark the end of an old regime and the beginning of a new revolutionary order. It was the lodestar of the revolutionary movement.[2]

A quick survey of how and why colonial Whigs developed and used the concept of natural rights indicates just how important it was in the development of America's revolutionary mind. In the years before 1776, colonial Americans used the principle of natural rights to evaluate the Sugar, Stamp, Declaratory, Townshend, Tea, and Coercive Acts. In 1764, in response to the Sugar Act and the impending Stamp Act, James Otis announced in his *Rights of the British Colonies Asserted and Proved* that the American colonists were "entitled to all the natural, essential, inherent and inseparable rights of our fellow subjects in Great-Britain." Such rights, he claimed, "no man or body of men, not excepting the parliament, justly, equitably and consistently with their own rights and the constitution, can take away." Two years later, in the wake of the Stamp and Declaratory Acts, Richard Bland spoke for most Americans in his *Inquiry into the Rights of the British Colonies* when he proclaimed that his countrymen "must have recourse to the law of nature, and those rights of mankind which flow from it." In response to the Intolerable Acts of 1774, Thomas Jefferson declared in his *Summary View of the Rights of British-America* that man has rights that "nature has given to all men" and that no man-made law can take away or abridge. Such rights, he continued, are "derived from the laws of nature" and "human nature" and are not the "gift of their chief magistrate." From the beginning of the imperial crisis to its end, the Revolution was about protecting rights—the natural, unalienable rights of man. As the summation of all the discussion of rights prior to July 4, 1776, the Declaration of Independence was, as Jefferson put it in an 1819 letter, the "declaratory charter of our rights, and of the rights of man."[3] America's revolutionary mind—and the *novus ordo seclorum* it established—was built on the foundation of man's natural rights.

America's revolutionary founders also used the doctrine of natural rights in the decade after 1776 as the foundation on which to build and establish their constitutional structures. Political liberty, noted Virginia's "Democraticus" in 1776, "will always be most perfect where the laws have derogated least from the original right of men." America's constitutions, Jefferson wrote in a 1797 letter, were premised on "the immovable basis of equal right and reason"; such rights of nature, he wrote in another letter later that year, are "the objects for the protection of which society is formed and municipal laws established." Man's natural rights, James Wilson declared, are the "great pillars on which chiefly rest the criminal and civil codes of the municipal law."[4] Many of the state constitutions adopted during the Revolutionary period began with, included, or were accompanied by a formal declaration of rights, including, most importantly, man's natural rights.[5] In their attempt to "fix" their constitutions as fundamental law, America's revolutionary constitution-makers searched for and found in the natural-rights philosophy that permanent, unmovable moral foundation on which to build their governments. Grounding their constitutions on a permanent moral foundation was possible, Jefferson insisted, because "nothing is unchangeable but the inherent and unalienable rights of man."[6]

The historical record demonstrates unequivocally that colonial and revolutionary Americans were obsessed with their rights, which they claimed were the rights of nature. Ironically, it may very well have been Thomas Hutchinson, the American Loyalist, who best captured the importance of rights to eighteenth-century Americans when, in his capacity as Massachusetts chief justice, he told the 1769 session of the Suffolk County (Boston) grand jury, "The bare Mention of the Word *Rights* always strikes an Englishman in a peculiar Manner." Hutchinson went on to define what would become the central theoretical and practical problem of the American Revolution: "In Order to support and defend the Rights, of which we are so fond," he continued, "we ought to have a just Apprehension of what they are, and whereon they stand."[7]

In many ways, the whole course of the American Revolution followed Hutchinson's challenge. From 1760 until at least 1776, the dispute between British imperial officials and their American provincials was one long inquiry into and debate about what rights are and where they come from. "Perhaps there never was a Time since the Discovery of this new World," noted an anonymous writer in the *Boston Gazette*, "when People of all Ranks every where show'd so eager a Spirit of Inquiry into the Nature of their Rights and Privileges, as at this Day." According to Richard Wells of Philadelphia, the "long disputes...between England and her colonists" compelled American Whigs "into a close search after their natural rights." For him personally, Wells notes that the Tea Act inspired him to set out "by reason alone" in search of his *"rights as a man."*[8] In hindsight, Hutchinson might very well have regretted raising the issue at all.

✴ ✴ ✴

How did eighteenth-century Americans develop and understand the concept "rights of nature"? Why did revolutionary Americans adopt the doctrine of natural rights?

As a juridical concept, the doctrine of rights had a long lineage dating back many centuries.[9] English common-law rights were certainly recognized and respected long before John Locke wrote the *Second Treatise* in the last quarter of the seventeenth century. The principle of rights also had a history of practical recognition and development in the American colonies dating back to the early seventeenth century.[10] When the first English settlers landed at Jamestown and Plymouth, they brought with them certain rights, liberties, and privileges afforded to all Englishmen from time immemorial. The so-called "rights of Englishmen" were said to be fundamental, unalienable, and indefeasible, and they were the rights to which all Englishmen could lay claim as beneficiaries. The authority of these rights was derived from history—from their ancientness. The degree to which the ancient rights of Englishmen were grounded on the rights of nature became a question of profound importance in the debate between American colonists and British imperial officials.

From the beginning of their New World settlements, English provincials in America asserted, compiled, enumerated, and institutionalized their traditional rights and liberties. The Massachusetts Puritans' Laws and Liberties of 1648, William Penn's 1677 Laws, Concessions, and Agreements for the province of West New Jersey, and New York's 1683 Charter of Liberties and Privileges are only the most famous of the proto–bills of rights drafted by the colonists up and down the Atlantic seaboard during the seventeenth century. The purpose of these abridgments was to enumerate, declare, and preserve a sphere of freedom for the individual against the omnipresent and omnipotent power of government force. These proto–bills of rights put up a barrier around the individual, protecting him from the arbitrary power of the state—that is, from unlawful arrest and imprisonment, arbitrary taxation, martial law and support of standing armies during peacetime, feudal dues, and so on. They also guaranteed individuals due process of law through the institution of trial by jury. The fundamentality of these rights derived from their ancient lineage and from their instantiation in certain time-honored charters (e.g., Magna Carta), statutes (e.g., Petition of Right), and court decisions (e.g., *Bonham's Case*). The rights tradition claimed by colonial Americans formed a continuous whole going back centuries, running through the first founding of the colonies in the seventeenth century, and then on up to the eve of the Stamp Act.

In the decades after 1689, and particularly in the four decades after 1720, traditional Anglo-American thinking about rights was supplemented and eventually supplanted by a new philosophic idiom that replaced history with a radically new understanding of rights: rights grounded in or derived from nature. During the middle decades of the eighteenth century, colonial Americans became the most rights-obsessed people in the world.[11] Many Britons throughout the empire recognized both the "rights of Englishmen" and the "natural" rights of man, and for some these two concepts were synonymous. The situation was even more complicated by the fact that some colonials also spoke about the "rights of Americans," which they saw as extensions of the rights of Englishmen *refracted* by the context of life in the New World. For virtually all the English-speaking peoples in both the Old and the New World, it was the common law in its pure English and Americanized forms that made these natural rights known, accessible, and operative.

Still, British Tories and British legal institutions did not fully understand or recognize the relationship between the laws and rights of nature, on one hand, and the common law and the rights of Englishmen, on the other. In the decades after the Glorious Revolution and up through the middle of the eighteenth century, the doctrine of parliamentary sovereignty took precedence in the British mind over the doctrine of fundamental law and rights born of nature and history. The Americans, by contrast, sought to ground their Anglo-American common laws in the laws of nature, and their traditional English rights in the rights of man.

At the deepest philosophical and jurisprudential level, this difference in the nature and origin of rights was the ultimate source of the conflict between the colonists and British imperial officials. Beginning sometime in the 1760s, American revolutionaries began to view the modern British constitution as deficient—as unable to protect their most basic rights. Its fatal flaw was that it did not properly identify or protect the natural rights of man. Grounding their English rights and liberties in something more fundamental than the laws of Parliament or the English common law became the most important task of America's best thinkers during the years of the imperial crisis.

RIGHTS IN THEORY

The revolutionaries' view of rights began with five basic assumptions. First, they assumed that the core of human nature was, as Benjamin Rush put it, everywhere "the same in all Ages and Countries." The moral-political implication of this teaching clearly suggested that the differences between any and all individuals "in respect to Virtue and Vice, Knowledge and Ignorance, may be accounted for from Climate, Country, Degrees of Civilization, form of Government, or other accidental causes."[12] This meant that, despite differences of time and space, geography, climate, and culture, there was a common human nature that was permanently fixed, and with a common nature there could be universal and eternal standards of moral action and justice.

Second, Revolutionary-era Americans assumed that there is an intimate relationship between what man *is* and how he *ought to act.* They were serious students of man's natural constitution. American Whigs viewed man's nature most often as defined by two primary qualities: rationality and free will. Their view of human nature was probably best summed up in the pre-Revolutionary period by the Reverend Elisha Williams of Connecticut, who wrote in 1744 that man's nature is such that he has been given "an understanding to direct his actions" and a "freedom of will and liberty" in acting. Man's freedom and "liberty of acting according to his will (without being subject to the will of another) is," Williams continued, "grounded on his having reason, which is able to instruct him in that law he is to govern himself by, and make him know how far he is left to the freedom of his own will. So that we are born free as we are born rational." Virtually every leading member of America's revolutionary generation would have agreed with the Reverend Daniel Shute of Hingham, Massachusetts, when he explained to his congregation in 1768 that man is a "rational moral agent." They believed that freedom—the freedom to think, choose, and act—is both a fact of human nature and a necessary condition of human flourishing. They assumed that reason is man's only means for living and living well, and so he must be free to use it. Likewise, according to John Perkins of Lynn, Massachusetts, "moral freedom" is the "exclusive property of the rational nature." That man is endowed "with reason and understanding, instead of more instinctive powers," Perkins wrote in 1771, "shows that we were ordain'd for self-direction."[13]

Freedom is that state in which men have the power and authority to act on their own judgment without direction or coercion from other men or from government. Freedom is also that condition in which individuals have the liberty to choose from an array of optional actions. As Lord Rokeby, a British Whig and supporter of the American cause put it: The "primary, essential, inherent rights of human nature" that sanction and protect man's freedom are grounded on the "faculties of man, with the perception of good and evil, with the means of self-preservation and self-defence, with the organs of reason and of speech and with a capacity to associate themselves for their mutual protection and support." In other words, individuals must be free to pursue their own rational self-interest unhindered by the coercion of others. As Jefferson opined, this requirement of freedom is precisely why "no one has a right to obstruct another exercising his faculties innocently for the relief of sensibilities made a part of his nature." Thus, the great achievement of the American Revolution, Jefferson noted, was to issue "finally in that inestimable state of freedom which alone can ensure to man the enjoyment of his equal rights."[14]

Third, American revolutionaries assumed that the individual is the primary unit of moral and political value. Given their view of man as a rational and volitional being and given their view of human equality, they assumed that each man is a morally autonomous and sovereign agent, which means that each man is an end in himself and not the means to someone else's end. "It is this sense of equality which gives to every man a right to frame and execute his own laws" in the state of nature, wrote a Virginian in 1776, "which alone can secure the observance of justice, and diffuse equal and substantial liberty to the people."[15] Rights apply to individuals and only to individuals.

The assumption that each individual is morally self-owning and self-governing was made forcefully in 1774 by Dan Foster, a pastor in Windsor, Connecticut. In a theoretically sophisticated but now long-forgotten essay, Foster declared that every single man has, by nature, "a principle of *individuation; i.e.* he hath such natural and undoubted right to, and property in some things, as no other man upon earth has: He has something he may justly call his own, and may appropriate it to himself, in such a sense as no other man may call it his, or appropriate it to himself." According to Foster, the single most important thing that each and every man owns is his own *self*—his body and soul. And as Connecticut minister Moses Mather argued the following year, "man hath an absolute property in, and right of dominion over himself, his powers and faculties; with self-love to stimulate, and reason to guide him, in the free use and exercise of them, independent of, and uncontrollable by any." Every man is, by nature, according to Mather, "his own legislator, judge, and avenger, and absolute lord of his property."[16] In 1776, Jacob Green of Philadelphia, following the arguments of John Locke's *Second Treatise*, declared that "every man" in a state of nature has "a right to enjoy himself, and the work of his hands, and what he took in hunting" as long as he does not injure his fellow men who have the very same right. Each and every man in the state of nature has "a right to defend and vindicate himself, if assaulted or injured by others."[17]

Fourth, the revolutionary generation assumed that, as one New York paper put it, "*Self Interest* is the grand Principle of all Human Actions." Many thought it "unreasonable and vain to expect Service from a Man who must act contrary to his own Interests to perform it. This is why, said "An American" in a Philadelphia paper, they did not think that government could "be wise or good, unless the Interests of Individuals is made co-incident with the Interest of the Publick." From the American viewpoint, it was both a fact, and, increasingly for many, a moral imperative that man's strongest "motive, is private interest," wrote the pamphleteer "Americanus." They considered it to be the "most powerful impulse of the human breast"; "one finds it at the foundation of all actions; it pierces into all discussions." During his trip to America, Alexis de Tocqueville observed that Americans "are pleased to explain all the actions of their life with the aid of self-interest well understood." In fact, most Americans "think that knowledge of one's self-interest well understood is enough to lead man toward the just and the honest."[18]

The leading thinkers of the American Revolution all understood that self-interest had to be "enlightened" or "well understood," as Tocqueville put it. Enlightened self-interest taught men "that to be happy in life one ought to watch over one's passions and carefully repress their excesses; that one can acquire a lasting happiness only in refusing a thousand passing enjoyments, and finally that one must constantly triumph over oneself to serve oneself better." They assumed that enlightened self-interest was a virtue, although they likewise knew that corrupted self-interest was a vice, which meant that it should be both set free and tamed. This was the principal theme of James Madison's *Federalist* No. 10. The founders' recognition that self-interest had to be both liberated and harnessed was their entry point to understanding and developing the concept "rights" as requiring a certain kind of relationship between individual men and society. The idea of pursuing one's own enlightened self-interest necessarily led to the pursuit of happiness as a right. The founding generation viewed self-interest as the motive and happiness as the end. The puckish and ever-irritable William Findley of western Pennsylvania declared that the moral "law of nature indispensably obliges every man to pursue his own happiness," and that it was "the moral duty of the people, at all times, to pursue their own happiness." According to Tocqueville, the doctrine of self-interest ("well understood") had become "universally accepted" in America by the 1830s.[19]

Fifth, revolutionary Americans also assumed (at least by implication) that the only thing that can destroy a man's natural liberty and right to act is the initiation (or the threat) of physical force against him, either by other individuals or by governments. Force is that state or condition in which physical coercion is used or threatened against individuals to prevent them from thinking and acting on their judgment. "No man has a natural right to commit aggression on the equal rights of another," Jefferson asserted, "and this is all from which the laws ought to restrain him."[20] Ultimately, force represents the denial of judgment and choice. For the Americans, such was the meaning of the Stamp, Townshend, Tea, and Coercive Acts. Even worse, the Declaratory Act (1766) represented an ever-impending threat of force without right.[21]

In sum, because individual men are naturally equal and free, because they are not by nature subordinate to others, because they are naturally autonomous and independent from others, and because reason and freedom are necessary for human flourishing, men must be free to exercise and follow their reason. The revolutionary generation assumed, therefore, that individuals are morally self-owning, self-governing, self-regulating, and self-sustaining, which means that they must be the beneficiaries of their own ideas and actions.[22] "Every man, and every body of men on earth," Jefferson wrote, "possesses the right of self-government. They receive it with their being from the hand of nature." In fact, he thought it would be "ridiculous to suppose that a man has less rights in himself than one of his neighbors, or all of them put together." *That*, he continued, "would be slavery." This is why no person is legitimately the master or the slave of another; this is why Jefferson would not grant even Sir Isaac Newton the authority to declare himself "lord of the person or property of others." A generation after the end of the War of Independence, the Reverend Alexander McCleod described man as a "free" and "moral agent," who has a moral right by nature to "dispose of himself, and be his own master in all respects."[23]

At the deepest philosophical level, then, the ultimate goal of the Revolution was, as Jefferson put it, to banish "all arbitrary and unnecessary restraint on individual action," thereby leaving men "free to do whatever does not violate the equal rights of another."[24] The initiation of physical force is the only means by which the rights of individuals can be violated, which means that offensive (as opposed to defensive) force must be abolished from a free society. American revolutionaries assumed that all individuals in civilized societies would be free from coercion to think, speak, act, produce, trade, assemble, worship, and pursue their own happiness as long as they respected the rights of others to do the same.

★　★　★

Based on these five assumptions, it is now possible to reconstruct the way in which American revolutionaries defined the concept of *natural* rights. Such a reconstruction involves elucidating the characteristics they associated with the rights of nature, the context in which they thought such rights arose, and what they saw as the ultimate purpose of rights.

Eighteenth-century Americans took for granted that all men everywhere have natural rights that are characterized by certain attributes. The rights of nature are indefeasible, inherent, universal, eternal, and absolute. They are not the subjective creation of human will. Colonial Whigs rejected the view that rights are man-made or a creation of kings and legislatures. The rights of nature were not and could never be, according to James Otis, matters of "favor and grace." Man's rights, John Adams wrote in his "Dissertation on the Canon and Feudal Law," are "undoubtedly, antecedent to all earthly government," and they "cannot be repealed or restrained by human laws." Certainly the rights claimed by the colonists, Adams insisted, were "not the grants of princes or parliaments." Indeed, they are "original rights," "inherent and essential," and "established as preliminaries, even before a parliament existed." In 1769, John Mackenzie, a South Carolinian, spoke for all Americans when he described the rights of nature as "latent" and "inherent," and "which no climate, no time, no constitution, no contract, can ever destroy or diminish." Three years later, a Boston writer calling himself "Centinel" declared that man's natural rights are "ABSOLUTE," and they "existed long before men formed into communities." And in 1774, the freeholders of Granville County, North Carolina, published the following resolve: "That those absolute rights we are entitled to as men, by the immutable Laws of Nature, are antecedent to all social and relative duties whatsoever." That same year, the Reverend Dan Foster of Connecticut wrote that man's rights have been "espoused, asserted, and vindicated in all ages of the world, as might be abundantly shewn from history." Thomas Jefferson summed up the revolutionaries' view of natural rights in declaring "that there exists a right independent of force."[25] Man's rights were therefore understood by American revolutionaries to be prepolitical and synonymous in some way with nature and human nature.

From the middle of the eighteenth century through to the early decades of the nineteenth century, American statesmen and political writers thoroughly embraced the idea that rights are derived from nature. Just as the Stamp Act crisis was beginning in 1765, for instance, John Dickinson, one of the most respected lawyers and writers in the American colonies, claimed that the liberties of men are "founded on the acknowledged rights of human nature." The following year, John Adams located the source of man's rights "in the frame of human nature" and "in the constitution of the intellectual and moral world." Philip Livingston, a New York delegate to the Continental Congress and a signer of the Declaration of Independence, declared in 1774 that the "great charter" of man's rights "may be read in the human frame." It was a charter "sealed with the breath of life. To this right every man is and must be entitled; it is annexed as an inseperable appendage to our existence, and altho' the English law hath secured it to the English subject, yet a Frenchman or Turk is as much entitled to it, by the law of nature." Likewise, Thomas Jefferson identified man's rights with the "hand of nature," and elsewhere he said they were "founded in our natural wants" and "sanctioned by the *laws of our being*." In discovering their rights, Jefferson noted, American revolutionaries "had no occasion to search into musty records, to hunt up royal parchments, or to investigate the laws and institutions of a semi-barbarous ancestry." Instead, he continued, they appealed to the principles of "nature, and found them engraved on our hearts." In 1790, James Wilson delivered a series of lectures attended by George Washington, John Adams, Thomas Jefferson, and Alexander Hamilton in which he sought to demonstrate how the rights of man are "laid deeply in the human frame" and on the "immovable basis of nature.[26]

But what is it that makes a natural right natural? America's revolutionary generation understood that recognizing the rights of nature was a *necessary* and an objective requirement of human life. That is why they were willing to fight and die for them. The Americans, explained Judge William Henry Drayton to a Charleston, South Carolina, grand jury in October 1776, were "acting upon natural principles" in declaring their independence from Great Britain. For American revolutionaries, nature was the standard for right and wrong and hence for political life. They understood a right to be a principle that recognizes the moral requirements of human life in the context of society. The rights of nature recognize what man is (i.e., a rational and a volitional being who must act on his judgment) and the unique way he relates to nature, and they define his moral requirements (i.e., freedom) in the context of living in society. Men have rights by virtue of the fact that they are "rational and free agents," wrote Philip Livingston in 1774. Thomas Jefferson viewed man's natural rights in the very same way as did Livingston. "Man," he wrote, "[is] a rational animal," which is why he is and must be "endowed by nature with rights."[27] By virtue of the fact that the free exercise of his rational faculty is man's fundamental mode of survival, he and those with whom he lives in civil society must therefore discover, recognize, and institutionalize certain moral principles that sanction and protect the use of his rational faculty.

In his 1791 lecture on "The Natural Rights of Individuals," James Wilson captured the essence of what rights are. A natural right is "whatever is *necessary* for the safety of life." For Wilson, that which is necessary must be recognized as right or good. The concept "rights" recognizes that it is necessary and therefore *right* that man should be free to choose and pursue those actions that are required to support his life; that it is necessary and therefore *right* that he freely exercise his rational faculty in order to gain knowledge, choose values, and act in accordance with his own judgment; that it is necessary and therefore *right* that he act in order to acquire, keep, use, and dispose of the property he has created to support his life; and that it is necessary and therefore *right* that he benefit or suffer materially and spiritually from the consequences of his value choices. In his *Lectures on Moral Philosophy*, developed and delivered many times at Princeton in the years 1768 to 1794 and almost certainly attended by his most famous student, James Madison, John Witherspoon professed that the rights of nature "are essential to man." A man has a "natural right," Witherspoon continued, "to act for his own preservation, and to defend himself from injury." Rights correspond to the necessities involved in our preservation and well-being.[28] They are a requirement of human flourishing. It is in this sense, Witherspoon argued, that it is proper to speak of man's rights as "natural."

The revolutionary generation understood a right of nature to be a rationally discovered moral *principle* necessary for the establishment, preservation, and protection of the social conditions required for human prosperity. Rights are morally unalienable precisely because their exercise is necessary to life itself. A man's life, liberty, and property are his by natural right and possession because without them he cannot truly be said to exist as a free man. Rights as such, America's revolutionary statesmen held, are owned by each and every individual as a form of moral property, that is, as a title, which means that their violation by individuals, groups, or governments should be treated as a crime. Man's natural *right* to property and freedom, wrote Richard Henry Lee, is a "possession" that is founded "on the clearest principle of the law of nature." In a 1792 essay on "Property," James Madison made the point even more forcefully: "In a word, as a man is said to have a right to his property, he may be equally said to have a property in his rights."[29] To have property in one's rights is to say that each and every individual has sovereignty over his choices and conduct within the limits agreed to by all individuals in a particular civil society. In other words, men are, by nature and right, self-owning and self-governing.

America's deepest revolutionary thinkers understood rights to be a moral concept, that is, a specific kind of identification of what freedom is (the freedom to think and act) and why it is important (to preserve and promote one's own life). Rights define spheres of freedom and human action in the context of a social setting. The founders treated rights and freedom as one, as necessarily and logically connected as a unity. Without freedom, there can be no rights and vice versa. Man's right (i.e., that which is the right course of action necessary to sustain his life and achieve his chosen values) necessitates freedom (i.e., the power to act free from the physical compulsion of other men). At the core of Jefferson's philosophy was the belief that there is a "right independent of force," and that "right" is connected to freedom of action. This is what the founding generation called justice, which, in the words of Witherspoon, "consists in giving or permitting others to enjoy whatever they have a perfect right to—and making such a use of our own rights as not to encroach upon the rights of others."[30]

The founders' use of the concept "rights" can therefore be viewed as having a dual character: it served as both a *license* and a *fence*. As a "license," rights provide a moral and legal sanction recognizing the freedom of individuals to act in a social context in the pursuit of their values. To be clear: a right is a *prerogative*; it is not a *permission* to act. It is the legal recognition of the fact that liberty is a necessary requirement of human well-being. As Jefferson put it with his usual felicity: "Under the law of nature, all men are born free, every one comes into the world with a right to his own person, which includes the liberty of moving and using it at his own will. This is what is called personal liberty, and is given him by the Author of nature, because *necessary* for his own sustenance."[31]

As a "fence," rights define and erect for each and every individual defensive barriers against the initiation of physical force by others. The "rights of mankind," Stephen Johnson told the Connecticut legislature in his election sermon, provide men with "the safe and unmolested enjoyment of life, liberty and property, and to the best improvement of all their powers, with every reasonable and equitable advantage they have to promote their present and everlasting welfare." In this sense, rights restrain individuals from acting in certain ways. The revolutionary generation's view of rights as fences is neatly summed up in the old proverb "good fences make good neighbors," made famous in Robert Frost's poem, "Mending Wall." Rights provide boundaries and barriers around each man's life, liberty, and property in order to protect them from other men. Rights are, as Jefferson once said in an exchange with Noah Webster, "fences which experience has proved peculiarly efficacious against wrong." They serve as barriers protecting individuals from criminals and governments. Rights as fences, Jefferson continued, were institutionalized in America through "instruments called declarations of rights and constitutions." Rights recognize and protect men, according to James Wilson, from "different degrees of aggression," including "threatening, assault, battery, wounding, mayhem, homicide."[32]

In this sense, rights establish limits on human action between individuals in their relations with each other and between individuals in their relations with their government.[33]

In sum, the concept "rights" means a morally and legally recognized license to act freely in order to produce, acquire, possess, use, and trade property or values for the purpose of attaining happiness, and it means a morally and legally recognized barrier against the arbitrary initiation of physical force against oneself or anyone else living privately and peaceably behind one's "fence." In this sense, the liberty of each and every person in society is both expanded and protected.

In order for a rights-based society to function properly, the rights of nature must be universally recognized as *reciprocal*. A truly civilized society, Jefferson claimed in his *Notes on the State of Virginia*, is one that respects "those rights in others which we value in ourselves." Rights provide the moral boundary lines by which society marks out and prevents one man from "violating the similar rights of other sensible beings." Along lines similar to those staked out by Jefferson, John Witherspoon professed in his *Lectures on Moral Philosophy* that "as our own happiness is a lawful object or end, we are supposed to have each a right to prosecute this; but as our prosecutions may interfere, we limit each other's rights, and a man is said to have a right or power to promote his own happiness only by those means which are not in themselves criminal or injurious to others."[34]

On this view, the discovery, recognition, and protection of man's natural rights is the necessary precondition for a civilized society. Human nature and the requirements of human flourishing provide men with an absolute and permanent benchmark with which to determine moral principles of good conduct and political principles of civil association, which in turn permit and encourage them to pursue the values (e.g., trade, voluntary associations, wealth) necessary for their well-being. The concept "natural rights" therefore provides the fundamental principle by which individuals in civil society can simultaneously be set free and yet live together under a common political authority.

✷　✷　✷

In addition to defining what a right of nature is and the role it plays in society, American revolutionaries also went far in addressing several corollary questions concerning the nature of rights.

First, how are such rights known, promulgated, and validated? The rights of nature are not created by kings or parliaments but are, rather, *discovered*—discovered by the use of human reason as it explores the nature of reality. Via this exercise of reason, rational principles that promote human flourishing can be discerned through a study of man's natural constitution. "If any thing in nature is capable of proof," declared the Reverend Dan Foster, the basic rights of nature "are capable to be proved, and of being set in a most convincing and clear point of light before all reasonable and impartial minds." The rights of man, he continued, are "as capable of demonstration, as any proposition in Euclid."[35]

America's most enlightened revolutionary leaders believed that the study of man and society should be treated as a science that uses the same modes of reasoning and methods of investigation as the natural sciences. The study of man and society is, according to Josiah Quincy, "the most extended in its nature, and the most important in its consequences of any in the circle of erudition." Given its importance, such a science, he continued, "ought to be an object of universal attention and study." In fact, should this branch of knowledge become widely studied, "the rights of mankind would not remain buried for ages, under systems of civil and priestly hierarchy, nor social felicity overwhelmed by lawless domination."[36]

According to John Dickinson, the American colonists considered their pre-1776 charter rights to be "*declarations* but not *gifts* of liberties." In his 1776 *Address to the Committee of Correspondence in Barbados*, Dickinson summed up the American revolutionary position on the source and means of promulgating rights. Kings and parliaments could never "*give* the *rights essential to happiness*," he announced. Instead, the Americans

> claim them from a higher source—from the King of kings, and
> Lord of all the earth. They are not annexed to us by parchments and
> seals. They are created in us by the decrees of Providence, which
> establish the laws of our nature. They are born with us; exist with
> us; and cannot be taken from us by any human power, without tak-
> ing our lives. In short, they are founded on the immutable maxims
> of reason and justice.

The rights of nature are not a product of human will and cannot be legislated. And if man's rights were not given to him as the favors or gifts of kings and parliaments, there was just one way in which they could be brought to life: they must be first *discovered* through reason and then publicly *recognized*, which means defined, declared, and protected. This is what the Reverend Stephen Johnson described as the "rational foundation" of man's natural rights.[37]

The revolutionary generation viewed the rights of nature as the foundation or standard for all legislation. Thus, the "Business of *Legislation*," Abraham Williams announced in 1762, is to "investigate," "discover," and "publish the Rules of Equity...and to annex such Sanctions as Reason directs, to secure the Rights and Properties of the Society, and of every Individual." Similarly, the primary purpose of a bill of rights, according to William Whiting of Berkshire County, in Massachusetts, was to "*ascertain* and clearly describe the rights of nature, including the rights of conscience, and that security of person and property." Even the best-written laws and proclamations—including Magna Carta, the English Bill of Rights and the Declaration of Independence—authored by the wisest and most virtuous men do not create rights. Instead, such laws "must be considered as only *declaratory* of our rights," announced Silas Downer of Providence, Rhode Island, in 1768, "and in affirmance of them." Thomas Jefferson, discussing the "rightful limits" of legislators' power, pronounced "their true office is to *declare* and enforce only natural rights and duties, and to take none of them from us."[38] Rights discovered and declared are rights that exist by virtue of man's nature independent of human will.

Second, how did American revolutionaries view the relationship among the different rights of nature? The Declaration of Independence lists three natural rights as fundamental—life, liberty, and the pursuit of happiness—to which all revolutionary Americans added a fourth: property. Are the rights to life, liberty, property, and the pursuit of happiness coequal, or are they ordered hierarchically? Do they form a coherent whole, or are there tensions and contradictions among them?

America's revolutionary founders viewed nature's rights as a logically ordered and unified whole that serves the fundamental right: the right to life. Man's natural rights are, as Samuel Adams put it in 1772, "evident branches of, rather than deductions from, the duty of self-preservation, commonly called the first law of nature." The right to life cannot be separated from the right to liberty, property, or the pursuit of happiness and vice versa. The *right* to life requires liberty—the *right* to liberty, liberty being necessary to think and act on one's own judgment in order to exercise one's right to life. The right to liberty necessitates property—the *right* to keep and/or to trade the fruits of one's labor, this property being necessary to sustain one's life and liberty. The right to property culminates in the right to the pursuit of one's happiness—the *right* to pursue one's own material and spiritual values, as one takes them to be necessary to live a satisfying, self-fulfilling life. Or, as John Dickinson put it in the context of the imperial crisis:

> It would be an insult on the divine Majesty to say, that he has given or allowed any man or body of men *a right to make me miserable*. If no man or body of men has *such a right*, I have a *right to be happy*. If there can be no happiness without freedom, I have a *right to be free*. If I cannot enjoy freedom without security of property, I have a *right to be thus secured*. If my property cannot be secure, in case others over whom I have no kind of influence may take it from me by taxes, under pretence of the public good, and for enforcing their demands, may subject me to arbitrary, expensive, and remote jurisdictions, I have an *exclusive right* to lay taxes on my property, either by myself or those I can trust; of necessity to judge in such instances of the public good; and to be exempt from such jurisdictions.—But no man can be secure in his property, who is "liable to impositions, that have NOTHING BUT THE WILL OF THE IMPOSERS to direct them in the measure;" and that make "JUSTICE TO CROUCH UNDER THEIR LOAD."[39]

Nature's rights—particularly the rights to liberty, property, and the pursuit of happiness—are corollaries of the fundamental right: the right to life. Taken together, they are a logically connected, unified whole without internal contradiction. They build and rely on each other and progress in a systematic order. Man's rights, according to Jefferson and the revolutionary generation, do not and cannot conflict because they do not impose reciprocal or positive obligations or duties on individuals. If the Declaration said, for instance, that individuals have a "right to happiness," then it follows that others would have a moral duty to help satisfy that right. But this is not what the Declaration says, and such a claim would have been utterly mystifying if not repugnant to the eighteenth-century Americans. In sum, there is no right to violate the rights of others. According to Jefferson, every man is free to pursue his happiness, but he is not promised that it will be satisfied by the labor of others.[40]

Third, what did Jefferson and his fellow revolutionaries think was the source of man's rights? The revolutionary generation was somewhat ambiguous on this question. However, they did not think that man's *natural* rights come from history, culture, parliaments, or the Bible. In 1772, a writer in the *Massachusetts Spy* told his fellow Bostonians that he did "not ground" the rights claims of the colonists "on old antiquated records, but on *the law of nature and nations*." Likewise, as Alexander Hamilton put it in 1775: "The sacred rights of mankind are not to be rummaged for, among old parchments, or musty records. They are written, as with a sun beam in the whole *volume* of human nature, by the hand of the divinity itself."[41]

Most revolutionaries assumed that God was the ultimate source of man's rights just as he was the source of nature's laws. The first obvious thing to note is that the Declaration of Independence announces that man's rights are *endowed* or given to man by his "Creator"—by Nature's God, even though we do not find those rights listed anywhere in scripture. Jefferson's "Creator" is the source of man's rights, but his "Creator" is also "Nature's God"; and "Nature's God" is virtually synonymous for Jefferson with nature pure and simple.[42] Jefferson's God is obviously not the stern, omnipresent, and vengeful God of the Old Testament. Rather, his Creator is the philosophers' god of the Enlightenment. Jefferson's God acts through and is known to man via the study of the physical laws of nature, and man's rights are a gift of nature or of nature's God so revealed.

Nature is the metaphysical order to which the Declaration appeals and the ground on which it establishes its moral principles. Whereas English Whigs deduced their view of rights from an "Anglo-Saxon source" and English Tories deduced their view of rights from a "Norman" source, American revolutionaries induced and then deduced their rights by studying and cataloguing "nature" itself, or what Jefferson referred to as the "laws of our being," the "order of nature," the "moral law of our nature," and "universal law." Samuel Adams spoke for most Americans in 1765 when he wrote of "those inestimable rights which are derived to all men from nature." Likewise, a writer in Boston declared that the rights of nature "have their foundation in the reason of things" and in "the laws of our being." The rights of nature are validated in and by "reality," according to Jefferson. By appealing "to the true fountains of evidence," he believed that "every rational and honest man" could discern and verify the order of nature for himself. "It is there that nature has written her moral laws," he continued, "and where every man may read them for himself."[43] In this last iteration of man's rights, Jefferson cut God out of the picture entirely. The rights of nature can be known apparently without reference to God's intervention or assistance.

Lastly, how did the founders understand the relationship, and the differences, between a "*law* of nature" and a "*right* of nature"? This is a difficult question to answer because none of the founding fathers addressed it directly or in any meaningful way. To the degree that even a few mentioned the relationship in passing, they did seem to suggest that the rights of nature issue from the laws of nature but without explaining the precise nature of that relationship. There can be little doubt that most references to the laws of nature and natural rights during the Revolutionary period seem to suggest that the former create the latter.

In 1764, James Otis, the first great thinker of the Revolution, argued in his *Rights of the Colonies Asserted and Proved* that the "law of nature and the grant of GOD Almighty," has given "to all men a natural right to be *free*." The following year, in response to the Stamp Act, the Massachusetts Assembly resolved,

> 1. That there are certain essential Rights of the British Constitution of Government, which are founded in the Law of God and Nature, and are the common Rights of Mankind—Therefore

> 2. That the Inhabitants of this Province are undeniably entitled to those essential Rights in common with all Men: And that no Law of Society can consistent with the Law of God and Nature divest them of those Rights.

In 1766, in the wake of the Sugar, Stamp, and Declaratory Acts, Richard Bland declared in *An Inquiry into the Rights of the British Colonies* that the Americans "must have recourse to the Law of Nature, and those Rights of Mankind which flow from it." Eight years later, Thomas Jefferson claimed in *A Summary View of the Rights of British-America* that the rights of nature are "derived from the laws of nature," and that same year the Continental

Congress in its Declaration and Resolves asserted that the colonists' rights to "life, liberty, & property" were grounded in the "immutable laws of nature." A few months later, Alexander Hamilton argued in his *Farmer Refuted* pamphlet that the "natural rights of mankind" depend on the laws of nature.[44] The evidence is compelling that, at least before 1776, most revolutionary Americans saw the moral rights of nature as deriving from the moral laws of nature.

The revolutionaries' view on this matter is, however, open to questioning if not a decisive criticism. The rights of nature recognize certain facts of human nature. They are moral principles, grounded in man's nature, that sanction and protect his freedom of action. The laws of nature are, by contrast, moral and legal principles, the purpose of which is to recognize and protect man's rights. The laws of nature would seem therefore to be a consequence of, or follow from, the rights of nature. Logically, the moral laws of nature must be deductions from the rights of nature.

RIGHTS IN PRACTICE

The first indication that American colonists would use the principle of natural rights as their standard of justice occurred in late 1760 and early 1761. This was the moment of the once-famous but now mostly forgotten writs of assistance case in Boston in which James Otis distinguished himself as the harbinger of the American Revolution. (A writ of assistance was a kind of search warrant issued by provincial courts to assist British imperial officials in the enforcement of the trade and navigation laws.) Consider the facts of the case. According to John Adams's first-hand account, British imperial officials initiated the writs of assistance case in 1760—and with it their "design" and "resolution" to conquer England's American colonies and subject "them to the unlimited authority of Parliament"—after they had received word of General James Wolfe's victory over Montcalm at Quebec City and Montreal, thereby effectively ending the Seven Years' War with France.[45] With the goal of tightening their control over the American colonies, British officials sent orders to imperial customs agents in Boston to begin issuing *general* as opposed to *specific* writs of assistance. Traditionally understood, a writ of assistance was a document granted to a litigant in a British court, granting him authority to have a sheriff assist him to collect a debt known to the court or to obtain possession of property that was due to

him. Courts granted these limited and controlled writs on oath and probable suspicion. By contrast, the writs sought by Boston customs officials in
1761 were *general* standing warrants, which permitted local customs officials
to go into any private residence or warehouse at any time with a constable
to search for *suspected* contraband. General writs were valid from the time
of issue until six months after the death of the issuing monarch, and the
holder needed no special permission from a court to initiate a search. They
also gave customs officials far-reaching powers that were clearly open to
abusing local property rights. Both customs commissioners and local merchants petitioned the court for relief, and the case went to court.

The ensuing legal case held in front of the Massachusetts Superior
Court pitted—certainly from the American perspective—the forces of
unlimited, arbitrary government power against the property rights of
individuals. James Otis, presenting on behalf of American merchants,
argued against general writs on the grounds that they gave the government
potentially tyrannical power over the lives and property of individuals.
He described these writs as "the worst instrument of arbitrary power," a
"monster of oppression," and a "remnant of Starchamber tyranny." Such an
unlimited and arbitrary power, he argued, "places the liberty of every man
in the hands of every petty officer." The open-ended nature of these writs
posed a genuine threat to the rights of American colonists. They violated
the ancient English right against unreasonable searches and seizures. More
fundamentally, "one of the most essential branches of English liberty,"
Otis insisted, "is the freedom of one's house." Otis then summed up the
threat posed by these writs of assistance to rights of Englishmen, which
he believed rested on the natural rights of man:

> A man's house is his castle; and while he is quiet, he is as well
> guarded as a prince in his castle. This writ, if it should be declared
> legal, would totally annihilate this privilege. Custom house officers
> may enter our houses when they please—we are commanded to
> permit their entry—their menial servants may enter, may break
> locks, bars and everything in their way, and whether they break
> through malice or revenge, no man, no court can inquire—bare
> suspicion without oath is sufficient....What a scene does this
> open! Every man prompted by revenge, ill humor or wantonness to
> inspect the inside of his neighbor's house may get a writ of assis-
> tance; others will ask it from self-defence; one arbitrary exertion

will provoke another until society will be involved in tumult and blood.

For Otis, even if the writ were recognized in the law and supported with long-standing precedent, it would still be illegal—illegal not based on its standing in the law, but illegal because it violated reason, natural equity, and the fundamental laws of justice, which means the rights of nature as expressed in the common-law rights of Englishmen. Otis then drew a revolutionary conclusion. Drawing on the famous argument of the great English jurist Sir Edward Coke in *Dr. Bonham's Case* (1610), Otis asserted: "An Act against the Constitution is void; an Act against natural Equity is void; and if an Act of Parliament should be made, in the very Words of this Petition, it would be void. The executive Courts must pass such Acts into disuse."[46]

From Adams's perspective, the event that triggered the American Revolution was not the passage of an illegal tax but the issuance of an illegal writ of assistance. Instead of "no taxation without representation," the rallying cry of the American Revolution might very well have been "no illegal searches and seizures." Either way, the common denominator shared by general writs of assistance and the Stamp Act tax was that both violated the colonists' fundamental rights. Both cases involved the common-law and natural right to private property. Otis's address to the court against these writs, Adams claimed, "breathed into this nation the breath of life."[47] It was the first shot of the American Revolution, the beginning of what Adams later called the *true* American Revolution—that revolution in the minds of the American people. Still, Otis's argument did not make an explicit case for the rights of nature, although the principle of natural rights was implicit in his argument. Three years later, in his influential pamphlet *Rights of the Colonies Asserted and Proved*, Otis used the very same arguments from his oration at the writs of assistance case, but he now explicitly grounded them on the foundation of Lockean natural rights.

Transitioning from the traditional rights of Englishmen to the rights of nature came with remarkable ease and speed for the American colonists. Over the course of the next few years, they searched for a more permanent grounding for their rights—rights abstracted from their embodiment in ancient common law. In 1762, the year after the writs of assistance case, the Massachusetts Assembly, quoting directly from Locke's *Second Treatise*, sent the following instructions to its London agent, Jasper Mauduit: "The natural rights of the colonists we humbly conceive to be the same with those of all other British subjects, and indeed of all mankind. The ...principal purpose of these rights is to be 'free from any superior power on earth, and not to be under the will or legislative authority of man, but to have only the law of nature for his rule.'"[48] In the context of the time, one could hardly imagine a statement that would have been more alien to British officialdom than this one. The Americans were claiming a principle of moral right higher than the law of the British constitution, but the British constitution—the polestar of all British legal thought and practice—did not recognize the Americans' moral law and rights of nature idiom. The Americans were expressing their grievances and core moral and political philosophy in a language so distant from the comprehension and experience of Whitehall's tradition-bound, legalistic ruling elite that the new vocabulary must have seemed either oddly quaint or potentially dangerous to English ears.

Still, it was only as a result of their constitutional and political battle with Great Britain that the Americans came to understand the natural-rights teaching. It was in reaction to the Sugar and Stamp Acts that American revolutionaries discovered, as William Pierce put it in an oration, "how to define the rights of nature,—how to search into, to distinguish, and to comprehend, the principles of physical, moral, religious, and civil liberty." From the beginning of the imperial crisis, declared Joseph Warren, the "attempt of the British parliament to raise a revenue from America, and our denial of their right to do it, have excited an almost universal enquiry into the rights of mankind in general, and of British subjects in particular." By contrast, the king's ministers "were looking into their laws and records, to decide what should be the rights of men in the colonies," said Samuel Williams, while "nature was establishing a system of perfect freedom in America," which the king's men "could neither comprehend or discern."[49] In the end, it was the failure of George III to protect the rights of his American subjects from the repeated usurpations of Parliament and then his own acts of violence against the colonists that ultimately justified revolution.

✷ ✷ ✷

When the Stamp Act was passed in 1765, Britain's American colonists responded with an arsenal of rights-based arguments. The debate was launched with a bitter polemical exchange between Judge Martin Howard of Rhode Island and James Otis of Massachusetts. Howard staked out the traditional view of rights held by many Anglo-American Tories. In order to determine the rights of the colonies and the mother country, he declared that right-thinking men must "shun the walk of metaphysics." Instead of beginning with an abstract individual who possesses theoretical rights in a hypothetical state of nature (an obvious reference to Locke), Howard began with natural political communities and man's "true natural relation[s]" as the primary unit of moral and political value. The judge did not think of man as an isolated individual but as one who is born and lives his life entwined in a variety of social relationships. Such relations are ordered, according to Howard, not by man's natural rights but by his natural, "reciprocal duties." To the extent that man has rights, they are derived from history, from man's social and political relations that have developed over the course of centuries. Howard thus eschewed the idea of natural rights for what he and most Englishmen spoke of as "the rights of Englishmen." He did recognize what he called "personal" rights"—"those of life, liberty, and estate"—that are "every subject's birthright," but such rights are not "self-existent." Instead, they are grounded in and defined by English common law. In the end, however, Howard and most Anglo-American Tories believed that the common law was synonymous with the "sense and virtue of the British parliament," which meant that the "rights of Englishmen" were ultimately human creations subject to the vicissitudes of parliamentary whim.[50]

James Otis's utter contempt for what he called Howard's "Filmerian" performance (suggesting that Howard was promoting the views of Sir Robert Filmer, the 17th-century English political theorist who advocated absolute monarchy grounded in a theory of divine rights) demonstrates just how far American Whigs had come in their understanding of rights in a short period of time. Howard and his Tory friends saw no difference, according to Otis, between "power and right," which means that they did not and could not understand the concept "*natural* rights." For Anglo-Americans, the failure of British imperial officials to recognize the provincials' natural rights represented an unbridgeable gulf that became the deepest source of the conflict between mother country and colonies. Nature's rights, according to Otis, are "inherent" and "indefeasible," and they are derived not from history and the actions of kings and parliaments but from the "laws of God and nature." Otis rejected Howard's characterization of the rights to life, liberty, and estate as "personal" rights, which suggested to him that they are derived from the relationship that Englishmen have with their king and with each other through the common law. Furthermore, man's natural rights, Otis claimed, provide the fixed, unchanging foundation of man's civil rights, particularly the civil rights of Englishmen. Indeed, the "natural absolute personal rights of individuals are so far from being opposed to political or civil rights that they are the very basis of all municipal laws." Otis and his Whig compatriots saw the common law as representing the instantiation and application of man's natural rights to the particular circumstances of life in Old and New England.[51]

At the deepest level, the imperial crisis was about where to locate the source of man's rights to life, liberty, and property: Anglo-American Tories located the fundamental rights in history, while Anglo-American Whigs located man's rights in nature. Forty years after the Howard-Otis exchange, Otis's sister, Mercy Otis Warren, felt the need to fight the intellectual battles of the 1760s and 1770s over again as though they were still living issues, particularly those that involved the question of rights. In her *History of the Rise, Progress, and Termination of the American Revolution*, published in 1805, Warren lashed out at the estimable English jurist and arch-Tory William Murray, 1st Earl of Mansfield, for what she took to be his corrupt view of the relationship between politics and principle. More to the point, she exploded with righteous indignation when she recalled that Mansfield, a man of "superior talents, profound erudition, law knowledge, and philosophical abilities," had claimed in the House of Commons in 1775 "'that the original question of *right* ought no longer be considered'" as Parliament pondered what to do with the colonies. Instead, the English jurist continued, "'the justice of the cause must give way to the present situation.'" Warren rejected Mansfield's pragmatic relativism and what she called his "sophistical reasoning," insisting instead that questions of truth and right should be resolved only by the "dictates of justice" and by appeals to "the immutable laws of justice" and the "principles of rectitude."[52] For Warren and her fellow revolutionary Whigs, the "original question of *right*" was the single most important question.

By 1774, the debate over the nature and source of rights became an intramural quarrel as American revolutionaries debated the question among themselves. In September of that year, just after the first Continental Congress convened in Philadelphia, a congressional committee was appointed to draft a statement of the colonists' "rights, grievances, and means of redress." Committee members immediately launched a probing discussion of the most important question relating to the nature of their rights: Where do rights come from?

The debate started with Richard Henry Lee of Virginia, who claimed that "Rights are built on a fourfold foundation—on Nature, on the British constitution, on Charters, and on immemorial usage." Lee emphasized how important it was for the Americans to "Lay our Rights upon the broadest Bottom, the Ground of Nature." John Adams and New York's John Jay seconded Lee's argument that the Americans' rights are and should rest primarily on the "Law of Nature." John Rutledge of South Carolina, James Duane of New York, and Joseph Galloway of Pennsylvania disagreed with Lee, Adams, and Jay. The more conservative Rutledge thought America's rights claims were better grounded "on the british Constitution" than "on the Law of Nature," and Duane supported "grounding our Rights on the Laws and Constitution of the Country from whence We sprung, and Charters, without recurring to the Laws of Nature—because this will be a feeble Support." Galloway claimed that he had "looked" for the Americans' "Rights in the Laws of Nature—but could not find them in a State of Nature, but always in a State of political Society."[53] The final draft of the Declaration and Resolves of the First Continental Congress closed the issue by grounding the rights of the Americans on the broadest foundation possible—on the "immutable laws of nature, the principles of the English constitution, and the several charters or compacts."[54] Within two years, though, American opinion shifted toward Lee, Adams, and Jay, which meant grounding their rights on the law of nature.

From the passage of the Stamp Act in 1765 to the final battle at Yorktown in 1781, the Americans conceptualized their conflict with Great Britain in the language of *natural* rights.[55] The vocabulary and philosophy of natural rights was the heart and soul of the revolutionary lexicon from the very beginning. The colonists, a Boston writer announced in 1765, "have a just value for those inestimable rights which are derived to all men from nature, and are happily interwoven into the British constitution." In fact, another Bostonian argued two years later, "To enjoy our natural Rights, and the Liberties of English subjects, is the supreme felicity of mankind....Natural Right, and the liberty of English subjects, undoubtedly belong to Americans, and are essentially comprised in this, a freedom from all taxes and laws not consented to." The Americans never once wavered during the entire imperial crisis from defending their natural rights as the spring of all their civil rights. In *A Few Political Reflections*, published in 1774, Richard Wells looked back to 1765 and surveyed the American reaction to the Stamp Act, and what he found was that virtually every colony from South Carolina to New England had published resolves that rested their claims "on the just principles of 'natural right.'" The colonists argued that their English "privileges" were founded "in the law of God and nature, and the common rights of mankind; rights which no law of society can consistently divest them of."[56] And on it went like this throughout the entire Revolutionary period. Indeed, the principle of natural rights provided the philosophic grammar of the Revolution from day one of the American resistance.[57]

✭ ✭ ✭

The founders' understanding and use of the concept "rights" consisted of four interconnected elements: first, the rights of nature served as principles grounded in a recognition of what man is—that is, of his metaphysical nature (e.g., what he requires and must use for his survival and well-being); second, rights defined the conditions necessary for man to act in association with other individuals; third, rights sanctioned his freedom to act so that he might pursue those values necessary to living and living well; and fourth, rights established boundaries around each and every individual that defined his range of action in a social context. Thus, when the Americans declared their independence from Great Britain, they were claiming a sphere of freedom unavailable to them under the rule of king and Parliament—a sphere of freedom in which each man could declare his independence from his fellow citizens. Even more radically, the long-term consequence and meaning of the Revolution was to liberate men from unchosen obligations to each other as they were freed from the arbitrary commands of government.

During the years of the imperial crisis, American colonists launched a searching examination into the nature of their rights. Initially, they sought to defend their traditional English rights, liberties, and privileges, which they claimed as a birthright. They scoured English and colonial history for precedents in order to justify their rights' claims against the actions of the British Parliament. Very quickly, though, the Americans realized that an argument based on the so-called "rights of Englishmen" was inadequate to the task at hand. The "rights of Englishmen" were, they realized, as uncertain historically, legally, and philosophically as was the status of the British constitution. Something more fundamental and permanent was needed. The critical moment came when they realized that the rights of Englishmen were simply a historically determined instantiation and refraction of a more fundamental moral principle: the rights of nature. Little did they know that they stood on the verge of a discovery that would herald the dawn of a new era in the history of civil society and government. Ironically, this new conception of rights would liberate men from the past and turn the course of human events in a new direction.

The Declaration of Independence was the culmination and the ultimate expression of the Americans' sixteen-year search into the nature of their rights. In the years after independence, many Americans pondered the meaning and ramifications of their studies and actions. In 1783, in his Circular Letter to the States, George Washington reflected on the philosophic and existential meaning of what he and his fellow Americans had achieved:

> The foundation of our empire was not laid in the gloomy age of ignorance and superstition, but at an epoch when the rights of mankind were better understood and more clearly defined, than at any former period, the researches of the human mind, after social happiness, have been carried to a great extent, the treasures of knowledge, acquired by the labors of philosophers, sages and legislators, through a long succession of years, are laid open for our use, and their collected wisdom may be happily applied in the establishment of our forms of government.[58]

When John Adams said that the true American Revolution was in the "minds of the people" in the years from 1760 to 1775, this is precisely what he meant. During that fifteen-year period, the American people were, under the pressure of events, forced to search into the nature and meaning of their rights; then they had to learn how to "distinguish," "comprehend," and "define" their natural rights and the "principles of physical, moral, religious, and civil liberty"; and, finally, they had to defend their rights with words and then with guns. The revolution in thought and practice brought about by colonial Americans would have enormous implications for the creation of America's new revolutionary constitutions, for the future development of a new American society in the nineteenth century, and then for the world in the twentieth and twenty-first centuries.[59]

CHAPTER 7

Life, Liberty, and
the Pursuit of Happiness

"We hold these truths to be self-evident, that all
men…are endowed by their Creator with certain
unalienable Rights, *that among these are Life, Liberty
and the pursuit of Happiness.*"

*A*merican revolutionaries in the 1760s and 1770s developed and
radicalized the Enlightenment theory of natural rights handed
down to them in the writings of John Locke, Samuel von Pufendorf,
Jean-Jacques Burlamaqui, Jean Barbeyrac, and many others. Whereas the
older English notion of historic rights was inherently conservative and
backward-looking, the provincials' new understanding of rights as anchored
in nature was inherently revolutionary and forward-looking. It provided
the Americans with a moral standard by which to organize their society
and political system—and with an elevating, inspiring, transforming vision
of what a free and just society should look like.

The subjection of government to the natural rights of individuals
formed the essence of American-style republicanism, and it provided
guideposts for the construction of republican constitutions and governments. To better understand what a right of nature is, it is important to
know what the particular rights of nature are and how the Americans
understood them.

The Declaration of Independence announced that life, liberty, and
the pursuit of happiness are man's unalienable rights. These are the fundamental rights of nature, although the Declaration says they are "among"
man's unalienable rights, suggesting that there are others not listed. Private

property was not listed in the Declaration, but all Americans recognized it as a fundamental, if not the central, right. They also thought there were subsidiary natural rights that followed logically from these fundamental ones (e.g., the rights to free emigration, free trade, free exercise of religion, freedom of conscience, speech, press and assembly, to bear arms, and to one's reputation).[1]

The revolutionary generation viewed the different rights of nature as fulfilling certain functions: the right to life is the *standard*; the right to liberty is the *means*; the right to property is the *actualization*; and the right to the pursuit of happiness is the *end*. Taken as an integrated whole, the natural-rights philosophy was viewed by American revolutionaries as the moral foundation of a free and just society.

THE RIGHT TO LIFE

American revolutionaries considered the right to life to be the fundamental right from which all others are derived. It is the moral standard by which all human action must be judged. The right to life means the right of each and every individual to take the actions necessary for the support, development, and well-being of his or her own life. The right to life means the right to self-ownership, self-sustenance, self-governance, self-preservation, and self-defense.

In one of the most penetrating and remarkable pamphlets written during the Revolutionary period, the Reverend Dan Foster, of Windsor, Connecticut, delved as deeply as any founding father into the question of what rights are. In his long-forgotten *A Short Essay on Civil Government*, published in 1774, Foster cut to the core in identifying the nature and purpose of rights, particularly the fundamental right—the right to life—and its implied corollary—the right to property. His analogous moral reasoning begins, hypothetically, with two individuals whom Foster identifies as *A* and *B*:

> *A*, HATH a right to, and property in, his hand, in such a sense as *B* hath not, nor can have; he may with great justice call his hand his own, and he hath an individual and entire right to, and property in his hand, which *B* cannot have. And it would be a manifest and intolerable invasion of *A*'s right and property, if *B* should pretend

to lay claim to his hand, or presume to use it as though it were his own, and as though he had a just right to, and property in it. This pretence, and this conduct in *B*, would be downright injustice, a pretence and action plainly contradictory to truth, which is always unjust. If *A* hath such right to, and property in his hand, as he is now said to have, it follows, that he hath a right to make use of his hand, for his own ends and purposes, and according as he shall please: and *B* can have no right or authority to rise up and forbid *A* the use of his hand, or to dispute with him his liberty and authority to use it according to his own pleasure. For such conduct would evidently declare that *B* has some right to *A*'s hand, evidently contrary to truth, for he has none: for if *B* has no right to *A*'s hand, according to the supposition, then certainly he can have no just right or authority to forbid *A* that use of it he shall please to put it to: For all authority and dominion are founded in right and property.

Foster next draws out the moral logic of his core principle. If a man has a right to his hand (and what his hand produces) that no other man can claim a right to, then it follows that he has a right to both hands, and to the rest of his body, including the workings of his mind. In sum, each and every man "hath an individual and indisputable right to himself," that is, to all his "powers and faculties," and with that right he may use these powers and faculties "as he shall judge it convenient, and for his own interest, and purposes of life."[2] This is the core argument in support of man's right to life.

If individuals have a right to sustain their lives, the correlative responsibility dictates that no man may violate or impinge on anyone else's life. As a legal concept, the right to life provides a barrier protecting the life of each individual from physical compulsion, coercion, or interference by other men. In the most important respect, it protects a man from having his life ended, assaulted, interfered with, or threatened by another person. Thus the right to life serves also as a legal "fence" protecting individuals from the initiation of force by others—against murder, manslaughter, assault, rape, and so on. The correlative rule forbids individuals from initiating force against the life of another person.

The purpose of the first law of nature—the law of self-preservation— is to sanction and protect man's natural right to life. "Self-preservation" is "a great and primary law of nature," Jonathan Mayhew declared in 1766, "and to be considered as antecedent to all civil laws and institutions, which are subordinate and subservient to the other." This means that individuals have an unalterable right to defend their lives, liberties, and properties according to the "great laws of nature and self-preservation." Quoting the great eighteenth-century English jurist Sir Michael Foster, a writer in Boston declared that the "primitive law of self-preservation" applies to men in both the natural state and in civil society, where "'in cases of great and urgent necessity, and where no other remedy is at hand, (says a great Crown lawyer,) is perfectly understood and universally assented to; a right which the law of nature giveth, and no law of society hath taken away.'" In April 1776, Judge William Henry Drayton told Charleston, South Carolina, jurors that George III had unleashed the fury of war against his American subjects "with swords, fire, and bayonets" in order to destroy them. "Nature cried aloud" that "self-preservation is the great law," Drayton noted, and the Americans have simply "obeyed" nature's call in defending their lives, their fortunes, and their sacred honor. Three months later, after the British army had landed in New York with the largest expeditionary force ever sent to America, the Americans were "led by the first law of nature, the innate principle of self-preservation," claimed a writer in Massachusetts calling himself "Plain Truth," to defend themselves and repel the invaders. In 1793, in his "Opinion on the French Treaties," Jefferson made clear that the "moral law" of man's nature dictated that if and when performance of an obligation "becomes self-destructive to the party" who has engaged to assume it, then "the law of self-preservation overrules the laws of obligation in others."[3]

THE RIGHT TO LIBERTY

Liberty is the first corollary of the right to life. The revolutionary generation's theory of individual rights said that man, given his nature, has a right to liberty, which means the unobstructed freedom to think, judge, choose, speak, act, assemble, worship, produce, and acquire values material and spiritual. Liberty means to be free of physical constraint or force. It is the right of voluntary action *versus* action by physical compulsion. According to Thomas Jefferson, it means "the rights of thinking, and publishing our thoughts by speaking or writing; the right of free commerce; the right of personal freedom."[4]

Life and liberty are inseparably linked by moral necessity. As Jefferson put it, "The God who gave us life, gave us liberty at the same time: the hand of force may destroy, but it cannot disjoin them." The right to life means the right to liberty, and the right to liberty makes the right to life possible. This is why one colonial American thought "there is no one Thing, which Mankind are more passionately fond of—which they fight with more Zeal for—which they possess with more anxious Jealousy, and Fear of losing, than LIBERTY." It is the "inherent right of all *mankind*," according to an anonymous author in the *Boston Gazette*. Indeed, virtually all Americans during the Revolutionary period would have agreed with John Tucker of Massachusetts, who considered the "love of liberty" to be "natural," and they would have likewise agreed with Thomas Dawes that liberty is a "palladium to the place of her dwelling" and "something to protect."[5]

In 1774, Nathaniel Niles argued in his *Two Discourses on Liberty*, a sermon delivered in Newburyport, Massachusetts, that it was "natural to enquire, in the first place, concerning the general nature of liberty; and indeed it is as *necessary* as natural." Only by determining what liberty is and the role it plays in human affairs could American revolutionaries understand the metes and bounds of liberty in civil society. "For until we determine" what good liberty is, Niles wrote, "we have no rule by which we may estimate the quantity of liberty in any particular constitution: But when once we have found the standard, we shall be prepared to examine our own constitution, or any other, at pleasure, and to determine what part of the constitution should be supported, and what may be given up with safety."[6]

American revolutionaries used the concept "liberty" in two different but related senses: first, they understood liberty to be an existential fact of human nature (i.e., man is a volitional being by nature), and, second, they also understood liberty to be a moral requirement of human flourishing (i.e., man must have and use his liberty in a social context in order to flourish).

Men are distinguished from "beasts" by virtue of the fact that they have free will or free agency and do not have instincts or an automatic code of survival.[7] Men must *choose* to act, and they must choose to act in certain ways, at certain times, and in certain places. Liberty in this sense refers to man's free will, agency, or volition.

The revolutionary generation's understanding of volitional liberty was usefully explained in 1771 by John Perkins, a physician from Lynn, Massachusetts, who authored one of the most philosophically interesting pamphlets published during the entire founding period. The purpose of his *Theory of Agency: Or, An Essay on the Nature, Source and Extent of Moral Freedom* was to determine "the reality of Liberty, particularly by a discovery of what it consisted in, and how it originated in the operations of the mind." Perkins did not think that proper liberty was synonymous with "absolute liberty" or "absolute will," that is, the liberty in which "a person has been supposed capable of determining differently, all circumstances remaining the same." Liberty is not synonymous, he argued, with bending reality to our whims and wishes. Nor did Perkins think that man has "innate ideas," which would obviate the existence of free will and agency. Following the "great Mr. Lock," Perkins argued that "Moral Freedom" is the "power of determining according to apprehended good and evil; opposed to a state of moral necessity, either natural, or induced by long custom, habit, passion, or some special depravity." Moral action is a choice, which means that liberty is the capacity to choose between right and wrong, good and bad, just and unjust. The clear implication is that moral freedom is the "exclusive property" of man's "rational nature," which is his unique method for seeing and choosing between alternatives. Man, Perkins claimed, "was form'd for self-direction" and his method of self-direction was his rational faculty and "intellectual powers," by which he "can govern the sensitive clues in the use of proper means; rectify errors in judgment; disengage himself from prejudices; foresee events, and conduct accordingly."[8] All men could be Socrates, Perkins argued, if they would just learn to tame their passions.

Similarly, in 1774 the Reverend Levi Hart delivered a highly theoretical sermon to his Connecticut congregation, in which he defined liberty as

a power of action, or a certain suitableness or preparedness for exertion, and a freedom from force, or hindrance from any external cause; *Liberty* when predicated of man as a moral agent, and accountable creature, is that suitableness or preparedness to be the subject of volitions, or exercises of will, with reference to moral objects; by the influence of motives, which we find belongeth to all men of common capacity, and who are come to the years of understanding.

THIS Liberty is opposed to that want of capacity, by which there is a total ignorance of all moral objects, and so, a natural incapacity of chusing with regard to them. *Again*, the term Liberty is frequently used to denote a power of *doing as we please*, or of executing our acts of choice; this refers principally to external action, or bodily motion; and is opposed to force or opposition:— thus the prisoner who is bound in fetters, and secured with bolts and bars of a prison, is not at liberty to go out, he is deprived of this kind of liberty, and is in bondage.[9]

Most other American Whigs agreed with this understanding of moral liberty. Liberty, as John Adams defined it, is "a self-determining power in an intellectual agent." Rightly understood, liberty "implies thought and choice and power; it can elect between objects, indifferent in point of morality, neither morally good nor morally evil." But liberty also implies, Adams continued, the ability and the free will to choose good or evil, right or wrong, just or unjust.[10] Such liberty or free will is not, however, automatic, innate, or instinctual. It must be consciously activated and self-directed.

The revolutionary generation also viewed liberty as a moral and political requirement of human flourishing. Liberty is to moral action what oxygen is to breathing. Given that man is a rational and a volitional being, to deny him the freedom to think, choose, and act is to deny him his nature and his means of survival. Thus the "is" of liberty implies the "ought" of liberty: Because liberty is a fact of his nature (part of his toolkit for survival), man must be permitted to make moral choices and to act on them. "The society whose laws least restrain the words and actions of its members," wrote a "Freeborn American" in the *Boston Gazette* in 1767, is "most free." As Simeon Howard of Boston put it in 1773, liberty is opposed "to external force and constraint, and to such force and constraint only, as we may suffer from men." More to the point, wrote Levi Hart, civil liberty does "not consist in a freedom from all law and government,—but in a freedom from *unjust* law and tyrannical government."[11]

Though the revolutionary generation viewed liberty as a requirement of human flourishing, they did not think it unproblematic. They did not mean the Hobbesian liberty to do as one lists. "It is a saying of Hobbs," noted a writer in Boston's *Independent Advertiser*, "that when some Men talk of Liberty, they mean THEIR OWN LIBERTY," by which is meant the liberty "to oppress without Controul."[12] This is not true liberty, however. The natural right to liberty implies the freedom of choice and action for every individual in respect of all others.

Ironically, the right to liberty means limits on the natural freedom of the precivil condition. For Nathaniel Niles, "good government is not inconsistent with liberty"; in fact, "good government" was "essential to the very being of liberty." Likewise, John Joachim Zubly told the Georgia provincial congress the following year that liberty "does not consist in living without all restraint; for were all men to live without restraint, as they please, there would soon be no liberty at all; the strongest would be master, the weakest go to the wall." Thomas Jefferson captured the twofold nature of the right to liberty, as both license and fence. On one hand, liberty is "in the whole plenitude of its extent,...unobstructed action according to our will." On the other hand, said Jefferson, "*rightful liberty* is unobstructed action according to our will within limits drawn around us by the equal rights of others. I do not add 'within the limits of the law,' because law is often but the tyrant's will, and always so when it violates the right of an individual."[13] For liberty to be socially "activated," it must be defined by boundaries—boundaries that protect the liberty of all men.

The Reverend John Tucker explained the intellectual and existential challenge presented by liberty in his election sermon to the Massachusetts government in 1771. Liberty is a passion, Tucker argued, and "like all other original principles of the human mind,"

> is, in itself, perfectly innocent, and designed for excellent purposes, though, like them, liable, through abuse, of becoming the cause of mischief to ourselves and others. In a civil state, the genius of whose constitution is agreeable to it, this passion, while in its full vigor, and under proper regulation, is not only the cement of the political body, but the wakeful guardian of its interests, and the great animating spring of useful and salutary operations; and then only is it injurious to the public, or to individuals, when, thro' misapprehension of things, or by being overballanced by self-love, it takes a wrong direction.

True or good liberty must be tamed and corralled by laws that serve an educative function in civil society. Such laws indicate what true or good liberty is not. Liberty corrupted by the "spirit of faction and discontent" leads first to anarchy and then to tyranny. By contrast, liberty rightly understood and rightly institutionalized is the "*animating soul* of a free state."[14]

Though published fifteen years before the beginning of the imperial crisis, a piece by a writer in Boston offering "some general Thoughts upon LIBERTY" summarized this view as well as any revolutionary writings. Following John Locke's lead, our anonymous writer argued that "every Man has a Right" in the state of nature "to think and act according to the Dictates of his own Mind: which in *that State*, are subject to no other Controul, and can be countermanded by no other Power, than the Laws and Ordinances of the great Creator of all Things." Liberty is perfected in the natural state when "every Man" is free "from any external Force" and can "perform such Actions, as in his own Mind and Conscience" is determined to be best for his life. This liberty, however, is thwarted not only by external forces, but by internal forces as well. True liberty—rational liberty—is lost when men allow their minds to be corrupted and "enthralled, by irregular and inordinate Passions: Since it is no great Privilege, to be free from external Violence, if the Dictates of the Mind are controuled by a Force within, which exerts itself above Reason." Thus unlimited liberty in the Lockean state of nature is insecure, which is why it must be placed "upon a more solid Foundation." The "true Notion" of liberty must be ordered, institutionalized, and constitutionalized through laws that protect it; its "just bounds" must be settled "in a State of Society and Civil Government."[15]

At this point, our unknown colonial writer considers and distinguishes the properties of liberty as they apply to the body politic as well as to each individual. Political liberty is

> enjoyed, when neither the *legislative* nor the *executive* Powers…are disturbed by an internal Passion, or hindered by any external Force from making the wisest Laws and executing them in the best Manner:—When the Safety, the Security and the Happiness of ALL, is the real Care and steady Pursuit of those, whose Business it is, to care for and pursue it:—in one short Word,—when no Laws are carried through Humour or Prejudice, nor controuled in

their proper Execution, by *Lust of Power* in the Great, or *wanton Licentiousness* in the Vulgar.

And once proper political liberty is established, individuals can experience and live out personal liberty, which occurs when a man "Freely enjoys the Security of the Laws, and the Rights to which he is born:—When he is hindered by no Violence, from claiming those Rights, and enjoying that Security: But may at any Time demand the Protection of the Laws under which he lives, and [be sure] when demanded to enjoy it."[16] The ideas expressed by this anonymous Boston writer in 1749 were replicated scores if not hundreds of times in the years between the passage of the Sugar Act in 1764 and the ratification of the Massachusetts constitution in 1780.

A prime example, fast forwarding now to 1773, is a New York Patriot writing under the pseudonym "Poplicola," who sought to prove that "*liberty* can have no existence without obedience to laws." In the state of nature, liberty is subjective and absolute, which ultimately means insecure. Because there is no common judge with the authority to identify, recognize, and protect man's rights, justice is either denied or dispensed by "private revenge," which leads ultimately to a war of all against all. Civil society and the government that comes with it seek to remedy this unsustainable situation by "adjusting the rights of individuals by a common wisdom, and protecting the exercise of them by a common power." The purpose of laws in a just society is to protect and expand human freedom by restricting "every man from acting in such a manner as to injure others, as it restrains others from injuring him." Freedom-promoting law—what Aristotle called "The Empire of Laws"—is synonymous with, and a precondition for, expanding the sphere of liberty. Civil liberty, then, is "nothing else but natural liberty so far restrained by human laws." Liberty without just law would "render society a rope of Sand." In fact, if men in civil society were to remove the "barrier of laws," the state of nature—in other words, the state of war—would return.

> For if every man could act as he pleased, no one would be secure. The arbitrary decision of right, and license of exercising it, which *you* assumed, would be assumed by your neighbor also. The same violence which one part of the community employed to vindicate what they had determined to be their privileges, would be on equal

ground employed by another. Power then would be the only criterion of right, and, instead of a common object, every branch would
have a distinct interest in view.[17]

For virtually all Americans during the Revolutionary period, liberty was
synonymous with law, but not just any law. As the colonists were then
experiencing with the laws passed by Parliament since the Sugar Act, laws
can be unjust and even tyrannical. In a free society, the law must be objective, which means to be demonstrably connected to the rights of nature
held by each and every individual. The laws of a free society as defined by
the Declaration of Independence will bar the initiation of physical force
from the relationships between individuals in civil society. The law of liberty must be publicly declared and written, so that all individuals know
the boundaries of liberty—the actions that constitute a crime against the
rights of others—before they act.

THE RIGHT TO PROPERTY

Private property is not listed in the Declaration's trinity of rights, but there
can be no doubt that all eighteenth-century Americans regarded property to be a fundamental right of nature.[18] The right to acquire, keep, use,
transfer, trade, and dispose of one's own property was a core *moral* principle
universally acclaimed by Americans of all descriptions.

How did colonial and revolutionary Americans understand what
property rights are, their source, their validation, and their relationship to
life, liberty, and the pursuit of happiness?

James Wilson, one of the deepest thinkers of the revolutionary generation, defined property as "the right of lawful power, which a person has to a
thing." Property, he continued, has three levels of complexity: "The lowest
degree of this right is a right merely to possess a thing. The next degree
of this right is a right to possess and to use a thing. The next and highest
degree of this right is a right to possess, to use, and to dispose of a thing."
James Madison defined property in a 1792 essay devoted exclusively to
the topic. Property, "in its particular application," he wrote, quoting from
William Blackstone's discussion of property in *Commentaries on the Laws of
England*, "means, 'that dominion which one man claims and exercises over
the external things of the world, in exclusion of every other individual.'"[19]

In its purest sense, private property means the right to possess legally, to the exclusion of all others, that which one has produced or earned. Americans of the Revolutionary era did not view the right *to* property as guaranteeing a right to *have or to be given* property; that is, they did not recognize that one man could have a moral or legal claim to the labor and property of another.

For eighteenth-century Americans, the source and validation of property rights was found in human nature and the related moral fact of self-ownership. The natural right to property, Jefferson wrote in 1816, is founded "in our natural wants, in the means by which we are endowed to satisfy those wants, and the right to what we acquire by those means without violating the similar rights" of others.[20]

American revolutionaries validated the right to property by connecting it to the most fundamental form of property: *self-ownership*. Madison's view of property as the ownership of *external* things was grounded in the *internal* ownership of one's own self. In his essay on "Property," Madison elaborated:

> In its larger and juster meaning, [property] embraces everything to which a man may attach a value and have a right; and *which leaves to everyone else the like advantage....*
>
> In the latter sense [the "larger and juster meaning"], a man has a property in his opinions and the free communication of them.
>
> He has a property of peculiar value in his religious opinions, and in the profession and practice dictated by them.
>
> He has a property very dear to him in the safety and liberty of his person.
>
> He has an equal property in the free use of his faculties and free choice of the objects on which to employ them.
>
> In a word, as a man is said to have a right to his property, he may be equally said to have a property in his rights.[21]

The revolutionary generation learned to ground property rights in self-ownership from John Locke's chapter on property in the *Second Treatise*, where the Englishman argued "every man has a *property* in his own person" such that no man "has any right to but himself." Each man, he continued, is "master of himself, and *proprietor of his own person*, and the actions or labor of it." In other words, man has "in himself, the great foundation of property." And because man owns himself (i.e., the "labour of his body, and the work of his hands," and by extension, his mind), every time he mixes his labor with material things he transforms them by injecting some part of himself into them. That is, he gives value to that which formerly had no value, and thereby comes to own them, as an extension of his right to self-ownership. Later in the *Second Treatise*, Locke argues that man by nature has a "power" and a right to "preserve his property," by which he means man's "life, liberty, and estate." In other words, property for Locke is the fundamental and inclusive concept that includes even life and liberty. Self-ownership is the building block from which Locke constructs his moral and political principles.[22]

One of the most developed American explications of Locke's theory is Dan Foster's brilliant *A Short Essay on Civil Government*. Recall that Foster describes hypothetical individuals by letters of the alphabet. He begins with "*A*," who owns his hands; and if he owns his hands, he owns his feet; and if he owns his hands and feet, then he has "an individual right, to his head and heart, and his whole body," to which "*B*" has no claim, "nor can pretend to have, without great and intolerable injury and injustice." The right that each man has in his own person leads to the right of property in possessions as individuals mix their labor with worldly entities:

> Accordingly, *A* labours with his hands, uses them in various secular employments, and is industrious in his business, for his support and maintenance. We will suppose for the sake of clearness and conviction, that *A* takes a piece of unoccupied land, which is claimed by no inhabitant of the earth; upon this ground he settles and builds, brings on cattle, so soon as prepared for them, and other living creatures, for his support and conveniency. Here he lives a number of years, manages his business alone, and separate from all near society with any other rational beings, and gains a considerable estate. Now *A* while he dwells here alone, hath an individual right to his land, and all that he hath brought upon it, and the effects of his own labour and toil upon it; to the Land he hath the right of prime occupancy, a very just and good right; and to all the fruits and effects of his labours, he hath just as good a right, as he hath to his hands, with which he laboured.

Foster's Lockean description of the nature and origin of property could just as easily have described the process by which property was established in the colonies during the seventeenth and eighteenth centuries as the ever-expanding frontier pushed farther westward. Through their "labours, industry and frugality," America's pioneers and settlers came to "have an absolute and individual right, and property in all they have earned."[23]

Foster and the revolutionary generation viewed the right to property as *absolute*. It was not to be violated by anyone, and government most especially:

> No man, or number of men have a right to disturb *A* in the enjoy-ment of his family and estate, or property: For to suppose them to have such right, would be to suppose them to have some property in *A*'s family and estate; for if they have no such property, the sup-position that they have right to molest or disturb *A* in the enjoy-ment of his family, and the possession of his estate, is impossible: for if one man has no property in the possessions of another, he certainly can have no *right* to give any molestation to this other man in the enjoyment of them: which is a very plain case to every one, who thinks ever so little. If *B* has no right to begin to give molestation to *A*, who is quietly and peaceably enjoying his own estate, then neither has *C*, *D* or *E*, or any other; for *E* has as much right to *A*'s estate as *B* has, that is, none at all; and so it is with *C*, *D*, and all the rest. For what any one man hath as just a right to, as any other, every man in the world, or all men, have as just a right to; but what every man hath a just right to, one as much as any other, none of them all has any just right to; for in such case, an equal right among all mankind, cannot be accounted any right at all. So that no man upon earth hath any just right to begin to disturb A in the enjoyment of his family and estate.[24]

Foster recognized the moral right of "*A*" to resist and repel every attempt of "*B*" to invade his property. This moral right was the heart of the Americans' resistance to the Stamp Act. Because a man owns himself, he owns the property that he has made or mixed his labor with and therefore acquired a right to. His property is his by right and can be taken from him only with his *consent*, which is derived from his self-ownership.

Dan Foster's view of property was the most sophisticated to have developed during the Revolutionary era, but his basic principles were shared by his entire generation. No one in the American colonies, with the possible exception of a few Tories, would have disagreed with Samuel Adams in 1768 when he told General Henry Conway, the British Secretary of State for the Northern Department, "It is acknowledged to be an unalterable law in nature, that a man should have the free use and sole disposal of the fruit of his honest industry, subject to no controul." Private property should be held as a "sacred" right, Adams claimed, that many have "fought, and bled, and died for."[25] Writing for the *Massachusetts Spy* in 1773, the pseudonymous "Massachusettensis" summed up quite powerfully the American position:

> So great, is the regard of the law for private property, that it will not authorize the least violation of it, unless applied to the detriment of the Society.—That men have a natural right to retain their justly acquired property, or dispose of it as they please without injuring others, is a proposition that has never been controverted to my knowledge: That they should lose this right by entering society is repugnant to common sense and the united voice of every writer of reputation upon the subject. All agree that no man can be justly deprived of his property without his consent in person or by his representative.[26]

And where does the right to property fit in the relationship to the rights to life, liberty, and the pursuit of happiness? America's eighteenth-century Whig revolutionaries viewed the right to property as the linchpin connecting life and liberty on one hand and the pursuit of happiness on the other. They considered the right to property to be an extension of the right to life and liberty, for the purpose of living and living well. Given that man does not live in the Garden of Eden or have an automatic means of survival, he must *produce* the material goods necessary for survival and flourishing.

Colonial and revolutionary Americans viewed liberty and property as indissolubly connected. In his 1774 *Summary View of the Rights of British-America*, Jefferson argued that property was intimately connected to, and fulfilled the promise of, life and liberty: "Still less let it be proposed that our properties within our own territories shall be taxed or regulated by any other power on earth but our own. The God who gave us life gave us liberty at the same time; the hand of force may destroy, but cannot disjoin them." In fact, according to one anonymous writer in the *Boston Gazette*, "*Liberty* and *Property* are not only join'd in common discourse," they "are in their own natures so nearly ally'd, that we cannot be said to possess the one without the enjoyment of the other." Liberty is, he continued, the "source and pillar of all true property." In his 1775 speech commemorating the Boston Massacre, Joseph Warren declared that "personal freedom is the natural right of every man; and that property or an exclusive right to dispose of what he has honestly acquired by his own labor, necessarily arises therefrom, are truths which common sense has placed beyond the reach of contradiction."[27]

Eighteen years later, Nathaniel Chipman, in his *Sketches of the Principles of Government*, one of the first American works of political science, defined what he called man's "primary rights," which included the "right which men have of using their powers and faculties, under certain reciprocal modifications, for their own convenience and happiness." The central "primary" right for Chipman was "the right of acquisition."[28] Chipman and virtually all eighteenth-century Americans viewed private property as the precondition for the right to pursue happiness. They repeated time and again that if government has the right to take one's property without one's consent, it therefore has the power to take away one's liberty, which means one's life and happiness.

For colonial and revolutionary Americans, the right to private property was not primarily an economic principle; it was first and foremost a *moral* principle, and it was the central right around which the others pivoted. In 1775, Arthur Lee, an American diplomat and statesman during the War of Independence, summed up the importance the revolutionary generation placed on the centrality of property as a fundamental right when he declared, "The Right of property is the guardian of every other Right, and to deprive the people of this, is in fact to deprive them of their Liberty."[29]

Self-ownership leads to liberty, liberty leads to private property, and property leads to the principle of consent, which is the moral midwife providing the link between the principle of rights and government. (The principle of consent is discussed at much greater length in chapters 8 and 9.) In a constitutional republic devoted to the protection of individual rights, consent is the only moral principle that can legitimately relieve a man of his property. As Joseph Warren put it in his Boston Massacre oration, "no man or body of men can; without being guilty of flagrant injustice, claim a right to dispose of the persons or acquisitions of any other man, or body of men, unless it can be proved that such a right has arisen from some compact between the parties in which it has been explicitly and freely granted." At the heart of the American Revolutionary position was this one moral-political principle repeated countless times during the years of the imperial crisis, "that no man shall have his property taken from him, but by his own consent, given by himself or by other deputed to act for him."[30]

The revolutionary generation was in universal agreement that the principle of consent leads to a certain kind of government (i.e., the republican form), the chief purpose of which is "the Protection of Property from Injuries within and without."[31] This principle defines and limits the better-known revolutionary slogan, "no taxation without representation." Consent and representation do not, however, give governments the unlimited right to arbitrarily take or destroy the property of their citizens. Rather, consent and representation give governments merely the highly limited authority to raise some minimal revenue for the purpose of protecting the rights of its citizens.

✳   ✳   ✳

The American Revolution was about defending the right to private property, but the Declaration of Independence does not list it as an unalienable right. The evidence, however, is overwhelming that Jefferson and his fellow signers of the Declaration viewed private property as a core natural right inseparable from life, liberty, and the pursuit of happiness. In fact, they probably wrote more words defending property as a right than they did the other three natural rights.

As the principal author of the Declaration, Jefferson was certain that property was one of man's most "sacred and undeniable" rights. His written instructions to the Virginia delegates to the Continental Congress warned that "the end of government would be defeated by the British Parliament exercising a power over the lives, the property, and the liberty of American subjects, who are not, and, from their local circumstances, cannot be, there represented." The American people above all others, Jefferson noted in his First Inaugural Address, have a "due sense of our equal right to…the acquisitions of our own industry." In fact, in 1816 Jefferson told Samuel Kercheval that the "true foundation of republican government is the equal right of every citizen in his person and property, and in their management."[32]

In addition to recognizing private property as a fundamental moral principle, America's revolutionary statesmen understood the salutary effects of protecting this principle. To a man (and woman), they would have accepted James Madison's claim that a legal-political order that protects the right to property "encourage[s] industry by securing the enjoyment of its fruits."[33] By contrast, a legal-political order that did not protect private property—or, worse, one that instituted communal property—was viewed by the founding generation as injurious to human life. They knew that if men were not permitted to keep what they have earned, they would not produce, at least not at the level necessary to achieve prosperity and happiness.

In his legal commonplace book (which he kept while studying the law as a young man), Jefferson wrote out extensive notes, drawn from Lord Kames's *Historical Law Tracts*, on the origin and history of property. Jefferson viewed with horror a collectivist society wherein "every man shall be bound to dedicate the whole of his industry to the common interest." Such a society, he continued, "would be unnatural and uncomfortable, because destruction of liberty and independency; so would be the enjoyment of goods of fortune in common." The forced sharing of property would likewise cause all generosity, benevolence, and charity to wither on the vine. If such "noble principles" were "destitute of objects and exercise," Jefferson added, they would "forever lie dormant."[34] In his *Autobiography*, written decades later, Jefferson finished Madison's thought when he noted that wealth creation and prosperity result only when individuals are left free to think, act, and produce. By contrast, "were we directed from Washington when to sow, and when to reap," he warned, "we should soon want bread."[35]

James Wilson agreed with Jefferson and Madison. In his essay "On the History of Property," Wilson noted that a social order grounded in the right to private property better secures, preserves, and *multiplies* the "productions of the earth and the means of subsistence." It was a basic truth, according to Wilson, that "what belongs to one man in particular is the object of his economy and care." Contrariwise, in a society where property is not respected and protected, "what belongs to no one is wasted by every one." Wilson then went on to explain the "superiority of separate over common property." Foreshadowing the twentieth century's various experiments with socialism, Wilson used the historical example of seventeenth-century Plymouth to demonstrate how and why property owned in common rather than individually leads inexorably to penury and misery. During the first seven years of the Plymouth experiment,

> all commerce was carried on in one joint stock. All things were common to all; and the necessaries of life were daily distributed to every one from the publick store. But these regulations soon furnished abundant reasons for complaint, and proved most fertile sources of common calamity. The colonists were sometimes in danger of starving; and severe whipping, which was often administered to promote labour, and was only productive of constant and general discontent.

As soon as the colony abandoned its disastrous experiment with primitive socialism, its fortunes increased exponentially, noted Wilson. With the introduction of private property, the colony underwent a miraculous transformation. The shift to individually owned property "produced the most comfortable change in the colony," Wilson noted, "by engaging the affections and invigorating the pursuits of its inhabitants." In fact, the right of individual, private property, according to Wilson, "seems to be founded in the nature of men and things; and when societies become numerous, the establishment of that right is highly important to the existence, to the tranquility, to the elegancies, to the refinements, and to some of the virtues of civilized life." Thus, private property is "essential," he declared, "to the interests of civilized society."[36]

For both moral and economic reasons, then, the revolutionary generation believed that government existed, in large part, in order to protect property. In *Federalist* No. 10, Madison suggested that the "first object of government" is to protect the "diversity in the faculties of men, from which the rights of property originate." By faculties, Madison here means both endogenous qualities such as intelligence, creativity, energy, and strength, and exogenous qualities such as knowledge, experience, and work ethic. Madison recognized, as an observable fact of reality, that men have different and sometimes unequal faculties that, when combined with the equal right to property and the right to choose, will lead to different and unequal possessions. Not only is there nothing wrong with the recognition and protection of unequal property; in Madison's view, government in a free society recognizes and protects unequal property as an act of justice. "The protection of these faculties [i.e., recognizing and protecting the unequal faculties of man, liberty, and fruits that result from both] is the first object of government. From the protection of different and unequal faculties of acquiring property, the possession of different degrees and kinds of property immediately results." Several years later, Madison restated the argument of *Federalist* No. 10 even more starkly: "Government is instituted to protect property of every sort; as well that which lies in the various rights of individuals, as that which the term particularly expresses. This being the end of government, that alone is a *just* government, which *impartially* secures to every man, whatever is his *own*." Madison understood man's natural right to property as an extension of his need to think and to think rationally. And as John Adams well knew, the "Pleasures of Property, arise from Acquis[it]ion more than Possession, from what is to come rather from what is."[37] The right to property, in other words, is as much a spiritual right—the right to exercise one's creativity, judgment, abilities, and labor—as it is a material right to things.

Adams was in full agreement with Jefferson, Lee, and Madison on the centrality of property rights as a natural right. "Property," he argued, "is surely a right of mankind as really as liberty." In *A Defence of the Constitutions of Government of the United State of America* (1787–88), Adams argued forcefully that constitutions, the rule of law, and properly constructed republican governments exist in a free society primarily to protect man's natural right to property:

> *Res populi*…signified a government, in which the property of the public, or people, and of every one of them, was secured and protected by law. This idea, indeed, implies liberty; because property cannot be secure unless the man be at liberty to acquire, use, or part with it, at his discretion, and unless he have his personal liberty of life and limb, motion and rest, for that purpose. It implies, moreover, that the property and liberty of all men, not merely of a majority, should be safe; for the people, or public, comprehends more than a majority, it comprehends all and every individual; and the property of every citizen is a part of the public property, as each

citizen is a part of the public, people, or community. The property, therefore, of every man has a share in government, and is more powerful than any citizen, or party of citizens; it is governed only by the law.[38]

It is hard to find a statement then or now more powerful in its articulation of property as a fundamental right. Adams thought the laws of property should be treated as "sacred as the laws of God." In fact, no nation could be considered civilized or free, Adams wrote, until it had institutionalized and made inviolable the "precepts," "'THOU SHALT NOT COVET,' and 'THOU SHALT NOT STEAL.'" The property rights of the rich were just as important, just as "sacred" to Adams, as those of the poor.[39] These basic moral rules are at the heart of civil society and hence of civilization.

Adams, Jefferson, Lee, Madison, and the rest of the founders could not and would not have recognized, on principle, an intrinsic and positive rights-claim to some*thing*, to the means of existence—to food, shelter, daycare, health care, a job, an education, and so on. With the glaringly obvious exception of chattel slavery, they did not recognize the right to life to mean that one man has a rights-claim on the liberty and property of another. Jefferson argued that extra or excessive taxes on the wealthy would violate natural right: "To take from one, because it is thought that his industry and that of his fathers has acquired too much, in order to spare to others, who, or whose fathers have not exercised equal industry or skill, is to violate arbitrarily the first principle of association, the guarantee to every one of a free exercise of his industry, and the fruits acquired by it." Likewise, in his Second Inaugural Address, Jefferson told the American people that his administration would be guided by principles of justice rather than by social envy. He assured the American people that under his presidency "equality of rights" would be maintained, as well as "that state of property, equal or unequal, which results to every man from his own industry, or that of his fathers."[40]

America's revolutionary founders believed and hoped that property ownership in America would be as widespread as possible. This does not mean, however, that they supported equality over inequality or the redistribution of property from the wealthy to the poor. They were opposed to laws that promoted artificial inequalities and artificial equality. Instead, they sought to establish a private property order that would allow all men the freedom to acquire, keep, and trade their property as they saw fit. By abolishing laws that perpetuated inequality through primogeniture and entail, for instance, they sought to break up artificial barriers to property ownership and wealth creation. They were also opposed to using the coercive force of the state to achieve an equality of property. In 1792, Vermont's Nathaniel Chipman summed up the revolutionary generation's view of the relationship between private property and the use of government coercion for the purpose of redistribution:

> If we make equality of property necessary in a society, we must employ force against both the industrious and the indolent. On the one hand, the industrious must be restrained from every exertion which may exceed the power or inclination of common capacities; on the other hand, the indolent must be forcibly stimulated to common exertions. This would be acting the fable of Procrustes, who, by stretching, or lopping to his iron bedstead, would reduce every man to his own standard length.[41]

The founding generation universally considered property a fundamental, natural right. Such a right served as a barrier against any claim by some citizens seeking any part of any other's property for their private advantage. Americans would spend the next eighty years, however, debating the nature and content of the property right—a debate that ended in 1863 with Abraham Lincoln's Emancipation Proclamation.

THE RIGHT TO THE PURSUIT OF HAPPINESS

The founders' theory of rights said that man, given his nature, has a *right to the pursuit of happiness*. The origin and meaning of this phrase and Jefferson's reasons for including it in the Declaration of Independence have confounded scholars for over two centuries. The right to the pursuit of happiness is the most difficult of the fundamental natural rights to understand because the revolutionary generation said very little about it. Only a few of the major pamphlets of the era even mentioned happiness in passing. Jefferson gave no serious account of what he meant by happiness, or from whence he might have derived the idea of a right to the "pursuit of happiness."[42]

Despite the relative paucity of writings on the meaning of happiness in the revolutionary literature, Americans took the subject seriously. Some described happiness as the highest end of government, and most described it as the purpose of life. In *Common Sense*, Thomas Paine quoted an obscure Italian writer, Giacinto Dragonetti ("that wise observer on governments," Paine called him), who, in a 1766 essay on "Virtues and Reward," told his readers, "The science of the Politician consists in fixing the true point of happiness and freedom. Those men would deserve the gratitude of ages, who should discover a mode of government that contained the greatest sum of individual happiness, with the least national expense." In his influential 1776 pamphlet *Thoughts on Government*, published a few months after Paine's *Common Sense* and several months before Jefferson sat down to write the Declaration, John Adams equated "the divine science of politicks" with the "science of social happiness." Indeed, "the happiness of society is the end of government," he continued, and the "happiness of the individual is the end of man." Decades later, Thomas Jefferson told the Polish-American general Thaddeus Kosciusko that a group of young men (presumably students at Mr. Jefferson's university in Charlottesville) had moved into the village next to Monticello in order to study with the author of the Declaration. "In advising the course of their reading," Jefferson wrote to his friend, "I endeavor to keep their attention fixed on the main objects of all science, the freedom and happiness of man." Freedom and happiness were, after all, "the sole objects of government," he told Kosciusko.[43] It is not known what Jefferson had these young men read nor what they talked about, but the letter does indicate that Jefferson thought happiness to be a serious subject of scholarly investigation. In fact, readers will note that Paine, Adams, and Jefferson all suggested that there was a "science" of happiness, which was connected to both the science of government and the science of freedom.

✳   ✳   ✳

The meaning that Jefferson and the revolutionary generation attributed to the "right to the pursuit of happiness" can be teased out through a series of questions concerning the nature and meaning of *happiness*, *pursuit*, and *right*. The answers to these questions are elusive and must be reconstructed from fragmentary evidence. The phrase "pursuit of happiness" is not listed as a natural right in any of the petitions, resolves, declarations, or major pamphlets published by the Americans in the years between 1764 and 1776. It does not appear in the list of English rights and liberties enumerated by either the Stamp Act Congress in 1765 or the declaration of the First Continental Congress in 1774. Even discussions on the nature and meaning of happiness are rarely raised in the revolutionary literature.[44]

The closest that any formal public document comes to Jefferson's formulation is wording contained in section 1 of George Mason's Virginia Declaration of Rights, published just weeks before Jefferson completed the Declaration of Independence. Jefferson was almost certainly familiar with Mason's document when he sat down to write on behalf of the Continental Congress. According to Mason and the Virginia Declaration, "all men are by nature equally free and independent and have certain inherent rights, of which, when they enter into a state of society, they cannot, by any compact, deprive or divest their posterity; namely, the enjoyment of life and liberty, with the means of acquiring and possessing property, and pursuing and obtaining happiness and safety."[45] Mason's wording is close to Jefferson's, and the comparative meaning is virtually identical. It is possible—indeed, it seems likely—that Jefferson simply compressed Mason's language for stylistic reasons. Still, the phrase "pursuit of happiness" seems to be uniquely Jefferson's—at least in an American context.

On a deeper, philosophical level, it seems clear that Jefferson borrowed the phrase from John Locke's 1690 *An Essay Concerning Human Understanding*, where the Englishman used it repeatedly. Locke's discussion of happiness and its pursuit is too long and complex to be considered here, but his central point is worth is considering:

> As therefore the highest perfection of intellectual nature lies in a
> careful and constant pursuit of true and solid happiness, so the care
> of ourselves, that we mistake not imaginary for real happiness, is
> the necessary foundation of our liberty. The stronger ties we have to
> an unalterable *pursuit of happiness* in general, which is our greatest
> good, and which, as such, our desires always follow, the more are we
> free from any necessary determination of our will to any particular
> action...[46]

There is much in this complex paragraph worth unpacking in order to understand what Locke meant by the "pursuit of happiness." The

Englishman begins with an empirically observable truth claim: all men everywhere pursue "true" happiness, but not all men attain it. Some are led astray by the siren song of "imaginary" happiness, and some simply fail for a variety of reasons in their pursuit of "real" happiness. Also, with true and imaginary happiness there are "infinite degrees of happiness."[47] Most men pursue some form or degree of happiness every day, but even the happiest of men experience its antipode, misery, or some degree of it, throughout their lives. Happiness, for Locke, is the end result of men pursuing their self-interest, rightly understood, which in turn is the foundation of liberty.

How precisely does the "pursuit" of happiness work for Locke? It begins with the mind, with reason's "power to *suspend* the execution and satisfaction of any of its desires." Man's reason, Locke says, "is at liberty to consider the objects" of its desires, to "examine them on all sides, and weigh them with others." With this liberty to think, which, in part, means the ability to pause and suspend our desires, men have "the opportunity to examine, view, and judge of the good or evil of what [they] are going to do" in the pursuit of their happiness.[48] This means that man must first choose to rate and judge certain values, and then he must choose among the available objects of his desires.

Because men experience pleasure in different ways, the objects of happiness and the means of pursuing them differ from one man to another. Some choose "study and knowledge," others "hawking and hunting" or "luxury and debauchery," still others prefer "sobriety and riches," while some find happiness in "virtue" or "contemplation" or "glory" or "honour" or "immortality." Still, identifying things that make men happy does not necessarily result in happiness. In some cases, men realize that certain values do not give them happiness, and in other cases they fail to achieve their values and thus their happiness. Because man is neither omniscient nor infallible, there results "all that variety of mistakes, errors, and faults which we run into in the conduct of our lives and our endeavours after happiness."[49] The great challenge for men as they pursue their true happiness is in overcoming their passions, which resist and fight against their right reasoning. They must use their reason to choose the object of their happiness and the path to pursue it. The pursuit of happiness is a process, which, if not properly conducted, can actually lead to its opposite—namely, misery and suffering.

Thus it is important for the "care of ourselves," Locke writes, that men not mistake "imaginary for real happiness." There is nothing innate about the pursuit of happiness precisely because of the complexity of man's daily life; a man makes a myriad of choices that incline toward either "imaginary" or "real" happiness.[50] For Locke, the distinction between real and imaginary happiness is the distinction between acting in one's long-term self-interest versus acting in the pursuit of short-term pleasures that can have unintended, long-term negative consequences. True happiness—the highest form of self-interest, rightly understood—is both euphoric and long lasting. It is the result of good choices and right action—that is, rational evaluation and judgment, and virtuous behavior. Imaginary happiness provides short-term pleasure but oftentimes long-term misery. Imaginary happiness results from irrational or faulty reasoning, and it leads ultimately to its antipode: misery or suffering.

Locke does not directly identify the virtues necessary to achieve happiness, but he certainly implies that they include rationality (including wisdom and prudence), temperance, fortitude, productiveness, and a host of other virtues. As such, the pursuit of happiness, rather than serving as the basis of hedonism, is the foundation of moral action and therewith of civilization.

☆   ☆   ☆

The revolutionary generation accepted as a fundamental truth Locke's distinction between "true" or "real" happiness and "imaginary" happiness.[51] In 1771, Samuel Adams told his nephew Joseph Allen that he hoped the young man would "meet with all that prosperity which shall be consistent with your *real* happiness." The following year, he told another correspondent, "We too often mistake our true Happiness, and when we arrive to the Enjoyment of that which seemd to promise it to us, we find that it is all an imaginary Dream, at the best fleeting & transitory."[52]

In one form or another, the entire revolutionary generation understood happiness to be the *summum bonum* of life and the highest object of human action. Despite its elusiveness and the work required to achieve it, it is what each of us strives for throughout our lives. As such, the pursuit of happiness is the architectonic or capstone natural right. The rights to life, liberty, and property are integral to, support, and are sustained by the right to pursue happiness.

American revolutionaries believed that each and every individual experiences, defines, and pursues happiness differently. It is a law of man's nature, Jefferson wrote, that each and every man will "pursue his own happiness" in the same way he pursues his interests. Individuals, rather than governments or seminaries of wise men, are the best judges of their own happiness. Man has been left free, Jefferson opined, to pursue his own happiness "in the choice of place as well as mode; and we may safely call on the whole body of English jurists to produce the map on which nature has traced for each individual the geographical line which she forbids him to cross in pursuit of happiness."[53]

However, for Jefferson and the other revolutionary founders, the individual right to the pursuit of happiness did not imply simple "subjectivism," in either means or ends. Though each and every man will pursue happiness as he defines it because each person experiences it in different ways, Jefferson did not think that all pursuits and forms of happiness were equal. Some forms of happiness are fleeting and some are permanent, some are infantile and some are uplifting, some are vulgar and some are ennobling. Jefferson did think that there is a hierarchic ordering of those values that give happiness, which means there is also a hierarchy in the forms of happiness.

Jefferson and America's revolutionary statesmen did not think there was a tension or dichotomy between property and happiness, that is, between material and spiritual values. Indeed, quite the opposite. By definition, the right to the pursuit of happiness also includes the right to pursue, acquire, keep, own, and transfer property. This is why Jefferson could write, in a letter to Francisco Chiappe, that it was a "great truth that industry, commerce and security are the surest roads to the happiness and prosperity of [a] people." Benjamin Franklin, more than any other eighteenth-century American, was a proponent of the necessary connection between the acquisition of property and the pursuit of happiness. Following Aristotle, Franklin believed that the attainment of happiness was certainly enhanced by a certain minimum level of life's conveniences. "Wherein consists the Happiness of a rational Creature?" he asked, and to which he answered: "In having a sound mind, a healthy body, a Sufficiency of the Necessaries and Conveniences of Life, together with the Favour of God, and the Love of Mankind." Industry and commerce are a prerequisite for the accumulation of property, which contributes to happiness and prosperity. Happiness therefore includes both material and spiritual values. And even though Jefferson did not think "Perfect happiness" was attainable to man in this world, as he wrote to John Page, he did think that it was very much in his power to approach or approximate complete felicity.[54]

Jefferson was of two minds on the source of happiness and its outcomes. In a famous letter to Maria Cosway, he constructed a dialogue between his head and his heart, which demonstrates his own uncertainty as to what happiness is and where it comes from. Jefferson's head tells him that happiness is a matter of weighing and calculating the costs and benefits, the pleasures and pains, associated with any object or value that one seeks to gain. Jefferson's head is stoical and anti-Epicurean. "The art of life"—that is, the art of happiness—"is the art of avoiding pain," says his reason. And since an excess of pleasure often precedes pain, Jefferson's head advises him to stay clear of "the rocks and shoals" associated with an overabundance of physical, material, or even emotional pleasure. Thus, the surest path to happiness, according to Jefferson's head, is to "retire within ourselves, and to suffice for our own happiness." It is only the "intellectual pleasures" that men create for themselves that can be relied on and can never be taken away by others: "Ever in our power, always leading us to something new, never cloying, we ride, serene and sublime, above the concerns of this mortal world, contemplating truth and nature, matter and motion, the laws which bind up their existence, and that eternal being who made and bound them up by these laws."[55]

Jefferson's heart speaks a different language and sees the source and substance of happiness in a different way. Whereas Jefferson's mind emphasizes the avoidance of pain, misery, and misfortune, his heart emphasizes the pursuit of pleasure, goodness, and beauty. Fortunately, he says, the greater part of our lives is to be found not in darkness or shade, but in "sunshine." Jefferson's heart rejects the pleasures associated with monks and philosophers:

> Let the gloomy monk, sequestered from the world, seek unsocial
> pleasures in the bottom of his cell! Let the sublimated philosopher
> grasp visionary happiness while pursuing phantoms dressed in the
> garb of truth! Their supreme wisdom is supreme folly; and they
> mistake for happiness the mere absence of pain. Had they ever felt
> the solid pleasure of one generous spasm of the heart, they would

exchange for it all the frigid speculations of their lives, which you have been vaunting in such elevated terms.

In the end, Jefferson believed that both the head and the heart must play a role in man's pursuit of happiness. This fact is a reflection of man's nature for Jefferson, or what he called man's "divided empire." He understood that man is a being of body and soul, which means that physical pleasure can and must be reconciled with intellectual pleasure in order for one to achieve the highest and most sustained levels of happiness. The man who comes closest to true happiness will reconcile the motivations and the desires of his head and his heart.[56]

✯　✯　✯

If happiness is the *summum bonum* of a life well lived, how is it attained? The Declaration of Independence does not say, and Jefferson did not think, that happiness is innate or automatic to man. The Declaration clearly states that man has a right to *pursue* happiness; it does not say that man has a right to happiness. For Jefferson, happiness, to be attained, must be pursued. But how does one pursue it? Is man naturally impelled toward happiness, or must he consciously choose to pursue it and to pursue it in a certain way? Is there a relationship between the pursuit of happiness and moral virtue? Are the moral demands of virtue in conflict with happiness?

For Jefferson and America's revolutionary statesmen, the *pursuit* required to attain happiness involves a *method*. Happiness does not just happen through wish or incantation, nor can it be achieved arbitrarily without deliberate action. To achieve long-lasting happiness at the highest levels requires sustained effort of rational thought, strength of character, and moral action. To pursue happiness, however, does not guarantee its satisfaction. Men can pursue rational and life-enhancing values but fail to achieve them as the result of error, evasion, or lethargy, or they can pursue destructive values that do not lead to happiness. The result either way can be depression, misery, and suffering rather than happiness.

Jefferson and his fellow Americans saw moral action as inextricably connected with happiness, as was immorality with suffering. For both Aristotle and Cicero—the greatest ancient influences on Jefferson as he wrote the Declaration—virtue is a critical component of happiness. As John Adams put it: "Happiness can never be found without virtue."[57]

We can see what the revolutionaries meant by the *pursuit* of happiness by examining the moral advice they gave to young people. Consider the counsel that Jefferson gave to his nephew Peter Carr and to his grandson Thomas Jefferson Randolph. The "first object" of a proper education in happiness, Jefferson told Carr in 1785, is "the purest integrity" and "the most chaste honour." He advised the young man to give up "money," "fame," "science," and even "the earth itself" rather than to engage in any kind of "immoral act" or "dishonourable thing." Dishonorable behavior, Jefferson suggested, would eventually lead to a life of misery and suffering. He told his nephew that whenever he was about to do something,

> though it can never be known but to yourself, ask yourself how you would act were all the world looking at you, and act accordingly. Encourage all your virtuous dispositions, and exercise them whenever an opportunity arises; being assured that they will gain strength by exercise, as a limb of the body does, and that exercise will make them habitual. From the practice of the purest virtue, you may be assured you will derive the most sublime comforts in every moment of life, and in the moment of death.[58]

The man of constant virtue, Jefferson told his young nephew, is the happy man or the man who most often achieves happiness.

Virtue's path to happiness is, however, always full of obstacles and challenges. In a complex world where temptations are continuously thrown in front of men to distract them from the path to true happiness, Jefferson advised the young man to always "do what is right, and be assured that that will extricate you the best out of the worst situations." He continued: "Though you cannot see, when you take one step, what will be the next, yet follow truth, justice, and plain dealing, and never fear their leading you out of the labyrinth, in the easiest manner possible. The knot which you thought a Gordian one, will untie itself before you." There is no self-interest in and nothing to be gained by lying, cheating, and stealing, he insisted:

> Nothing is so mistaken as the supposition, that a person is to extricate himself from a difficulty, by intrigue, by chicanery, by

dissimulation, by trimming, by an untruth, by an injustice. This
increases the difficulties ten fold; and those who pursue these methods, get themselves so involved at length, that they can turn no way
but their infamy becomes more exposed. It is of great importance
to set a resolution, not to be shaken, never to tell an untruth. There
is no vice so mean, so pitiful, so contemptible; and he who permits
himself to tell a lie once, finds it much easier to do it a second and
third time, till at length it becomes habitual; he tells lies without
attending to it, and truths without the world's believing him. This
falsehood of the tongue leads to that of the heart, and in time
depraves all its good dispositions.[59]

Two years later, Jefferson admonished his nephew to "be good," to "be
learned," and to "be industrious," so that he could be "happy within
[himself]." And twenty-one years later, he advised his grandson Thomas
Jefferson Randolph to look inside himself and introspect every now and
then about the kind of man he would like to be. "Be assured," he told the
boy, "that these little returns into ourselves, this self-catechising habit, is
not trifling nor useless, but leads to the prudent selection & *steady pursuit
of what is right.*"[60]

Abigail Adams offered remarkably similar advice to her thirteen-
year-old son, John Quincy, who was living in Europe at the time with
his father, John Adams, and being tutored at home. In 1780, Abigail
wrote an extraordinary letter to her young son, in which she asked him
to ponder his purpose in life. After explaining his moral responsibilities
to the "Great Preserver," to "Society in General," to his "Country," and
to his "Parents," she expatiated at some length about his moral responsibilities to himself:

To become what you ought to be and, what a fond Mother wishes
to see you, attend to some precepts and instructions from the pen
of one who can have no motive but your welfare and *happiness*, and
who wishes in this way to supply to you, the personal watchfulness,
and care which a separation from you, deprives you of at a period of
Life when habits are easiest acquired, and fixed, and tho the advise
may not be new, yet suffer it to obtain a place in your memory, for
occasions may offer and perhaps some concurring circumstances
give it weight and force.

She informed John Quincy that a "knowledge and study of yourself" is one of life's "most usefull Lessons." Indeed, "there is no knowledge so hard to be acquired, nor of more benefit when once thoroughly understood." And yet it was here, she warned her son, "you run the greatest hazard of being deceived." The greatest threat to his moral character and ultimate happiness in life is man's "ungoverned passions." If not controlled by reason, they will "render the possessor unhappy in himself and disagreeable to all who are so unhappy to be witnesses" to raging passions or who suffer their "effects." This is why the "due Government of the passions has been considered in all ages as a most valuable acquisition." And it is why young John Quincy, a boy whose "passions are strong and impetuous," must learn to control them. "Having once obtained this self-government, you will find a foundation laid for happiness to yourself and usefulness to Mankind." Quoting from Alexander Pope's chapter in the *Essay on Man* on "The Nature and State of Man, with Respect to Happiness," Abigail tells her son, "'Virtue alone is happiness below,' and consists in cultivating and improveing every good inclination and in checking and subduing every propensity to Evil."[61]

The actual content of the moral instruction offered by Thomas Jefferson and the Adamses was drawn from the same source. Most educated eighteenth-century Americans derived their ideas about virtue and character formation from the classical Greek and Roman moralists and historians. Franklin's aspiration to achieve moral perfection was derived from Pythagoras and Socrates. For moral instruction, Jefferson advised his nephew Peter Carr to "read Epictetus, Xenophontis, memorabilia, Plato's Socratic dialogues, Cicero's philosophies."[62] Likewise, John Adams told John Quincy that in "Company with Sallust, Cicero, Tacitus, and Livy," his son would "learn Wisdom and Virtue." In 1781, the father told his fifteen-year-old son that he should have "Books of Morals" as his "most constant companions" throughout the "whole Course" of his life. In particular, the elder Adams recommended Jean Barbeyrac's *An Historical and Critical Account of the Science of Morality* (1729), and he always recommended in letter after letter the writings of Cicero and Seneca. The year after John Quincy graduated from Harvard College, his father offered this advice to his son: "you should have some Volume of Ethicks constantly on your Table. Morals, my Boy, Morals should be as they are eternal in their nature, the everlasting object of your Pursuit." In addition to a few modern moralists such as Joseph Butler and Francis Hutchinson, the father recommended to the son the writings of "Socrates and Plato, Cicero and Seneca."[63]

Eighteenth-century Americans understood the importance of moral education and its connection to happiness. They accepted as a fundamental moral tenet the proposition that the good man is invariably the happy man, a view that they learned from their reading of the classical Greek and Roman moralists.

Jefferson, for one, understood that there could be no admixture between happiness on one hand and either amoral or immoral action on the other. "Morals," Jefferson wrote to Maria Cosway, are "of man," and true happiness was connected to virtue. He likewise told J. Correa that the "order of nature" is such "that individual happiness shall be inseparable from the practice of virtue." Happiness was not possible to man, he told Amos Cook, a preceptor at Fryeburg Academy in Maine, "without virtue." In 1819, Jefferson reminded his old friend and former secretary, William Short, that "Happiness is the aim of life," virtue is "the foundation of happiness," and the four pillars of virtue consist in "1. Prudence. 2. Temperance. 3. Fortitude. 4. Justice."[64]

Jefferson's understanding of what virtue is and how one should live by its precepts was complicated and evolved over time, but this much can be said with confidence: he believed, as he wrote in *Notes on the State of Virginia*, that the "first elements of morality," combined with wisdom, were the necessary preconditions for individuals to "work out their own greatest happiness." Indeed, in a letter to Amos Cook, he equated the "wise" man with the "happy man," and both with virtue. Virtue and the "greatest happiness" were, he continued in the *Notes*, attainable by all men, rich or poor, independent of the "condition of life in which chance has placed them." Happiness "is always the result of a good conscience, good health, occupation, and freedom in all just pursuits." For Jefferson, happiness went beyond the individual's immediate self-interested pursuit of it. As a "moral agent," he told Miles King in 1814, men are concerned not only for their own happiness but for that of others as well, particularly for those closest to them. Our experience of it can be increased and intensified when it is shared voluntarily with others "by acting honestly towards all, benevolently to those who fall within our way, respecting sacredly their rights, bodily and mental, and cherishing especially their freedom of conscience, as we value our own."[65]

Virtually all eighteenth-century Americans agreed. In 1728, a twenty-two-year-old Benjamin Franklin announced as one of his "first principles" that "without Virtue Man can have no happiness in this world." In *Poor Richard's Almanack*, Franklin declared: "virtue and happiness are mother and daughter." In one of the most influential pamphlets published during the Revolutionary era, John Adams wrote that all of the great philosophers throughout history—those "sober inquirers after truth, ancient and modern"—have "declared that the happiness of man, as well as his dignity, consists in virtue." In his First Inaugural speech to the American people as their first-ever president, George Washington declared "there is no truth more thoroughly established, than that there exists in the economy and course of nature, an indissoluble union between virtue and happiness." The four pillars of national happiness, he told the Marquis de Lafayette, are "harmony, honesty, industry, and frugality." And in his 1789 letter to America's Episcopal bishops, clergy, and laity, Washington declared, "human happiness and moral duty are inseparably connected."[66]

★ ★ ★

The Declaration of Independence lists the "pursuit of happiness" as an "unalienable right." It does not say that man has a right to happiness, nor does it say that government should define what happiness is. The Declaration says only that individuals have a right to pursue it, which means that individuals should be left free to pursue it.

But how and why is the pursuit of happiness a right? The right to the pursuit of happiness is corollary to the right to liberty. Liberty is a precondition for the pursuit. The freedom to pursue happiness must be recognized as a right, which means identifying and establishing the sociopolitical conditions necessary for all individuals to pursue their own happiness. This is why Jefferson, Adams, and Paine all spoke of happiness in the context of the science of politics and the science of freedom.

But what is the relationship between the individual's pursuit of happiness and the role of government in society? The signers of the Declaration of Independence did not think that the coercive force of government should be used to define, dictate, maximize, satisfy, or guarantee individual happiness. Jefferson was unable "to conceive how any rational being could propose happiness to himself from the exercise of power over others." In

1771, a Massachusetts author calling himself "Scipio" summed up what Americans meant by a right to the pursuit of happiness when he wrote: "That every rational man is the best guardian of his own interest, is so obvious a truth, that one would deem it an affront to the public understanding to suggest it needed so much as a repetition."[67]

The right to pursue happiness is therefore best fulfilled in a certain kind of society with a certain kind of government. What kind or form of government did the revolutionary generation think best promoted the rights of individuals to pursue their happiness? For Jefferson and his fellow Americans, happiness is most easily pursued and attained in a society in which the government's role was limited simply to providing a moral-legal framework in which individuals could be left alone to seek their own happiness as they saw fit—as long as said individuals do not violate the freedom of other individuals to pursue their own happiness. Beyond that government should not go.

"Misgovernment," Jefferson lamented late in life, diverts men from using their "energies" for achieving the proper object of life—that is, "the happiness of man"—and from establishing a "paradise of the whole earth." This is why he was sometimes tempted to suggest "those societies [e.g., of American Indians] which live without government, enjoy in their general mass an infinitely greater degree of happiness than those who live under the European governments." The golden mean between the political anarchism of Native American societies (with all of their vices) and political absolutism of European societies (with all of their vices) was embodied by America's limited constitutional republics, which are "more friendly," Jefferson argued, "to the happiness of the people at large, and especially of a people so capable of self-government as ours" than any other form of government. A government defined by a "noiseless course, not meddling with the affairs of others, unattractive of notice" was the best "mark that society is going on in happiness." It was therefore necessary for American statesmen to "prevent the government from wasting the labors of the people under the pretense of taking care of them" so that the people can "become happy."[68]

The "pursuit of happiness" was the Declaration's capstone right that defines and guides the human experience. To identify, liberate, and protect this right was the great moral achievement of the American Revolution. Jefferson and his fellow revolutionaries understood that the *pursuit* of happiness provides no guarantees, but they also knew that without happiness man's life would be intolerable.

The Stamp, Townshend, Tea, and Coercive Acts violated the colonists' rights to liberty and property, but in the end these laws also violated the Americans' right to the pursuit of happiness. American revolutionaries knew that a free society—one that guarantees to each and every person the freedom and the right to pursue happiness as he defines and seeks it—greatly enhances the possibility of each person's successfully ascending to a life full of happiness and joy.

CHAPTER 8

The Consent of the Governed

*"We hold these truths to be self-evident, that all men
are...endowed by their Creator with certain unalienable
Rights,... That to secure these rights, Governments are
instituted among Men, deriving their just powers
from the consent of the governed."*

*T*he Declaration's first two self-evident truths—equality and rights—
are relatively simple truths that announce the existence of objective
moral principles grounded in the observable facts of human nature. These
two truths are intimately connected and can be summed up as a single
principle: all men have an equal right to govern themselves. The revolutionaries' philosophy of equal rights says that no man is by nature the slave
or the ruler of another. The Declaration's third self-evident truth, which
says—"That to secure these rights, Governments are instituted among
Men, deriving their just powers from the consent of the governed"—is
considerably more complex than the first two truths.

The Declaration's third truth is complex in that it incorporates and
mixes three interrelated claims about government: (1) that the purpose
of government is to protect rights, (2) that governments are necessary to
secure rights, and (3) that the just powers of government are derived from
the consent of the governed. The complexity of the Declaration's third self-
evident truth is compounded by the fact that it is built on several unstated
assumptions, which include the following: (a) that man has rights that
exist prior to the creation of government; (b) that there exists a prepolitical
"state of nature"; (c) that man's rights are insecure in natural society; (d)
that the consent of the governed is a necessary mechanism for establishing
legitimate government; (e) that legitimate political societies are created by

a social contract that defines government's just powers; and (f) that government is a man-made rather than a naturally occurring phenomenon. Unlike the Declaration's first two self-evident truths, which state principles as moral facts (i.e., equality and rights), the third truth indicates human action, which includes individuals *consenting* to and *instituting* governments for the purpose of *securing* rights.

This chapter and the next illuminate the meaning of the two key concepts of the Declaration's third self-evident truth: consent and government. The discussion here focuses on the idea and practice of consent in two contexts: in the broader philosophical context of the seventeenth and eighteenth centuries, and in the political context of the imperial crisis. Chapter 9 examines how the revolutionary generation understood the origin and nature of government.

CONSENT IN THEORY: IT USUALLY BEGINS WITH JOHN LOCKE

The best-known principle of the American Revolution prior to the publication of the Declaration of Independence was the famous battle cry associated with the Stamp Act crisis of 1765: "No taxation without representation." The genesis of America's revolutionary mind can be traced to that year, but surely its principal ideas did not spring up just then out of nowhere. Where did the principle of "no taxation without representation" come from?

The fountainhead of this principle can be traced to three sources: first, to English political and constitutional practice dating back to Magna Carta and earlier; second, to the outpouring of English political writings first published during the Exclusion Crisis (1679–81) and then during and after the Glorious Revolution (1688); and, third, to philosophical ideas developed during the seventeenth-century Enlightenment, particularly in the writings of the "law of nature" theorists, such as Hugo Grotius, Samuel von Pufendorf, Jean-Jacques Burlamaqui, Emmerich de Vattel, and, most especially, John Locke. The theory of consent developed in Locke's *Second Treatise* profoundly shaped the development of the American mind. Like a cultural tsunami, the philosophic ideas that swept over Europe in the seventeenth and eighteenth centuries soon crashed on American shores. These New World provincials drew from this wellspring of ideas from the start of the imperial crisis. The Stamp Act triggered a deep-seated moralism that was latent in colonial culture to rise to the forefront of the American mind. The insurrection of 1765 was the first cause of 1776, but it was also a consequence of seismic shifts that had been taking place in Anglo-American intellectual culture for decades.

From the beginning of the imperial conflict in 1765, colonial America's leading thinkers (as well as scores of newspaper writers and pamphleteers) interpreted what they took to be the unjust actions of the British Parliament through the lens of Lockean consent theory. There is no point in reciting or analyzing the Lockean argument as it was presented in the *Second Treatise* because it was copied and used almost verbatim by eighteenth-century Americans. In fact, the Lockean argument was the colonists' default position from the moment the Sugar and Stamp Acts were announced. A pure Lockean theory of consent had been steadily gaining ground throughout eighteenth-century America, particularly among Protestant ministers, which then culminated in its crystalline presentation in the Declaration's third self-evident truth.

How did the Lockean argument develop in colonial America? The first known use of Locke's ideas in the colonies occurred in 1701, when John Montague, a London representative of several hundred New York landowners, published a pamphlet defending his clients' land claims from the grasping hands of the governor and the provincial legislature. In his *Arguments Offer'd to the Right Honourable Lords Commissioners for Trade & Plantation*, Montague contended that the Crown had no legitimate claim to New York lands held by private settlers who owned the contested land by virtue of having mixed their labor with it or purchased it from Native American tribes (e.g., the Mohawks). Citing Locke, whom he describes as "a very worthy and learned Author," Montague quotes directly from the *Second Treatise* to the effect that a just government "cannot take from any Man any part of his Property without his own consent." Then, paraphrasing Locke, Montague notes that the "great motive and inducement" for individuals "to unite themselves into Politick Societies, and to submit to Government, was the Preservation & Protection of their Properties, and rendering them more certain and secure than they could be in a state of Nature."[1] What is important about Montague's position is that his Lockean philosophy largely explained the lived experience of colonial Americans in the seventeenth and early eighteenth centuries.

In 1744, Elisha Williams, the Connecticut pastor and jurist, openly presented the pure Lockean theory of a social contract grounded on consent in his pamphlet *The Essential Rights and Liberties of Protestants*. The work is a brilliant condensation of the key principles outlined in chapters 1–5 and chapter 9 of Locke's *Second Treatise*. Offering "a short sketch of what the celebrated Mr. Locke in his *Treatise of Government* has largely demonstrated," Williams begins his pamphlet with a thoroughly Lockean discussion of "*the Origin and End of Civil Government*." Virtually replicating *in toto* Locke's discussion of man in the state of nature (but with his own emendations), Williams notes what "Reason teaches," namely, that "all men are naturally equal in respect of jurisdiction or dominion one over another."[2] For Williams, as for Locke, reason first identifies a fact of human life.

The fact of human equality leads to a second fact connected to human nature: man has been given "an understanding to direct his actions," which means he also has a "freedom of will and liberty of acting." Williams identifies three attributes of human nature—reason, equality, and free will—that serve as his philosophic starting point, which can be restated as follows: all men have reason to guide their free will. Williams makes the point this way: "For the freedom of man and liberty of acting according to his own will (without being subject to the will of another) is grounded on his having reason, which is able to instruct him in that law he is to govern himself by, and make him know how far he is left to the freedom of his own will. So that we are born free as we are born rational." Williams induces a core moral principle from these facts: men have moral rights by nature. All men, he notes, have "an equal right to their preservation," which means "to such things as nature affords for their subsistence." The natural rights to life and liberty lead logically to the right of property, which is born of self-ownership:

> And every man having a property in his own person, *the labour of
> his body and the work of his hands* are properly his own, to which
> no one has right but himself; it will therefore follow that when he
> removes any thing out of the state that nature has provided and left
> it in, he has mixed his labour with it and joined something to it that
> is his own, and thereby makes it his property. He having removed it
> out of the common state nature placed it in, it hath by this labour

something annexed to it that excludes the common right of others; because this labour being the unquestionable property of the labourer, no man but he can have a right to what that is once joined to, at least where there is enough and as good left in common for others. Thus every man having a natural right to (or being the proprietor of) his own person and his own actions and labour and to what he can honestly acquire by his labour, which we call property; it certainly follows, that no man can have a right to the person or property of another: And if every man has a right to his person and property; he has also a right to defend them, and a right to all the *necessary means of defence*, and so has a right of punishing all insults upon his person and property.[3]

Following Locke, Williams's moral claims are situated within the context of a metaphorical state of nature, which is that place where there is no civil government.

Williams next quotes Locke verbatim on the inadequacies of the state of nature, which lacks three things: (1) "an established known law received and allowed by common consent to be the standard of right and wrong," (2) "a known and indifferent judge with authority to determine all differences according to the established law," and (3) "a power to back and support the sentence when right, and give it due execution." The state of nature's inadequacies make civilized life impossible because not all men follow nature's moral laws all the time. Thus the state of nature is reduced to a state of war. In order to remedy this untenable situation, men use their reason to figure out that they must bring some kind of order and stability to their common social life. Hence they come together through common consent, and their "reason" teaches them

> to join in society, to unite together into a commonwealth under some form or other, to make a body of laws agreable to the *law of nature*, and institute one common power to see them observed. It is they who thus unite together, viz. the people, who make and alone have right to make the laws that are to take place among them; or which comes to the same thing, appoint those who shall make them, and who shall see them executed. For every man has an equal right to the preservation of his person and property; and

so an equal right to establish a law, or to nominate the makers and executors of the laws which are the guardians both of person and property.[4]

Implicit in Williams's recounting of man's escape from the state of nature is the role played by consent, which is the philosophic linchpin in the transition between the state of nature and the state of political society.

While still living in the state of nature, men, through mutually expressed and shared reason, agree among themselves to give up and transfer to a constitutionally bound government certain natural powers, which are:

> 1st. The power that every one has in a state of nature *to do whatever he judgeth fit*, for the preservation of his person and property and that of others also, within the permission of the law of nature, he gives up to be regulated by laws made by the society, so far forth as the preservation of himself (his person and property) and the rest of that society shall require.

> And, 2. The power of punishing he wholly gives up, and engages his natural force (which he might before employ in the execution of the law of nature by his own single authority as he thought fit) to assist the executive power of the society as the law thereof shall require.

This consent to transfer these powers is and must be universal (those who do not consent are excluded from the new community), and, when agreed upon collectively, it creates a new form of sovereignty—the sovereignty of the people, which is the "fountain and original of all civil power."[5]

The institution of government follows deductively, according to Locke and Williams, from the facts and principles derived from their shared account of human nature. To secure man's rights—rights owned by each individual—is the raison d'être of government. Consent delivered through a social contract is the bridge linking man's fundamental rights (which are insecure in the state of nature) with government, the sole purpose of which is to protect man's rights. The consent of the governed is therefore the necessary principle that grounds the just powers of all legitimate governments. This means that government is not a naturally occurring phenomenon as it was for ancient thinkers such as Plato and Aristotle, but is a man-made artifact because it is based on human agreement and convention.

Locke's theory of consent continued to define how colonial Americans in the 1760s and 1770s thought about questions of political legitimacy and the moral foundations of government. In 1766, Jonathan Mayhew, quite likely New England's most influential minister during the years of the imperial crisis, delivered a powerful and influential sermon at Boston's West Church in which he applied the moral core of the Lockean teaching to the Stamp Act. The aim of Mayhew's lesson was to "express" what he took "to be the general sense of these colonies." At the heart of his representation of American views was the Lockean moral premise that all men are "free-born," which means they "have a natural right" to their own property unless they "have freely consented to part with it, either in person, or by those whom *we* have appointed to represent, and to act for us." Consent was the bridge linking man's natural rights with the actions of government. The right to self-ownership and therewith private property is, according to Mayhew, "declared, affirmed, and secured to us, as we are British subjects, by Magna Charta," and any law that violates that fundamental right is "*ipso facto* null and void." The principle of consent is built into and is an extension of the right to self-ownership, which means that legitimate governments may tax their subjects or citizens only with their express consent or through their representatives. To Mayhew and the Americans, the Stamp tax violated this basic principle, and thus reduced the colonists to a state of "perpetual bondage and slavery." This state of vassalage, he continued, was seen when a people "are obliged to labor and toil only for the benefit of others," or when the fruits of their labor can be "lawfully taken from them without their consent."[6]

For colonial Americans, it was a self-evident truth that, as John Adams said, "the only moral foundation of government is, the consent of the people." Likewise for them, the statement by Benjamin Church in his oration commemorating the Boston Massacre—"That state only is free, where the people are governed by laws which they have a share in making"—was axiomatic.[7] The principle of consent and its relationship to taxation and representation had deep roots in English law. It was common during the 1760s for American newspapers to reprint the classic statements of English rights and liberties, such as Magna Carta (1215), the Petition of Right (1628), Edward Coke's *Institutes of the Laws of England* (1628–44), and the Bill of

Rights (1689) in their arguments against the Sugar, Stamp, and Townshend Acts and the claims of parliamentary sovereignty. In August 1767, the *Boston Gazette* reprinted these seminal documents along with William Molyneux's *The Case of Ireland Being Bound by Acts of Parliament in England, Stated* (1698), which argued against Parliament's authority to make laws for Ireland. The *Boston Gazette* editors then adapted Molyneux's argument (Molyneux was a personal friend of John Locke's) to the present situation in the colonies by simply substituting the word "America" wherever the word "Ireland" appeared. A few weeks later, the *New-York Journal* republished all of this same material from the Boston paper. The crucial concept from Molyneux adapted by the Americans to their situation was that of consent. "Consent only," argued Molyneux and his American fans, "gives human laws their force." The principle of consent is in turn grounded on the self-evident principle (which Molyneux borrows directly from Locke) that "All men are by Nature in a state of Equality, in respect of jurisdiction or Dominion," a principle he thought "stands in Need of little Proof." The fact of human equality implies the moral principle that no man "should be subordinate and subject one to another," which leads to that "Right which all Men, claim, of being free from all Subjection to Positive Laws, till by their own *Consent* they give up their Freedom, by entering into Civil Societies for the common Benefit of all the Members thereof." And from the principle of consent, argued the Americans via Molyneux, "depends the *Obligation* of all *Human Laws*."[8]

Starting with the premise of consent, Molyneux and his colonial admirers then built the scaffolding of their case against parliamentary usurpation by using Coke's defense of traditional English liberties as presented in the great English jurist's *Institutes of the Laws of England*. The principle of consent was built into the very fiber of English common law. It was the birthright of every free-born English subject, they insisted, that men shall not be subject to laws to which they have not given their direct or indirect consent. Drawing on Coke, the *Boston Gazette* and the *New-York Journal* argued that the principles and institutions of the common law apply to America, which means that the Stamp and Townshend Acts were "repugnant to all natural reason and equity." Using the same arguments applied by James Otis in the writs of assistance case, Bostonians and New Yorkers argued that laws against natural reason and equity are laws against law, and thus void.

The moral logic of the American position was clearly marked out in the Molyneux reprints in the two newspapers, which declared with no sense of exaggeration that a people "bound by a Law to which [they] do not consent" are slaves. Consent is the only true and proper source of political legitimacy and obligation. For trans-Atlantic Whigs, there was a clear line to be marked in the sand:

> The obligation of all laws having the same foundation, if *one* law may be imposed *without our consent*, any *other* law whatever, may be imposed on us without our consent. This will naturally introduce taxing us *without our consent*; and this as necessarily destroys our *property*. I have no other Notion of *property*, but a *power of disposing my Goods as I please*, and not as another shall command: Whatever another may *rightfully* take from me *without my consent*, I have no *property* in. To tax me without consent, is little better, if at all, than *down*-right *robbing me.*[9]

The Americans used this Lockean logic time and again during the imperial crisis. It was the core of their argument against Parliament. Indeed, it was the rare American argument that did not use it in some form. Typical was the writer in the *Pennsylvania Gazette* who wrote that Locke, with "much pregnancy of reason, developed the ends for which [men]" left the state of nature and entered into civil society, which was to protect their property—the property men have in their lives, liberties, and possessions. This American Whig declared, quoting from chapter 11 of Locke's *Second Treatise*, that the "supream power cannot take from any man any part of his property, without his own consent." The connection between property and consent was a moral absolute for the Americans. As the pseudonymous "Hampden" wrote from New York: "The chief End of all free Government, is the Protection of Property, from Injuries within and without it." Property, he continued, "*is here used in the Large Sense in which Mr. Locke uses it, as comprehending Life, Liberty, and Estate.*"[10]

Why were the Americans so deeply committed to this Lockean understanding of property and consent? Why were they unwilling to compromise? In part, Locke's reasoning both shaped and spoke to their deepest and most fundamental moral convictions. The American sense of life and the moral constitution that went with it were rooted in a system of beliefs that viewed right and wrong in black and white. Moral action rooted in a defense of the laws and rights of nature was viewed as a moral necessity for American Whigs of the revolutionary generation.

This line of reasoning can be seen clearly in Joseph Warren's Boston Massacre oration, in which he reduced the constitutional issue of Parliament's authority to tax the colonists to its moral common denominator. The Sugar, Stamp, and Townshend Acts, according to Warren, reduced the Americans into "absolute SLAVES," who "have no property of [their] own" that is not subject to the "arbitrary *commands of those* over whom [they] have no controul or influence." This degraded state puts their property "entirely at the disposal of another." Thankfully, the Americans would not succumb, according to Warren, to voluntary abasement:

> Such gross absurdities I believe will not be relished in this enlight-
> ened age: And it can be no matter of wonder that the people
> quickly perceived, and seriously complained of the inroads which
> these acts must unavoidably make upon their *Liberty*, and of the
> hazard to which their *whole property* is by *them* exposed; for, if they
> may be taxed without their consent even the smallest trifle, they
> may also without their consent be deprived of every thing they pos-
> sess, although never so valuable, never so dear.[11]

The Lockean ethos explained the world in terms that made sense to the Americans. The Englishman's moral reasoning and political principles were not just formulaic principles to be trotted out whenever the colonists found them useful. Locke's moral logic cut to the core of the colonists' sense of life; it gave voice to their deepest values and principles; and it also explained and justified the reality of life in America and how it had developed over time.

A few years later and in the wake of the Coercive Acts, Moses Mather, a direct descendant of one of New England's most influential Puritan families, explained to his fellow Americans the philosophic foundations and meaning of the doctrine of consent. In his 1775 *America's Appeal to the Impartial World*, Mather begins by asserting that man's "Free agency" is synonymous with and reliant on his "rational existence," which means that his "powers and faculties, and freedom of enjoying and exercising them," are under the sovereignty of his rational faculties and will. Following Locke and his American students, Mather claims that all men are, morally speaking, entirely self-owning and self-governing; they "hath an absolute property in, and right of dominion" over their "powers and faculties," including the fruits of their mental and physical labors. All men, he noted, stimulated by "self-love" and guided by "reason" in the "free use and exercise" of their various "powers and faculties," have an absolute property claim to whatever they have freely chosen to create, acquire, or trade for. And no man, Mather continued, can be "divested" of his property "but by his own voluntary act, or consent, either expressed, or implied." Likewise, when a man enters into a social compact to create a civil society with rules regulating property and contracts and a government to enforce those rights-protecting rules, he consents explicitly or implicitly to live by the laws created by that government. Consent, then, is the moral-political passkey by which man's individual rights are recognized and protected. In free governments consent is embodied in the institution of political representation, which secures to each man a voice in making the laws that he must live by. The genius of the English system, according to Mather, was to have grounded its constitution and political institutions on "these first great principles of natures dictates," thereby erecting a "system of civil government correspondent thereto." And the core constitutional-political principle of the British government, which extended back in time over five hundred years to Magna Carta, was of course the principle of "no taxation without representation." No man "could be deprived of [his] rights or properties but by [his] own consent in parliament, and no laws could be made, or taxes imposed, but such as were necessary, and in the judgment of the three estates in parliament, for the common good, and interest of the realm."[12]

The principle of consent was at the heart of the Anglo-American moral, political, legal, and constitutional tradition, and it was in defense of this principle that American revolutionaries were eventually forced to take up arms. Thus, for Mather and the American Whigs in 1775, the entire question of the imperial crisis could be reduced to a single point:

> Either the parliament hath no such power over the persons and
> properties of the Americans as is claimed, or the Americans are
> all slaves. Slavery consists in being wholly under the power and
> controul of another, as to our actions and properties: And he that
> hath authority to restrain and controul my conduct in any instance,

without my consent, hath in all. And he that hath right to take one penny of my property, without my consent, hath right to take all. For, deprive us of this barrier of our liberties and properties, our own consent; and there remains no security against tyranny and absolute despotism on one hand, and total abject, miserable slavery on the other. For power is entire and indivisible; and property is single and pointed as an atom. All is our's, and nothing can be taken from us, but by our consent; or nothing is our's, and all may be taken, without our consent.[13]

From the American perspective, Mather's logic was simple and irrefutable. From the perspective of American and British Tories, it was incomprehensible.

The power of Locke's logic and the principles it conveyed via Williams and others were planted deeply and broadly in American soil. In the five-and-a-half decades between 1720 and 1776, Lockean moral and political philosophy was baked into the American psyche. Locke's arguments and those of his best American students were repeated countless times in the colonies, particularly in the years after 1764. It is easy to see how and why a culture that had become thoroughly imbued with these kinds of ideas by the 1760s would respond to the Stamp Act as it did. Psychologically, Locke's philosophy served as a kind of early warning system alerting these Anglo-American provincials to even the slightest threat to their liberties and rights. The genesis of the American mind begins with John Locke.

CONSENT IN PRACTICE: THE IMPERIAL CRISIS

The American Revolution began at a time when the colonists were among the wealthiest and freest people anywhere in the world. They were also loyal subjects of the Crown, and they reveled in their Englishness. However, Parliament's passage of the Stamp Act in 1765 struck the colonists like a thunderbolt. It was a shock to their moral sensibilities, and it crystallized ideas that had been seeping into the American consciousness for several decades.

The colonists were certain that Parliament did not have the authority to tax them for purposes of raising revenue. They assumed their customary rights were protected by the British constitution and its core principle, according to which only their elected representatives could tax them. On a deeper level, American resistance to the Stamp Act and later to the Townshend, Tea, and Coercive Acts was a response to unjust acts of power deemed arbitrary and potentially without limit. The Stamp Act unleashed a torrent of rebuke, much of it in a moral idiom that spoke, remarkably, of tyranny and slavery. The first convulsion of the American rebellion thus did not occur for economic or even for political reasons. It was primarily a *moral* uprising against political legislation passed by the British Parliament. The colonists had every reason, certainly every political and economic reason, to want to resolve this controversy as quickly as possible. Instead, they precipitated first a moral and then a political revolution that would turn the greater Britannic world upside down.

Though the Americans viewed the Stamp Act as unprecedented, they did have a foreshadowing of the coming storm the year before when Parliament passed the Sugar Act, which cleverly cut in half Britain's duty on imported foreign molasses into the colonies. The problem with this new postwar legislation is that it created new enforcement mechanisms, the purpose of which was not to direct trade but to raise revenue to help defray the costs of maintaining a new imperial bureaucracy and an increase in Britain's military presence in America. The Sugar Act was an ominous signal to the Americans. They viewed it therefore with concern and skepticism.

The colonists believed there was a necessary connection between taxation and representation, property and consent. Their Lockean moral logic taught them that what a man has honestly acquired through his own mental and physical labor cannot be taken from him without his consent. They believed this principle to be the most important guarantee of English liberty extending back to the time of Magna Carta and beyond. Furthermore, all Americans agreed with their British cousins that the "Right to legislate is originally in every Member of the Community."[14] It was the core principle of British constitutionalism. The problem was in determining how to extend the principle of consent to a political community of more than a few hundred people living in close proximity to one another. In other words, how does one ensure the consent of the governed given the impossibility of convening all the people all the time?

The great discovery and development of representation by the Saxons in the five centuries before Magna Carta was the uniquely English solution to the problem of converting the individual consent of all into the very practical need for just a few to design just laws. The Americans told themselves time and again throughout the 1760s and 1770s, "Representation is the feet on which a free government stands."[15] It was the foundational principle of the British constitution that united all Britons and all Americans. Tragically, it was also the primary principle that divided them during the years of the imperial crisis.

For trans-Atlantic Britons, property and liberty had been linked as one for centuries. For subjects of the realm, Parliament was their representative body and thus was the only legitimate authority to tax their property. But virtually no one in America presumed that Parliament's authority to tax extended to the colonists' property. For almost 140 years, the colonists had taxed themselves in their local assemblies, which they claimed as a fundamental right and not as a privilege. According to one writer in New York's *Constitutional Gazette*, "it has been the established and unimpeached practice, ever since the foundation of the British Empire in America, for the King to make requisitions for supplies to the provincial representatives, and levy taxes by the authority of the provincial legislatures." The Americans claimed they were prepared to "contribute towards the expenses of the state," but the real question came down to "how they [were] to contribute, whether they [were] to be taxed by their own representatives, or by representatives chosen by the people of Great-Brtiain." From the provincials' perspective, their local assemblies were the equivalent of Parliament with regard to taxes, which meant that only their elected representatives could tax them. But now Parliament was attempting to tax them through the Sugar Act, as the New York Assembly claimed, "upon the subjects *here*, by Laws to be passed *there*." The Americans searched the historical record for a precedent but could find none. History, they insisted, "can furnish" no "Instance of a Constitution to permit one Part of a Dominion to be taxed by another, and that too in Effect, but by a Branch of that other Part."[16]

In a forceful petition sent to the House of Commons in 1764, the New York Assembly claimed a total exemption from parliamentary taxation. The New Yorkers insisted that "the People of this Colony, inspired by the Genius of their Mother Country, nobly disdain the thought of claiming that Exemption as a Privilege.—They found it on a Basis more honourable, solid and stable; they challenge it, and glory in it as their Right." They claimed this right by virtue of being Englishmen but also as a *natural* right: "An exemption from the Burthen of ungranted, involuntary Taxes, must be the grand Principle of every free State.—Without such a Right vested in themselves, exclusive of all others, there can be no Liberty, no Happiness, no Security; it is inseparable from the very Idea of Property, for who can call that his own, which may be taken away at the Pleasure of another?" This right, they continued, is "the natural Right of Mankind." It was established

> in the first Dawn of our Constitution, founded upon the most substantial Reasons, confirmed by invariable Usage, conducive to the best Ends; never abused to bad Purposes, and with the Loss of which Liberty, Property, and all the Benefits of Life, tumble into Insecurity and Ruin: Rights, the Deprivation of which, will dispirit the People, abate their Industry, discourage Trade, introduce Discord, Poverty, and Slavery; or, by depopulating the Colonies, turn a vast, fertile, prosperous Region, into a dreary Wilderness; impoverish *Great-Britain* and shake the Power and Independency of the most opulent and flourishing Empire in the World."[17]

The Americans' concern became outrage a year later with passage of the Stamp Act, which imposed taxes on a variety of legal and commercial documents. The new tax required the colonists to purchase officially stamped paper sent from the central stamp office in London to be sold in the colonies by Crown-appointed local agents. The colonists immediately saw the burden of the new tax: they would now be required to pay stamp fees to conduct the ordinary business of life: for wills and contracts at every stage of a lawsuit, for leases, deeds, diplomas, land grants, mortgages, insurance policies, customs papers, almanacs, pamphlets, and newspapers, and even for dice and playing cards. The stamp tax affected nearly all areas of economic life. And it came with heavy fines for those who violated the law. Even worse, violators would now be tried in admiralty courts without jury trials. More fundamentally, the colonists saw the Stamp Act as an assault on their private property because it taxed them without their consent: if Parliament could levy and collect this tax, there was seemingly no limit to what it might demand in the years ahead.

✳   ✳   ✳

News of the Stamp Act reached America in April 1765. Patrick Henry sparked the American response the following month, when he introduced a series of resolutions in the Virginia House of Burgesses denouncing parliamentary taxation in America. Henry's first two resolutions simply asserted the right of all Virginians to their traditional British liberties, privileges, and immunities as guaranteed by common law and their royal charter. His third resolution announced the principle that taxation and representation were indissolubly linked in the ancient British constitution, calling this principle the "distinguishing Characteristick of British Freedom." The fourth resolution declared that Parliament had no right to legislate for the colonies. Henry's final resolution completed the third: it resolved that the "General Assembly of this Colony have the *only and sole exclusive* Right and Power to lay Taxes and Impositions upon the Inhabitants of this Colony." Attempts to place that power elsewhere, he argued, have "a manifest Tendency to destroy British as well as American Freedom."[18]

The Burgesses eventually dropped Henry's fifth resolution, passing the first four in slightly revised form. (Henry is alleged to have had two even more radical resolutions at the ready in his pocket.) Henry was not finished, though. Adding fuel to his fire, he accompanied his resolutions with something more than a lèse-majesté of the king: "Tarquin and Ceasar each had his Brutus, Charles the First his Cromwell," Henry thundered, and then he crossed the line into treasonous territory when he suggested that he doubted not "that some good American would stand up" to George III "in favor of his country." Interrupted by cries of treason, Henry is alleged to have retorted: "if *this* be treason, make the most of it."[19] It was an electric and unforgettable moment. The young Thomas Jefferson, who attended the House of Burgesses that day, declared that Henry appeared to "to speak as Homer wrote." Years later, Jefferson also noted that the passage of the Virginia Resolves "may be considered as the dawn of the revolution."[20]

Henry's resolutions lit a fuse up and down the Atlantic seaboard. Ironically, though not approved by the Virginia Burgesses, all seven of Henry's resolutions (including the two he did not present) were printed in the other colonies as though the Virginians had in fact passed all of them. The sixth resolution boldly declared that Virginians were not legally obliged to obey laws not passed by their legislature (surely a call for civil disobedience), and the even more radical seventh resolution declared that individuals who supported the right of Parliament to tax the colonies were traitors to the colony of Virginia. From the beginning, the American position that emerged in 1765 was latent with revolutionary intent.[21]

Virtually every colonial assembly followed Virginia's lead by issuing a series of resolutions in response to the Stamp Act as did the continent-wide Stamp Act Congress, all of which bore a remarkable similarity to Henry's first five resolutions. In fact, the colonists responded to the Stamp Act with arguments that would carry them through all the way to the Declaration of Independence. The most interesting characteristic of these statements is that none were concerned with the tax per se. They all opposed the authority of Parliament to tax the colonies in any amount on moral and constitutional principles. The Pennsylvania Resolves declared that "the Constitution of Government in this Province is founded on the natural Rights of Mankind, and the noble Principles of *English* Liberty, and therefore is, or ought to be, perfectly free." The Stamp Act was, according to Pennsylvania legislators, a direct violation of those fundamental moral principles. Likewise, the Massachusetts Assembly declared that there are "certain essential Rights of the *British* Constitution of Government, which are founded in the Law of God and Nature, and are the common Rights of Mankind," and thus the people of the Bay Colony are, the Assembly continued, "*unalienably* entitled to those essential Rights in common with all Men: And that no Law of Society can consistent with the Law of God and Nature divest them of those Rights."[22]

Building on these fundamental moral principles, the Massachusetts legislature went on to declare that the British constitution and the colonial charters guaranteed to all British subjects that "no Man can justly take the Property of another without his Consent: And that upon this *original* Principle the Right of Representation in the same Body, which exercises the Power of making Laws for levying Taxes, which is one of the main Pillars of the British Constitution, is evidently founded." The Pennsylvania, Maryland, Connecticut, South Carolina, and New Jersey resolves all declared that no man can be taxed without his consent as a right of nature and of Englishmen. Translated historically and politically, this fundamental right not to be taxed without one's consent was "Granted by Magna Charta," declared the Maryland Assembly, and "Confirmed by the Petition and Bill of Rights." Finally, the American position was ably summed up in 1765 in "The Declaration of the Stamp Act Congress," which announced that "it is inseparably essential to the freedom of a people, and the undoubted rights of Englishmen, that no taxes should be imposed on them, but with their own consent given personally, or by their representatives."[23]

Collectively, these statements from the colonial assemblies and the Stamp Act Congress express the state of the American mind in 1765. From the very beginning, the rallying cry "no taxation without representation" was a nonnegotiable principle for the Americans as it was based on the fundamentals of their beloved British constitution and, more importantly, on the unalienable rights of nature. From this position, the colonists would not budge over the course of the next eleven years.

The Stamp Act triggered a full-scale debate in Britain and America over the extent of parliamentary authority in the colonies. The specific constitutional issue dividing the Britannic world for the next ten years concerned the authority of Parliament to tax the colonies, and, more generally, its authority to legislate for the colonies, as the Declaratory Act of 1766 put it, "in all cases whatsoever." In either case, the contest between Great Britain and America concerned the twin principles of consent and representation. The principle of consent and its application to government and politics in the form of the slogan "no taxation without representation" was more than just a rallying cry in 1765. To repeat: it was a fundamental principle of the British constitution extending back to Magna Carta, and it was held dearly even by those men who supported the Stamp Act. All Britons, regardless of which side of the Atlantic they lived on, held this principle as a pillar of British constitutionalism. In the end, the divide between mother country and colonies in 1765 came down to one question: Were the colonies represented in Parliament? The answer to this question was not so obvious. One thing, however, was clear to the Americans, said Alexander Hamilton: "The foundation of the English constitution rests upon this principle: that no laws have any validity or binding force without the consent and approbation of the *people*, given in the persons of *their* representatives, periodically elected by *themselves*."[24]

British defenders of parliamentary sovereignty assumed that the colonists were represented in Parliament. The most sophisticated British argument defending the Stamp Act came from its principal author, Thomas Whately, a confidant of Prime Minister George Grenville.[25] At Grenville's urging, Whately quickly wrote and rushed into print his pamphlet *The Regulations Lately Made*, which was a full-throttled defense of both the

Sugar and Stamp Acts. Whately answered those American writers who argued against the Stamp Act and the constitutionality of parliamentary taxation. He made clear that he supported the principal that no Englishman can be taxed without the consent of his representative, which he regarded as a palladium of British liberty. "No new Law whatever can bind us," he declared, "that is made without the Concurrence of our Representatives." But according to the "Principles of our Constitution," he claimed, the colonists *were* represented in Parliament. They may not choose their representatives, but the fact is that "Nine Tenths" of the inhabitants of Great Britain did not have the franchise. Wealthy London merchants and the inhabitants of major cities such as Leeds, Halifax, Birmingham, and Manchester could not vote, while uninhabited "rotten boroughs" such as Old Sarum sent a representative to Parliament. Because of the peculiarities of the British electoral system, the vast majority of Britons did not vote and yet were nevertheless represented in Parliament.[26]

This notion of representation—what was called *virtual* representation—assumed that all Britons everywhere were a single people united as a homogenous whole by common values and interests. It did not matter whether one voted for a representative or not because all laws made by Parliament affected electors and nonelectors in the same ways. All Britons—voters and nonvoters, Londoners and Bostonians—shared a common political heritage that was embodied in the principles of the British constitution. The most celebrated articulation of virtual representation was Edmund Burke's letter to his Bristol constituents in 1774, wherein he argued that Parliament was not a "*congress* of ambassadors from different and hostile interests, which interests each must maintain, as an agent and advocate, against other agents and advocates; but Parliament is a *deliberative* assembly of *one* nation, with *one* interest, that of the whole, where, not local purposes, not local prejudices ought to guide, but the general good, resulting from the general reason of the whole." Under the principle of virtual representation, the role of a legislator was not to *re*-present the views of those who elected him but to deliberate on the interests of the nation or empire as a whole.[27]

Working implicitly with this conception of virtual representation, Whately argued that the colonists were in exactly the same situation as nine-tenths of those Britishers who could not vote. Indeed, there was no fundamental difference between a nonvoting Englishman and an

American. These New World provincials were, by Whately's account, "an important Part of the Commons of *Great Britain*: they are represented in Parliament in the same Manner as those Inhabitants of *Britain* are, who have not Voices in Elections: and they enjoy, with the Rest of their Fellow-subjects the inestimable Privilege of not being bound by any Laws, or subject to any Taxes, to which the Majority of Representatives of the Commons have not consented."[28] For this reason, he argued, the Stamp Act is constitutional precisely because the British Parliament *virtually* represents all Britons everywhere, and thus it is an expression of common consent. Whately had to work very hard to make this claim believable to the Americans.

American Whigs found Whately's argument for "virtual" representation specious. The most impressive American argument against virtual representation was Daniel Dulany's best-selling pamphlet, *Considerations on the Propriety of Imposing Taxes in the British Colonies, for the Purpose of Raising a Revenue* (1765). Dulany, an English-educated (Eton, Cambridge, and Middle Temple) lawyer from Maryland, began his response to Whately by examining the historical relationship between consent, taxation, and representation in the British constitution. Taxation had been throughout British history, he argued, a freely given "gift" time out of mind from the people to their representatives in the House of Commons. The constitutionality of the Stamp Act therefore rested on a single question: "Whether the commons of *Great Britain* are *virtually* the representatives of the commons of *America* or not?" By "what right," Dulany asked, had the British people and their representatives in Parliament to "be munificent at the expense of the commons of *America*?" As a matter of general principle, he countered, it is a "flagrant injustice" to "give property not belonging to the giver, and without the consent of the owner."[29]

Dulany then reconstructed and deconstructed the argument for virtual representation. The problem was that its proponents had not "defined, or precisely explained what they mean by the expression, *virtual representation*." Instead, he argued, they simply asserted it in "fanciful" language as though presumptively true when in fact it was disconnected from reality. As best he could tell, the argument for virtual representation could be reduced to three claims: first, British nonelectors have the capacity to become electors by acquiring freehold property; second, there was an identity of interests between British electors (one-tenth of the British population) and nonelectors (nine-tenths of the British population); and third, nonelectors were secure from oppression because the elected must live by the laws they make. Thus, the argument went, members of Parliament represent all Britons whether they are elected by all of them or not. Dulany summed up what he called the "only rational explanation" for virtual representation this way: "Under this constitution then, a double or virtual representation may be reasonably supposed. The electors, who are inseparably connected to their interests with the non-electors, may be justly deemed to be the representatives of the non-electors, at the same time they exercise their personal privilege in the right of election; and the members chosen, therefore, the representatives of both." Dulany rejected these arguments as little more than a "mere cob web, spread to catch the Unwary, and intangle the weak."[30] He conceded that the flawed concept of virtual representation might apply to the local circumstances of Great Britain, and it might even be a salutary institution there, but it simply could not apply to the American colonies. To do so would be to sanction an absurdity, he argued. The difference between British and American nonelectors was one of kind and not one of degree.

Dulany then offered three reasons why virtual representation could not apply to the colonies. First, it was impossible under the current system for the colonists to become electors to the House of Commons even if they owned the requisite freehold property. Second, there was and could be no identity or harmony of interests between the commons in Britain and in America. They were places and peoples separated by more than three thousand miles of ocean. It may once have been true that there was a harmony of interests between Britons on both sides of the Atlantic, but those days were gone. "There is not that intimate and inseparable relation between the electors of Great-Britain, and the Inhabitants of the colonies," Dulany noted, "which must inevitably involve both in the same taxation." Finally, it was possible and even likely that Parliament could pass tax legislation directed specifically at the colonies (e.g., the Stamp Act) that would not affect the electors in the realm who supported it. In other words, the former "might be oppressed in a thousand shapes, without any Sympathy, or exciting an alarm" in the latter. The conclusion for Dulany was obvious: "the notion of a double or virtual representation, doth not with any propriety apply to the people of *America*," which of course means that "the principle of the *Stamp act*, must be given up as indefensible on the point of representation." The Stamp Act was, therefore, an unjust act of "power" and a violation of the core principles of Britain's ancient constitution.[31]

★   ★   ★

Following the Stamp Act, the colonists developed a different understanding of representation. They assumed that all legitimate government rests on the direct and *actual* consent of the governed, which was built on a tradition of political representation that had deep roots in their colonial past. The provincials combined the ideas of Locke with the reality of their lived experience. Their arguments gave expression to that which had already existed in fact. Almost from the moment the colonies were first founded and then over the course of the next 150 years, the Americans had developed an understanding of representation very different from that of their British cousins. Local conditions unique to the colonies led the Americans to believe that the people "must be represented actually—not 'virtually,'" which meant they must be "consulted in the most particular manner that can be imagined."[32] Ironically, the American view of representation had more in common with a much older, pre-feudal conception of the relationship between constituents and representatives.[33]

The Stamp Act directly threatened the Americans' understanding of consent, which is why they reacted to it with such immediate ferocity. For the colonists, taxes constituted a special form of legislation that required ongoing and direct consent. Because they were not represented in the British Parliament, the colonists did not recognize the right of any political body other than their own legislatures to tax them. Parliament had "no right to tax the Americans any more than they have to tax the inhabitants of France," declared an anonymous writer in the *Massachusetts Spy*. The Americans mocked ruthlessly the idea that "members of the British Parliament" could be "representatives of the whole British Empire." According to the colonists, the principle of virtual representation contradicted the "avowed principles" of true English Whigs, namely, that "Property and residence within the Island, alone [constitute] the right of election." The idea of virtual representation was, according to Benjamin Church, "futile and absurd" and could be taken as nothing more than the "Idea of a political visionary." It was ludicrous, he continued, to suggest that an "*unlettered British Elector*," who was "possessed of a turnip garden," should have the power to "appoint a legislator, to assess the ample domains, of the most sensible opulent *American* planter." Church refused to recognize virtual representatives "in whose nomination or appointment I have no choice."[34]

The great English abolitionist Granville Sharp supported the American position on representation and taxes. In *A Declaration of the People's Natural Right to Share in the Legislature* (printed four times in America during the imperial crisis), Sharp argued that the inequality of representation in Great Britain could provide "no just argument for setting aside the Representation of the people in other parts of the British empire." The fact is that Britain's colonies had no representation in Parliament, including virtual representation. Sharp was one of the few English writers who grounded his theory of representation on underlying moral principles. "No tax can be levied," he argued, "without manifest robbery and injustice where his legal and constitutional Representation is wanting; because the English law abhors the idea of taking the least property from freemen without their free consent." Such a law is "iniquitous," which means that it "can never be made lawful by any authority on earth; not even by the united authority of King, Lords, and Commons." For Sharp, the political-constitutional principle was simple: "In every point of view, the making laws for the subjects of any part of the British Empire, without their participation and assent, is iniquitous, and therefore unlawful." Sharp joined with American Whigs in rejecting the British presumption that the Stamp Act might be unjust but constitutional because it was legal. Sharpe and his American allies argued that the Stamp Act was unconstitutional precisely because it was unjust. His argument is worth quoting at length:

> For if the inhabitants of one part of the empire might determine a
> question, or enact a law, for the peculiar advantage only of that one
> part, though to the manifest detriment and injury of another part,
> without the Representation of the latter, the former part would
> be made judges in their own cause, a circumstance that would be
> literally partial! the very reverse of justice and natural equity, and
> which must, therefore, be esteemed iniquity, even to a fundamental
> maxim, viz. it is iniquitous for any one to be a judge in his own
> cause. Partiality is, therefore, such an abomination in the eye of the
> law, that no power on earth can make it lawful; for "even an Act of

Parliament" (says the learned Judge Hobart, Rep. 87.) made against natural equity, as to make a man judge in his own case,…is void in itself; for *jura naturae sunt immutabilia* [the laws of nature are immutable], and they are *leges legum* [law of laws].[35]

A violation of the Lockean principle of consent and the moral principles on which it rested, the Stamp Act also violated the English constitution's most basic conceptions of justice and the rule of law. For the Americans, it violated every moral, political, and constitutional ideal they held dear. Thus, as one American writer argued, it was "the duty of every loyal subject, of every honest man, to treat the authors, aiders and abettors of such ruinous, illegal and unconstitutional usurpations, as traitors and public enemies."[36]

Faced with this fervid backlash, Parliament repealed the Stamp Act less than a year after it was passed. Still, British politicians could not resist trying to invent new ways to tax the colonies in the succeeding years, forcing the Americans to deepen their views on the nature and meaning of consent and representation. One such response came from Silas Downer of Providence, Rhode Island, who stated with admirable clarity the American case on the role of consent within British constitutionalism:

> It is of the very essence of the *British* constitution, that the people
> shall not be governed by laws, in the making of which they had no
> hand, or have their monies taken away without their own consent.
> This privilege is *inherent*, and cannot be *granted* by any but the
> Almighty. It is a natural right which no creature can give, or hath a
> right to take away. The great charter of liberties, commonly called
> Magna Charta, doth not give the privileges therein mentioned, nor
> doth our Charters, but must be considered as only declaratory of
> our rights, and in affirmance of them.[37]

The principle of consent and all the moral principles contained in it are not given to men as gifts by government but are inherent in man's nature and then are discovered and declared by government.

The following year, Georgia's leading spokesman in the dispute with Great Britain, John Joachim Zubly, wrote and published one of the clearest pamphlets defending the American position against the Declaratory and Townshend Acts. In his *An Humble Inquiry into the Nature of the Dependency of the American Colonies upon the Parliament of Great-Britain and the Right of Parliament to Lay Taxes on the Said Colonies,* Zubly reminded his readers that "taxes are a free *gift* of the people to the crown," which means "the crown hath no right to them but what is derived from the givers." By viewing taxes as a gift, Zubly began with the individual and not Parliament as the primary unit of moral and political value. This means the individual must determine and freely choose why and when the government deserves his endowment and how much. On the principle that "no man can give what is not his own," the British constitution has, with the consent of the people, transferred the taxing authority to the House of Commons. That power, however, is neither unlimited nor universal. It must meet certain conditions, the most important of which is that individuals be actually or virtually represented in the House of Commons. According to Zubly, "it seems to be a prevailing opinion in America, that to be taxed without their consent, and where they are not and cannot be represented, would deprive them of the rights of Englishmen, nay, in time, with the loss of the constitution, would deprive them of liberty and property altogether."[38]

For the Americans, there was no legitimate taxation without representation, and there was no representation without the people's actual consent (direct or indirect). This view was not new. It expressed, systematized, and gave a moral sanction to a reality that had been developing in the colonies since their foundings in the seventeenth century.

✯ ✯ ✯

In addition to the problem of taxation and representation, colonial Whigs used the doctrine of consent in a second important way during the years of the imperial crisis. The theoretical and practical problems first raised by the Declaratory Act forced America's best minds to reconceptualize the nature of the constitutional relationship between the mother country and the colonies. More precisely, American thinkers sought to disconnect any relationship (other than trade) between the colonies and the British Parliament. To that end, in the seventeenth-century political foundings of various American colonies they rediscovered historical laboratories in which to observe the proper legal relationship between the provinces and the mother country. America's most perceptive intellectuals discovered in the original colonial charters decisive evidence that the provinces were built on something like a Lockean social contract that bound the colonies to the mother country through a personal relationship with the king. Two of the most insightful and original American essays in this vein were Richard Bland's *Inquiry into the Rights of the British Colonies* (1766) and John Adams's Novanglus letters (1774–75). Bland and Adams articulated what might be called a disguised Lockeanism, one veiled in the more traditional language of English constitutional jurisprudence.

In his pamphlet, Bland presented the most original American argument on this count to emerge before 1774.[39] He made clear that it would be "in vain to search into the civil constitution of England for directions in fixing the proper connection between the colonies and the mother-kingdom." There was no case in the "ancient laws of the kingdom," he wrote, that could account for the planting of new colonies by private citizens. English emigrants established colonies in America at their own expense in blood and treasure. The new colonies, he noted, were founded by "private adventurers," who "established themselves, without any expense to the nation, in this uncultivated and almost uninhabited country."[40] The colonists were under no obligation to the mother country except those they chose of their own free will.

On what basis, then, were mother country and colonies associated? Bland's answer turned to "the law of nature, and those rights of mankind which flow from it." He thus transformed the historical founding of the colonies into a quasi-Lockean moment, when a company of New World adventurers found themselves in a state of nature, where all men "recover their natural freedom and independence." When such men "unite and by common consent take possession of a new country, and form themselves into a political society," they become members of a new sovereign state separate and distinct from the one they left. These New World settlers had vacated an existing state and settled in a place where there was no state, and hence were temporarily in a state of nature with all of the natural rights that come with it. Most importantly, they were now free to form new governments, which they did based on the consent of those locally assembled. The colonists formed social compacts first among themselves and then as a community with a sitting king in England in the form of their charters. The terms of these new social compacts "must be obligatory and binding upon the Parties." Interestingly, Bland referred to these new social and charter compacts as "constitutions," as the New World equivalents of

"Magna Charta." Ultimately, wrote Bland in his 1764 pamphlet *The Colonel Dismounted*, the American charters gave the colonists the right to govern themselves fully, which they had done "by a constant and uninterrupted usage and custom" for close to 150 years. This prescriptive right was legally recognized in English jurisprudence by Sir Edward Coke's decision in *Calvin's Case*, in which he ruled that colonial charters were compacts by which the king had granted colonists either "the laws of England or a power to make laws for themselves." And just as every liberty-loving Englishman would defend the Magna Carta, so the American colonists would defend their local constitutions against any infringements, including those by their British cousins.[41]

By 1775, the most sophisticated American argument synthesizing Cokean constitutionalism and Lockean social contract theory was that of John Adams in the letters written under the pseudonym "Novanglus."[42] Adams built on Bland's arguments, but he also teased out their more radical implications. The Novanglus letters were a systematic attempt to describe the origins, nature, and jurisdictional boundaries of the imperial constitution. The colonists' political connection to Great Britain and their rights and liberties were derived, according to Adams, from two different sources: "the law of nature and the compact made with the king in our charters."[43] The fact of the matter, according to Adams, is that the colonies were discovered, explored, purchased, settled, and cultivated by free Englishmen who had exercised their Lockean right of free exit and self-government. The colonists did so, as Locke put it, by "withdrawing themselves, and their obedience, from the jurisdiction they were born under, and the family or community they were bred up in, and *setting up new governments* in other places."[44] When a subject left the realm with the king's permission, "he carried with him as a man all the rights of nature," Adams argued. Indeed, English liberties were nothing but "certain rights of nature reserved to the citizen by the English constitution," which cleaved to the colonists when they left England.[45]

The early history of the Plymouth colony provided Adams with an instructive example of how the colonies were founded on the laws of nature:

> The first planters of Plymouth...had no charter or patent for the
> land they took possession of, and derived no authority from the
> English Parliament or Crown, to set up their government. They

purchased land of the Indians, and *set up a government of their own, on the simple principle of nature,* and afterwards purchased a patent for the land of the council at Plymouth, but never purchased any charter for government of the Crown, or the King: and continued to exercise all the powers of government, legislative, executive and judicial, upon the plain ground of an *original contract* among independent individuals for 68 years.[46]

The colonies were first founded through a social compact among freely consenting individuals and then through a second compact in the form of charters, which established a political and personal relationship between the colonists and their king. The charters were to be treated with the same solemnity that Edward Coke had given the Magna Carta—that is, not as a "new declaration" but rather as "declaratory of the principall grounds of the fundamentall Laws of England." The colonists, using terms that might have been borrowed from James Otis's *Rights of the British Colonies Asserted and Proved,* had established their charters in a manner commensurate with the principle *jus dicere* (to declare the law) rather than *jus dare* (to make the law). In other words, their charters declared and embodied the laws of nature.[47]

English laws—statutory or common—did not therefore bind the Americans, excepting those laws to which the colonists had consented (e.g., Parliament's regulation of trade within the empire) and that they agreed to live by. The colonists, Adams said, had a "right by nature" to establish English common law or any other law system in America as long as it was not inconsistent with their professed allegiance to the king. Those who discovered and founded the American colonies could begin tabula rasa, he said, with "eternal reason, and the law of nature" as the basis of their constitutional and legal codes. The first colonists could have "erected in this wilderness a British constitution, or a perfect democracy, or any other form of government they saw fit."[48] From the beginning, the colonies were independent of Parliament and were self-governing realms in their own right. The charters therefore defined the relationship between king and colonists.

This argument from the charters took on a special importance in Adams's mind. By casting the colonists' expatriation from England and first settlement in America in Lockean terms, Adams seemed to be saying that the charters represented an original social contract. In other words, these social compacts were more than *pactum subiectionis*; they were also *pactum societatis*.[49] The bonds that tied individuals together in these new communities were contractual and volitional as opposed to natural and perpetual. Then, in a subtle move, Adams trimmed the colonists' allegiance to the king from one grounded on Coke's quasi-medieval teaching in *Calvin's Case* to one squarely within the radical social-contract tradition of Locke's *Second Treatise*. He summarized his final teaching in this way:

> There is no provision in the common law, in English precedents, in the English government or constitution, made for the case of the colonies. It is not a conquered but a discovered country. It came not to the king by descent but was explored by the settlers. It came not by marriage to the king but was purchased by the settlers of the savages. It was not granted by the king of his grace, but was dearly, very dearly earned by the planters in the labor, blood, and treasure which they expended to subdue it to cultivation. It stands upon no grounds, then, of law or policy, but what are found in the *law of nature*, and their express contracts in their charters, and their implied contracts in the commissions to governors and terms of settlement."[50]

Ingeniously, Adams conflated a historical argument about the founding of the colonies with a theoretical claim about natural rights and consent. In sum, American Whig thinkers were now Lockeanizing their argument against the claims of British imperial officials.

✳ ✳ ✳

The American theory of consent culminated with Tom Paine's incendiary *Common Sense*, published in early 1776. For Paine, the constitutional debate over the imperial constitution was finished. The time had come for the Americans to sever their ties with Great Britain and to establish new governments on the simple principles of nature. Paine thus begins his manifesto with an account of the origins of government. Following in the Lockean tradition, he posits that "Some writers have so confounded society with government, as to leave little or no distinction between them; whereas they are not only different, but have different origins."[51] Paine, more than any other American thinker, drew a radical distinction between society (mostly good) and government (mostly bad). Society, he argued, is a voluntary association produced by man's naturally occurring social passions and virtues and is united by his affections, whereas government is an artificial institution produced by man's wickedness and vices and is united by commands and coercive power.

Man's fallible nature makes government a "necessary evil" for Paine, one that man creates in order "to supply the defect of moral virtue." Cooperating and consenting individuals in the state of natural liberty and civil society eventually find "it necessary to surrender up a part of [their] property to furnish the means for the protection of the rest." Prudence dictates, Paine concludes in good Lockean fashion, that "security being the true design and end of government, it unanswerably follows, that whatever form thereof appears most likely to insure it to us, with the least expense and greatest benefit, is preferable to all others."[52] Protecting man's security, liberty, and property constitutes the end of government for Paine, and the particular form of government best suited to those purposes is one that is small in size and miserly in its expenditures. Paine's theory of government thereby extended Locke's argument by suggesting that government exists solely to promote and protect the freedom associated with man's natural condition.

The phenomenal success of *Common Sense* in America can be explained by the fact that Paine's separation of society and government described an actual social reality being lived by many people in the colonies. This was particularly so in western Massachusetts, where there was no legally functioning government for almost six years, between 1774 and 1780. Paine's view of natural society provided nervous patriots with a positive model of what was possible should they decide to declare their independence from Great Britain, and it calmed the fears of moderates that anarchy and disorder would necessarily follow from the dissolution of the empire.

Finally, *Common Sense* was the first truly revolutionary pamphlet published before the Declaration of Independence. Unlike the pamphlets of Otis, Bland, Dulany, Dickinson, Wilson, Jefferson, and Adams, *Common Sense* was not trapped in the categories of eighteenth-century English jurisprudence, and it did not need to describe the historical conditions of the colonies' first foundings. Instead, Paine begins with a theoretical state of nature that described an extant American frontier life. Paine uses

Locke to describe the actual conditions on the ground; he transports Locke to America and infuses his ideas into the American political discussion, making them part of the language of American political life. From this point forward, Locke's theory of consent would be used to construct new governments rather than dismantle old ones.

CHAPTER 9

Consent and the Just Powers of Government

"We hold these truths to be self-evident, that all men are...endowed by their Creator with certain unalienable Rights,... That to secure these rights, Governments are instituted among Men, deriving their just powers from the consent of the governed."

T he Declaration's third self-evident truth is concerned primarily with the origin and nature of government. Built into its language, logic, and principles are several implicit assumptions drawn from John Locke's political philosophy.

To begin with, the third self-evident truth assumes the existence of a Lockean state of nature, which is that place where there is no government. If governments are instituted to secure rights, then the obvious inference is that there was a time and place before governments were instituted.[1] Further, the third self-evident truth assumes the idea of a Lockean social contract, which is the mechanism by which men leave the state of nature and create governments. If governments are instituted by the consent of those in a state of nature who wish to live under a just government, then the soon-to-be governed must devise some procedure through which to express their consent to create a government. Further still, the third self-evident truth assumes two derivative political principles concerned with the form of government—sovereignty and representation, which are applications of the consent principle. If consent provides the moral foundation of a free government, then its political manifestation will be grounded on the sovereignty of the people and expressed in their ongoing representation in government. Finally, the third self-evident truth assumes a view of the powers of government, which must be shaped by the purposes of government. If the sole or primary end of government is to protect the rights of individuals, then its powers must be commensurate with that end.

The best way to access the meaning and implications of the Declaration's third truth is to subject its implicit assumptions and explicit principles to a cluster of questions. First, why did American revolutionaries think that men could not live in a state of natural liberty without government? Second, how did revolutionary Americans think they should move from the state of nature in which they found themselves in 1776 to a state of civil society with a just government? Third, what form of government is implied by the Declaration's related principles of equality, rights, and consent? Finally, how much political power did the revolutionary generation give to their new governments?

THE STATE OF NATURE AND CONSENT

Why did American revolutionaries think that government was necessary to securing their rights? Why did they think that men could not live permanently in a state of natural liberty? Their answer was simple: they did not think it possible to have a *civil* society over time where there was no government.

In Enlightenment literature this prepolitical state was known as a state of nature. Locke's state of nature, described in his *Second Treatise* as one of radical, arbitrary subjectivism, is inherently unstable. On one hand, the "*state of nature* has a law of nature to govern it, which obliges everyone: And reason, which is that law, teaches all mankind, who will but consult it, that being all equal and independent, no one ought to harm another in his life, health, liberty, or possessions." The problem is that not all men are able or willing to "consult" or follow nature's law. Thus, "though the law of nature be plain and intelligible to all rational creatures," Locke argues, "yet men being biased by their interest, as well as ignorant for want of study of it, are not apt to allow of it as a law binding to them in the application of it to their particular cases." The fact is that some men are not rational (or, at least not all of the time), some do not study the law of nature, some are "quarrelsome and contentious," and some err in their study of nature's law or misapply it.[2]

In his Massachusetts election sermon, Jonas Clark strongly echoed Locke's ideas, telling Governor John Hancock and state legislators that "reason teaches the propriety, convenience points out the advantages, and all the social affections concur to urge the importance of civil government." The problem, however, is that these arguments appeal only "to the wise, the benevolent, or judicious" and thus are a "feeble support to the peace and order of society." The sad fact is that reasoned arguments in support of justice and peace do not appeal to the "lawless lusts of vicious, aspiring, or blood-thirsty men." Every society contains men who are grasping, avaricious, envious, and indolent, all of whom seek to take advantage of their fellow citizens. This is why "*Necessity alone*" brings men together in society and "gives rise to civil government."[3]

Men are also fallible and prone to interpret the law of nature through their own subjective interests. They are not good judges in their own causes. "In whatever situation we take a view of man," wrote "Democraticus" of Virginia, "whether ranging the forests in the rude state of his primeval existence, or in the smooth situation of polished society; wheresoever we place him—on the burning sands of *Africa*, the freezing coasts of *Labrador*, or the more congenial climes of the temperate zones—we shall everywhere find him the same complex being, a slave to his passions, and tossed and agitated by a thousand disagreeing virtues and discordant vices." Even Benjamin Church, the part-time patriot and part-time traitor, argued in his Boston Massacre commemorative oration that in the state of nature men's lives are defined by a "SENSE of their wants and weakness." Man in the state of nature was "actuated by a savage ferocity of mind, displayed in the brutality of his manners," and the "necessary exigencies of each individual naturally impelled him, to acts of treachery, violence, and murder."[4] The state of nature for Locke and his American students was a metaphor for human nature: fallible and flawed, man is not fit to live in freedom and peace without a system of enforceable justice.

Not all Americans, though, used the pure Hobbesian or even the Lockean version of the state of nature. Some described what might be called an Edenic, before-the-Fall state of nature. Thomas Dawes, who also gave an oration commemorating the Boston Massacre, claimed "descriptions" of "primeval man" in his "Arcadian state" are "numerous." Man in Dawes's prepolitical state was a simpler being living in a simpler time, who had "but few desires," and these were controlled by the "works of virtue."

Man's passions in the Edenic state of nature served a good end: they "were as the gales of their own Eden—enough to give a spring to *good* actions—to keep the waters of life in motion without inducing storm and whirlwind." They were guided by reason "to acquire, secure and enjoy all possible happiness." Over time, during the "morning of man," the wise patriarchs of man's natural state met under "some aged oak" and with benevolence of heart explained to each other their "misunderstandings," and "charity and peace kissed each other." Such a state could not and did not last, though. Given that man is neither omniscient nor infallible, "misunderstandings" naturally arose, explained Dawes, which were "quarrels in embrio." Over time, man's worst passions were unleashed, and "depravity grew enraptured with strife."[5]

Others, such as the pseudonymous "Spartanus" from New Hampshire, applied a Christianized state of nature to American circumstances:

> In the days of Adam and Noah, every man had an equal right to
> the unoccupied earth, which God said he had given to the children
> of men. The whole world was before them, there was much more
> land than they could occupy or enjoy.—Each man had a right to
> occupy new land where he pleased, and to take wild beasts by hunt-
> ing. This was what civilians call a state of nature. In this state every
> man had a right to enjoy himself, a right to his enclosure, to what
> he took in hunting, and to feed his flocks where he pleased, so that
> in any of these, he did not interfere with any pre-occupant. In such
> a state every man had a right to defend himself and repel inju-
> ries, as he thought best….Every man had an equal right to judge
> between himself & his neighbour, and to do that which was right in
> his own eyes.[6]

In the end, Dawes's and Spartanus's state of nature suffered from the same fatal flaw as that of Hobbes and Locke. Missing was a neutral arbiter to settle disputes among individuals. And the problems of the natural state were exacerbated by the fact that men—including moral and rational men—have incomplete knowledge and sometimes make mistakes, which leads to disagreements and sometimes to conflict. When and where individuals are judges in their own causes, conflict will inevitably arise, leading eventually to violence and sometimes to a war of some against some. As

Dan Foster from Connecticut put it in his remarkable 1774 essay on civil government:

> I THEREFORE conclude, that every man in a state of nature, or where no civil government is yet erected, hath an individual and most just right to an equivalent to any injury that shall be done his person, or any invasion and seizure of his property; and that wheresoever he shall find it, in the possession of him who did the wrong, and whensoever he shall have an opportunity, to take it to himself. And all the mischief and bloodshed, if there should be any, while the injured man defends his person, or is taking to himself his equivalent for the seizure of his estate or property, must forever lye at the door of him who did the injury.[7]

Foster clearly describes the central problem of that place where there is no government, including those pre-Fall states described either in Genesis or in Jean-Jacques Rousseau's *Discourse on the Origin and Foundations of Inequality among Men*. In the state of nature, men are bound to come into conflict.

☆   ☆   ☆

The idea of a state of nature was not a fiction or a hypothetical construct for American revolutionaries. It described their social reality and explained much of their lived experience throughout the colonial period. As long as there was an American frontier, there would be something like a state of nature along the western boundaries of the provinces or in those places where the long arm of British or provincial law did not extend.

Consider the towns of western New Hampshire along the eastern shore of the Connecticut River—towns such as Hanover, home of Dartmouth College. Much of this area was subject to disputed land claims between New York and New Hampshire during the middle decades of the eighteenth century. The former royal governor of New Hampshire, Benning Wentworth, had incorporated all of these new towns (beginning in 1749) pending resolution of the competing land claims, but with the passage of the Declaration of Independence everything was thrown into legal and political chaos. The situation was compounded by the fact that many residents of the western towns did not recognize the legitimacy of the revolutionary assembly then running the colony's affairs. After July 4, 1776, there was "no legal power subsisting in the Colony," which meant, certainly in the eyes of the frontiersmen, that sovereign power was "still in the hands of the people." The people of the border towns along the Connecticut River now claimed the authority, as the author of a "Public Defence" put it, "to look out for themselves, and assert their natural rights and privileges in common with their brethren in the American states." An author writing as "The Republican" observed, "the people of the different colonies slid back into a state of nature, and in that condition they were to begin anew."[8]

The following year, a convention of the Connecticut River towns told the state's revolutionary assembly that the people living in the territory granted by former Royal Governor Wentworth were now "unconnected with the former Government of New Hampshire or any other incorporated State as to any compact of theirs, or any Grant or charter whatever, and are so far reverted to a state of nature." Finally, rejecting the authority of both the Crown and New Hampshire's revolutionary government, a writer calling himself "Republican" argued that the residents of the Connecticut River valley had "in point of social compact" reverted "to a state of nature." Not all of these river Lockeans believed they were in a pure state of nature. The writer of the "Public Defence" did not think that the publication of the Declaration released the Americans from all political ties. He asked: "*Did they revert to a State of nature?*" His answer: "*Not wholly so.*" After the king's colonial authority ended, the American "*people made a stand at the first legal stage, viz. their town incorporations.*" In other words, government still existed at the town level. The problem was that the towns were in a state of nature relative to each other. Eventually, they would have to incorporate with a larger state in order to escape that state of nature.[9]

Even more confused were the land and political claims over the territory west of the Connecticut River (an area that would later become the state of Vermont). In the years between 1763 and 1777, this territory was contested by competing claims from New Hampshire and New York and was thus governed by no one. Strictly speaking, it was a state of nature. According to Samuel Williams in his highly regarded *The Natural and Civil History of Vermont* (1794), the residents of the Vermont territory preferred to live with no government than to be absorbed into the colony or state of New York. For well over a decade, the "situation of the inhabitants…seems to have approached nearly to what has been called by some, a state of nature." Williams described life in the Vermont territory in terms that would have met Locke's definition: a "large number of people were scattered over a large tract of country, in small settlements, at a great distance from each other, without any form of government, any established laws, or civil officers."[10] In 1777, Vermonters formed the Vermont Republic, under which they lived until 1791, when they were admitted into the Union as the fourteenth state.

And it was not just frontier communities that seemed to be in a Lockean state of nature. With the passage of the Coercive and Prohibitory Acts in 1774 and 1775, the settled colonies reverted to a condition that could have been so described. In his *Summary View of the Rights of British-America* (1774), Thomas Jefferson suggested that the actions of Parliament in suspending the New York legislature in 1767 and passing the Massachusetts Government Act of 1774 had reduced the colonies "to a state of nature." The Massachusetts Government Act, in particular, abrogated the colony's governing charter, suspended its legislature, forbade local town meetings, and substituted a military government under General Thomas Gage. Massachusetts Patriots responded by essentially shutting down all extant royal government functions in the colony by pressuring sheriffs, judges, and juries either to resign their positions or to not enforce the law. As a result, courts were unable to conduct business and it was impossible to form juries for trials. At the first Continental Congress in September 1774, Patrick Henry told his fellow delegates: "Government is dissolved....We are in a State of Nature." Even General Gage was forced to admit, "Civil government is near its end, the courts of justice expiring one after another." In October 1774, James Warren, a leader of the Boston Whigs, wrote to Adams, then in Philadelphia: "It can be no longer a question whether any People ever subsisted in a State of Nature. We have been and still remain in that Situation."[11]

In December, Adams, back in Massachusetts, confirmed Gage's portrait of the state of affairs there. "We are, in this province," he wrote, "at the brink of a civil war": "We have no Council, No House, No Legislative, No Executive. Not a Court of Justice, has sat Since the Month of September. Not a Debt can be recovered, nor a Trespass rebufed, nor a Criminal of any Kind, brought to Punishment." In January 1775, three months after his letter from Warren and three months before the battles of Lexington and Concord, Adams wrote to a British correspondent, explaining that, in Massachusetts, "four hundred thousand people are in a state of nature." The province, he added, was without any legally functioning government.[12]

Remarkably, there would be no legally recognized government in Massachusetts for six years, from 1774 to 1780. Some residents of Massachusetts, particularly those living at its western end, announced their preference for no government (at least temporarily) than to have either a despotic government or even an illegitimate republican government. These independent and sometimes rebellious inhabitants were preternaturally mistrustful of *all* central government, not just royal government. By long tradition, they were accustomed to mostly governing themselves at the local town level. In 1775, the town of Pittsfield sent a petition to the province's temporary and extralegal revolutionary assembly, declaring: "We have been led to wish for new previleges which we still hope to obtain, or remain so far as we have done for some Time past in a State of Nature." They much preferred their current situation to being ruled either "with a rod of Iron" or even by their "antient Mode of Government." Since the abolition of a legally functioning government in the province, they claimed to live "in peace, Love, safety, Liberty & Happiness," and they were content to stay in that situation until "the formation of a fundamental Constitution as the Basis and ground work of Legislation." Despite rumors back east, the residents of Berkshire County were not anarchists. They understood the "destructive nature of Tyranny & lawless power, & the absolute necessity of legal Government to prevent Anarchy & Confusion."[13] These hardscrabble, yeoman farmers were Lockean purists. They wanted a constitution and a functioning government, but only one grounded on the moral rights of nature, individual sovereignty, a social contract, and the full consent of the people.

In response to the claims of Pittsfield and Berkshire County, the eastern political establishment (all of whom were revolutionaries) enlisted William Whiting, a resident of Berkshire County, to report on the state of affairs there. His objective was to persuade these farmer-legislators that their state of nature was unsustainable and that they still owed political allegiance to the majority of their fellow citizens in Massachusetts. Whiting used a more conservative reading of Locke against the radical libertarian Lockeans of Berkshire County. First, he drew a distinction between a "state of nature" and a state of "civil society." Western Massachusetts was not in a state of nature, he argued, but in a state of civil society even though an extra- or nonlegal government governed it. The Declaration of Independence may have rendered obsolete the province's existing royal government, but it did not "annihilate or materially affect, the union or compact existing among the people." The inhabitants of Berkshire County were still obliged "to obey the rules, and orders prescribed by the major part of the society," as it makes laws "for the good of the whole," even if the state has not yet formed any "particular constitution, mode, or form of government whatever." They cannot be "justified in withdrawing their allegiance, or refusing to submit to the rules and orders of the society."[14] Whiting then drew the intellectual sword on the Berkshirites: if they were not currently a part of the civil society of Massachusetts, then they could have no say in the forming of its future constitution and government. Eventually, both sides came to terms after they agreed to establish a process for creating a constitution grounded on a Lockean theory of consent and sovereignty.

Back in New Hampshire, the contest between the defiant river towns and the revolutionary assembly eventually ended in accommodation very much as it did in Massachusetts. The radical Lockeans of the western frontier insisted that the current relationship between the grant towns and the state government was "founded in force and compulsive power, and not in compact and agreement." In the wake of the Declaration of Independence, the extant government in New Hampshire was "null and void, and therefore, there being no compact or agreement of the People whereby they became united" with either New Hampshire or New York, they now "reverted to a State of nature as to Government, and stand entirely unconnected to them." The river radicals' options were twofold: they could either unite with an existing state, or they could create "a new and distinct State." Some radicals wanted to create a new state.[15]

Timothy Walker, a member of the state council, responded to the Lockean frontiersmen by telling them that their core principle, which "is the basis of [their] whole superstructure"—that is, "that the Declaration of Independence dissolves all political relations and connections"—was false and dangerous. Should they admit this principle as "true in theory, but also carried into practice," the whole edifice of American independence, he argued, "will be laid prostrate, jumbled into a huge heap of sand, without any cement to hold it together." Walker reminded the westerners that in each of their communities was a minority of fellow residents who wished to remain connected to the state of New Hampshire. How and why, he asked, would these minorities be compelled to obey the majorities of their tiny-town republics? Walker feared that these Lockean republics along the river, rather than escaping the state of nature, would return to it with a vengeance. They could expect, he concluded, "another Civil War."[16]

✶   ✶   ✶

American revolutionaries were not anarchists. They all believed the state of nature is a "state of mere anarchy" and a "state of perpetual war," where there is "no security, or social happiness." According to Josiah Quincy, regular government is necessary in order to preserve "private property and personal security." Without a single, neutral arbiter to resolve disputes among individuals on the basis of settled and known laws universally recognized as common to all, the right of individuals to defend themselves and to prevent what they consider to be designs against their lives, liberty, and happiness would result in a state of nature more like the one Hobbes described in *Leviathan*—that is, a state of war, which reduces human life to being "solitary, poor, nasty, brutish, and short."[17]

In his *A Short Essay on Civil Government*, Dan Foster assumed that he was speaking for all Americans in asserting what he took to be a common truism: "a people cannot live in society without civil government of some kind and form or other." Likewise, John Joachim Zubly in his 1775 essay on *The Law of Liberty* summed up a view held by virtually all American Whigs *and* Tories: "Wherever there is society, there must also be law; it is impossible that society should subsist without it. The will, minds, tempers, dispositions, views and interests of men are so very different, and sometimes so opposite, that without law, which cements and binds all, every thing would be in endless disorder and confusion." Where there is no civil government for the "preservation of peace, the guard of liberty, the protection of property and the defence of life," warned Jonas Clark, the result is predictable: "that anarchy, confusion, blood and slaughter, waste and destruction, would soon take place in the earth....and the longest sword must quickly determine the fate of mankind." Continental Army chaplain John Hurt likewise described the state of nature to Virginia troops then stationed in New Jersey in terms they were unlikely to forget:

The miseries of the state of nature are so evident that there is no
occasion to display them; every man is sensible that violence, rapine
and slaughter must be continually practised where no restraints are
provided to curb the inordinancy of self-affection. To society then
we must owe our security from these miseries, and to a wisely constructed and well regulated government we must stand indebted for
our protection against those, who would encroach upon the equal
share of liberty which belongs to all, or would molest individuals in
the possession of what is fairly appropriated, or justly claimed.[18]

Throughout the 1760s and 1770s, American Whigs up and down the
Atlantic seaboard quoted a well-known passage from Locke's *Second
Treatise*, in which, in summary, the Englishman established three necessary
preconditions and loci of power for a free and just society that are absent
from the state of nature: first, objective laws that are established, settled,
and known; second, impartial judges committed to objective law; and, third,
the execution of objective laws.[19]

In order to overcome and escape the problems associated with the
state of nature, men must establish and enforce common rules of justice,
and they must find a way to secure peace and protection. To that end, they
must design and build an artificial institution known as government. In the
words of Joseph Warren, civil government "hath its origin in the *weakness* of
individuals, and hath for its end, the *strength* and *security* of all." Benjamin
Church described the movement from the state of nature to the state of
civil society in these terms: "The miseries of mankind thus proclaiming
eternal war with their species, led them probably to *consult certain measures*
to arrest the current of such outrageous enormities."[20] Building certain
kinds of social and political institutions was therefore necessary to overcome the weaknesses of human nature. But the theoretical and practical
problems raised by man's attempt to leave this state of social entropy were
innumerable. Thus, to fully understand the Declaration's third self-evident
truth, more precise questions must be asked and answered.

How, for instance, did revolutionary Americans think societies of free,
autonomous, and rights-bearing individuals move from a state of nature to
a state of government, from a state of absolute freedom to a state of ordered
freedom? What did American constitution-makers think individuals consent to when they join with others to create constitutions and governments?

Why did they think free individuals would voluntarily submit to the compulsions of government? By what authority does government bind men with coercive laws? In sum, how did American revolutionaries address the perennial problem of political obligation?

These are hard questions to which American revolutionaries devoted considerable thought, particularly in the years just before and just after 1776. Although their philosophic teacher, John Locke, provided them with much wisdom in identifying the moral foundations of a free society and the motives for escaping the state of nature, he provided little to no guidance on the nature and terms of the kind of social contract that moves groups of individuals from the state of nature to a free and just society. In the *Second Treatise*, Locke is enigmatic in explaining both the substance and process by which the social contract is formed, particularly when men have dissolved one government and seek to create a new one. In such a state, Locke says, "the people are at liberty to provide for themselves, by erecting a new legislative, differing from the other, by the change of persons, or form, or both, as they shall find it most for their safety and good."[21] Locke's advice was largely worthless to American revolutionaries, both theoretically and practically.

With the signing of the Declaration of Independence, Anglo-Americans found themselves in a Lockean state of nature without a Lockean solution to escape it and advance to a state of civil society. American revolutionaries were therefore forced to develop theoretical and practical devices to help them move from one state to another. The freemen of Lexington, Massachusetts, saw the problem and the solution in purely Lockean terms:

> It appears to Us, 'That, in emerging from a State of Nature, into a State of well regulated Society, Mankind give up some of their natural Rights, in order that others, of greater Importance, to their Well-being, safety & Happiness, both as societies & Individuals, might be the better enjoyed, secured & defended:—
> 'That a civil Constitution or Form of Government, is of the Nature of a most sacred Covenant, or Contract, entered into by the Individuals, which form the Society, for which such Constitution, or Form of Government is intended, whereby the[y] mutually and solemnly engage to support & defend each other, in the Enjoyment of those Rights, which they mean to retaine.'[22]

The American conception of a social contract was developed over the course of fifteen years in response first to the imperial crisis and then to the condition in which they found themselves after the publication of the Declaration of Independence. Remarkably, not only America's best thinkers and statesmen but ordinary Americans of all social descriptions—farmers, cordwainers, mechanics—engaged in a serious national conversation about how to create new constitutions and governments via a social contract.

THE SOCIAL CONTRACT AND CONSENT

The idea of a social contract provided American revolutionaries with the means by which order would emerge from disorder. According to Locke and his American students, a social contract was made operative through the principle of consent.[23] These two principles are integrally connected. "The first steps, in entering into society and toward the establishment of civil government among a people," according to Reverend Jonas Clark, "is the forming, agreeing to, and ratifying an original compact, for the regulation of the State, describing and determining the mode, departments and powers of government, and the rights, privileges and duties of the subjects." The creation of civil society and civil government through these mechanisms is a process, which Benjamin Church described in Lockean terms:

> Men then began to incorporate; subordination succeeded to independence; order to anarchy; and passions were disarmed by civilization: Society lent its aid to secure the weak from oppression, who wisely took shelter within the sanctuary of law.
>
> Encreasing society afterwards exacted, that the tacit contract made with her by each individual at the time of his being incorporated, should receive a more solemn form to become authentic and irrefragable; the main object being to add force to the laws, proportionate to the power, and extent of the body corporate, whose energy they were to direct.
>
> Then *society* availed herself of the sacrifice of that liberty, and that natural equality of which we are all conscious superiors and magistrates were appointed, and mankind submitted to a civil and political subordination. This is truly a glorious inspiration of reason,

by whose influence, notwithstanding the inclination we have for independence, we accept controul, for the establishment of order.

Church makes clear that some kind of explicit or "solemn form" of social agreement is required to move men from a natural society to a state of civilization, which in turn necessitates the "establishment of order." The process was achieved in America through the "inspiration of reason."[24]

Locke's social contract theory was a central component of the Americans' philosophic arsenal during the entire Revolutionary period. For the Americans, though, the idea of a social contract was not a fiction born in the mind of an English philosopher. It was not a mythical event that took place in an imaginary place or imagined past. It was real. As Oliver Wolcott, a signer of the Declaration from Connecticut, remarked, the Americans intended to provide "an instance Real not implied or Ideal of a Government founded in Compact Express and Clear." Levi Hart, also of Connecticut, contended that "human society is founded originally in compact, or mutual agreement." The social compact, according to Hart, "implieth certain rules and obligations which neither of the parties may violate with impunity." An unknown writer in Philadelphia defined a civil society as "a number of proprietors of land within certain limits, united by compact or mutual agreement for making laws, and appointing persons to execute those laws for their common benefit." All lawful government, he continued, "is founded in compact."[25]

Locke summarizes his teaching on how and why men leave the state of nature to join in civil association and form governments in chapter 9 of the *Second Treatise*. The logic of his argument works this way: the doctrine of consent rests on the principle of sovereignty; sovereignty rests on the principle of individual rights; rights rest on the principle of man's metaphysical equality and independence, which says that each individual has the means (i.e., the rational faculty and the free will) and thus the right to govern himself. Locke's argument appealed to the Americans because it gave philosophic expression to their lived experience.

The Americans' obsession with the Lockean principle of consent as the source of political authority, obligation, and legitimacy can be seen in Massachusetts over a fifteen-year period, where the connection between consent and the legitimate government was worked out with great clarity. In 1765, the *Boston Gazette* published an extraordinary letter signed by none other than the pseudonymous "John Locke" and quoting verbatim from the English philosopher's chapter on conquest in the *Second Treatise*:

> No government can have a RIGHT to obedience from a people, who have not *freely consented* to it, which they can never be supposed to do, till either they are put in a full state of *liberty* to choose their government and governors, or at least till they have such stand-ing laws to which they have by *themselves* or their *representatives given their consent*, and also, till they are allowed their due *property*, which is so to be *proprietors* of what they have, that no body can take away any *part* of it without their *consent*, without which men under any government are not in the *state of freedom*, but are *direct slaves*, under the force of war. The nature of *property* is, that without a man's own consent it cannot be taken from him.

This was a stunningly radical statement in the context of 1765 because it brought into question not only the legitimacy of the Stamp Act but also the legitimacy of all governments everywhere. Likewise, eight years later in 1773, the inhabitants of Mendon, Massachusetts, passed the fol-lowing resolve: "That all just and lawful Government must necessarily originate in the free Consent of the People." In 1778, as Massachusetts was desperately attempting to create a constitution for the state, the resi-dents of Essex County defined political liberty as "the right every man in the state has, to do whatever is not prohibited by laws, TO WHICH HE HAS GIVEN HIS CONSENT." And finally, the meaning of the Declaration's understanding of consent was perfectly summed up by and embodied in the Massachusetts Constitution of 1780, which announced: "The body politic is formed by a voluntary association of individuals. It is a social compact, by which the whole people covenants with each citizen, and each citizen with the whole people."[26] The purpose of this social compact is to exchange allegiance and obedience on the one side for protection and peace on the other.

American thinking on the subject can be summed up rather simply: Sovereignty precedes consent, consent precedes compact, compact precedes obligation, and obligation precedes government. Men agree to obey the laws made by their government because they have voluntarily consented to obey it. They have promised to themselves and to each other to obey it because they see it as in their rational self-interest to do so. "Consent only," wrote the editor of the *Boston Gazette* in 1767, "gives human laws their force."[27] This agreement or social contract establishes a relationship not between rulers and ruled but between sovereign individuals, who voluntarily agree with each other on how they shall govern themselves as a civil society. This principle was a core ingredient of America's revolutionary mind.[28]

*   *   *

Revolutionary Americans defined the consent necessary to complete a social contract by two characteristics: first, it must be unanimous, and, second, it must be enlightened. They grounded the unanimity of consent on the moral premise that all men are self-owning and self-governing, which means that all men who choose to live in this new civil society under a rights-protecting government must directly consent to do so, and they must subsequently obey the laws they have agreed to live by. Those who refuse their consent to join this new political society are, by definition, alien to it. Consent that is not unanimous would mean that some men would have unequal and unjust power over others.

American revolutionaries also thought that the kind of consent necessary to create a free and just society must be enlightened. The source of American republicanism, noted Thomas Dawes, "is our laws of *Education*." In a republican government "where the *people* fill all the branches of the sovereignty, *Intelligence* is the life of Liberty." The strongest safeguard for liberty in a constitutional republic is that "*learning* which is necessary" for each American to have the "knowledge" required to understand his constitution. Only those who have knowledge of the moral rights of man as well as the difference between the just and unjust powers of government can actually give the kind of enlightened consent that is the necessary precondition for establishing a free government. "An *elective despotism* was not the government we fought for," Jefferson declared in his *Notes on the State of Virginia*. Fortunately, the discovery of the moral rights of nature made government by consent more possible. "All eyes are opened, or opening, to the rights of man," Jefferson wrote at the end of his life. "The general spread of the light of science has already laid open to every view the palpable truth, that the mass of mankind has not been born with saddles on their backs, nor a favored few booted and spurred, ready to ride them legitimately, by the grace of God."[29]

To *what* precisely do men consent in the original social contract? What are its terms and conditions? What do individuals give up and what do they gain in the transition from the state of nature to that of civil society?

At a minimum, individuals consent to three things: first, they all agree to renounce their right to execute the primary law of nature—that is, the law of self-preservation and the corollary right to self-defense, unless their life or property is in imminent danger; second, they agree to respect the rights of their fellow citizens; and third, they agree to live by the rights-protecting laws determined by their newly created legislatures. Connecticut's Dan Foster described the social transaction this way:

> In a state of nature, each individual man hath a just right to defend
> his own person against all assaults, and to repel force with force,
> and to secure his person from any injury that may be offered to
> it. But a civil state being entered into, and civil rulers chosen, and
> invested with power and authority to make and execute laws for the
> defence and security of every man's person who belongs to the state;
> each individual man has no longer a right inherent and personal, to
> defend his own person, and to resist force with force, when he shall
> be assaulted and violence offered to his person. This right to defend
> his own person, which he before had, while he lived in a natural
> state, he hath given up to the civil state, and it is now the duty
> and business of the state to defend and protect the person of each
> individual in it.

The "very Reason of man, and the Nature of Things," according to Archibald Kennedy, the son of a Scottish nobleman who immigrated to America and served as a member of the New York Council and a royal collector of customs, "shew us the necessity of such Agreements."[30] Nature, necessity, and convention are united in the Lockean social contract.

In his election sermon delivered to the Massachusetts government in 1771, the Reverend John Tucker explained the moral meaning of the social contract. Civil government, he noted, "is founded in the very nature of man, as a social being, and in the nature and constitution of things....It is the dictate of nature:—It is the voice of reason." Such a social compact, he continued, is an *"ordinance of man,"* which means that it is an act of "choice." Then, in what must surely have been an affront to Governor Thomas Hutchinson, Tucker laid out the American view explaining how and why government is created:

> All men are naturally in a state of freedom, and have an equal claim to liberty. No one, by nature, nor by any special grant from the great Lord of all, has any authority over another. All right therefore in any to rule over others, must originate from those they rule over, and be granted by them. Hence, all government, consistent with that natural freedom, to which all have an equal claim, is founded in compact, or agreement between the parties;—between Rulers and their Subjects, and can be no otherwise. Because Rulers, receiving their authority originally and solely from the people, can be rightfully possessed of no more, than these have consented to, and conveyed to them.[31]

It was ten years later, just after the new Massachusetts constitution was put in effect, that Jonas Clark delivered the election sermon in which he explained to the governor and legislature that the institution of civil government "takes its rise from *Necessity*." Only necessity can teach lawless, lustful men, prone to ruthless competition and violence, to see the importance of establishing civil government. All just governments must therefore be founded "in *compact alone*." Clark then pulled together all the pieces of his Lockean rationale for the creation of the new Massachusetts government:

> The first steps, in entering into society and toward the establishment of civil government among a people, is the forming, agreeing to, and ratifying an *original compact*....
>
> This should be done by the whole body of the people; or by princes, leaders, or delegates, by their choice, appointment, or consent.
>
> This right in the people, whether emerging from a state of nature, or the yoke of oppression, is *an unalienable right*—a right which cannot be given up by a people, even though ever so much inclined to sell or sacrifice it.

In 1775, a writer "from the County of Hampshire" explained in the *Massachusetts Spy*: "Personal liberty, personal security, and private property are the three only motives, the grand objects for which individuals make a partial surrender of that plentitude of power which they possess in a state of nature, and submit to the necessary restrictions, and subordinations of government."[32]

Across the border in New Hampshire, the pseudonymous "Spartanus" summed up what it is that "men *relinquish*, and what they *obtain*," when they enter a state of civil society and government. The most important right men give up when they leave the state of nature and enter into civil society is "their right to judge between themselves and those that offend or injure them, and leave this to the civil magistrate; consequently they give up the right to vindicate or revenge themselves any other way than by the magistrate or proper officers." What they gain when they enter into civil society is "*protection*, the protection of our lives and properties; that we may without violence enjoy our *own*."[33]

To the south in Rhode Island, an "American Whig" wrote one of the clearest statements of social-contract theory. In a series of five essays written for the *Providence Gazette* in 1779, this pseudonymous author extended Locke's theory by claiming that there were actually three distinct steps and covenants in the creation of a body politic. Civil government, he claimed, is "established for the good of the people, by their *voluntary submission and agreement*." To that end, men must first "unite in the establishment of a commonwealth"; second, they must "submit to the form of government agreed upon by the majority"; and, finally, the social contract is completed when men agree to "support and maintain the government established by the rulers and subjects agreeable thereto."[34]

The principal message offered by Locke, Jefferson, and the founders is that the retaliatory use of force must be removed from the realm of subjective whim and transferred to a neutral, nonarbitrary, constitutionalized authority that can define, codify, and administer objective laws. Those rules must be validated by their connection to nature's rights. "Our rulers," wrote Jefferson in *Notes on the State of Virginia*,

> can have no authority over such natural rights, only as we have submitted to them. The rights of conscience we never submitted, we could not submit. We are answerable for them to our God. The legitimate powers of government extend to such acts only as are

injurious to others. But it does me no injury for my neighbor to say
there are twenty gods, or no God. It neither picks my pocket nor
breaks my leg.[35]

Picking pockets and breaking legs are, however, violations of an individual's rights, and these are the crimes that government is created to
punish. In his charge to a Charleston, South Carolina, grand jury, Judge
William Henry Drayton drove home the point to his jurors:

> Every outrage and violence against the person, habitation or prop-
> erty of an individual, is a crime, a misdemeanor, or a contempt, and
> therefore an injury against the State, bound by original compact to
> protect the individual in his rights. For no man, conceiving him-
> self injured, has any authority, or shadow of it, to redress himself;
> because the State has established courts which are *vindices inju-
> riarum* [avengers of injuries]. Hence, every criminal injury against
> the individual must ultimately wound the State; and be included in
> the offences against the body politick, which must be more impor-
> tant in their nature than those relating to the individual, because
> they are more extensive, and of a higher degree of criminality.[36]

With the creation of a new civil society and government comes a new class
of rights that are not natural but civil. These new rights are conventional
manifestations of nature's rights. The most comprehensive and important
of these civil rights is the individual's right to be protected *by* the state from
the criminal actions of others (i.e., the right to be protected by the laws
with regard to one's life, liberty, property, and contracts) and to be protected
from the state (e.g., the right to due process, writs of habeas corpus, and
jury trials). From these general civil rights flow a myriad of particular civil
rights, which apply the general rights to an endless variety of particular
situations. Such rights are contextual: the civil rights of one country might
not be recognized in another country at another time, which is not necessarily a violation of the underlying rights of nature. The best-known system
of civil rights and the one that was predominant in eighteenth-century
America was the English system of common law. Traditional common-law
rights recognized in England and America included the rights to vote, to
bear arms, to habeas corpus, to jury trials, to petition, to free assembly, to
representation, and so on.

In sum, virtually all American revolutionaries from Massachusetts to Georgia viewed the principle of consent as the linchpin of their political theory. The American mind on this subject was ably expressed in 1775 by an anonymous writer for the *Massachusetts Spy*, who argued that consent is the "necessary link in the chain of events, which forms the transition from a condition of nature, to that of civil societies founded on constitutions; and in the order of nature, and the view of the mind must always precede it." Consent is the primary mechanism by which men entering into civil society establish a two-step process by which they design and implement republican constitutions: first, they agree to "divest themselves to a certain degree of their natural powers, and in the same proportion to confer them on others, as their representatives in different measures," and, second, they also agree to establish "the number of rulers; their several degrees of power; the objects on which it is to operate, the sphere and manner of its exertion; its limits and duration, all arranged with such harmony, as tenderly to feel the interest of the people, and fairly represent their majesty and power."[37] As Samuel Lockwood told the Connecticut General Assembly in 1774, a proper social contract "limits the power of the rulers—secures the rights of the people—is the standard of justice for rulers, and subjects—and the regulating measure of duty to both, mutually."[38]

Interestingly, unknown and pseudonymous authors in colonial newspapers published many of the best American arguments explaining the role of consent in the theoretical transition from the state of nature to the creation and running of a state of civil society. In 1775 the Hampshire County writer told readers in the *Massachusetts Spy* that an "agreement or compact, virtually or personally, fully or reciprocally, either expressed or implied between every individual of a community, is absolutely essential to his becoming one of her members."[39]

BUILDING REPUBLICAN GOVERNMENT

America's revolutionary founders viewed government as an artificial, man-made institution, the sole purpose of which was the protection of man's natural rights. Just as the über-Lockean Reverend Tucker emphasized that just governments are "an human institution," so several years later, Thomas Paine, writing under the pseudonym "The Forester," wrote that government "should always be considered as a matter of convenience, not of right."[40]

But what kind of government is implied by the Declaration's third self-evident truth? What form of government is best suited to protecting man's natural and civil rights?

American revolutionaries were proponents of the republican form of government. Traditionally understood, republicanism was concerned mostly with the question of *who* should rule. While republican government could assume innumerable forms, including adopting elements of democracy, aristocracy, and monarchy, it was most often defined as the rule of the people through representative institutions. Thomas Jefferson defined republicanism in the traditional way: "It means a government by its citizens in mass, acting directly and personally, according to rules established by the majority." But this definition was not quite precise enough. Jefferson further refined it by suggesting that republicanism is the degree of the people's "*control*…over the organs of government," which is somewhat different from rule by the people. The people's control over the use and abuse of government power, he said, was the "measure of its republicanism."[41]

Jefferson's amendment to the traditional definition of republicanism was illustrative of a change that had taken place in the American revolutionary mind. This change actually transformed republicanism into something very different from the historical understanding of the term associated with ancient and early modern thought and practice. For Jefferson and his fellow revolutionaries, republicanism was more than a form of government, and it meant considerably more than substituting an elective system of government for a king. As Thomas Paine put it, "What is called a *republic*, is not any *particular form* of government." This new American-style republicanism was a way of life grounded in certain moral and social principles as much as it was a political form. The Americans' republican revolution led them, according to the Reverend Samuel Williams in 1774, to "form a new era and give a new turn to human affairs."[42]

For traditional republicans going back to ancient Greece and Rome, the sacrifice of individual interests for the common good was the ultimate standard of moral and political value, which meant that the public and the private were drawn together as tightly as possible. The republican state was viewed as a unified and homogenous whole. For American revolutionaries, by contrast, the individual and his right to self-government and the pursuit of happiness was the standard of moral and political value, which meant that the public and the private were to be separated as much as possible. The new republican state was defined by its diversity and heterogeneity. Revolutionary republicanism thus shaped the Americans' conception of how to view the individual's relationship to government; it defined how they viewed the structure and operation of their society and government. This new conception of republicanism pointed to a reordering of the moral, social, and political principles and institutions that would dominate American life for a century. This was no utopian vision, however. The Revolution of 1776 and the new republican ideology that came with it reflected and gave philosophic expression to a society that largely existed in America already.[43]

Jefferson was not alone in his modification of the traditional definition of republicanism. There developed in America during this period a new and improved understanding of republicanism that shifted the focus away from the question of who should rule toward the question of how men should live their lives in a republican society. Illustrative statements supporting Jefferson's recasting of republicanism can be found in John Adams's *Defence of the Constitutions of Government of the United States of America* and in James Madison's tenth essay of *The Federalist*.

Adams distinguished between free and unfree republics. He defined unfree republics as those that violated the rights of individuals. A free republic—what he called "the best of governments, and the greatest blessing which mortals can aspire to"—adds two crucial criteria to the standard definition of the term "republic." The most important criterion for Adams revises the general definition of a republic to include the requirement that it be "an Empire of Laws, and not of Men." He distinguished a free from an unfree republic in these terms: "An empire of laws is a characteristic of a free republic only, and should never be applied to republics in general." The rule of law, then, establishes the necessary but not the sufficient condition in the definition of a free republic. Adams well knew that majority-rule republicanism combined with the rule of law could still lead to unjust laws and an unfree republic. A second criterion was necessary. For Adams, the rule of law exists primarily to protect individual rights, particularly the right to private property. He defined a republic as that form of government "in which the property of the people predominated and governed; and it had more relation to property than liberty."[44] This American-style republicanism secured and protected private property by law, and it protected the property of all men, including the wealthy. Adams offered what is surely one of the most sophisticated definitions of a republic written during the Revolutionary period. His definition goes beyond a description of institutional arrangements or defining the locus of social power. Instead, Adams demands of republics that they fulfill certain ends or social goods. He defined a free republic as that form of government in which the rule of law protects the property and therewith the liberty of *all* citizens, not just those who rule.

James Madison was another influential proponent of the new American-style republicanism. His greatest contribution to republican theory and practice was to constitutionalize it. In the tenth and fifty-first essays of *The Federalist*, Madison sought to solve the traditional problems typically associated with the republican form of government, particularly the problem of majority faction. Too often, Madison lamented, popular governments ancient and modern (including America's postrevolutionary republics) had passed laws "not according to the rules of justice, and the rights of the minor party; but by the superior force of an interested and over-bearing majority." In other words, the traditional form of republican government too often inclined toward democracy (defined by Madison as "a Society, consisting of a small number of citizens, who assemble and administer the Government in person"), which means that a majority faction was able to "sacrifice to its ruling passion or interest, both the public good and the rights of other citizens."[45] The intellectual and practical challenge Madison set for himself was to reconcile the republican form with the natural rights of individuals.

Like the views of Jefferson and Adams, Madison's view of republicanism was shaped by the underlying moral philosophy of the Revolution and by the modern science of politics. Republican government was the form of government most likely to promote and protect the moral laws and rights of nature listed in the Declaration of Independence, but it still was not good enough. Madison therefore set out to devise institutional arrangements that could ameliorate the problems inherent in the republican form. He famously constitutionalized the republican form through a series of mechanisms meant to defang majority factions. In *Federalist* No. 10, Madison proposed two solutions to the problem of majority tyranny. The first was representation, the purpose of which was to "*refine* and *enlarge* public views, by passing them through the medium of a chosen body of citizens, whose wisdom may best discern the true interest of their country, and whose patriotism and love of justice, will be least likely to sacrifice it to temporary or partial considerations." The second was to extend the geographical sphere of the republic and thereby "take in a greater variety of parties and interests," which would dilute the strong impulses of passions and interests that lead to majority factions bent on violating the rights of minorities.[46]

In *Federalist* Nos. 48 and 51, Madison identified several other mechanisms that can be used to prevent majority tyranny, the most important of which is separation of powers with checks and balances. By 1787, many American statesmen came to realize that the most dangerous branch of government in the republican form of government was not the executive but rather the legislative. It was "against the enterprising and ambition of this department, that the people ought to indulge all their jealousy and exhaust all their precautions." In *Federalist* No. 51, Madison explained how the new Constitution sliced (separation of powers) and diced (federalism) the powers of the government, thereby limiting the power and the ability of republican legislatures to violate the rights of individuals. He identified a variety of checks and balances built into the federal government (e.g., giving to each department a "will of its own"; giving to each department an independent source for the "emoluments annexed to their offices"; giving to the administrators of each department "the necessary constitutional means, and personal motives, to resist encroachments of the others"; as well as a variety of "auxiliary precautions" and "inventions of prudence" such as a bicameral legislature, an executive veto, and a division of powers between the state and federal governments) that would tame, channel, and sometimes smother the ambitions of unhinged majorities.[47]

Madison summed up the broad outlines of how he and America's republican constitution-makers reformed and transformed the republican theory of government by securing liberty and justice. American constitution-makers created what they variously called complex or compound republics, defined by Madison in the following way: "In the compound republic of America, the power surrendered by the people, is first divided between two distinct governments, and then the portion allotted to each, subdivided among distinct and separate departments. Hence a double security arises to the rights of the people. The different governments will controul each other; at the same time that each will be controuled by itself."[48] Defined and institutionalized by a written constitution, America's new form of republican government represented a revolutionary advance in the theory and practice of government. The Americans reconfigured the traditional idea of republican government by resting it on a new moral philosophy summed up in the first and second truths of the Declaration, then by adapting this philosophy to the institutional developments brought forth by the Enlightenment's new science of politics (e.g., representation and separation of powers). Even the rancorous debate between Federalists and Anti-Federalists in 1787 and 1788, which was fought largely over the nature of republicanism, was notable for what both sides held in common. To a man, they believed that the purpose of republican government was to secure the rights of individuals, and to one degree or another they all assumed that their republican governments should be controlled by written constitutions with separation of powers, federalism, bicameral legislatures, and various checks and balances. The differences between the two sides lay primarily in the amount of power they were willing to give to the state and federal governments.

American-style republicanism was unique because of the emphasis it put on limiting the political power of those who rule—including the rule of the majority—so that individuals could rule themselves more efficaciously. They well knew the truth of Madison's observation that, "had every Athenian citizen been a Socrates[,] every Athenian assembly would still have been a mob."[49] In contrast to the ancient Greek and Roman republics, the new American republics shrank the public sphere and expanded the private sphere. This American-style republicanism was better defined as *self*-government in the fullest sense of the term. It meant the people controlling the growth and power of government so that individuals could have greater freedom to be left alone and govern themselves.

THE JUST POWERS OF REPUBLICAN GOVERNMENT

The Declaration of Independence claims that legitimate governments are instituted to secure the rights of individuals. But how does government secure rights? How much power should republican governments have to achieve their ends? And how should that power be limited so that the government itself does not become the principal vehicle by which the rights of individuals are violated?

The greatest achievement of the American Revolution was to free individuals from the arbitrary commands of government. The radical transformation in thought and practice that followed would have enormous implications for the development of a new American society in the century that followed.[50] Morally, the founders' American-style republicanism insisted that men have a right to be free—free to pursue their individual happiness (material and spiritual) without the interference of others. Politically, it declared that government should be limited to protecting individual rights. By default and by intention, the Declaration draws a line between the public realm (what government may do and what individuals may not do) and the private (what individuals may do and what government may not do). The public realm is necessarily narrow and shallow, and the private realm is necessarily broad and deep. The purpose of the public sphere is to protect and expand the private sphere.

The success or failure of republican government was measured by the degree to which the government left individuals alone to govern themselves. Jefferson had more to say on this subject than any other revolutionary founder. During the second year of his presidency, he told the English theologian and natural philosopher Joseph Priestley that he regarded the American people as acting "under the unrestrained and unperverted operation of their own understanding[s]," and thus demonstrating to mankind that "degree of freedom and self-government in which a society may venture to leave its individual members."[51] The role of republican government, Jefferson told another correspondent, was to expand man's freedom and his ability for self-rule. It was therefore the responsibility of republican legislators to be "sufficiently apprised of the rightful limits of their power" and to "declare and enforce only our natural rights and duties, and to take none of them from us." In a free society, he continued, the actions of men should be limited in two ways: first, "no man has a natural right to commit aggression on the equal rights of another; and this is all from which the law ought to restrain him," and, second, "no man having a natural right to be the judge between himself and another, it is his natural duty to submit to the umpirage of an impartial third." Finally, after legislators and their laws "have declared and enforced all this, they have fulfilled their functions; and the idea is quite unfounded, that on entering into society we give up any natural right."[52]

There was no single American mind on the question of the various forms that republican government might take, but there was universal agreement about the purpose of republican government. Not a single American revolutionary believed that government could legitimately transgress man's natural rights. They all believed that the goal of government was to protect men in their peace and security, thereby expanding their freedom to govern their lives as they see fit. "The true foundation of republican government," Jefferson declared, "is the equal right of every citizen, in his person and property, and in their management."[53] In a free state, laws must therefore be "reasonable, that is, not violative of first principles, natural rights, and the dictates of the sense of justice."[54] In 1818, Jefferson reported to the Commissioners for the University of Virginia that the purposes of a proper university education included the study of the basic principles and structures of government, which should promote "a sound spirit of legislation, which, banishing all arbitrary and unnecessary restraint on individual action, shall leave us free to do whatever does not violate the equal rights of another."[55]

In this new republican theory of government, the individual replaced the government or any part of it as the primary unit of moral and political sovereignty. American-style republicanism mandated the securing rights as the sole criterion by which to judge whether any particular government is legitimate or not. This criterion is, Samuel Lockwood of Massachusetts said, the "standard of justice for rulers, and subject—and the regulating measure of duty to both, mutually."[56] The first responsibility of government in a free society is to protect the natural rights of individuals from their violation by other individuals in society, which means that government must therefore serve as both a police officer and a judge in order to arrest, convict, and sentence criminals in society. Governments that do not serve this primary function are illegitimate.

In his *Essay on the Government of the Colonies*, Archibald Kennedy claimed that the "Design of Civil Government is to secure the Persons and Properties, and Peace of Mankind, from the Invasions and Injuries of their Neighbours"; it is to "protect the People in their Lives, Liberties, and Properties, by restraining or punishing those who injure, attack, or assault them." In the preface to his proposed revision of Virginia's criminal law in 1778, Thomas Jefferson wrote of the need for government to restrain "wicked and dissolute men" who have "resigned themselves to the dominion of inordinate passions" and therefore "commit violations on the lives, liberties and property of others." Given that men "enter into society" to "secure enjoyment of their rights," Jefferson argued that "government would be defective in its principal purpose were it not to restrain criminal acts, by inflicting due punishments on those who perpetuate them."[57]

America's revolutionary statesmen understood that a government was necessary to protect man's rights, but they also knew that government poses the greatest threat to those rights. In a political state, the sphere of rights is extended to include not only the relationship between individuals but also between the individual and governments. This is why the "sole end and design of government," according to Samuel Cooke in his sermon on "The True Principles of Civil Government," is "not to ennoble a few and enslave the multitude, but the public benefit, the good of the people; that they may be protected in their persons, and secured in the enjoyment of all their rights, and be enabled to lead quiet and peaceable lives." According to Connecticut's Dan Foster, "Tis very plain in reason" that when men agreed through a social compact to enter into a civil state with civil rulers holding civil swords of power and the authority to wield it, they did so in order to "defend and secure to them the quiet and peaceable enjoyment of their persons and properties; *i.e.* of their persons and all their worldly good, estates, and chattles, which they had gotten by fatigue, labour and industry." The purpose of lawmaking in a rights-respecting republic is to make laws that reflect the "maxims and laws of reason and the nature of things." Those civil magistrates "who would consult and promote the peace and happiness of the state are solemnly and forever bound to make truth and reason, the laws of God and the nature of things, their standards in making civil laws, and very scrupulously to abide by them."[58]

Laws imply power, and the great challenge for the revolutionaries was to design a government that used power properly. "Unlimited power," Charles Turner told the assembled Massachusetts government in his election-day sermon, "has generally been destructive of human happiness." Jefferson likewise understood that politicians are always grasping for more power. Government, he believed, was the greatest threat to individual liberty. "It should be remembered, as an axiom of eternal truth in politics," he wrote to Judge Spencer Roane in 1819, "that whatever power in any government is independent, is absolute also; in theory only, at first, while the spirit of the people is up, but in practice, as fast as that relaxes."[59]

As serious students of the history of freedom and tyranny, the architects of the American republic would have uniformly accepted the wisdom of an unknown Marylander who, writing pseudonymously as "An American," declared that "all men, by nature fond of power, are unwilling to part with the possession of it." Man's lust for power is insatiable, he wrote, and the "desire to command increases every day." This is why "no man, or body of men, ought to be intrusted with the united powers of Government, or more command than is absolutely necessary to discharge the particular office committed to him." Such ideas were common currency in eighteenth-century America. In 1771, a writer for the *Massachusetts Spy* spoke for virtually all Americans when he told his readers, "Power is of such an encroaching nature, that it is impossible to guard against it."[60]

America's founding generation understood that government is defined by one fundamental fact: the power of government officials to bend the will of a man without his consent to their wishes and commands. Throughout history, government coercion had been used to demand obeisance and obedience from its citizens. In America, by contrast, the founding fathers sought to limit—if not eliminate—the ability of governments to *initiate* force against innocent citizens. This is why, after America's purchase of the Louisiana Territory, President Thomas Jefferson could tell the nuns in a New Orleans convent that "the principles of the constitution and government of the United States are a sure guarantee...that your institution will be permitted to govern itself according to its own voluntary rules, without interference from the civil authority."[61]

Here then is the great paradox confronted by America's founders: government is necessary to protect the rights of individuals, but the coercive power of government is most often the greatest threat to the rights of individuals. The challenge implicit in the Declaration's third truth was to establish a government with the power necessary to protect the rights of all individuals while at the same time not giving the government so much power that it could be used to violate the rights of individuals. Madison put forward probably the best description of this general problem in a well-known formulation in *Federalist* No. 51: "In framing a government which is to be administered by men over men, the great difficulty lies in this: you must first enable the government to control the governed; and in the next place oblige it to control itself."[62] After July 4, 1776, the revolutionaries' principal task was to create a government strong enough to protect, but not so strong as to oppress—to make the compulsory power of the state the servant, rather than the master, of a free people.

But *how* could a limited government remain limited in its powers? The founders' solution to the problem was to institutionalize the rule of law by creating written constitutions. Or, as Stephen Johnson put it in his 1770 election-day sermon to Connecticut's General Assembly, "A good constitution of civil polity…is of very interesting importance to every free state; without which, all the rights and privileges of subjects, rest upon a very weak foundation, and are held by a very slippery and uncertain tenure, the will and caprice of rulers in power." It was a standard maxim of the entire Revolutionary period (borrowed from Locke's *Second Treatise*) that "wherever law ends, tyranny begins."[63] The political system of liberty required the replacement of arbitrary political rule with the rule of law—laws objective, known, certain, and applied equally to all citizens. Government officials would be denied discretionary power in applying the law, and the law applied to one man would apply to all men.

In 1771, a writer in the *Massachusetts Spy* defined a free state as that form of government where "the balance of power is rightly and justly poised—Where the power of the governors, and the liberty of the subjects are well understood and uniformly supported—Where *justice has a free and uninterrupted course*, no man being above the *law*, and none below it." That same year, John Tucker recounted to Governor Thomas Hutchinson and the Massachusetts House of Representatives in his election-day sermon that "fine expression of a Spartan Ruler…who, upon being asked, 'who governed at *Sparta?* answered the laws, and the magistrates *according* to these laws.'" The constitutional laws of the state, are, he continued, "properly, the supreme power, being obligatory on the whole community,—on the highest officer, as well as the lowest subject."[64]

Shortly after the Declaration of Independence was signed, the states began the process of converting the moral theory of the Revolution into functioning governments by writing constitutions. Between 1776 and 1780, eleven states drafted written constitutions, and then of course the Philadelphia convention drafted a national constitution in 1787 that was ratified by the states the following year. American revolutionaries attached great importance to having a written document that specified the limited powers of the government and the personal and property rights of the citizens. The great virtue of a written constitution (in contrast to the unwritten

British constitution) is that it established, limited, and defined the powers of government, and it served as a permanent standard by which the people could measure the actions of the government. Jefferson described the importance of a written constitution in this way: "It is still certain that though written constitutions may be violated in moments of passion or delusion, yet they furnish a text to which those who are watchful may again rally and recall the people; they fix too for the people the principles of their political creed."[65]

The framers of the United States Constitution created a government that limited, separated, and divided power. American constitutional republicanism meant limited government, which resulted in the creation of social and economic spheres of activity where individuals and their voluntary associations would be left free to think, act, produce, and trade. America's revolutionary statesmen were, in other words, proponents of a free society.

CHAPTER 10

Revolution

"We hold these truths to be self-evident, that all men are...endowed by their Creator with certain unalienable Rights... *That whenever any Form of Government becomes destructive of these ends, it is the Right of the People to alter or to abolish it; and to institute new Government, laying its foundation on such principles and organizing its powers in such form, as to them shall seem most likely to effect their Safety and Happiness.*"

*T*he Declaration's fourth and final self-evident truth—the revolution truth—represents the logical conclusion of the antecedent three truths. It builds indirectly on the principles of equality and rights and directly on the principle of consent.

The fourth self-evident truth applies the principle of consent in two ways: there is *negative* consent (i.e., consent withdrawn) and there is *positive* consent (i.e., consent given). Put differently, this final truth calls for opposite kinds of action, one destructive (i.e., to alter or to abolish one's government) and one constructive (i.e., to institute a new government). More broadly, it teaches, first, that revolution is justified when governments become tyrannical and violate the rights of their citizens, and, second, it implies that just as *any* form of republican government may become despotic (including democratic republics), so *any* form of republican government (including monarchic and aristocratic republics) can be legitimate as long as the rights of its citizens are guaranteed and protected.[1] It would be possible to have a rights-respecting monarchic republic.

The revolutionary generation was unanimous in its collective belief that republican governments are instituted to secure individual rights.

(Many American Loyalists held this position as well.) Governments that fail to secure rights over time lose their legitimacy, and governments that actively violate rights should be judged as tyrannical. The people in their collective capacity always reserve "the right to alter or abolish" illegitimate governments. This right is otherwise known as the "right to revolution," which, though not described this way in the Declaration, is nonetheless a direct inference from man's unalienable rights. Like the rights to life, liberty, property, and the pursuit of happiness, the right to revolution is a fundamental political right. This is what makes the right to revolution so revolutionary: it is valid for all political societies everywhere and always.

According to the Declaration, the fourth self-evident truth includes not only the right to abolish illegitimate governments but also the right to alter old governments or to build new ones. Since altering or abolishing government can leave man's rights in a precarious state, societies of men must reassert their "Right...to institute new Government" as they or their forebears once did. The right to alter or abolish government does not, however, mean returning to a state of nature. In fact, it implies quite the opposite. For Jefferson, invoking the right to revolution is a temporary step on the road to reestablishing a just government founded on proper principles. American revolutionaries were not proponents of permanent revolution.

The Declaration's right to revolution indicates the conditions under which revolution is justified by establishing certain standards of natural justice. Whereas the right to life is simply absolute, the right to revolution is *contextually* absolute—that is, it is absolute but its application is contextual. Revolutions are never easy, nor should they be taken lightly. Unlike the first three self-evident truths, which are stated directly and without reservation, the fourth, after being stated, is then immediately qualified and further explained. Interestingly, the first word that follows the fourth self-evident truth is "prudence," which is the practical virtue that determines when revolution is both justified and propitious. Prudence, Jefferson wrote, dictates that revolution is and must be the last resort of the people against governments that violate their rights. There are times when exercising the right to revolution would be imprudent or foolish, though one might be justified in doing so. Likewise, there are times when not exercising the right to revolution would be imprudent or foolish. Most revolutionary

Americans understood that "human prudence is to be our guide in the concerns of time."[2]

Determining why, when, and how a government should be overthrown is a remarkably complicated question. The Declaration identifies the challenge as twofold: first, governments with long and venerable histories "should not be," according to Jefferson, "changed for light and transient Causes"; and, second, history teaches that men "are more disposed to suffer, while Evils are sufferable, than to right themselves by abolishing the Forms to which they are accustomed." There will always be individuals ready with their pitchforks at the slightest infraction of their rights by the government, and there will always be inherently cautious individuals who are reluctant or refuse to act when governments violate rights. The question of timing, therefore, is critical to Jefferson's theory of revolution.

The question raised by the Declaration is, when exactly is revolution both justified and prudent?

Revolution is justified when a government ceases to be the protector of the rights of its citizens and becomes the chief destroyer of those rights. Knowing when it is prudent to overthrow a government is not, however, self-evident. Is it appropriate to rebel against a government that is simply incompetent? Is it prudent to abolish one's government every time it raises taxes, however small the increase, or imposes minor regulations? Was revolution justified in 1765 after the passage of the Stamp Act, or after the Tea Act in 1772, or the Prohibitory Act in 1775?[3] Alternatively, is it more prudent to obey unjust acts and to do whatever it takes to achieve reconciliation? Were American Loyalists right in arguing that declaring independence in 1776 was both imprudent and even suicidal?

REVOLUTION IN THEORY

The American theory of revolution was inspired by the practice of Britain's Glorious Revolution and the philosophic ideas that supported it. Eighteenth-century Americans were steeped in the literature of English revolutionary thought. They read the so-called English Real Whigs with great interest, men such as John Milton, Algernon Sidney, Robert Molesworth, and the coauthors of the immensely popular *Cato's Letters*, John Trenchard and Thomas Gordon. These Real Whig writers (sometimes also known as Commonwealthmen) distinguished themselves in English thought with their intrepid defense of the people's right to disobey and throw off unjust rulers. Their philosophy of revolution was grounded on the view that government is an artificial construct created by a social contract. By the terms of the contract, government was created to protect the natural and inherent rights of individuals living in a particular civil society.

For virtually all trans-Atlantic Real Whigs, the particular instantiation of this theory of government was an idealized version of the mixed and balanced English constitution, which its defenders sought to safeguard from corruption and decay. When the people's rulers violated the fundamental rights of their citizens or subjects, when they broke the contract and violated the trust that justified their power, when they damaged the constitution that gave them power, the people had a right to resist and ultimately to reclaim their original right to self-government. It is important to note, however, that the Real Whig authors were also careful to define and insist on certain preconditions, procedures, and rules that defined the grounds on which resistance and revolution were both justified and prudent. These "rules for radicals" were typically presented in the form of limits and constraints. Revolution was the option of last resort and even then it must proceed with caution.[4]

Without question, the philosopher of revolution turned to most often by eighteenth-century Anglo-Americans, the one who most influenced the Real Whig tradition, was John Locke. In the concluding two chapters of his *Second Treatise of Government*, Locke carefully presented the conditions under which revolutions are justified and sometimes necessary. The Englishman's burden was to demonstrate the role played by prudence in determining the how and when of revolution. His argument for revolution begins by defining the nature of illegitimate government and tyranny. In his chapter "Of Tyranny," Locke defines tyranny in the most general sense as the "exercise of power beyond right, which no body can have a right to." Tyranny is present, he continues, when a government (and Locke here means *any* form of government, including democracy) takes and applies the property of its citizens to ends to which they have not consented, and/or if a government impoverishes, harasses, subdues, or subjects the citizenry "to the arbitrary and irregular commands of those that have it." In Locke's more famous formulation, he states, "Wherever law ends, tyranny begins."[5]

The concepts "right" and "law" are therefore inextricably connected in Locke's mind, and they must be constitutionalized in order to stand as barriers to grasping power. Thus, whoever would exceed the political authority given him by the people and the law (i.e., the constitution) and abuses that power and trust by violating the rights of the citizenry is, Locke says, a tyrant and may be opposed for the same reason that one has a right to resist a criminal "who by force invades the right of another."[6] The fundamental issue on which the right to resistance and revolution is based is the conflict between right and force.

With this general standard in mind, Locke raises an obvious question: Do individual citizens have a right to oppose a king, or any other form of government for that matter, every time they feel themselves aggrieved by their rulers or government?

Locke's answer is a definitive no, and he then adduces several particular cases in which it would be inappropriate to oppose a king or any other form of government. If every individual had a right to resist or abolish his government every time it did something he did not like, this would, he argues, "unhinge and overturn all polities, and instead of government and order, leave nothing but anarchy and confusion." Such a right would devolve very quickly into subjective whim and political antinomianism. Ultimately, anarchy results in just another form of tyranny. Generally speaking, armed resistance should not be used where an appeal to justice and law is possible. "For where the injured party may be relieved, and his damages repaired by appeal to the law," Locke argues, "there can be no pretense for force, which is only to be used, where a man is intercepted from appealing to the law."[7] There can be no appeal to force where the constitution is still operative and claims to justice have a chance of being heard. But when all else fails, necessity requires using just force to resist the unjust use of force by government.

But what of those cases in which injustice is real and prolonged? Is revolution justified if government acts unjustly against just one man or a minority? The truth is that a lone malcontent or a small minority of distressed citizens who feel unjustly abused by their government will not pose a threat to the authorities and to the social order, either because they will be crushed or do nothing for fear of being crushed. And "where the body of the people do not think themselves concerned in it," as when "a raving madman, or heady malcontent" attempts "to overturn a well-settled state," the government will remain secure, with "the people being as little apt to follow the one, as the other." The situation changes entirely, however, when the government's "illegal acts" extend "to the majority of the people," or when the majority can be persuaded by an oppressed minority that the precedent set by the government's unjust actions, though affecting only a few individuals or a minority, could eventually have consequences for everyone. In this situation, Locke warns, it is difficult to stop people from "resisting illegal force used against them." Arriving at the point where a majority are prepared to openly resist the enforcement of unjust laws or arbitrary decrees is something that, as Locke recognizes, usually occurs over a long period of time. Governments rarely become tyrannical in one fell swoop. Locke recognizes that the transition from a free government to despotism is slow and sometimes unseen or unfelt for a considerable period. Thus he elucidates a list of telltale signs that a free people should look for in determining whether a government is moving toward tyranny or not. Most importantly, the people should determine whether a ruler evinces a "*long train*" of actions that "*show the councils* all tending" toward despotism."[8]

In his chapter "Of the Dissolution of Government," Locke's goal is to establish objective criteria for judging whether the citizens or subjects are justified in resisting the laws and actions of their rulers, or even altering or abolishing their government.[9] Locke's first criterion justifying revolution concerns "when the *legislative is altered.*" The legislative power is critically important to Locke because it provides the "umpirage" regulating human action in civil society. Its primary responsibility is to make laws that protect the rights of nature relative to life in civil society. Thus the "*constitution of the legislative* is the first and fundamental act of society"; it "is the soul that gives form, life, and unity to the commonwealth." Without it, society collapses eventually into tyranny or anarchy. The constituted legislative authority is altered, according to Locke, in four ways: first, when a ruler "sets up his own arbitrary will, in place of the laws, which are the will of the society"; second, when a ruler "hinders the legislative from assembling in its due time, or from acting freely, pursuant to those ends"; third, when a ruler arbitrarily alters the "electors, or ways of election" without the people's consent; and fourth, when a ruler delivers his subjects or citizens "into the subjection of a foreign power."[10]

Locke's second criterion sanctioning revolution arises when rulers "act contrary to their trust." By this he means that governments lose their legitimacy when they systematically "endeavor to invade the property of the subject, and to make themselves, or any part of the community, masters or arbitrary disposers of the lives, liberties, or fortunes of the people." Governments that repeatedly violate the fundamental rights of their citizens not only deserve no respect or allegiance, but they are in fact, from Locke's perspective, criminal institutions that must be overturned. Curiously, Locke's ire on this point is directed not against monarchs but at legislatures. The purpose of the legislative authority is to make laws that will serve as "guards and fences to the properties of all the members of society, to limit the power, and moderate the dominion of every part and member of the society." When democratically elected legislatures confiscate or destroy the people's property, or attempt to "reduce them to slavery under arbitrary power, they put themselves into a state of war with the people, who are thereupon absolved from any farther obedience." Under these conditions, if the legislative authority "transgresses the fundamental rule of society" and attempts to establish "absolute power" in violation of the people's natural rights, it thereby forfeits its power, which then devolves back to the people, "who have a right to resume their original liberty" and to establish a "new legislative" power.[11]

Having established the conditions that justify revolution, Locke turns next to the all-important prudential question: whether the people can be wise and responsible enough to be entrusted with the power to cashier their rulers. The Tories of Locke's time wondered whether it would not lead to "certain ruin" to endow the people with the authority to establish a new legislative every time they took "offence at the old one." But Locke made sure to explain that whim and fancy were not his standard for determining when a revolution is justified. His argument is that the people, rather than being volatile, are, in general, lethargic, passive, and bound by their traditional political forms and formalities. As evidence for this claim, Locke points to the general reluctance of various peoples throughout history to "amend the acknowledged faults, in the frame [of government] they have been accustomed to." And even if their traditional constitution has obvious "original defects, or adventitious ones introduced by time, or corruption," the people are still rarely inclined to do anything about it, which is precisely why English revolutions are never radical, according to Locke. Indeed, they are almost always profoundly conservative in purpose and outcome. The English people, Locke claims, always seek to restore their "old constitutions" through revolution and their "old legislative of kings, lords and commons."[12]

The fact of the matter is that revolutions are, historically speaking, rare occurrences, according to Locke, and they do not result from "every little mismanagement in public affairs." Indeed, the people are willing to tolerate all kinds of faults and shortcoming in their rulers along with "many wrong and inconvenient laws, and all the *slips* of human frailty." And then, in a sentence that would be echoed in the Declaration of Independence eighty-six years later, Locke asserts that, although revolutions may be rare occurrences in the historical record, they will come about "if a long train of abuses, prevarications, and artifices, all tending the same way," make a tyrannical "design visible to the people." Locke's point is that while it typically takes the people a long time to overcome their natural deference and "rouse themselves," they will eventually "endeavour to put the rule into such hands which may secure to them the ends for which government was at first erected."[13]

The people's moral right to alter or abolish the standing government actually serves a profoundly conservative function in Locke's political philosophy. Rulers who violate the rights of their citizens and who violate the "constitutions and laws of the government" are, according to Locke, "truly and properly *rebels*." Rather than preserving and conserving society, such men violate the true principles of civil government and return society to the state of nature. Like the Sword of Damocles, Locke's moral right to revolution is meant to hang over the rulers' heads as a constant reminder to hew to the principles that make their positions legitimate and to justify the people's trust. Ironically, then, the people's right to revolution is an inherently conservative principle. It is the "*best fence against rebellion*, and the probablest means to hinder it."[14] In Locke's hands, the ultimate purpose of the right to revolution is to protect men's rights and to preserve their traditional constitutions.

✴   ✴   ✴

The first American thinker to seriously consider the question of "Lockean" resistance to unjust government was Jonathan Mayhew.[15] During his tenure as the minister of Boston's Old West Church, from 1747 to 1766, Mayhew infused Lockean epistemological and political principles into the heart of New England culture through his preaching and writing. Most historians regard Mayhew's 1750 *A Discourse Concerning Unlimited*

Submission and Nonresistance to the Higher Powers to be the most influential political sermon published during the late colonial period. His sermon challenged the authoritarian doctrine of unlimited submission and passive obedience to rulers. His conclusion spoke to the necessity and virtue of civil disobedience and the need for resistance to tyranny. It defined for an entire generation the conditions under which the people may resist illegitimate governments. Late in life, John Adams told Thomas Jefferson that he had read Mayhew's political pamphlet when he was fourteen and then reread it "till the Substance of it was incorporated into my Nature and indelibly engraved on my Memory." Adams also said of Mayhew's sermon that it was "read by everybody, celebrated by friends, and abused by enemies."[16]

Though published a quarter-century before America's revolutionary Whigs declared their independence from Great Britain, Mayhew's sermon—along with Locke's *Second Treatise*—served as a guidebook for revolution. It established the standards by which governments could be judged as legitimate or not, and it elucidated the grounds on which the people might resist or alter their governments. The sermon sought to explore "the general nature and end of magistracy" along with "the grounds and extent of that submission which persons of a private character ought to yield to those who are vested with authority." Mayhew's innovative argument represents a transitional moment in late Puritan thought, when the traditional New England doctrine of passive obedience, unlimited submission, and nonresistance to duly appointed political rulers, described by St. Paul in Romans 13:1–7, was liberalized if not totally demolished in the light of Locke's revolutionary political philosophy. The Boston minister made it clear that citizens must show obedience to civil rulers who properly exercise their duly constituted responsibilities. To do otherwise would be a violation of the divine will. That said, he also made it clear that he disagreed with the common opinion extant in both England and America that scripture in general, and Romans 13:1–7 in particular, "makes all resistance to princes a crime, in any case whatever." Mayhew considered this interpretation of Romans 13 to be both wrong and dangerous. Had it been followed, Tarquin, Julius Caesar, Charles I, and James II would not have faced their just deserts. Instead, Mayhew argued that men owe obedience only to those rulers "who *actually* perform the duty of rulers by exercising a reasonable and just authority for the good of human society." He went on to make the point even more forcefully and clearly: "If those who bear the title of civil rulers do not perform the duty of civil rulers but act directly counter to the sole end and design of their office; if they injure and oppress their subjects instead of defending their rights and doing them good, they have not the least pretense to be honored, obeyed, and rewarded according to the Apostle's argument." Mayhew made it quite clear that "common tyrants and public oppressors are not entitled to obedience from their subjects by virtue of anything here laid down" by St. Paul.[17]

As with Locke, Mayhew's challenge was to determine *when* rulers become tyrants and oppressors. This line is not easily drawn. Mayhew concedes that even good rulers make mistakes, and mistakes are not grounds for resistance. If error were the standard, government would be impossible. Government could not function, according to Mayhew, if resistance were permitted or encouraged when governments were not managed "in the best manner possible." If such a principle were allowed to govern political life, the community would be thrown "into confusion and anarchy." The boundary line between the occasional mistake and active oppression is defined by rulers "acting so *habitually*, and in a manner which plainly shows that they aim at making themselves great by the ruin of their subjects."[18]

The seventeenth-century England of Charles I provided Mayhew with guidance on when and how rebellion is justified. England had "been patient under the oppressions of the crown even to *long suffering*, for a course of many years; and there was no rational hope of redress in any other way." In such a case, "resistance was absolutely necessary in order to preserve the nation from slavery, misery, and ruin." Mayhew actually interpreted St. Paul to say, in the scriptural passage under consideration, that when a ruler "turns tyrant and makes his subjects his prey to devour and to destroy instead of his charge to defend and cherish, we are bound to throw off our allegiance to him and to resist," including "forcibly" if necessary. He goes further: passive obedience in the face of tyranny and oppression would be, in effect, "to join the sovereign in promoting the slavery and misery of that society the welfare of which we ourselves as well as our sovereign are indispensably obliged to secure and promote as far as in us lies."[19]

After establishing the criteria (the "why" question) by which rulers may be adjudged and resisted, Mayhew took up the more difficult prudential questions (the "how," "when," "where" questions): "How far are we obliged to submit? If we may innocently disobey and resist in some cases, why not in all? Where shall we stop? What is the measure of our duty?" The theoretical standard that defines and distinguishes between legitimate and illegitimate government can be established with clear-cut certainty, but the application of that standard to a myriad of different circumstances is difficult and often uncertain. Mayhew noted that there are "petulant, querulous men in every state—men of factious, turbulent, and carping dispositions—glad to lay hold of any trifle to justify and legitimate their caballing against their rulers and other seditious practices." Fortunately, such men are a distinct minority. By way of contrast, the great majority of men "have a disposition to be as submissive and passive and tame under government as they ought to be—witness a great, if not the greatest, part of the known world, who are now groaning, but not murmuring, under the heavy yoke of tyranny."[20] Between the extremes of sectarianism and tolerationism lies a kind of revolutionary golden mean that is neither anarchic nor slavish. But knowing exactly when resistance or revolution is justified and exactly the form by which such action should take place is a difficult matter.

Persistent oppression that points clearly in the direction of despotism is the tripwire justifying revolution. If that unfortunate moment ever arrives, the people have not only the right but also the duty to overthrow the tyrant. "For a nation thus abused to arise unanimously and to resist their prince, even to the dethroning him, is not criminal, but a reasonable way of vindicating their liberties and just rights; it is making use of the means, and the only means, which God has put into their power for mutual and self-defense. And it would be highly criminal in them not to make use of this means."[21] There are times, Mayhew wrote, when revolution is not only justified, but it remains a moral obligation for those who refuse to live as slaves. Mayhew's sermon, largely forgotten today, served as the connecting link between Locke's theoretical arguments for revolution and the actions of New England revolutionaries in the 1760s and 1770s.

THE PROBLEM OF POWER

The passage of the Sugar and Stamp Acts in 1764 and 1765 set in motion the formation of America's revolutionary mind. British legislation inspired the colonists to launch a searching investigation into the nature of power and liberty, justice and injustice. Their distrust of government power subsequently became ingrained in the American character and has shaped the nature of American politics ever since the Revolutionary era.

Colonial opposition ideology grew out of the tension between the use and abuse of power on one hand and the requirements of justice and freedom on the other. In 1766, Richard Bland assumed that "Right and Power have very different Meanings, and convey very different Ideas." He illustrated this distinction by noting, "every Act of Parliament that imposes *internal* Taxes upon the Colonies is an Act of *Power*, and not of *Right*." American Whigs began with a basic assumption grounded in their study of history: that there was a natural tendency for men in positions of political authority to seek more and more power and therewith to destroy liberty and right. This meant for John Adams that there were "but two sorts of men in the world, freemen and slaves." Adams defined a freeman as "one who is bound by no law to which he has not consented." By 1775, the Americans found themselves in a desperate situation in which they were forced to obey laws to which they had not given their consent. Worse: they were bound to laws made not only by distant British ministers but ultimately by an entire nation corrupted by "luxury, effeminacy, and venality." In this situation, Adams, writing as Novanglus, warned his audience, "you would not only be slaves, but the most abject sort of slaves, to the worst sort of masters!" John Dickinson made a similar point when he warned that the Tea Act of 1773 had given an immoral monopoly to the East India Company in America—but he made it in much more pungent terms: "It is something of a Consolation to be overcome by a Lion," he noted sarcastically, "but to be devoured by Rats is intolerable."[22]

America's revolutionary Whigs were deeply pessimistic about the relationship between power and politics. They saw the corrupting desire for power as wrought deeply into man's natural constitution. Mercy Otis Warren summed up the standard American view of the relationship between human nature and power lust in these terms: "Ambition and avarice are *the leading springs* which generally actuate the restless mind. From these *primary sources of corruption* have arisen all the rapine and confusion, the depredation and ruin, that have spread distress over the face of the earth from the day of Nimrod to Cesar, and from Cesar to an arbitrary prince of the house of Brunswick."[23]

In every colonial act passed by the British Parliament in the years between 1764 and 1775, American Whigs saw power and compulsion encroaching on their rights and liberties. They saw malevolent power as a kind of moral cancer that grows and spreads, largely invisibly, until it eventually consumes and destroys its victim. It thus had to be constantly resisted to prevent it from metastasizing. In his First Inaugural Address, Thomas Jefferson debunked the notion that men should trust themselves with power: "Sometimes it is said that man cannot be trusted with the government of himself. Can he, then, be trusted with the government of others? Or have we found angels in the forms of kings to govern him? Let history answer this question."[24]

Revolutionary Whigs typically described power as restless, aggressive, insatiable, grasping, imperialistic, and malignant. Its natural prey was liberty and right, which were seen as passive, isolationist, and defenseless. The lust for power never sleeps and advances by stealth; thus the defense of liberty requires constant vigilance. In any battle, though, between power and liberty, power was bound to win. That said, as John Joachim Zubly of Georgia noted in his 1769 pamphlet *An Humble Inquiry*, "No power can alter the nature of things, that which is wrong cannot be right, and oppression will never be productive of the love and smiles of those that feel it." In 1772, John Adams warned that "Liberty, under every conceivable Form of Government is always in Danger....Ambition is one of the more ungovernable Passions of the human Heart. The Love of Power, is insatiable and uncontroulable....There is danger from all men. The only maxim of a free government ought to be to trust no man living with power to endanger the public liberty." Likewise, Thomas Jefferson believed that it was a "law of our general nature" for all men in power to "become wolves." Regrettably, experience taught Jefferson, "man is the only animal which devours his own kind."[25]

Colonial and revolutionary Americans typically viewed the preservation of liberty as resting on the ability of the people to tame, check, and channel the sphere of power through a mixed and balanced constitution. In the years between 1765 and 1774, most Americans viewed the English constitution as the greatest political check on the abuse of political power ever invented by man. The idea of a constitution and the meaning behind it was of central importance to the American revolutionary mindset. Indeed, the colonists' entire understanding of the imperial crisis rested on it. American Whigs, even those, such as John Dickinson, who would eventually become reluctant revolutionaries, understood that liberty was a state or condition that was secured only by constitutionalizing power. With a subtle dig at the British constitution, Dickinson wrote: "For WHO ARE A FREE PEOPLE?

Not *those*, over whom government is reasonably and equitably exercised, but *those*, who live under a government so *constitutionally checked* and *controuled*, that proper provision is made against its being otherwise exercised." Likewise, Zubly understood the necessary connection between liberty and a properly constructed constitution: "When constitutional liberty is once lost, the transit is very short to the loss of property; the same power that may deprive of the one may also deprive of the other, and with equal justice; those that have not liberty enough to keep their property in reality have no property to keep. Some that look no further build right upon power, and insist the Parliament can do so." Indeed, he continued, "If power is all that is meant very like it may, so it may alter the constitution."[26] In the early years of the imperial crisis, the Americans praised the English constitution for its ability to thwart the advance of unjust power.

A quarter century later, Thomas Jefferson declared intellectual and political war on the growth of governmental power, which derived too much confidence in individual men. For Jefferson, the primary role of a constitution was to check grasping political power.

> It would be a dangerous delusion were a confidence in the men
> of our choice to silence our fears for the safety of our rights: that
> confidence is everywhere the parent of despotism—free govern-
> ment is founded in jealousy, and not in confidence; it is jealousy
> and not confidence which prescribes limited constitutions, to bind
> down those whom we are obliged to trust with power: that our
> Constitution has accordingly fixed the limits to which, and no
> further, our confidence may go....In questions of powers, then, let
> no more be heard of confidence in man, but bind him down from
> mischief by the chains of the Constitution.[27]

It was their fear of power and love of liberty together that colored the way American Patriots viewed the actions of Parliament and king in the years after 1764. Some American commentators saw the embrace of power as a natural human phenomenon that cuts in two directions. A few of the more sophisticated colonial thinkers distinguished between the legitimate and illegitimate use of power. Power can be a force for good and bad. Power corrupted leads to tyranny, but power tamed can lead to liberty. As Richard Bland noted, "Power abstracted from Right cannot give a just Title to

Dominion," suggesting that Bland thought there to be a legitimate form of power connected to "Right." Early in the imperial crisis, John Adams equated power with "dominion," which he characterized as that "encroaching, grasping, restless, and ungovernable Principle in human Nature." Traditionally, dominion meant the force and compulsion that some men use to dominate others. Still, Adams also knew that power constitutionally tamed and controlled "within the limits of *equity* and *reason*" was necessary for establishing a rights-protecting and freedom-promoting government.[28]

Communities of individuals create legitimate power in order to expand the sphere of freedom and to diminish the sphere of dominion, and with it the encroachments of princes, nobles, or democratic majorities. The voluntary transfer of legitimate power by all men in their natural state, through consent and compact, to a government strong enough to protect their rights is the mode by which illegitimate power is prevented. This new government serves as a trustee and guardian of the powers delegated to it by each and every individual. The Americans believed they had created a realm of freedom in their New World colonies greater than that known in any other part of the world. "They think that the Liberties of Mankind and the Glory of human Nature is in their Keeping," John Adams declaimed in his diary, and they "know that Liberty has been skulking about in Corners from the Creation, and has been hunted and persecuted, in all Countries, by cruel Power."[29]

A HISTORY OF THE CONSPIRACY

The colonists' understanding of the relationship between power and liberty was not, however, part of some lofty philosophic discussion disconnected from the realities of day-to-day life. It was forged during the pressing events of the 1760s and early 1770s. The provincials' intellectual rebellion developed as a result of their assessment of what they believed was an active and organized conspiracy of power led by British imperial officials and their Loyalist supporters against liberty. American Patriots discerned in the various laws passed by British officials what they took to be evidence—irrefutable and overwhelming evidence—of a conscious pattern of malevolent intent. In fact, America's revolutionary leaders claimed to see a deliberately organized plan to destroy the English constitution and to enslave them through several coordinated steps.[30] "The system is formed with art," claimed John Dickinson, "but the art is discoverable." Throughout the years of the imperial crisis, American Patriots searched high and low for all the evidence they could collect of such a "system" and the motives that lay behind it. Such fateful events, Moses Mather claimed in 1775, such "intolerable calamities spring not of the dust, come not causeless."[31] The provincials' search for the moral causes that motivated the actions of British imperial officials and their American supporters is the distinguishing feature of the American response to the events of the 1760s and 1770s.

In order to see the development of the American revolutionary mind prior to 1776, several questions concerning the colonists' motives, modes of moral analysis, and rhetoric must be asked. Why, for instance, did they become permanently disaffected in their relationship with the mother country? How did they go from thinking in 1764 that they were the freest people in the world to thinking just a few years later that they were in the process of being enslaved? Was the American response to the Sugar, Stamp, Townshend, Tea, and Coercive Acts reasonable? Were the revolutionaries' claims of a British conspiracy to enslave them justified or hyperinflated rhetoric? Were such grandiose charges a sign of the revolutionaries' distempered minds, as suggested by the American Loyalists and some twentieth-century historians?[32]

From the Sugar Act to the Coercive Acts, the leaders of the American Revolution examined, measured, and judged the meaning of every piece of colonial legislation and how it affected their rights and liberties. Remarkably, some of the most astute provincials saw a British design to steal their freedom literally from the beginning of the imperial crisis. In 1765, just after the passage of the Sugar and Stamp Acts, John Adams was either prescient or paranoid when he declared, "There seems to be a direct and formal design on foot, to enslave all America."[33] On the face of it, the charge seems ludicrous.[34] But Adams saw immediately the implications of a tax commanded without the colonists' consent and backed up with the force of Britain's imperial state—for example, enforcement by an increased British naval presence in American waters, increased and financially incentivized customs officials armed with new writs of assistance, and, most ominously, the replacement of common law jury trials with non-juried vice-admiralty courts. According to Adams, "the most grievous innovation of all" was not the tax but rather the alarming extension of the power of courts of admiralty. In these courts, one judge presides alone! No juries have any concern there! The law and the fact are both to be decided by the same single judge, whose commission is only during pleasure, and with whom, as we are told, the most mischievous of all customs has become established, that of taking commissions on all condemnations; so that he is under a pecuniary temptation always against the subject.... We cannot help asserting, therefore, that this part of the act will make an essential change in the constitution of juries, and it is directly repugnant to the Great Charter itself.

Few, however, saw what he saw—or imagined. It took almost a decade for most Americans to connect the dots and catch up to Adams, who had been waiting for them somewhat impatiently. He understood that America's revolutionary progress would necessarily be slow: It is, he noted, "like a large Fleet sailing under Convoy. The fleetest Sailors must wait for the dullest and slowest. Like a Coach and six—the swiftest Horses must be slackened and the slowest quickened, that all may keep an even Pace."[35] With every passing year, the evidence of a design to restrict and then to destroy the colonists' liberty mounted with frightening weight and urgency.

With the passage of the Declaratory Act in 1766 and the Townshend Acts in 1768, more Americans began to see and understand what was happening to them. In addition to the taxing elements of the Townshend duties, the colonists were no less alarmed by the dramatic increase in Whitehall's bureaucratic control of the colonies through the use of increased customs officials and standing armies, not to mention Parliament's suspension of the New York Assembly. John Dickinson summed up the American position in these terms:

What man who wishes the welfare of America can view without pity, without passion, her restricted and almost stagnated trade, with its numerous train of evils—taxes torn from her without her consent—her legislative Assemblies, the principal pillars of her liberty, crushed into insignificance—a formidable force established in the midst of peace, to bleed her into obedience—the sacred right of trial by jury violated by the erection of arbitrary and unconstitutional jurisdictions—and general poverty, discontent, and despondence stretching themselves over his unoffending country.[36]

All of these developments combined, it was feared, would upset the constitutional balance by extending ministerial influence and executive patronage, and with that a new class of parasitic officeholders, into America at the expense of the colonists' own self-governing institutions. Even worse, the greatest threat to Anglo-American freedom came in the form of the Declaratory Act, which granted Parliament authority to legislate for the colonies "in all cases whatsoever." The Declaratory Act represented the naked essence of power. Thus the Americans regarded British authorities as the true innovators, as the true revolutionaries against the principles and institutions of the English constitution.

In 1770, in the wake of the Townshend Acts and then the Boston Massacre, the Boston Town Meeting sounded the alarm in a report to its representatives in the Massachusetts Assembly:

> A series of occurrences, many recent events,...afford great reason
> to believe that a deep laid & desperate plan of Imperial despotism
> has been laid, and partly executed, for the extinction of all civil
> liberty....The august and once revered, fortress of english free-
> dom—the admirable work of ages,—the BRITISH CONSTITUTION
> seems fast tottering into fatal & inevitable ruin. The dreadful catas-
> trophe threatens universal havock, and presents an awful warning to
> hazard all if, peradventure, we in these distant confines of the Earth
> may prevent being totally overwhelm'd and buried under the ruins
> of our most established rights.[37]

By 1773, however, just when it seemed that the political crisis between colonies and mother country might have reached a state of political stasis and that it might resolve itself through dissipation, Parliament passed and the king approved the Tea Act. Suspicion turned into outright hostility. In the wake of the Boston Tea Party in December 1773, Parliament took swift retribution by passing a series of coercive measures—the Boston Port Act, the Administration of Justice Act, the Massachusetts Government Act, the Quartering Act, and the Quebec Act—that finally exposed for all with eyes to see the ultimate motives and goals of British officialdom.

By passing these punitive measures, known in America as the Intolerable Acts, the British government had finally raised its political Jolly Roger. From this point forward, the tide shifted in America as a consensus began to build denying the authority of Parliament to legislate for the colonies in all cases whatever.

By 1774, the Americans had all the proof they needed of a conspiracy of British lawmakers and ministers to enslave them. For most, Parliament's passage of the Coercive Acts was the smoking gun. They saw in the ministry's actions nothing less than a systematic program for the establishment of tyranny. The Coercive Acts presented all the harbingers of despotism that writers in the Real Whig tradition had warned about for decades. That year, two of America's most brilliant polemicists, John Adams and John Dickinson, published exposés of the malevolent designs of British imperial officials to enslave the colonies.

Adams's Novanglus letters proposed to show "the wicked policy of the Tories—trace their plan from its first rude sketches to its present compleat draught." More, he proposed to show "that it has been much longer in contemplation, than is generally known—who were the first in it—their views, motives and *secret springs of action*—and the means they have employed." Adams traced a twenty-year conspiracy from the administration of Governor William Shirley in the mid-1750s to that of Thomas Hutchinson in the early 1770s. His ultimate goal, he wrote, was to pursue the "Tories through all their dark intrigues, and wicked machinations; and to shew the rise, and progress of their schemes for enslaving this country." He accused the conspirators of nothing less than advancing the despotic "principles of Hobbes and Filmer." In lawyerly fashion, Adams detailed the seen and unseen actions and motives of the co-conspirators. The result: a "settled plan to deprive the people of all the benefits, blessings and ends of the contract, to subvert the fundamentals of the constitution—to deprive them of all share in making and executing laws."[38]

Likewise, Dickinson, the man who did as much as anyone to inspire the Americans to revolution but who also personally resisted independence until the bitter end, announced in a series of letters to the American people that he would "prove" to his readers "such a series of correspondent facts" that would convince them "that a plan had been deliberately framed, and pertinaciously adhered to, unchanged even by frequent changes of Ministers, unchecked by an intervening gleam of humanity, to sacrifice to a passion for arbitrary dominion the universal property, liberty, safety, honor, happiness and prosperity of us unoffending, yet devoted Americans."[39]

It was not just the intellectual and political elite that charged British imperial officials with a malevolent design to enslave them. Up and down the Atlantic seaboard, colonial Whigs of all stripes reacted with outrage at what they considered to be a virtual British declaration of war against Massachusetts. Not surprisingly, it was the Massachusettsians who most often spoke of a deliberate conspiracy to destroy their freedom. In Boston, the Suffolk Resolves (written by Joseph Warren) denounced a "licentious minister," a "parricide which points the dagger at our bosoms," and "the attempts of a wicked administration to enslave America." Likewise, the Boston Committee of Correspondence saw in the Coercive Acts "glaring evidence of a fixed plan of the British administration to bring the whole continent into the most humiliating bondage."[40]

Moving into lower New England, on May 19, 1774, a thousand Connecticut residents gathered at the local liberty pole in Farmington and there resolved, mincing no words: "That the present Ministry, being instigated by the Devil, and led by their wicked and corrupt hearts, have a design to take away our liberties and properties, and to enslave us for ever....That those pimps and parasites who dared to advise their master to such detestable measures, be held in utter abhorrence by...every American, and their names loaded with the curses of all succeeding generations." About fifty miles southwest of Farmington, the Rev. Ebenezer Baldwin of Danbury, Connecticut, likewise told his flock "that if we view the whole of the conduct of the ministry and parliament, I do not see how any one can doubt but that there is a settled fix'd plan for inslaving the colonies, or bringing them under arbitrary government." Another seventy or so miles southwest of Danbury, in New York City, the Association of the Sons of Liberty of New York accused the "commons of Great Britain" of a "diabolical project of enslaving America," and a nineteen-year-old Alexander Hamilton assumed that a "system of slavery, fabricated against America, cannot, at this time, be considered as the effect of inconsideration and rashness. It is the offspring of mature deliberation. It has been fostered by time and strengthened by every artifice human subtility is capable of."[41]

Likewise in the middle colonies, a committee of Philadelphia merchants announced "that the Ministry have formed a plan for subjugating the Americans and that they are determined to persist in it." James Wilson reminded his audience in Philadelphia that the British ministry had, in the years after the Stamp Act, "renewed their designs against us, not with less malice, but with more art." Under the cover of clever policies that distinguished between internal and external taxes, British officials "pursued their scheme of depriving us of our property without our consent." Only after it became clear to the Americans that the British attempt to "degrade" them "to a rank inferiour to that of freemen, appeared now to be reduced into a regular system," did it become necessary and proper on their part "to form a regular system for counteracting" British actions.[42]

Further south, Virginians George Washington, Richard Henry Lee, and Thomas Jefferson, careful analysts of the revolutionary situation, summed up the logic and direction of the leading American thinking on the motives and actions of British imperial officials. In a series of letters written in 1774, Washington responded to the passage of the Coercive Acts by suggesting that it was "as clear as the sun in its meridian brightness, that there is a regular, systematic plan formed to fix the right and practice of taxation upon us." Washington thought he saw in recent British legislation a "tyrannical system," and he then accused the government of "pursuing a regular plan at the expense of law and justice to overthrow our constitutional rights and liberties." Nay, worse: Washington saw nothing less than "self evident proofs of a fixed and uniform plan" designed to impose on the people of Massachusetts "the most despotic system of tyranny, that ever was practised in a free government." In one of the best and most advanced American arguments in 1774, Washington put his cards on the table. He told his correspondent that an "innate spirit of freedom" had inspired him, and averred

> that the measures, which administration hath for some time
> been, and now are most violently pursuing, are repugnant to every
> principle of natural justice; whilst much abler heads than my own
> hath fully convinced me, that it is not only repugnant to natural
> right, but subversive of the laws and constitution of Great Britain
> itself, in the establishment of which some of the best blood in the
> kingdom hath been spilt. Satisfied, then, that the acts of a British
> Parliament are no longer governed by the principles of justice, that
> it is trampling upon the valuable rights of Americans, confirmed
> to them by charter and the constitution they themselves boast of,

and convinced beyond the smallest doubt, that *these measures are the result of deliberation*, and attempted to be carried into execution by the hand of power, is it a time to trifle, or risk our cause upon petitions, which with difficulty obtain access, and afterwards are thrown by with the utmost contempt? Or should we, because heretofore unsuspicious of design, and then unwilling to enter into disputes with the mother country, go on to bear more, and forbear to enumerate our just causes of complaint? For my own part, I shall not undertake to say where the line between Great Britain and the colonies should be drawn; but I am clearly of opinion, that one ought to be drawn, and our rights clearly ascertained.[43]

Along with Washington, Lee saw nothing less than irrefutable evidence of the "tyrannous designs" of British ministers "for destroying our constitutional liberty." So too did Jefferson, who, in his 1774 essay *A Summary View of the Rights of British-America*, announced that "single acts of tyranny may be ascribed to the accidental opinion of a day; but a series of oppressions begun at a distinguished period, and pursued, unalterably through every change of ministers, too plainly prove a deliberate and systematical plan of reducing us to slavery."[44] The idea of a ministerial conspiracy against American liberty, when conjoined with the patriots' commitment to Lockean principles of government, activated the American spirit of liberty and inspired colonial patriots to resist every British injustice, real or perceived.

Until 1774 and the passage of the Coercive Acts, virtually all Americans hoped for some kind of reconciliation with Great Britain. When the First Continental Congress met in that year, it offered to submit to parliamentary regulation of imperial trade, but it denied Parliament's authority to legislate for the colonies. But the outbreak of armed hostilities at Lexington and Concord on April 19, 1775, and the passage in December of the Prohibitory Act, effectively removing the Americans from the protection of their king and declaring war against them, pushed the Americans to the breaking point. America's leading revolutionaries, who had once sworn fealty to king and constitution, now rejected both: they no longer had any desire to restore the constitutional and political relationship that had existed between the colonies and their mother country before 1764. After eleven years of serious and careful reflection, the vanguard of

American revolutionary thinking had come to a stark realization: not only did Parliament have no authority to tax and legislate for the colonies, but Parliament also had never held that authority in the first place, despite the fact that the forefathers of these New World provincials had occasionally indulged Parliament in its unjust actions. That is, the American people were and had always been politically and constitutionally independent of the British people and their Parliament. Henceforth, they were absolved from their obligation of allegiance to the British Crown.

In a letter to Horatio Gates dated March 23, 1776, John Adams laid bare the ultimate meaning of the Prohibitory Act:

> I know not whether you have seen the Act of Parliament call'd the restraining Act, or prohibitory Act, or piratical Act, or plundering Act, or Act of Independency, for by all these Titles is it call'd. I think the most apposite is the Act of Independency, for King Lords and Commons have united in Sundering this Country and that I think forever. It is a compleat Dismemberment of the British Empire. It throws thirteen Colonies out of the Royal Protection, levels all Distinctions and makes us independent in Spight of all our supplications and Entreaties. It may be fortunate that the Act of Independency should come from the British Parliament, rather than the American Congress: But it is very odd that Americans should hesitate at accepting Such a Gift from them.[45]

With George III having declared the colonies to be in a state of rebellion and then committing Britain in August 1775 to strong military measures to force the colonists to yield to parliamentary authority, the Americans were left with little choice. In 1776 the political Rubicon was forded on vessels supplied by John Locke's natural-rights philosophy and its corollary theory of revolution.

PRUDENCE AND REVOLUTION

The Declaration suggests that it is unwise to overthrow those governments that have been "long established" for "light and transient causes." But what are "light and transient causes"? In *A Summary View of the Rights of British-America*, published two years before he wrote the Declaration,

Jefferson indicated the conditions under which it would be inappropriate to alter or abolish a government long established. During the first fifty years of the eighteenth century, Parliament passed three laws—the Post Office Act (1710), the Hat Act (1732), and the Iron Act (1750)—all of which Jefferson thought were unjust violations of the colonists' rights; but he regarded them as "less alarming" because they were "repeated" at "distant intervals."[46] Such laws, either taken separately or together, did not meet the threshold to justify revolution against an otherwise good government long established. Jefferson and his fellow provincials viewed these laws as unfortunate single acts that evinced no design of tyranny. The ultimate standard employed by Jefferson to justify the necessity of revolution is defined first by the facts—"a long train of abuses and usurpations, pursuing invariably the same Object"—which must then add up to and evince "a design to reduce" a people under the arbitrary rule of "absolute Despotism." This means that single acts of oppression do not constitute grounds for revolution, particularly when citizens still retain the right to petition, to peacefully protest the government's actions, and to persuade said government to retract its mistake.

Colonial Americans did not think that the passage of the Sugar and Stamp Acts in 1764 and 1765 had placed them in a revolutionary situation. Consider the colonists' reaction to the passage of the Sugar Act and the subsequent rumor that Parliament was about to pass a stamp tax the following year. James Otis spoke for most Americans in 1764 when he declared in *The Rights of the British Colonies Asserted and Proved* that it would "be the highest degree of impudence and disloyalty to imagine that the King, at the head of his parliament, could have any, but the most pure and perfect intentions of justice, goodness and truth." In 1765, the idea of rebelling against and attempting to overturn their government because they thought the Sugar and Stamp Acts were unjust and therefore unconstitutional would have struck virtually all Americans as dangerously unhinged. Woven into eighteenth-century Anglo-American constitutional culture was the unwavering belief that the motives of king and Parliament were pure and good, that their only concern was for the "public good." It was therefore incumbent on the colonists that they demonstrate a "most perfect and ready obedience" to the king and to Parliament's laws as long as such laws "remain in force." In fact, the colonists' "duty," according to Otis, was "to submit and patiently bear" the enforcement of unjust laws until Parliament saw the error of its ways and corrected its mistake. Otherwise, "there would be an end of all government, if one or a number of subjects or subordinate provinces should take upon them so far to judge of the justice of an act of parliament, as to refuse obedience to it." The idea of altering or abolishing government in such situations was simply beyond the pale. In the face of an unjust law, the colonists, Otis continued, should assume that the king and Parliament have simply "erred" because they have been "misinformed and deceived." Virtually all colonists would have agreed with Otis that the only proper method of seeking the repeal of an unjust law passed by Parliament was to petition king and Parliament for redress, which is precisely what they did. Should that fail, Otis was confident that the king's executive courts would "adjudge such acts void." For Otis and most Americans, the "grandeur of the British constitution" was defined by its internal checks and balances, which made the idea or possibility of tyranny and therefore of revolution virtually irrelevant.[47]

Two years later, American theorists began to question the near-sacred status afforded the British constitution, particularly as it was developed in William Blackstone's influential *Commentaries on the Laws of England* (1766). Blackstone there argued that the British constitution was synonymous with Parliament's power and could not be altered or abolished by the people. The English jurist explicitly rejected Locke's theory that the people have a primitive power as logically impossible and practically dangerous. According to Blackstone, "No human laws will therefore suppose a case, which at once must destroy all law, and compel men to build afresh upon a new foundation; nor will they make provision for so desperate an event, as must render all legal provisions ineffectual."[48]

After Parliament's passage of the Declaratory Act in 1766, American Whigs began to develop a very different understanding of the British constitution, one that included a theory of resistance and revolution. Richard Bland of Virginia did not think the British constitution was infallible, above reproach, or divorced from natural justice, and he certainly did not think it was immune to alteration by the people. Following Locke's revolutionary logic, Bland moved the American argument a step closer to a full-throttled theory of revolution. "If a man invades my property," Bland reasoned, he

> becomes an aggressor, and puts himself into a state of war with me: I have a right to oppose this invader; if I have not strength to repel him, I must submit; but he acquires no right to my estate which he

has usurped. Whenever I recover strength, I may renew my claim, and attempt to regain my possession; if I am never strong enough, my son, or his son, may, when able, recover the natural right of his ancestor, which has been unjustly taken from him.

What Bland thought true in the state of nature was also true in civil society, whether in England or America. He recognized Parliament's sovereign authority in the political sphere, but it "cannot, constitutionally, deprive the people of their natural rights." If Parliament were to pass laws that violated the rights of British Americans, the colonists should "refuse obedience to such a vote, and may oppose the execution of it by force."[49] The right of resistance is an option of last resort, according to Bland, but it is an option.

When a government—including a formerly good government—becomes destructive of the ends for which it was created, when it becomes an arbitrary tyranny that violates the rights of its citizens (including free speech and peaceful assembly), then the people must seriously judge for themselves whether it is or is not "prudent" to rebel, given that they have the moral right to do so under defined conditions. There may be times when it is *not* prudent to openly attempt to overthrow the government. There are times, however, when the people not only have a right to overthrow their government but also have, according to the Declaration, a "duty" to do so. Thus, as Jefferson stated in the Declaration's first paragraph, it had become "necessary" for the Americans to dissolve their connection to Great Britain. The Americans had chosen to live their lives according to certain moral and political principles no matter what, which meant that by their own moral code they could not evade the responsibility to fight for those principles. Jefferson summed up his view of the matter in an eloquent statement to Madame de Staël. "When patience has begotten false estimates of its motives," he wrote to his French correspondent, "when wrongs are pressed because it is believed they will be borne, resistance becomes morality."[50] In the context of 1776, armed rebellion was ultimately a moral necessity for Jefferson.

It is important to note, however, that Jefferson did suggest that for governments long established, and especially for those governments that had been formerly just and good, the subjects or citizens should first resort to all peaceful and rational means by which to alert the government to their concerns. In the context of 1776, the Americans, according to the Declaration, had done just that: they had, during "every stage of these Oppressions," petitioned king and Parliament for a redress of their grievances and sent various resolutions and declarations, but to no good end. Over the course of ten years, the various resolves, petitions, and declarations written by the town councils, provincial legislatures, committees of correspondence, and the Continental Congress to George III and Parliament sought to make two points: first, that the colonists remained loyal to their king, and second, that they would *not* long endure violations of their "most sacred" rights and liberties. American provincials made it clear to George III that their goal was to return to the state of affairs they had known in 1763. Continued violations of their rights would cause them to invoke what John Adams called "revolution principles."

The final decision for independence did not come easily or lightly; indeed, it was done with great trepidation. After establishing the philosophic standards by which the king and Parliament were to be judged, the Declaration goes on to explain why the colonists were declaring their independence. It lays out in lawyerly fashion the "long train of abuses and usurpations" they have suffered, listing eighteen abuses by the king and an additional nine in conjunction with Parliament. The "history of the present King of Great Britain is a history of repeated injuries and usurpations" evincing a "design to reduce them under absolute Despotism" and "absolute Tyranny." The colonists' final judgment on King George was that his "character is thus marked by every act which may define a Tyrant." He was therefore "unfit to be the ruler of a free People."

For a decade, the colonists suffered patiently, without relief. Their "repeated Petitions" to king and Parliament were met by "repeated injury." The Declaration notes that the colonists had also appealed directly to the people of Great Britain. The Americans had warned their British brethren "from time to time of attempts by their legislature to extend an unwarrantable jurisdiction over us." The colonists reminded their British kin "of the circumstances of our emigration and settlement here"; they "appealed to their native justice and magnanimity," and, finally, they "have conjured them by the ties of our common kindred to disavow these usurpations, which, would inevitably interrupt our connections and correspondence." The colonists had done everything in their power to right repeated wrongs through all constitutional and political channels available to them, but to no avail. It was now "necessary" in the face of tyranny unmasked that the

Americans "declare, That these United Colonies are, and of Right ought to be FREE AND INDEPENDENT STATES."

By 1776, the colonists had come to the painful conclusion that rebellion and independence were morally necessary—that they must act out of fidelity to their principles. The Declaration announced independence as the final response to the imperial government's failure to take the steps necessary to redress the colonists' grievances.

PAINE'S REVOLUTION

The publication of Thomas Paine's *Common Sense* in January 1776 represents the climax of the American revolutionary response to the unfolding events of the imperial crisis. Utterly unique in the literature of the Revolution, Paine's pamphlet was the most provocative, the most partisan, the most widely read, and the most influential polemic written between 1765 and 1776. It "burst forth from the press," Benjamin Rush wrote, "with an effect which has rarely been produced by types and papers in any age or country." Leading revolutionaries such as Charles Lee claimed that it was *Common Sense* that brought them to the cause of revolution and independence. Even George Washington noted in a letter that the "sound doctrine and unanswerable reason" of Paine's pamphlet was working a "powerful change…in the minds of men."[51]

Unlike the logical and abstract pamphlets that preceded it, the language of *Common Sense* brims with indignation, rage, and hatred when it describes the present and the past, and waxes lyrical, inspirational, and urgent when it imagines the future. An assault on Western civilization as it then existed, it sought to give birth to new forms of social and political organization. In this respect, Paine's pamphlet had more in common with the pamphlet literature of the French Revolution than with constitutional arguments of the imperial crisis. *Common Sense* was the first public tract to call openly not just for American independence but also for the creation of a new kind of political society. It was the literary spark that ignited armed rebellion. The Revolution henceforth would no longer be about restoring something old; it was now about creating something new. *Common Sense* was the penultimate expression of America's revolutionary mind.

Paine's *Common Sense* was the most radical document of the Revolutionary era because it was the first to sever *all* ties with England

and the British throne. Much ink had been spilled by Richard Bland, James Wilson, Thomas Jefferson, and John Adams to delegitimize the politics of Parliament while elevating the authority of the king in the colonies. But with Paine, the severance of the last psychological and constitutional connection between the mother country and colonies was placed at the forefront of the colonial agenda. Until Paine, America's best thinkers sought to defend and restore some version of an idealized English constitution with the king at its head. *Common Sense* changed everything. Even an idealized English constitution was now under assault by Paine. The Americans were now interested in beginning the world anew.

Paine's radicalism began with his almost complete rejection of all received ideas on government. He was the first American (strictly speaking, Paine was an Englishman only recently transplanted to America) to denounce openly the revered British constitution and the very idea of monarchy. In fact, Paine even rejected the mythical ancient constitution that so many of his fellow revolutionaries sought to restore. The "much boasted constitution of England," even in its idealized Cokean form, was ultimately corrupt and degenerate, in Paine's view, and could not be fixed. *Common Sense* proposed therefore an "inquiry into the constitutional errors of the English form of government" because the Americans "remain fettered" by an "obstinate prejudice," the very same kind of prejudice in favor of traditional political forms and formalities noted earlier by Locke. Paine uncoupled that "prejudice" from the Americans' political self-understanding. A predisposition to favor a "rotten constitution of government," Paine wrote, "will disable us from discerning a good one." According to traditional Anglo-American belief, liberty rested on a constitutional equilibrium that balanced and institutionalized the three naturally occurring socio-constitutional orders of the one (the monarchy), the few (the aristocracy), and the many (the people), with each embodied in its corresponding organ of government: the Crown, the House of Lords, and the House of Commons. In challenging this belief, Paine, at the broadest level, rejected the idea of what he called "complex" government.[52]

Unlike Jefferson and Adams, Paine was not interested in recovering the ancient Saxon or even the seventeenth-century Cokean constitution.[53] His rejection of the British constitution was grounded on his utter contempt for two of its three socio-constitutional forms: the monarchy and the aristocracy. The notion of the nobility's moral legitimacy was, in Paine's view, beneath contempt. The nobility represented the living dead. The monarchical branch, however, was a much more serious matter, particularly given the fact that his revolutionary colleagues had recently reconnected the colonies to the mother country constitutionally through the person of the king. With spitting invective, he used a variety of stinging epithets to describe the idea of monarchy in general and the English monarchy in particular. He characterized the world's first king as "nothing better than the principal ruffian of some restless gang" and denounced William the Conqueror as a "French bastard," who invaded England with a gang of "armed banditti." In short, the principle of "hereditary succession" was an "evil" that had left "the world in blood and ashes." Paine then moved in for the kill: he argued that "one of the strongest *natural* proofs of the folly of hereditary right in kings, is, that nature disapproves it, otherwise she would not so frequently turn it into ridicule by giving mankind an *ass for a lion*."[54]

Paine was asking his fellow Americans to sever the constitutional head from the political body. Such an action was completely justified, he argued, after the events at Lexington and Concord and after the king had signed the Prohibitory Act, that is, after George III "hath wickedly broken through every moral and human obligation, trampled nature and conscience beneath his feet; and by a steady and constitutional spirit of insolence and cruelty, procured for himself an universal hatred."[55] For Paine, the objective criteria justifying revolution had been met. Revolution was now necessary.

Having severed all moral and political ties to Great Britain, Paine's last task was to draw certain boundary lines in America between those who supported independence and those who did not. The decision that all Americans had now to make was not to determine what kind of relationship they would have with the mother country but whether there would be any political relationship at all. If not, then the resort to arms would be necessary. The radicalness of Paine's position is clearly seen in his suggestion that by "referring the matter from argument to arms, a new æra for politics is struck," and "a new method of thinking hath arisen." In this new "æra," this "new method of thinking" would seek to establish relations between the colonies and Great Britain on an entirely different foundation—that of one independent nation to another. Therefore, reconciliation and subordination to an external power, Paine wrote, is unmanly, "repugnant to reason" and "to the universal order of things"—a hopeless and "fallacious dream," he wrote. "Nature," he continued, "hath deserted the connexion, and Art cannot supply her place." Armed resistance was not only justified, but it was also now imperative. The time was right for the Americans not only to declare their independence from Great Britain, but also to build new governments. For the first time in human history, he asserted, the moment had arrived "*To begin government at the right end.*"[56]

Paine's revolution was therefore not simply constitutional; it was psychological, moral, and political. He called for nothing less than the beginning of a new world: "Should an independency be brought about by the first of those means, we have every opportunity and every encouragement before us, to form the noblest, purest constitution on the face of the earth. *We have it in our power to begin the world over again.* A situation, similar to the present, hath not happened since the days of Noah until now."[57]

In terms of the American mind and the emerging national sentiment, *Common Sense* made the Declaration of Independence possible. America's impatient revolutionary, Thomas Paine, radicalized the gentlemanly revolution launched by Otis, Bland, Dickinson, Washington, Adams, and Jefferson. Paine's revolution does not seek to recover a pristine and virtuous past; instead, it seeks to destroy a corrupt past and replace it with an idealistic future governed by the monarchy of reason. Prudence, moderation, and caution played no part in Paine's revolution, which was instead driven by a kind of dyspeptic anger and systematic rage. As John Adams once said of Paine, he was good at tearing down constitutional buildings but not very good at building them up.[58] That task was left to America's more thoughtful constitutional architects. Still, it was the dawning of a new age.

CHAPTER 11

Rebels with a Cause

*"And for the support of this Declaration,…we mutually
pledge to each other our Lives, our Fortunes and
our sacred Honor."*

The Declaration of Independence was both a consequence and a cause of the American Revolution. As an "expression of the American mind," it was an *effect* with its own deep, underlying causes—the culmination of a long line of thinking and acting by many people over the course of many years. The Declaration, John Adams wrote to a family friend, "compleats a Revolution, which will make as good a Figure in the History of Mankind, as any that has preceeded it."[1] The text itself was the product of a thinking mind that attempted to express in written words the moral and political ideas, principles, and convictions of several million people as they had developed over the preceding decade.

The Declaration was also a *cause* with many effects. Its articulation of certain moral and political principles made a real difference in the lives of ordinary people. It motivated individuals to act in certain ways. It inspired and even obligated Americans to act in defense of its principles (and not just in 1776): it impelled them to resist the decisions and actions of the British king and his Parliament, to declare their independence from the mother country, to join George Washington's Continental Army, to fight a war of national liberation, and to construct new constitutions and governments. According to William Whipple, a signer of the Declaration from New Hampshire: "This Declaration has had a glorious effect—has made these colonies alive."[2]

To revolutionary Americans, the words used in the Declaration of Independence held real and important meaning. The Declaration's ideas were more than simply descriptive or illustrative rationalizations; they had a profound moral meaning that served as a causal force in motivating American revolutionaries to take certain actions. Ascertaining the moral values and principles that moved eighteenth-century Anglo-American provincials to act—what they were reacting against and what they were acting for—is the first task of any history of the Revolution. Historians must recreate and understand their problems, challenges, alternatives, modes of reasoning, values, motives, and judgments as they understood them. Then, and only then, can we determine *why* they thought and acted as they did.

The writing, signing, and public readings of the Declaration were themselves discrete acts that altered the course of human events. The Declaration brought a decade-long struggle to a single point, but it was more than just a symbol or an expression of the American mind. A mere 1,337 words transformed the subjects of a British king into republican citizens of an independent nation. The Declaration's principles served as the moral foundation for the creation of new republican governments. More immediately, it also inspired tens of thousands of Americans to fight and thousands to die on behalf of its principles. Moreover, by signing their names to the Declaration and thereby renouncing their allegiance to George III, the representatives to the Continental Congress were committing treason and thereby signing their own death warrants. From the British perspective, the Declaration of Independence was a declaration of American treason.

The United States became a different place after July 4, 1776.

*　　*　　*

The Declaration of Independence was both a consequence of thought and action and a cause of new thought and action. Its first sentence says that it is necessary for "one People" to do two things, one negative and one positive: they must end their constitutional relationship with Great Britain, and they must also assume the power and authority to create new governments, with the power to "levy War, conclude Peace, contract Alliances, establish Commerce, and to do all other Acts and Things which Independent States may of right do." In its concluding paragraph, the Declaration sums up what it is doing (as both fact and moral imperative) by announcing that America's "United Colonies are, and of Right ought to be FREE AND INDEPENDENT STATES." The publication of the Declaration of Independence is the necessary first step in achieving both goals. Thus the Declaration unites theory and practice.

The most interesting word in the opening sentence of the Declaration is one that readers typically glide over without a second thought. The key word is the adjective *necessary*. Consider the meaning of the word in the context of the sentence in which it appears: "When in the Course of human events, it becomes *necessary* for one people to dissolve the political bands which have connected them with another,...they should declare the causes which impel them to the separation." In the second paragraph, the Declaration also says that it is not only the "right" but the "duty" of the American people to "throw off such Government, and to provide new Guards for their future security." But why necessary, why a duty? Why in the course of events from 1765 to 1776 did it become "necessary"—even a duty—for the American colonists to dissolve their political connection to king and mother country and to build a new nation? Was separation really necessary?

In reality, there was none of the legendary tyranny in Britain's American colonies that stained the annals of history. Could the Americans of 1776 genuinely say they were an oppressed people? Surely not! For some, the stamp tax was a pittance not worth the pottage. In fact, it might be truer to say that, despite their political disagreements with George III and his government, the American people were freer and wealthier than any other people in history. The Americans felt none of the crushing weight imposed on the peoples of Europe by the canon and feudal laws. Certainly from the perspective of British officialdom, the Americans' response to parliamentary legislation was incomprehensible.

The Declaration's strange use of the word "necessary" raises even more philosophic questions. Why is separation said to be necessary rather than chosen or optional? Would it not be truer to say that the colonists had in front of them a whole range of options? In the wake of the Declaration, according to Thomas Paine, "all was choice."[3] But if so, how could their choice be necessary? Scientific laws of nature are necessary, but how does necessity work in a moral-political context? What will happen if the colonists do not separate? Why was it necessary to risk unspeakable suffering and even death itself? Imagine how the meaning of the Declaration would have changed if Jefferson had written not "When in the course of human

events, it becomes necessary..." but instead "optional," "possible," "expedient," "preferable," or even "prudent"?

These kinds of questions help bridge the artificial chasms that historians sometimes create between ideas and events, words and deeds, intentions and actions, rhetoric and reality—which is to say, causes and effects.
Such questions challenge us to see the origin of the American Revolution
and the motives that led American revolutionaries to act in a new light.
They permit us to dissolve the false dichotomy between the revolutionaries'
consciously chosen ideals and their consciously chosen actions.

Consider, for instance, how and why Jefferson and the signers
used some of the rhetorically powerful language that we see in the
text. When they invoked the inflammatory language of "despotism" and
"tyranny" or "equality" and "liberty," were they deploying manipulative
propaganda, or did those words and ideas reflect reality and certain
moral imperatives? By tracing the "history of the present King of Great
Britain" through an objective examination of his "repeated injuries and
usurpations" and by submitting "facts to a candid world," were the
Americans not judging and acting according to a moral standard that
they publicly announced?

The Declaration's first sentence goes on to say that the Americans are
now declaring the "*causes* which *impel* them to the separation." But how is
it that they are being impelled, and by what force? And what are the precise
"causes" that "impel" separation and independence? In order to explain
those causes, Jefferson demonstrated two things in the Declaration: first,
the unjust actions taken by king and Parliament (i.e., the twenty-seven
charges leveled against the king) in the years between 1764 and 1776, and,
second, the moral and political principles against which the actions of
king and Parliament were to be judged (i.e., the laws of nature and certain
self-evident truths). The colonists' moral principles and the king's actions
are presented dialectically. They are in conflict with one another, and one
is judged against the other. Taken together, they are the causes that impel
the Americans to the separation.

Readers of the Declaration are still left with a deeper question:
why should these particular causes lead to war? No one was forcing the
Americans to sever their ties with George III and go to war against
the world's most lethal military force. For many Americans, independence was a difficult, if not a tragic, choice. In the two years leading up to

independence, the colonists debated in the Continental Congress whether to separate or not. In 1774, the First Continental Congress reaffirmed the colonists' loyalty to the British Crown, and as late as July 5, 1775, the Second Continental Congress adopted John Dickinson's "Olive Branch Petition," which declared the colonists' genuine hope for reconciliation with their king and mother country. So the Americans did have the choice to *not* sever their ties with Britain and to seek reconciliation. Many political moderates and certainly the Loyalists took that position.[4] Even staunch Whigs such as Landon Carter and John Dickinson balked at the prospect of forever renouncing allegiance to their king and to a nation and constitution they had long venerated. To repeat our primary question: Why was separation said to be *necessary*?

THE SPIRIT OF LIBERTY

The American mind was forged in the 1760s and 1770s under the pressure of events provoked by the imperial crisis and as a result of the provincials' confrontation with certain philosophic ideas. As John Adams, Thomas Jefferson, and Thomas Paine knew very well, the American Revolution was primarily an intellectual and a moral revolution—it represented, as Adams noted, a *"radical change in the principles, opinions, sentiments, and affections of the people."*[5] It was a revolution that advanced new moral values and virtues, new manners and mores, and a new way to think about moral character and moral action. From this fundamental change in the Americans' moral values followed all of the subsequent social, political, and economic changes that would come to define a new way of life in America.[6]

This moral revolution is best seen by trying to understand *why* American revolutionaries thought it was *necessary* to dissolve a long-standing constitutional, political, and cultural relationship with Great Britain, and then by examining *how* they did it. Quite possibly the most intriguing element of the revolutionaries' moral reasoning and action was their view that it was necessary—absolutely necessary—that they dedicate their lives, their fortunes, and their sacred honor to separating from Great Britain and then to founding a nation de novo.

Our entry point for examining why this was so is a phrase the Americans of the 1760s and 1770s used often: the "spirit of liberty." The revolutionaries' dedication to the spirit of liberty as a cardinal virtue is a powerful theme that defines the American response to the issues of the imperial crisis.

To modern historians, the notion of a spirit of liberty might seem like little more than flowery rhetoric. To eighteenth-century Americans, however, it meant something specific and essential. The word "spirit" as used in the phrase signifies both an idea and action. As Levi Hart put it, the spirit of liberty means to "assert and maintain the cause of liberty." The phrase "spirit of liberty" united theory and practice for American revolutionaries; it implied an action in defense of a principle; it was characterized by certain virtues in the defense of liberty. In the words of an anonymous writer published in the *Boston Gazette*, "We know our rights, liberties, and privileges, and likewise men are determined to sacrifice all things else for their preservation."[7] The spirit of American liberty is a sentiment, a mindset, a disposition, a virtue. As a sentiment, it loves freedom and hates slavery. As a mindset, it is watchful, suspicious, and skeptical. As a disposition, it is active, jealous, restless, resolute, protective, and, most of all, vigilant. And as a virtue, it is defined by integrity, fortitude, perseverance, courage, and patriotism. The spirit of liberty, then, is a sense of life defined by independence in the fullest sense of the term.

The spirit of liberty almost seems to have been bred into the Americans' political subconscious. The first seventeenth-century settlers in the New World, wrote the historian Samuel Williams in 1794, were virtually forgotten by their kings and left alone without supervision. Without ruling structures from above, the result was predictable: the American settlers established and developed a "spirit of freedom" unique to them. And with time, "nature" established "a system of freedom in America," which British imperial officials "could neither comprehend or discern."[8] The spirit of American liberty developed slowly in the colonies, over the course of a century and a half, through barely detectable, piecemeal adaptations of thought to experience and experience to thought. As a result, colonial Americans developed certain habits and social conventions that grew out of and were compatible with the broad freedom that was unique to their culture.

They also developed what would come to be a new moral logic, with its own unique idiom, dialect, and vocabulary of thought. In 1774, in the wake of the Coercive Acts, Richard Wells called on his fellow provincials to "inject a little of the *spiritus Americani*" into their battle with British imperial officials. For himself, he hoped to purge "every narrow sentiment" from his "soul" so that the "pure unadulterated spirit of liberty" would give "vigor" to "[his] understanding." Likewise, Jonas Clark went so far as to suggest that the depredations of the British Parliament and army had rekindled the Americans' original moral spiritedness and been "the means of preserving and transmitting that *glorious spirit of liberty*."The American spirit of liberty was virtually synonymous with the moral constitutions of the colonists, and it provided the Americans with a worldview through which they interpreted and responded to the cascade of events between 1764 and 1776. No theme ran as broadly or deeply through American culture in the 1760s and 1770s. American Patriots like Virginia clergyman John Hurt were constantly reminding themselves and their fellow citizens that it was incumbent on all of them "to cherish and cultivate" the tree of liberty. They must, said Hurt, "fence it in and trench it round against the beasts of the field and insects of earth"; they must revere and conform all their actions to the "majesty of liberty."[9]

The spirit of liberty as a cause also had certain identifiable effects. According to Phillips Payson in his 1778 election-day sermon, "it is obvious to observe that a spirit of liberty should in general prevail among a people," and where it does "their minds should be possessed with a sense of its worth and nature." In those places where "the spirit of liberty is found in its genuine vigor it produces its genuine effects; urging to the greatest vigilance and exertions, it will surmount great difficulties; [so] that it is no easy matter to deceive or conquer a people determined to be free."[10]

The spirit of American liberty served as a kind of moral and psychological tripwire that was first triggered by the passage of the Stamp Act and kept active with the passage of every piece of British legislation aimed at the Americans in the decade leading up to 1776. During these years, American Whigs developed objective standards by which to measure the justice and injustice of British legislation. These standards, when combined with the provincials' spirit of liberty, provided the Americans with an early-warning system that alerted them day or night to the abuse or growth of arbitrary power.

By the early 1760s, this emerging moral awareness was taking root in the political consciousness of most Anglo-Americans. At the highest level of abstraction, the American Revolution, wrote Samuel Williams, "explained the business of the world, and served to confirm what nature and society had before produced."Thus their contest with Great Britain was not to create freedom de novo, but to restore and maintain a sense of lost freedoms. In 1774, the Americans reminded their king through the Continental Congress that they were "born the heirs of freedom." The American spirit of liberty meant discovering and resisting the forces of despotism before such forces could sink roots in the New World. The spirit of liberty was, according to Reverend John Tucker, the "*animating soul* of a free state."[11]

An excellent example of this kind of spiritedness can be seen in an essay published in the *Massachusetts Spy* in 1771. There the pseudonymous "Massachusettensis" warned his fellow countrymen about the advance of creeping power, "which is impossible to guard against" because it "appears in a variety of shapes." Encroaching power, he continued, corrupts a free society first "under the colour of law, and then it is christened with the name of *lawful authority*." Thus it is absolutely imperative for a free people who want to stay free to be on guard against and to watch for the first sign of power's appearance. "In order to do this," however, "the laws and rules of the constitution should be well examined," Massachusettensis told his fellow Bostonians, "and if we see an exercise of power not warranted by those laws and rules, it becomes our duty to remonstrate against it, and if this be ineffectual, to oppose it." Two years later, Simeon Howard, in a sermon preached to the Boston artillery company, reminded the soldiers that in every free state it was the right and responsibility of every subject to watch the quest for power by their rulers. It was "necessary," he said, that the people preserve their freedom from unreasonable restraints by government officials so that they might retain "a spirit of liberty" and a capacity to defend themselves.[12]

It was common for colonial Americans to view power as restless and sleepless, which meant they must be ever alert to its machinations. The colonists frequently invoked the famous Latin dictum *obsta principiis* (to nip in the bud, or to resist the beginnings), which they attributed to Machiavelli's *Discourses on Livy*. "Watch and oppose ought therefore," Josiah Quincy declared, "to be the motto" of the Americans if not the rest of mankind. In his 1781 election sermon to Governor Hancock and the Massachusetts legislature, Jonas Clark declared "*Obsta Principiis*...a good maxim" for all friends of liberty.[13] And in a series of essays written for the *Massachusetts Spy* in 1771 and 1772, the pseudonymous "Centinel" frequently if not obsessively cited Machiavelli's warning. "It is the declaration of a great man," he wrote in reference to the Florentine, that "a nation should often recur to its first principles." It is critically important, he warned, for the people to be vigilant against the "first motions" of power's relentless march. They must "keep the most watchful active eye on the times." Centinel pounded away at his neighbors week after week, reminding them over and over again "if there was a period of American history, that required vigilance, and a careful inspection of the time," now is that time. In fact, "we live in a day," he wrote, "when we must suspect every *thing*." To satisfy the point, he nagged and browbeat his fellow Bostonians time and again with the rallying cry, *obsta principiis*, which, he repeated as a kind of self-fulfilling prophecy, "should frequently be inculcated on a people."[14]

The keepers of America's vestal flame recognized that political power is an omnipresent force in all societies, which is why the liberty-loving temper of the people must be kindled, nurtured, and kept constantly on the alert. No infringement of their rights should be seen as too small to protest or resist. One day in 1774, an unknown man writing under the pseudonym "A Freeman" stopped by the Pennsylvania assembly, then in session, and left with the members a short, untitled essay in which he declared the "passion of Liberty" must be "implanted in every breast" and "awakened." The time had come, he continued, with an obvious reference to Machiavelli, to "nip this pernicious weed in the bud, before it has taken too deep root." It was built into the Americans' language and grammar of liberty that tyranny always begins with some seemingly small and insignificant violation of rights that goes unnoticed at first but that sets a precedent for further violations. The lust for power frequently works its way stealthily until it is too late to stop it. This is why a free people must be in a state of constant readiness to identify the unlawful or unjust use of power and to resist it. According to Samuel Adams (writing as "Vindex"), a true patriot should "keep the attention of his fellow citizens awake to their grievances" and in a constant state of agitation "till the causes of their just complains are removed."[15]

Rekindling and stoking the spirit of American liberty became a central theme repeated over and over again in the writings of leading American Patriots. Consider now two of the deepest explorations—the writings of John Adams and John Dickinson—of what that spirit was and how it was carried out in practice, particularly as it arose in response to the Stamp and Townshend Acts.

The first American essay to really examine the nature and meaning of the spirit of liberty during the 1760s was John Adams's "Dissertation on the Canon and Feudal Law," published in 1765. The ultimate purpose of the "Dissertation" was twofold: to identify the nature of the despotism inherent in the Stamp Act, and to inspire the Americans to defend their liberty. Adams's goal was to define and rekindle what he called the American "spirit of liberty," which for him was a certain kind of virtue that he characterized in his "Governor Winthrop to Governor Bradford" essays as "a jealous, a watchful spirit." The maxim that he chose to define the spirit of liberty was "*obsta principiis.*" A free people ought to be jealous of their rights and liberties, and they must be ready to resist encroachment on them at the earliest signs of malevolence on the part of rulers. This is why he warned his fellow Patriots in 1767 to be wary of "these early advances, these first approaches of arbitrary power, which are the most dangerous of all, and if not prevented, but suffered to steal into precedents, will leave no hope of a remedy without recourse to nature, violence, and war."[16]

In notes that he wrote in his *Diary* in 1772 for an oration at Braintree, Adams summed up the spirit of American liberty during the Revolutionary era:

> But this is an unalterable Truth, that the People can never be enslaved but by their own Tameness, Pusillanimity, Sloth or Corruption....The Preservation of Liberty depends upon the intellectual and moral Character of the People....Liberty, under every conceivable Form of Government is always in Danger....The Love of Power, is insatiable and uncontrollable....There is Danger from all Men. The only Maxim of a free Government, ought to be to trust no Man living, with Power to endanger public Liberty. Let Us guard against these dangers, let us be firm and stable,...but as daring and intrepid as Heroes..... Liberty depends upon an exact Balance, a nice Counterpoise of all the Powers of the state.

Adams understood that the long-term preservation of liberty required both a certain kind of political constitution sustained by a certain kind of moral constitution, that is, the moral vigilance of the people. He regarded the latter as more fundamental than the former. In the summer of 1775, he told Abigail that a "Constitution of Government once changed from Freedom, can never be restored." Once liberty is lost, he continued, it "is lost forever," which is precisely why those who love freedom must be vigilant in its defense. To that end, Adams appealed in his Novanglus letters to a "latent spark" in human nature, which is the "love of liberty." Connected to this "latent spark" was an additional aspect of human nature that felt "a resentment of injury and indignation against wrong. A love of truth, and a veneration for virtue." Ultimately, Adams argued in February 1775, "Liberty can no more exist without virtue and independence, than the body can live and move without a soul. When these are gone...if you look for liberty, you will grope in vain."[17]

The spirit of liberty is wrought into the constitution of human nature, but even so it is a spirit that must be continuously nourished and kept alive. And when this spirit of liberty is combined with certain moral and political principles—such as equality, natural rights, consent, popular sovereignty, the social contract, and rule of law—the architectonic principle that results is what Adams called the "revolution-principle." By 1775, the time had come for the Americans to invoke such revolution-principles, which were, he argued, "the principles of nature and eternal reason." He was therefore distressed to learn that some residents of Massachusetts could hold such principles to be "noble, and true" on one hand, but, on the other hand, considered the "application of them to particular cases" as somehow "wild and utopian." For Adams and fellow revolutionaries, moral principles should provide rational guidance to practice. The practically right action should result from the rationally true principle. There should be no dichotomy between theory and practice. American revolutionaries could not accept the idea that politics was a sphere sovereign unto itself without the need of guidance from rational thought or practical philosophy. The unification of theory and practice was central to Adams's self-understanding and moral constitution. He simply could not apprehend or appreciate a moral psychology that assumed that certain principles could be accepted as "in general true" but nevertheless "not applicable to particular cases." Adams wrote, "I thought their being true in general was because they were applicable to most particular cases."[18]

It was the provincials' unbending moral character, their dedication in practice to their moral and political ideals, that British imperial officials were never able to comprehend. Hence British imperial officials could never understand why for the Americans independence had become a moral necessity.

Adams's invocation of "revolution-principles" was remarkable for its somber, rational, and levelheaded appeal to facts, precedents, and historical conditions. If revolutions are not to be undertaken for light and transient reasons and must be pursued with caution, moderation, and prudence, then there must be rationally defensible principles and observable conditions that justify such a momentous step. For Adams, the boundary line between resistance and revolution was the nature of the existing political constitution. He always sought constitutional solutions to constitutional problems, but when that was no longer possible, then a "recourse to higher powers not written" was justified.[19] The colonists were now moved to open rebellion and independence under the sanctifying authority of these "higher powers." In other words, in the course of recent events it had become "necessary" for the Americans to declare their independence.

In 1767, John Dickinson penned his *Letters from a Farmer in Pennsylvania*, which many historians regard as one of the most influential pamphlets of the Revolutionary period. Dickinson's *Letters* present a powerful analysis of the ways in which unchecked power asphyxiates liberty. They also provide the best analysis of the American spirit of liberty written at the time.

Dickinson knew that the various acts of the British government should not be "regarded according to the simple force of each, but as parts of a system of oppression." His primary concern in the *Letters* was to sound the alarm against the Townshend Acts, particularly the New York Suspending Act and the Townshend duties. The Americans, he warned, must be vigilant and exert "THE MOST WATCHFUL ATTENTION" against Parliament's subtle designs; they must prevent a creeping form of slavery under the guise of legalities, otherwise "A NEW SERVITUDE MAY BE SLIPPED UPON US, UNDER THE SANCTION OF USUAL AND RESPECTABLE TERMS." He goes on to warn against those "artful rulers" who attempt to "extend their power beyond its just limits" by subtly manipulating language and legal technicalities. And with every passing generation the noose is tightened just a little bit more. Every usurpation, whether large or small, eventually requires additional usurpations to keep all prior usurpations in force: "A free people therefore can never be too quick in observing, nor too firm in opposing the beginnings of *alteration* either in *form* or *reality*, respecting institutions formed for their security. The first kind of alteration leads to the last: Yet, on the other hand, nothing is more certain, than that the *forms* of liberty may be retained, when their *substance* is gone." Thus it is absolutely necessary, Dickinson argued, that the people should always be on guard to protect their liberty as they protect their property. He encouraged them to "watch," "observe facts," "search into causes," and "investigate designs," and of course he insisted that they assert their "right of JUDGING from the evidence before them, on no slighter points than their *liberty* and *happiness*." He implored his fellow Americans to be ever vigilant. Quoting from Montesquieu's *Spirit of the Laws*, Dickinson reminded his readers that "SLAVERY IS EVER PRECEDED BY SLEEP."[20]

Invoking ideas and rhetoric similar to Adams's, Dickinson equated the American spirit of liberty with jealousy, watchfulness, and vigilance. "A PERPETUAL *jealousy*, respecting liberty," he told the American people, "is absolutely, requisite in all free states." They must keep up the "utmost vigilance," and they must be "watchful of their liberty." He went on to remind his fellow colonists of Machiavelli's famous chapter in *Discourses on Livy*, which "prove[s] that a state, to be long lived, must be frequently corrected, and reduced to its first principles." The lesson of all history proves "that every free state should incessantly watch, and instantly take alarm on any addition being made to the power exercised over them."[21]

Dickinson attacked the Townshend duties precisely because they were so comparatively small. It would be a "fatal error," he warned, to disregard and therefore to acquiesce in these new duties because of their trifling amount. In fact, the "smallness" of the duties is a trap. No matter how inconsequential the tax, no matter how reasonably and equitably applied, the colonists should regard the act with "abhorrence." He suggested that the Townshend duties were intentionally designed to be small so that the Americans would not notice or object and a precedent could therefore be established. He went on to posit that the British were testing the moral disposition of the colonists. The Townshend Act "is a bird sent out over the waters, to discover, whether the waves, that lately agitated this part of the world with such violence [Dickinson is here referring to the colonists' reaction to the Stamp Act], are yet *subsided*. If *this adventurer* gets footing here, we shall quickly find it to be of the kind described by the poet—'*Infelix vates*' ["A direful foreteller of future calamities," from Virgil's *Aeneid*]." He then raised the very real possibility that the goal of the British imperial officials in setting such a small tax was to establish a "PRECEDENT, the force of which shall be established, by the tacit submission of the colonies." Once the precedent is established, "the parliament will levy upon us such *sums* of money as they choose to take, *without any other* LIMITATION, than their PLEASURE." Thus it is imperative that the colonists resist every attempt to tax them without their consent regardless of the size.[22]

The Townshend Act "is founded," according to Dickinson, "on the destruction" of the colonists' "constitutional security." If members of Parliament "have a right to levy a tax of *one penny* upon us," Dickinson noted, then "they have a right to levy a *million* upon us." What this means, of course, is that the possession and control of American property depended not on the will of the colonists and their rights but on the pleasure of Parliament. Dickinson supported his contention by invoking the authority of Locke: "'There is nothing which' we can call our own; or, to use the words of Mr. Locke--'WHAT PROPERTY HAVE WE IN THAT, WHICH ANOTHER MAY, BY RIGHT, TAKE, WHEN HE PLEASES, TO HIMSELF?'" The Townshend duties are clearly a tax, Dickinson concluded, and "*Those* who are *taxed* without their own consent, expressed by themselves or their representatives, are *slaves. We are taxed* without our own consent, expressed by ourselves or our representatives. We are therefore—SLAVES." The logic of Dickinson's moral reasoning was simple, compelling, motivating, and explanatory. It's what made the American revolutionary mind unique. This idea of preserving natural liberty in its pristine form and so resisting even one small precedent against it had come close to the center of the American consciousness. This idea is precisely why the colonists viewed the rather trifling stamp tax and Townshend duties so ominously: they viewed each as the entering wedge of a broader campaign to deprive them of rights and liberties. Years later, James Madison borrowed Dickinson's moral logic and reconfirmed the spirit of American liberty in no uncertain terms: "Remember that precedents once established are so much positive power; and that the nation which reposes on the pillow of political confidence, will sooner or later end its political existence in a deadly lethargy."[23]

Third-party British observers of American affairs such as Edmund Burke also took note of, and attributed causal force to, American revolutionaries' notion of a "spirit of liberty." In his 1775 speech on conciliation with the colonies, Edmund Burke was moved to explain that the single most important factor in understanding the Americans' resistance to

British legislation was their *"Temper and Character."* By studying the moral character of the colonists, Burke thought he had located the deepest source of their behavior over the course of the previous decade. In the American temperament and moral character, he wrote,

> a love of Freedom is the predominating feature which marks and distinguishes the whole: and as an ardent is always a jealous affection, your Colonies become suspicious, restive, and untractable, whenever they see the least attempt to wrest from them by force, or shuffle from them by chicane, what they think the only advantage worth living for. *This fierce spirit of Liberty is stronger in the English Colonies probably than in any other people of the earth.*

The Americans' spirit of liberty, according to Burke, provided the primary causal explanation of why they reacted to the Stamp, Declaratory, Townshend, Tea, and Coercive Acts in such a determined and principled way. It rendered the colonists "acute, inquisitive, dexterous, prompt in attack, ready in defense, full of resources." By contrast, the people of other countries, he noted, "judge of an ill principle in government only by an actual grievance." These American provincials did not succumb to the same kind of moral lethargy so common to most people throughout history. They would have none of that. Instead, they anticipated the "evil," and they judged "of the pressure of the grievance by the badness of the principle." They saw and augured "misgovernment at a distance; and snuff the approach of tyranny in every tainted breeze."[24]

Burke's warning was not heeded. Like modern historians, his colleagues never understood the principles, temperament, and character of the American revolutionaries, which meant they never understood their deepest motives. They had no way to know that the revolution's trigger was embedded in the spirit of American liberty. British officials therefore could never understand why it was *necessary* for the Americans to dissolve the political bands that had connected them to Britain for over 150 years.

IDEAS HAVE CONSEQUENCES

Though the Declaration of Independence was a foreign policy statement inspired by certain philosophical principles drawn largely from John

Locke's *Second Treatise of Government*, it was also something more. It was a call to action. As Thomas Paine put it in *The American Crisis*, during some of the darkest days of the war, "those who expect to reap the blessings of freedom, must, like men, undergo the fatigues of supporting it." The Declaration was both the last step of a process to defend the old-style English liberty and the first step in a process to support the new-style American liberty. Moral principles require moral action, and as John Hurt said of the American colonists in a sermon to Virginia troops, "there never was a country" with "stronger *motives* to unite in active zeal than this, nor was there ever a time required it more than the present."[25] Samuel Adams repeated many times in the months leading up to July 4, 1776, that the time had come: it was now or never, and he chose now.

American revolutionaries permitted no dichotomy between words and deeds. The Declaration's signers knew that they were committing treason and that war would soon follow. And in order to support their commonly shared principles in the face of war, they mutually pledged to each other, on behalf of the American people, their lives, their fortunes, and their sacred honor. This meant they must now fight to defend their freedom, and they must create a new constitution and establish a government with the power to levy war and contract diplomatic alliances.

But the Declaration meant war not just for the fifty-six men who signed it. Tens of thousands of ordinary men and boys were, in effect, pledging to fight against the greatest military power in the world. Some would die, some would be maimed, some would be captured, imprisoned, and tortured, and virtually all would suffer from exhaustion, starvation, and exposure. And not just soldiers would suffer deprivations, but their families and communities would undergo great hardships as well.

Jefferson's words were therefore intended, in part, to inspire and motivate men to act in the context of the time. Initially, the great alternatives confronting the Americans on July 4, 1776, were, as one member of the Continental Congress wrote to another, "perfect freedom, or Absolute Slavery," and to choose freedom of course meant war. They had been left "no other alternative," said Jonas Clark, but the "SWORD or SLAVERY." Six months later, however, the options facing General George Washington and his troops were even more ominous. As Washington put it on Christmas Day, 1776, just before the Battle of Trenton, the choice to separate from Great Britain could now be reduced to an even more fundamental alternative: "Victory or Death."[26]

✷ ✷ ✷

After the Second Continental Congress unanimously approved the Declaration of Independence on the fourth of July, the document was printed and distributed throughout the United States. It was imperative that all Americans be told as quickly as possible that they were now an independent nation and that this new country would have to defend itself on the battlefield. The responsibility for printing and distributing the Declaration fell to John Hancock, who on July 6 commissioned a Philadelphia publisher to print over five hundred copies. In his letter to the states, Hancock spoke of the general purpose and hoped-for consequences of the Declaration: "The important Consequences...from this Declaration of Independence, considered as the Ground & Foundation of Government will naturally suggest the Propriety of proclaiming it in such a Manner, that the People may be universally informed of it."[27]

Fast riders were then instructed to deliver copies throughout the former colonies. Once received in cities, towns, and villages, the Declaration was read publicly to large civilian audiences in state after state, in public meetings up and down the Atlantic seaboard and from the coast to the Appalachian Mountains. The Declaration's effect on the spirit of the American people was electrifying. Parades, celebrations, fireworks, thirteen-gun salutes, and toasts typically accompanied each public reading. In the days and weeks after it was signed, distributed, and read around the country there was an outpouring of support for the document.[28] Its four self-evident truths served as a polestar for the members of Congress, the people at large, and, most importantly, for Washington's troops.[29]

On July 9, Joseph Barton of Delaware wrote to a correspondent that the Declaration "gives a great turn to the minds of our people declaring our independence." It provided the Americans, he continued, with a moral standard on which "to depend." Until the publication of the Declaration, he was torn, he said, between his fealty to the king and his desire to defend his country. For now, though, his "heart and hand shall move together." As for his neighbors, they had been sitting on the fence "until we declared a free State," but now they are "ready to spend their lives and fortunes in defense of our country." With the signing of the Declaration of Independence, wrote Joseph Elmer, a future member of the Continental Congress and the United States Senate, "a new era in politics has commenced." The future happiness or misery of the American people, he continued, depends "entirely upon ourselves." Ten days later, Tristram Dalton, a former Harvard classmate of John Adams's, wrote to congratulate Elbridge Gerry, one of the Declaration's signers:

> I wish you joy on the late full Declaration—an event so ardently
> desired by your good self and the people you particularly represent.
> We are no longer to be amused with delusive prospects. The die is
> cast. All is at stake. The way is made plain. No one can now doubt
> on which side it is his duty to act. We have everything to hope from
> the goodness of our cause.....We have put on the harness, and I
> trust it will not be put off until we see our land a land of security
> and freedom—the wonder of the other hemisphere—the asylum of
> all who pant for deliverance from bondage.

The exuberance generated by the Declaration around the country was contagious. Benjamin Rush, a last-minute delegate to the Continental Congress and thus a signer of the document, told Charles Lee, "The Declaration of Independence has produced a new aera in this part of America." It inspired the Pennsylvania militia, he wrote, to "be actuated with a spirit more than Roman" and because of it the "spirit of liberty reigns triumphant in Pennsylvania."[30]

The Declaration of Independence played a particularly important role in motivating George Washington's volunteer army. On July 6, two days after the Declaration was approved by Congress, Washington received a copy from John Hancock, whose accompanying letter urged the general to share it with his troops: "that our Affairs may take a more favourable Turn, the Congress have judged it necessary to dissolve the Connection between Great Britain and the American Colonies, and to declare them free & independent States; as you will perceive by the enclosed Declaration, which I am directed to transmit to you, and to request you will have it proclaimed at the Head of the Army in the Way, you shall think most proper." By Hancock's account, the Declaration was to be the banner that would lead Washington and his troops into battle.[31]

Three days later, on July 9, 1776, as the sun was setting over New York City, the commander in chief of the Continental Army ordered all the fighting brigades in the city to convene in lower Manhattan to hear one of the first-ever public readings of the Declaration of Independence. Before they began the fight to save New York City, the soldiers were told that General Washington "hopes this important Event will serve as a fresh *incentive* to every officer, and soldier, *to act* with Fidelity and Courage, as knowing that now the peace and safety of his Country depends (under God) solely on the success of our arms: And that he is now in the service of a State, possessed of sufficient power to reward his merit, and advance him to the highest Honors of a free Country."[32] The Declaration's words inspired and galvanized Americans to fight, and possibly to die, in the name of defending their homes and their most deeply held moral principles.

The Declaration was, as Jefferson would later say, an expression of the American mind—of the Americans' deepest moral and political aspirations. It gave voice to what few of them were capable of expressing in speech or print. On July 18, 1776, James Thacher recorded in his military diary what the Declaration meant to his fellow soldiers:

> When we reflect on the deranged condition of our army, the great deficiency of our resources, and the little prospect of foreign assistance, and at the same time contemplate the prodigious powers and resources of our enemy, we may view this measure of Congress as a prodigy. The history of the world cannot furnish an instance of fortitude and heroic magnanimity parallel to that displayed by the members, whose signatures are affixed to the Declaration of American Independence. Their venerated names will ornament the brightest pages of American history, and be transmitted to the latest generations.

What Jefferson did, as Ezra Stiles, president of Yale College, put it in a 1783 sermon to the Connecticut General Assembly, was to "[pour] the soul of the continent into the monumental act of independence."[33]

The Declaration inspired and motivated not only those Americans who supported the "glorious cause" but also those sitting on the fence. On July 15, Samuel Adams wrote to Richard Henry Lee in Virginia that "our Declaration of Independency has given Vigor to the Spirits of the People." It inspired many moderates, he continued, to change their minds and support independence and the "American cause." The next day, Adams wrote to his fellow Bostonian, James Warren, telling him "our Declaration of Independence has already been attended with good Effects." On August

1, summing up the meaning and influence of the Declaration to his colleagues in the Continental Congress, Adams said: "You are now the guardians of your own liberties....The hearts of your soldiers beat high with the spirit of freedom; they are animated with the justice of their cause." In the words of David Ramsay, one of the first historians of the Revolution, the Declaration motivated the American people to "bear up under the calamities of war," and to endure "the evils they suffered, only as the thorn that ever accompanies the rose."[34]

By energizing the spirit of the people, the Declaration also served to inspire men to join Washington's army. Sometime after the signing of the document, an unknown farmer in Pennsylvania gave a speech to a meeting of his neighbors in Philadelphia County to explain why he was signing up: "I am an American," he declared, "and am determined to be free." In fact, he had been "born free" and was not about to forfeit his birthright "for a mess of pottage" as Esau did in the Book of Genesis (25:29–34). This unknown but eloquent farmer went on to explain what the inescapable logic of his principles meant in practice: "We have no alternative left us, but to fight or die. If there be a medium, it is slavery; and ever cursed be the man who will submit to it! I will not." He added bluntly: "I, therefore, conceive myself as having taken up arms in defence of innocence, justice, truth, honesty, honour, liberty, property, and life; and in opposition to guilt, injustice, falsehood, dishonesty, ignominy, slavery, poverty, and death." Indeed, "I will part with my life sooner than with my liberty; for I prefer an honourable death to the miserable and despicable existence of slavery." He concluded: "Blest be the spirit of *American* liberty, wisdom, and valour."[35] This is a stunning example of actions taken on the motivation of clear principles.

Ideas have consequences, and the Declaration's ideas fired men up to fight and die for liberty in the years after 1776. Those who supported the Declaration viewed going to war as a moral and existential necessity. Compromise, slavery, or defeat were not options. American revolutionaries acted consistently in the name of a morally absolute principle. "The truth is," Samuel Adams wrote in 1771 as a premonition of what was to come, "all might be free if they valued freedom, and defended it as they ought."[36]

No man lived and exuded that spirit of liberty more than America's commander in chief, George Washington. More than any other revolutionary, he was the embodiment of Aristotle's vision of the magnanimous man—a man whose greatness of soul stood above all others and was fired by an animating love of liberty. His towering figure left most men—including many other truly great men—in awe. The example of his moral character did even more than his military tactics to inspire his troops. "I hope we shall be taught to copy his example," said Nathanael Greene, who himself became a sterling commander of the Continental Army, "and to prefer the love of liberty in this time of public danger to all the soft pleasures of domestic life and support ourselves with manly fortitude amidst all the dangers and hardships that attend a state of war."[37] Americans high and low, rich and poor, young and old understood the necessity to defend their country and their moral principles. And that is precisely what they did.

In the year after the signing of the Declaration of Independence, General Washington's army moved from Massachusetts to New York, and then to New Jersey and Pennsylvania. Before and after every battle, Washington spoke to his troops in order to fortify and renew their fighting spirit of liberty. In the late summer of 1776, now in New York City and preparing for several battles in defense of Manhattan, he once again addressed his troops: "The Enemy have now landed on Long Island, and the hour is fast approaching, on which the Honor and Success of this army, and the safety of our bleeding Country depend. Remember officers and Soldiers, that you are Freemen, fighting for the blessings of Liberty—that slavery will be your portion, and that of your posterity, if you do not acquit yourselves like men."[38] But words only go so far. They must be translated into action, and few men are truly ready for the brutality and horror that comes with actual fighting. Still, they fought.

After taking lower Manhattan, British forces pushed forward to the north end of the island on their way to New Jersey. The British goal was to take Fort Washington, which was the rebels' last redoubt on the lower Hudson. On November 15, William Howe, the commander in chief of British forces in America, sent one of his officers to deliver a message to Robert Magaw, the American commander at Fort Washington. Howe's message left no room for misunderstanding: surrender the fort or face total destruction. Magaw's reply to Howe's aide-de-camp summed up perfectly the spirit of American liberty:

If I rightly understand the purport of your message from Gen:
Howe…"this post is to be immediately surrendered or the garrison put to the sword["]—I rather think it a mistake than a settled

resolution in General Howe to act a part so unworthy [of] himself and the British nation—But give me leave to assure his excellency that actuated by the most glorious cause that mankind ever fought in, I am determined to defend this post to the very last extremity.[39]

"Give me liberty, or give me death," "Live free or die," "We hold these truths to be self-evident": these were more than highfalutin slogans to the Americans. They had genuine meaning for America's fighting men. Ideas and principles provided the motivation for action—sometimes life-or-death action. On November 16, 1776, some 8,000 British soldiers attacked Fort Washington. In the battle, 53 Americans were killed, 96 were wounded, and just over 2,800 were taken prisoner, most interned on British ships where hundreds would die of starvation, disease, or exposure.

After the loss of Fort Washington and New York City, General Washington and his army were on the run. Washington's increasingly ragtag soldiers were first driven to New Jersey; then, in early December 1776, with the British chasing close behind, the Americans commandeered every skiff, boat, and raft they could round up and escaped across the Delaware River into Pennsylvania. A brutal early winter had set in. Washington's citizen-soldiers were cold and miserable, and some were sick and starving. The American painter and inventor, Charles Willson Peale, watched the American landing from the Pennsylvania shore. Peale immediately made his way to the soldiers' camp and was left shaken by what he saw. Several soldiers were barely clothed. One soldier "was in an Old dirty Blanket Jacket, his beard long, and his face so full of Sores that he could not clean it." The man was so badly "disfigured" that Peale failed to recognize at first that he was looking into the eyes of his own brother, James. During the American soldiers' winter of despair, Major General William Heath from Massachusetts reported seeing troops from another regiment "so destitute of shoes that the blood left on the frozen ground, in many places, marked the route they had taken."[40]

In the winter of 1776, Thomas Paine, the author of the world's first bestseller, *Common Sense*, volunteered to serve as a civilian aide on General Nathanael Greene's staff. What he saw that winter was more than he could bear. Paine was so moved by the depredations suffered by the American troops and by their undaunted bravery that he wrote a series of essays in their honor. Two days before Christmas 1776, illuminated by the light of the campfire, he wrote the first essay in what would come to be known as *The American Crisis*. The essay begins with these immortal words: "These are the times that try men's souls. The summer soldier and the sunshine patriot will, in this crisis, shrink from the service of their country; but he that stands by it *now*, deserves the love and thanks of man and woman. Tyranny, like hell, is not easily conquered; yet we have this consolation with us, that the harder the conflict, the more glorious the triumph."[41]

☆   ☆   ☆

Ironically, the Declaration of Independence not only invokes the "Laws of Nature," but it is itself an instance of that very law—the law of self-preservation. The Declaration's moral law commands those who support its underlying principles to act in a certain way—to separate from Great Britain and to establish new governments. The Declaration's moral law of nature can be presented in the form of the *if-given-then* principle described in chapter 2: *If* the Americans want to live in a free and just society, *given* the arbitrary and unjust laws passed by Parliament and supported by George III, *then* they must declare their independence. Moral necessity demands of the colonists that they act in a certain way (i.e., with vigilance, integrity, and courage) given their chosen values (e.g., justice and freedom). Failure to do so means a concession to tyranny and will result in oppression, their likely enslavement, or worse. As Judge Drayton put it in his charge to the Charleston grand jury in October 1776, three months after the writing of the Declaration of Independence, freedom was the birthright of the American people by the "law of nature." The former colonists were therefore "authorized" by that same law to exert "the inherent powers of society" to resist "the edicts which told them they had no property" and that they were bound to obey Parliament's laws against their consent "in all cases whatsoever."[42]

The Declaration of Independence announced to the world that the Americans could not and would not renounce their most deeply held convictions. It also said that the Americans *must* act on their chosen values. They were impelled by moral necessity, according to the Declaration, to "alter their former Systems of Government." American revolutionaries permitted themselves no breach between their principles and their practice. Given their devotion to those principles, they saw no alternative.

Thomas Paine described the moral situation in which the American people found themselves in the months just before and after the signing of the Declaration of Independence: "All was choice, and every man reasoned for himself." The rationally necessary choice was to act in defense of their liberty and property. "It was in this situation of affairs, equally calculated to confound or to inspire," Paine continued, "that the gentleman, the merchant, the farmer, the tradesman and the laborer mutually turned from all the conveniences of home, to perform the duties of private soldiers, and undergo the severities of a winter campaign."[43]

The words John Adams wrote to a friend during some of the darkest days of the Revolutionary War serve as a kind of motto capturing who Adams and his fellow revolutionaries were as men and as patriots: "*Fiat Justitia ruat Coelum*" (let justice be done though the heavens should fall). In the powerful words of the Continental Congress's Declaration of the Causes and Necessity of Taking Up Arms, published in 1775, the Americans had been

> reduced to the alternative of chusing an unconditional submission
> to the tyranny of irritated ministers, or resistance by force.—The
> latter is our choice—We have counted the cost of this contest, and
> find nothing so dreadful as voluntary slavery....we will in defiance
> of every hazard, with unabating firmness and perserverance, employ
> for the preservation of our liberties; being with our [one] mind
> resolved to dye Free-men rather than live slaves.[44]

Having made their case *against* despotism and *for* freedom, it should be clear now why, for the Americans, revolution was necessary, why they would not compromise, why it was their duty to act, and why they were impelled to dissolve the political bands that had connected them to Great Britain. Based on their commitment to certain principles, they had no other option. They had to act because of who and what they were, because of the choices they had already made, because of the values they held, because of the moral law they chose to live by, because of the kind of society they chose to live in, and because George III and the British Parliament threatened to rob them of all that. Henry Knox, in the spring of 1776, put the matter this way:

> The future happiness or misery of a great proportion of the human
> race is at stake—and if we make the wrong *choice*, ourselves and our

prosperity must be wretched. Wrong choice! There can be but one choice consistent with the character of a people possessing the least degree of reason. And that is to separate—to separate from that people who from a total dissolution of virtue among them must be our enemies—an event which I de[v]outly pray may soon take place; and let it be as soon as may be![45]

The Declaration of Independence required action, the kind of action that leads in the short term to hardship, penury, and possibly even death, but in the long term to the blessings of a free society.

The Declaration also tells us a good deal about the men who signed it and led the Revolution. They declared to the world their right to self-government, and they backed it up with their lives, their fortunes, and their sacred honor. They demonstrated to the world that ideas and action can and must be unified. The Declaration and the war for independence that followed represent a heroic integration of thought and deed. The virtue of integrity was the linchpin that united theory and practice in the revolutionaries' moral universe. They held their moral principles as absolutes, and they attempted to practice them without compromise or contradiction. They chose to act in ways they thought right and just, regardless of the immediate consequences, precisely because they understood the value of acting in their long-term self-interest.

America's founding revolutionaries were thus rebels with a cause. Despite the many vicissitudes and challenges thrown at them by *fortuna*, they met their problems head-on and remained loyal to their principles. They attempted to lead an integrated moral life. If integrity is the principle of being principled, then the revolutionary generation of 1776 embodied that virtue in spades. As Joseph Reed, who became one of Washington's aides, put it to his wife, Esther, "My honor, duty, and every other tie held sacred among men, call upon me to proceed with firmness and resolution."[46]

At every stage of the Revolutionary crisis, the Americans held in focus their principles, the ways in which those principles were being violated, and the means by which they should protest and then fight to defend them. They refused to sanction British actions. They did not evade, rationalize, turn the other cheek, or shirk their commitment or responsibility to their highest values. Instead, they responded to the repeated violations of their rights and liberties by organizing boycotts and protesting and resisting usurpations, by writing letters, petitions, and remonstrances, by liberating boxes of tea, and eventually by going to war.

This uncompromising spirit of liberty can be seen in the attitude of John Adams, one of the earliest, most principled, and most articulate advocates for independence. In 1775, he saw what few others did. Writing in June from the Continental Congress, then meeting in Philadelphia, Adams told Moses Gill, "I am myself as fond of Reconciliation...as any Man...[but] the Cancer is too deeply rooted, and too far spread to be cured by any thing short of cutting it out entire." Adams rejected the position of the conciliationists and the pragmatists. "The Middle Way is none at all," he wrote to General Horatio Gates. "If we finally fail in this great and glorious Contest, it will be by bewildering ourselves in groping for this middle Way." For Adams, there was no turning back. In his letter to Gill, he also noted, "Powder and Artillery are the most efficacious, Sure, and infallibly conciliatory Measures We can adopt." The time had come to invoke what he called, in the Novanglus letters, "revolution-principles."[47]

At the fateful moment on August 2, when fifty-six men formally signed their declaration of independence, they heroically assumed full responsibility for the war that was sure to come. And when Patrick Henry the year before proclaimed, "Give me liberty, or give me death," it was no idle pledge. In February 1776, word arrived that Parliament had declared that all Americans who did not submit unconditionally to the principle of parliamentary sovereignty would be deemed traitors. Adams and the other members of Congress knew that the punishment for treason was death by hanging. To make matters worse, it was reported that the British navy was headed to America with a cargo of German mercenaries—the dreaded Hessians. Imagine having to tell your wife, as Adams did, that in "Case of real Danger...fly to the Woods with our children."[48] Several months later, when forty-five ships of the British armada had actually dropped anchor off the coast of Manhattan, General Henry Knox, along with hundreds of other New Yorkers, was forced to evacuate his wife, Lucy, and their infant daughter. The British bombardment and invasion of the city would begin any day. On July 11, 1776, seven days after the Americans declared their independence, Knox wrote to Lucy, telling her "the great being who watches the hearts of the children of men, knows I value you above every blessing, and for that reason I wish you to be at such a distance from the horrid scenes of war." As if to remind himself, he told her, "We're fighting for our country, for posterity perhaps. On the success of this campaign the happiness or misery of millions may depend."[49]

The moral universe inhabited by American revolutionaries might seem like a foreign place to twenty-first-century Americans, but we forget its moral lessons at our peril.

★　★　★

On July 3, 1776—the day after he had delivered one of the greatest speeches in American history, a speech that moved the Continental Congress to vote for independence and for which he was later called the "Atlas of Independence"—John Adams summed up the meaning of their declaration in language that captures perfectly the Americans' sense of life:

> You will think me transported with Enthusiasm but I am not.—I
> am well aware of the Toil, and Blood, and Treasure, that it will cost
> Us to maintain this Declaration, and support and defend these
> States.—Yet through all the Gloom, I can see the Rays of lavishing
> Light and Glory. I can see that the End is more than worth all the
> Means. And that Posterity will tryumph in that Days Transaction.[50]

Despite the vicissitudes that befell them—the hardships of war, the blood and toil, the starvation, the imprisonment and torture, the destruction of home and property, the loss of family and loved ones, and, for some, death itself—the American revolutionaries refused to compromise, or to surrender their lives, liberty, property, and sacred honor. *Their* revolution is surely one of history's greatest monuments to human virtue. It is *ours* to remember and celebrate.

CONCLUSION

*I*n 1782, just as the American War of Independence was coming to an end, Hector St. John de Crèvecoeur, who had come to North America from France in 1755 and by 1765 had settled in New York, published *Letters from an American Farmer*. In it he asked a fascinating and enduring question: "What then is the American, this new man?"[1] Crèvecoeur's question suggests that eighteenth-century Americans were somehow different from all other peoples, and thus he invites us, some 230 years later, to reflect on the nature and meaning of America.

Crèvecoeur's new man was the existential embodiment of Thomas Jefferson's "American mind." He practiced and made real the principles expressed in the Declaration of Independence. The moral, political, social, and economic philosophy associated with the American mind is sometimes reduced to a single word: "Americanism." The "ism" suggests that being an American is part ideology, part way of life, part attitude, and even part personality. Broadly defined, Americanism is that philosophy which identifies the moral character and sense of life *unique* to the people of the United States, and which, under distinctive conditions, was translated into practice by millions of ordinary men and women in late eighteenth- and early nineteenth-century America.

Interestingly, the idea of Americanism has no foreign counterpart. No other nation has anything quite like it. We may speak of a French, an Italian, or a Persian culture, but there is no Frenchism, Italianism, or Persianism. Americanism, by contrast, is more than just a culture steeped in historically evolved folkways (i.e., the forms and formalities associated with speech dialects, food, music, dress, architecture, etc.). America's traditional folkways are no doubt different from those of any other nation, but such cultural accoutrements do not capture the essence of the American mind.

This book has attempted to explain the revolution in thought that culminated in the creation of what Jefferson called the American mind. We now conclude with a brief overview of the world created by Crèvecoeur's new man—the world later described by Alexis de Tocqueville in his magisterial account of *Democracy in America*.

THE AMERICAN MIND IN THEORY

As we now know, the content of the American mind was synonymous with the self-evident truths of the Declaration of Independence. The Declaration forever associated the American way of life with a social system that recognized, defined, and protected as sacrosanct the rights of individuals. The greatest achievement of the American Revolution was to subordinate society and government to this fundamental moral law.

The radical transformation in thought and practice that followed would have enormous implications for the development of a new American society in the century that followed.[2] The revolutionaries' ethical individualism promoted the idea that human flourishing requires freedom—the freedom to think and act without interference, which means security from predatory threats against one's person or property. Freedom requires government, but only government of a particular sort—the sort that protects individuals from force and coercion and that defines a sphere of liberty in which individuals would be free to pursue their own welfare and happiness. Within that protected sphere, American revolutionaries and their nineteenth-century heirs created a new world unlike anything anywhere else.

The revolutionaries' natural-rights republicanism was the product of a relatively recent revolution in thought that had its source in seventeenth-century England, originating in the Enlightenment ideas of Bacon, Newton, and, most importantly, Locke. These ideas were first injected into the intellectual life of the colonies in the early eighteenth century through the universities and the book trade; polemical writings such as *Cato's Letters*, by John Trenchard and Thomas Gordon, then democratized these ideas through the newspapers. The radical individualism associated with the natural-rights philosophy armed the Americans with an entirely new morality that would provide the foundation for an unprecedented political, social, and economic system.

The moral philosophy of the American Revolution was closely associated with the idea of *self*-government—that is, with the idea that individuals must govern their own lives in the fullest sense of the term. Prior to the American Revolution, wrote John Taylor of Caroline, "the natural right of self-government was never plainly asserted, nor practically enforced; nor was it previously discovered, that a sovereign power in any government...was inconsistent with this right, and destructive of its value." Ultimate sovereignty rests with the individual and not government. After the Revolution, "the natural right of *self*-government" was made "superior to any political sovereignty." The Americans now believed, said Tocqueville, "that at birth each has received the ability to govern himself."[3]

In this new world, the individual replaced the government as the primary unit of moral and political value. This meant sovereign power began with self-governing individuals and extended outward in concentric circles of voluntary association, but never beyond the reach of a man's control. Thomas Jefferson described the relationship between individual self-government and the various layers of political government this way:

> The way to have good and safe government, is not to trust it all
> to one, but to divide it among the many, distributing to every one
> exactly the functions he is competent to. Let the national govern-
> ment be entrusted with the defense of the nation, and its foreign
> and federal relations; the State governments with the civil rights,
> laws, police, and administration of what concerns the State gener-
> ally; the counties with the local concerns of the counties, and each
> ward direct the interests within itself. It is by dividing and subdi-
> viding these republics from the great national one down through all
> its subordinations, until it ends in the administration of every man's
> farm by himself; by placing under every one what his own eye may
> superintend, that all will be done for the best.

All government in postrevolutionary America (local, state, or federal) was grounded on the free political association of individuals who retained ultimate authority and sovereignty over its power. Political power was imploded down to the local level. The Americans, Tocqueville observed, "have a secret instinct that carries them toward independence...where each village forms a sort of republic habituated to governing itself." Government was to have no power that was not explicitly delegated to it by the people and for specific purposes. Or, as John Taylor put it, the "sovereignty of the people arises, and representation flows out of each man's right to govern himself."[4]

The ideal of individual self-government set in motion forces that weakened the centralizing tendencies of government power. "What has destroyed liberty and the rights of man in every government which has ever existed under the sun?" asked Jefferson. His answer was clear: "The generalizing and concentrating all cares and powers into one body." The men who designed America's constitutional system understood and accepted the truth that Lord Acton's famous maxim would much later capture: "Power tends to corrupt and absolute power corrupts absolutely." In 1788, James Madison wrote in *Federalist* No. 48 that "power is of an encroaching nature, and ... ought to be effectually restrained from passing the limits assigned to it." A few months later, Jefferson noted pithily, "The natural progress of things is for liberty to yield and government to gain ground."[5]

Thus the great question confronted by America's revolutionary constitution-makers was this: How could the grasping power of government be tamed and harnessed in a way that would serve the legitimate functions of government? The founders' revolutionary solution to the problem posed by the expansionary nature of power was to subordinate governments (the rule of men) to constitutions (the rule of law). By *constitutionalizing* their governments, they would constrain arbitrary political rule with the rule of law—laws universal and objective, known and certain. Government officials would be denied discretionary power in applying the law, and the law applied to one man would apply to all men. "In questions of power," Jefferson declared, men were not to be trusted, and so they should be bound "from mischief by the chains of the Constitution."[6]

Between 1765 and 1788, American revolutionaries invented and then implemented the architectonic idea of the American Revolution: *the idea of a written constitution as fundamental law*. Written constitutions would capture and guide liberty-promoting subsidiary principles, such as the separation of powers, bicameralism, federalism, judicial review, bills of rights, and various limitations on executive, legislative, and judicial power. These were the principal means by which individual rights and the rule of law would be protected and promoted. By explicitly and exactly defining both the power that may be exercised by government and the rights of individuals, written constitutions would create protected spheres of human action that were knowable and predictable.

The founders' vision of government was the original version of what is sometimes called the "night-watchman" state—a government strictly limited to a few necessary functions, supported by low taxes, a frugal budget, and minimal levels of regulation. Ideally, government's role was to protect individuals in their rights by serving as a neutral umpire, sorting out and judging conflicting rights claims. Even Alexander Hamilton, the founding generation's greatest advocate of energetic government, saw the purpose and power of the national government as strictly limited to a few functions: "the common defence of the members—the preservation of the public peace as well against internal convulsions as external attacks—the regulation of commerce with other nations and between the states—the superintendence of our intercourse, political and commercial, with foreign countries." Jefferson offered the classic statement of the limited purpose of government in his First Inaugural Address: "Still one thing more, fellow citizens—a wise and frugal government, which shall restrain men from injuring one another, which shall leave them otherwise free to regulate their own pursuits of industry and improvement, and shall not take from the mouth of labor the bread it has earned. This is the sum of good government." The classical liberals of the early republic supported a form of government that would ensure their liberty and property by prohibiting murder, assault, theft, and other crimes of coercion and fraud. James Madison summed up the entire revolutionary generation's definition of a "*just* government" as one that "*impartially* secures to every man whatever is his own."[7]

Jefferson was particularly sensitive to the tendency of government officials to intervene in both the spiritual and material lives of their fellow citizens. This is why, on one hand, he claimed that the "*opinions of men are not the object of civil government, nor under its jurisdiction,*"[8] and, on the other, that the acquisition, production, ownership, and trade of men's property is not the proper purview of government. Jefferson therefore supported both the separation of church and state as well as the separation of economy and state. He did not think that government should be in the business of religion, nor did he think it should be in the business of business. He strongly inclined toward supporting a policy of religious and economic laissez-faire.

Jeffersonian Republicans envisioned a government that would function without a standing army, that would eliminate debt and dramatically reduce federal taxes and tariffs, that would shun public works projects and internal improvements, and that would reduce controls and regulations on the economy. The founders' emerging view of the purpose and role of government was most clearly described by William Leggett, one of the great antebellum, Locofoco individualists. "Governments," Leggett announced, "possess no delegated right to tamper with individual industry in a single hair's-breadth beyond what is essential to protect the rights of person and property."[9]

Like Leggett, most Americans of his time distrusted political power, believing that a good society was defined by the paucity of its laws. Accordingly, in the eighteenth and nineteenth centuries, there was little government in America relative to the major countries of Europe. In fact, government at all levels before the Civil War was Lilliputian compared to what followed in the postbellum period. Political power—what little of it there was—was concentrated in the states and localities.

In 1839, John L. O'Sullivan, editor of *The United States Magazine and Democratic Review*, memorably captured the postrevolutionary view of government:

> *The best government is that which governs least.* No human depositories can, with safety, be trusted with the power of legislation upon the general interests of society, so as to operate directly…on the industry and property of the community.…Legislation has been the fruitful parent of nine-tenths of all evil, moral and physical, by which mankind…since the creation of the world…has been self-degraded, fettered and oppressed.

The only proper purpose of legislation, according to O'Sullivan, was to protect individual rights. In domestic affairs, the action of legislatures

> should be confined to the administration of justice, for the protection of the natural equal rights of the citizen, and the preservation of social order. In all other respects, the *voluntary principle*, the

principle of freedom…affords the true golden rule. The natural
laws which will establish themselves and find their own level are
the best laws.…This is the fundamental principle of the philosophy
of democracy, to furnish a system of administration of justice, and
then leave all the business and interests of society to themselves,
to free competition and association—in a word, to the *voluntary
principle.*[10]

Government in America before the Civil War had limited power: its
primary responsibilities were to protect the nation from foreign invasion,
to preserve the peace, and to adjudicate disputes among citizens. Much
beyond that, it dared not go. William Leggett summed up the prevailing
political worldview with the following maxim, which he recommended "be
placed in large letters over the speaker's chair in all legislative bodies": "DO
NOT GOVERN TOO MUCH."[11]

Indeed, too much government was not a feature of life in the early
republic. As William Sampson, a recent émigré from Ireland, observed, "the
government here makes no sensation; it is round about you like the air, and
you cannot even feel it." Americans, said Leggett, were an independent lot
who wanted little to "no government to regulate their private concerns; to
prescribe the course and mete out the profits of industry." They wanted "no
fireside legislators; no executive interference in their workshops and fields."
In America, wrote the nineteenth-century individualist Josiah Warren,
"Everyone must feel that he is the supreme arbiter of his own [destiny],
that no power on earth shall rise over him, that he is and always shall be
sovereign of himself and all relating to his individuality."[12] America's new-
model man mostly just wanted to be left alone.

Wherever there was a frontier in the early republic, government was
especially thin, light, and weak. American pioneers, having broken free
from the mother country, began a process of declaring independence from
their own national and then their state governments, and, finally, from each
other as they migrated in ever-increasing numbers to the western frontier,
which continued to move toward the setting sun until the close of the
nineteenth century. What was happening politically in late eighteenth- and
early nineteenth-century America was unlike anything else seen anywhere
in the world.

In the end, the new world order created by America's founding fathers asked only three things of its citizens: first, that they not violate each other's rights; second, that they live self-starting, self-reliant, self-governing lives by practicing certain uniquely American virtues and character traits (e.g., independence, initiative, industriousness, frugality, enterprise, creativity, adventurousness, courage, and optimism); and third, that they deal with each other by means of persuasion and voluntary trade. In return, the free society made certain promises to those who lived by the American creed: it promised to protect all citizens' freedom and rights from domestic and foreign criminals; it promised to govern by the rule of law; and it promised a sphere of unfettered opportunity that made possible their pursuit of material and spiritual values undreamed of in other societies.

The changes wrought by the Revolution were truly momentous. The individual-rights revolution of 1776 launched the greatest moral, social, and political transformation not just in American history but also in world history. A new civilization—a republican civilization—was born, free from the dead weight of the past, free from the encrusted hierarchies of old-regime Europe, free from artificial privilege and haughty arrogance, free from ostentation, decadence, and corruption, free from vicious, medieval laws, free from overweening state power, and free from the cynicism of low expectations.

The society Tocqueville discovered in America did not experience a brutal revolutionary upheaval after 1776. There were no guillotines or revolutionary calendars that began with Year One. Instead, the moral, social, political, and economic revolution that followed the end of the War of Independence and the Treaty of Paris was unlike anything ever seen before. The revolution in thinking, principles, and sentiments that preceded 1776 resulted in a gradual, evolutionary, but thorough transformation in American life that blended the Revolution's libertarian philosophy and the circumstances of life on an ever-expanding frontier.

THE AMERICAN MIND IN PRACTICE

The American Revolution began as a revolution in ideas, but its ultimate success required that theory be translated into practice. Ultimately, as Alexis de Tocqueville noted, the "American mind turns away from general ideas; it does not direct itself toward theoretical discoveries."[13] The whole purpose of the Declaration's ideas was to liberate men to *act*.

The *way of life* associated with the American spirit of liberty was thus born of a fortuitous meeting between the ideas of men like Thomas Jefferson and James Madison and the actions of men like Daniel Boone and Davy Crockett. As the ideas of the Revolution spread westward through the Cumberland Gap, they were lived day by day on the frontier. Over the course of a century, the American idea of freedom and the experience of life on the frontier worked together to create and define the uniquely American spirit—a spirit defined by honesty, adventure, energy, daring, industry, hope, idealism, enterprise, and benevolence. American-style frontier republicanism was unlike anything ever seen anywhere in the world.

In Tocqueville's America, "hardy adventurers"—avatars of Crèvecoeur's new man—left the shelter of their "fathers' roofs" and plunged "into the solitudes of America," where they sought a "new native country." They marched westward toward the "boundaries of society and wilderness." Late eighteenth- and nineteenth-century American pilgrims chased a frontier that followed the direction of the setting sun. Living alone and far from the comforts of civilization, the "pioneer hastily fells some trees and raises a cabin under the leaves." While all "is primitive and savage around him," he brings with him the ideas that freed him to leave in the first place: he "plunges into the wilderness of the New World with his Bible, a hatchet, and newspapers." Through this process, according to Tocqueville, the Americans are habituated "little by little to govern themselves." Frontier life was partly defined by the absence of government (including legislatures, courts, police, and armies), all of which eventually followed. Until the end of the nineteenth century, a decent, law-abiding frontier American could pass through life and hardly see or feel a trace of government beyond the post office and the marshal. For the most part, the state left men and women alone. Despite the poverty and barbarism of his condition, America's new man knows "what his rights are and what means he will use to exercise them."[14]

In the half century following the Revolution, these pioneering adventurers—many of whom, at least in the first wave, were veterans of the War of Independence—created a society the likes of which had never been seen before. The Americans destroyed the remnants of the ancien régime, with its artificial hierarchies and unchosen duties, regulations, and social stasis; in its place they created a dynamic society defined by equal rights, freedom, the pursuit of happiness, competition, and social mobility. They built both that society and its governments on the premise that individuals are self-owning, self-making, and self-governing. Once men came to believe that they owned and controlled their own lives, free from the burden of overbearing government power, they began to pursue their own self-interested values and to explore new ways of conducting their lives. Freedom became the rallying cry for those seeking to challenge all forms of authority and to tear down traditional social, political, and economic barriers. In this new world, society preceded government, and the individual preceded society.

The new man who developed along with this new kind of political society was one of entrepreneurial energy and creativity. Nothing contributed more to this explosion of social vitality than the twin principles of freedom and rights. These conjoined ideas represented the most radical and most potent philosophical force let loose by the Revolution. Within a couple of decades following the Declaration of Independence, the United States became—at least in the northern states—the freest nation in world history (at the same time, paradoxically, that the existence of slavery made it one of the least free). The Revolution brought new producers and consumers into the emerging market economy. It aroused and liberated previously dormant acquisitive impulses, and it freed the "natural aristocracy" promoted by Thomas Jefferson to build a new kind of hustling and bustling society.

It was a society of individuals constantly on the move. The people of the early republic were restless, rootless, and sometimes homeless. It was not uncommon for individuals and families to move—almost always westward—every few years.[15] Nor was it uncommon for them to change jobs and professions. When Tocqueville toured the country, he encountered Americans "who [had] been successively attorneys, farmers, traders, evangelical ministers, doctors." In Tocqueville's America,

> a man carefully builds a dwelling in which to pass his declining
> years, and he sells it while the roof is being laid; he plants a garden
> and he rents it out just as he was going to taste its fruits; he clears
> a field and he leaves to others the care of harvesting its crops. He
> embraces a profession and quits it. He settles in a place from which
> he departs soon after so as to take his changing desires elsewhere.
> Should his private affairs give him some respite, he immediately
> plunges into the whirlwind of politics. And when toward the end of

a year filled with work some leisure still remains to him, he carries his restive curiosity here and there within the vast limits of the United States. He will thus go five hundred leagues in a few days in order to better distract himself from his happiness.[16]

In 1817, George Flower, an Englishman recently arrived on the Illinois prairie, was not convinced that the American people always lived up to the moral principles of the Declaration, but he was certain that the open space of the frontier environment aided in spreading freedom: "The practical liberty of America is found in its great space and small population. Good land, dog-cheap everywhere, and for nothing, if you will go for it, gives as much elbow-room to every man as he chooses to take," Flower wrote. He continued: "Poor laborers, from every country in Europe, hear of this cheap land, are attracted to it, perhaps without any political opinions. They come, they toil, they prosper. This is the real liberty of America."[17] The distinctively American ethos associated with frontier life held that individuals are morally sovereign and that they therefore must be self-starting, self-governing, and self-reliant in order to succeed in life. They just needed, as Flower noted, a little elbow room.

Life on the frontier unleashed in America's new man a primordial energy that would conquer a broad and wild continent and build a new kind of meritocratic society, defined by the natural aristocracy of ability, inventiveness, daring, and hard work. The new frontier ethos broke down Old World social barriers and hierarchies, replacing them with a social order that judged men not by their circumstances at birth but by what they made of their lives. The American frontier was the refuge where ambitious men and women could escape their past and the burden of living for others—the guilt, the pressure, and sometimes the compulsion to live one's life for family, tribe, church, king, or state. It was the place where men and sometimes even women could reinvent themselves. Only in America could a man who came from nothing prove his ability and worth and become a man of accomplishment and wealth. Only in America could there be such a creature as the "self-made man."

The ideal of the self-made man was a reality for many nineteenth-century Americans.[18] Ironically, the best exposition of the self-made man as ideal and fact is found in the speech of a runaway slave, Frederick Douglass. In an 1859 lecture titled "Self-Made Men," the former slave defined in unmistakable terms the story and the qualities of the quintes-sential American:

> Self-made men…are the men who owe little or nothing to birth,
> relationship, friendly surroundings; to wealth inherited or to early
> approved means of education; who are what they are, without the
> aid of any favoring conditions by which other men usually rise
> in the world and achieve great results. In fact they are the men
> who are not brought up but who are obliged to come up, not only
> without the voluntary assistance or friendly co-operation of society,
> but often in open and derisive defiance of all the efforts of society
> and the tendency of circumstances to repress, retard and keep them
> down. They are the men who, in a world of schools, academies,
> colleges and other institutions of learning, are often compelled by
> unfriendly circumstances to acquire their education elsewhere and,
> amidst unfavorable conditions, to hew out for themselves a way
> to success, and thus to become the architects of their own good
> fortunes. They are in a peculiar sense, indebted to themselves for
> themselves.

Douglass observed America's self-made men all around him, and of course he was the living embodiment of the ideal. Notably, he did not think that the success of the self-made man was due to accident or good luck. Instead, success in life could be explained, he insisted, "by one word and that word WORK! WORK!! WORK!!! WORK!!!!"[19]

A few Europeans who came to America were nonplussed by what they saw. In 1787, Charles Nisbet, a Scottish academic recently arrived in Pennsylvania, described the American Revolution as having "commenced on just and solid grounds." It was "carried on," he continued, "by honest, enlightened, noble-minded patriots" who were "prompted by a sincere love of rational liberty." Still, this Old World professor did not quite fully understand or appreciate the new world created by the Revolution, which was made up of "discordant atoms, jumbled together by chance, and tossed by inconstancy in an immense vacuum." Less than impressed, Nisbet com-plained that America lacked "a principle of attraction and cohesion."[20] He was mistaken.

This new American creed of "rational liberty" did not mean that its practitioners lived alienated and crabbed lives in atomistic isolation from one another. It did not mean that Americans were indifferent or unneighborly to each other, that they did not help each other during times of crisis or distress. Quite the opposite. These rugged American individualists joined together in bonds of civic friendship as they experienced and lived through seemingly never-ending disasters like floods, fires, tornadoes, earthquakes, native attacks, and diseases such as smallpox, measles, tuberculosis, yellow fever, and influenza. The moral and political philosophy by which they lived their lives was no antisocial creed that confined men to their own spiritual cages. Together, as friends and neighbors, the westward-moving Americans built—literally—cabins, houses, barns, roads, canals, libraries, schools, colleges, villages, towns, and cities. Freedom produced unparalleled social cooperation.

From the Revolution to the Civil War, American society developed its own principles of attraction and cohesion that naturally melded its individual atoms into a common culture. The country was unified through a commercial system of natural liberty and a harmony of economic interests. Instead of anarchy, the natural system of liberty encouraged and generated new associations and bonds of civil cooperation.

Tocqueville observed that "Americans of all ages, all conditions, all minds constantly unite." Ordinary Americans voluntarily united with each other to form all kinds of benevolent associations in order to improve their material and spiritual lives. According to Tocqueville, the Americans not only have "commercial and industrial associations in which all take part, but they also have a thousand other kinds: religious, moral, grave, futile, very general and very particular, immense and very small; American use associations to give fêtes, to found seminaries, to build inns, to raise churches, to distribute books, to send missionaries to the antipodes; in this manner they create hospitals, prisons, schools."[21]

This, then, was the great paradox of American society: it united radical individualism with tight bonds of civil association. The former was responsible for the latter. It was *e pluribus unum*.

What made this revolutionary society unique was that the force and authority of government and the ties of land and blood were not what held it together, as was true of most countries of the Old World. The American people were united instead by self-interest, rights, freedom, money, benevolence, voluntary associations, and—most importantly—by a common moral ideal that was expressed so eloquently in the ringing phrase: "We hold these truths to be self-evident..."

The American experiment in self-government truly was a *novus ordo seclorum*.

EPILOGUE

Has America Lost
Its American Mind?

The deepest questions raised by this book go beyond the merely anti-quarian. In the end, the Declaration of Independence was more than just a summing up of extant beliefs, principles, and attitudes. And it was more than just an "expression of the American mind" as it existed in 1776.

Initially, as we saw in chapter 11, the Declaration served to unite colonial Patriots and inspired many to fight and some to die in a brutal war for independence. But during the years of the early republic and beyond, it was held up and celebrated by Americans as a symbol of what America stood for and aspired to be. The Declaration's principles defined America's identity and her national destiny.

This was certainly Abraham Lincoln's position. Lincoln called the Declaration the "electric cord" that "links the hearts of patriotic and liberty-loving men together." Even recent immigrants to America who were not yet citizens and who had no blood connection to the founding generation felt its current, according to Lincoln:

When they look through that old Declaration of Independence they find that those old men say that "We hold these truths to be self-evident, that all men are created equal," and then they feel that that moral sentiment taught in that day evidences their relation to those men, that it is the father of all moral principle in them, and that they have a right to claim it as though they were blood of the blood, and flesh of the flesh of the men who wrote that Declaration,...and so they are.

The Declaration's "electric cord" inspired not only American citizens and recent immigrants to the United States, but its words could be felt "in the minds of all men everywhere."[1] That recent immigrants would feel the power of the Declaration is not surprising. They chose to come to America because of the freedom promised by the Declaration. But what of those Americans whose ancestors were brought to America as slaves and held in chattel bondage? What to the slave could the Declaration possibly mean?

Again, it was Lincoln who understood what the Declaration meant to all Americans, *especially* in the light of slavery. Responding to the claim of Senator Stephen Douglas and Chief Justice Roger Taney that the signers of the Declaration of Independence did not "intend to include negroes, by the fact that they did not at once, actually place them on an equality with the whites," Lincoln charged the pair with doing violence "to the plain unmistakable language of the Declaration." He captured both the intent and meaning of the Declaration's signers with cascading logic. The following passage, previously cited, bears repeating:

> I think the authors of that notable instrument intended to include *all* men, but they did not intend to declare all men equal *in all respects*. They did not mean to say all were equal in color, size, intellect, moral developments, or social capacity. They defined with tolerable distinctness, in what respects they did consider all men created equal—equal in "certain inalienable rights, among which are life, liberty, and the pursuit of happiness." This they said, and this meant. They did not mean to assert the obvious untruth, that all were then actually enjoying that equality, nor yet, that they were about to confer it immediately upon them. In fact they had no power to confer such a boon. They meant simply to declare the *right*, so that the *enforcement* of it might follow as fast as circumstances should permit. They meant to set up a standard maxim for free society, which should be familiar to all, and revered by all; constantly looked to, constantly labored for, and even though never perfectly attained, constantly approximated, and thereby constantly spreading and deepening its influence, and augmenting the happiness and value of life to all people of all colors everywhere.[2]

Frederick Douglass, the former slave and leading abolitionist, saw the meaning of the Declaration of Independence in the same way as did Lincoln. He believed that the Declaration was "the ringbolt to the chain" of America's "destiny," and he described its moral principles as "saving principles." Douglass challenged the American people to "stand by those principles, be true to them on all occasions, in all places, against all foes, and at whatever cost."[3]

The Declaration's promise of liberty and justice to all meant everything to the man who had once been held in chattel bondage as another man's property. It provided all Americans, including slaves, with a moral and political standard by which to judge the actions of government officials past, present, and future. It declared certain moral and political principles to be *true*—true for all men and women everywhere. Such a proposition assumed that reason is capable of knowing what is true and false, right and wrong, just and unjust. Thus, the revolutionary generation did not consider their principles to be mere opinions, equal in status to all other opinions. They viewed the Declaration's moral and political truths as grounded in an unchanging nature—absolute, certain, universal, and timeless. As Abraham Lincoln once said of the Declaration's principles: they are "the definitions and axioms of free society."[4]

✯   ✯   ✯

And what of the Declaration's fate in the nineteenth and twentieth centuries?

Beginning in the late 1830s, as new philosophic ideas began to seep into America from Europe, some Americans—most notably Southern slaveholders and their Northern allies—began to openly challenge whether the Declaration's self-evident truths were actually true. The two best-known criticisms of the Declaration were spoken by Northerners. In 1854, John Pettit, a Democratic senator from Indiana, famously announced during the debate on the Kansas-Nebraska Act that the Declaration's first self-evident truth, holding that "all men are created equal," was not a self-evident truth at all, but instead "is nothing more to me than a self-evident lie."[5] Two years after Pettit's speech in defense of allowing the extension of slavery into the Kansas Territory, Rufus Choate, the great intellectual voice of the American Whig Party, referred to the

Declaration's self-evident truths as little more than "the glittering and sounding generalities of natural right."[6]

Why had some antebellum Americans lost confidence in or simply rejected what Lincoln once called America's "ancient faith"?[7]

Beginning in the late 1830s, proslavery intellectuals in the South began to rethink the nature and meaning of their "peculiar institution" in response to the rise of the abolitionist movement in the North, which based its moral philosophy on the principles of the Declaration.[8] A new breed of Southern intellectual was no longer willing to treat slavery as a "necessary evil" in the face of abolitionist attacks. They now promoted it as a "positive good," which meant they were forced to rethink their relationship to America's revolutionary tradition, and, more particularly, to the moral principles that informed it. Eventually, proslavery thinkers came to realize that the greatest intellectual obstacle to promoting slavery in the United States was the Declaration of Independence and its psychic hold on the minds of ordinary Americans, including patriotic Southerners.

This realization put Southern intellectuals in a difficult spot. Like most Americans, they were proud of what their fathers and grandfathers had accomplished in 1776. But now, the Declaration was being used to condemn their way of life. Philosophically, this moment was the Southerners' Rubicon: they had to make a choice between slavery and the Declaration, and they chose slavery. Proslavery writers began to openly challenge the Declaration's understanding of truth, nature, and reason, as well as its four substantive truth claims about equality, rights, consent, and revolution, and they also turned against the political, social, and economic institutions of a free society.

At the philosophic heart of the Southerners' rejection of the Declaration was their rejection of "nature" for "history" as the standard of justice and right. Proslavery writers repudiated the Enlightenment proposition that there are absolute moral truths grounded in an unchanging nature that transcend time and place. Moral truth, they claimed, was discovered by studying real men as they live in actual political communities, and not by studying the abstraction "man" in a hypothetical state of nature. Following the methods of the nineteenth-century German Historical School, Southern intellectuals replaced the idea of an unchanging human nature as the standard of right with the idea of the historical process as the standard of right. Proslavery intellectuals were the first to introduce in

America the philosophy of *historicism*, which advanced the idea that truth (especially moral and political truth) is historically relative to one's own cultural horizon.

Many Southern intellectuals adopted a philosophy of history worked out by the most influential German thinker of the first half of the nineteenth century, Georg Wilhelm Friedrich Hegel. Proslavery writers embraced the Hegelian claim that history is necessarily unfolding toward higher levels of rationality, progress, freedom, and civilization.[9] The first-known mention of Hegel in Southern literature occurred in 1832, when Jesse Burton Harrison, who had just returned from Germany, where he is thought to have attended Hegel's lectures on the philosophy of history, wrote in the *Southern Review* on the "philosophical mind of Hegel."[10] Southern intellectuals over the course of the next three decades drank deep from the well of German philosophy and history.

Consider the views of the Reverend James Warley Miles of Charleston, South Carolina, the South's leading Hegelian. In a speech delivered to the graduating class of the College of Charleston on the topic "God in History," Miles applied Hegel's universal history, as outlined in *Lectures on the Philosophy of History*, to the situation of the South. By studying the "the conflicting phases of human history," one could see "the manifestation and embodiment of Supreme [i.e., God's] Thought," the "working out" of a "determinate plan in history," and the "progressive stream of civilization." Following Hegel's lead, Miles traced the revelation and history of freedom to its discovery first by the Greeks and Romans (i.e., freedom for some), then its expansion to all believers as spiritual freedom through the Germanic Christian world, and, then, finally, to its highest expression in the antebellum American South. Miles told his audience of graduating seniors, "the stream of humanity has always manifested its capacity for the development of higher civilization as it flowed westward from its Asiatic home—thus indicating a gradual unfolding of the divine plan or idea of man." For Miles, man should not be studied as "merely one of a collection of individual human beings, he is a member of the organic body of humanity." Miles's Hegelian philosophy of history studied "humanity as an organic whole, possessing one intelligence, allotted in different phases and degrees to nations as to individuals" in order to see "the idea of man which is being realized in human history." And like his German teacher, Miles believed that "man can only develop all of his capacities in the organism of the state."[11] He also believed that civilization was reaching its apex in the American South, and that the slave plantation (and not Hegel's Prussian monarchy) represented a new kind of state superior to all others. It is hard to imagine a philosophy or worldview more antithetical to the principles of the American Revolution and the Declaration of Independence.

Hegel's ideas even trickled down from the ivory towers of Southern intellectuals into the halls of the United States Congress. Speaking in the House of Representatives in 1860, Lucius Quintus Cincinnatus Lamar II of Mississippi saw fit to read on the House floor "from Hegel's Philosophy of History," which he described as "an imperishable monument of human genius." Lamar quoted Hegel to the effect that the institution of chattel slavery was, with regard to the enslavement of black Africans, a forward-looking and civilizing institution that was riding the crest of history. Lamar concluded his reading of Hegel with this thought from the German philosopher that spoke to the status of slavery in America: "But thus existing in a State, slavery is itself a phase of advance from the merely isolated sensual existence—a phase of education—a mode of becoming participant in a higher morality and the culture connected with it."[12] American slavery, Lamar went on to claim, is the vanguard of history's unfolding progress and civilization. In fact, the institution of slavery represented what Southern intellectuals might have called the "end of history."[13]

How did proslavery thinkers use and apply the new ideas imported from Germany to critique the Declaration of Independence and to defend slavery? The proslavery critique of the Declaration and the natural-rights philosophy first began in the late 1830s. In 1838, William Harper of South Carolina attacked America's revolutionary heritage and the Declaration of Independence with its "well-sounding but unmeaning verbiage of natural equality and inalienable rights." For the most part, Harper did not believe in the doctrine of individual natural rights. He and his proslavery colleagues did not view rights as timeless and placeless abstractions attached to hypothetical and isolated individuals in a state of nature, who themselves possessed a universal and fixed nature. Rights, he argued, were derived not from nature but from history, tradition, and "the conventions of society." A new generation of Southern thinkers viewed rights as particular manifestations of concrete human relationships attached to actual political communities. Each political society had its own unique history and development, which meant that each would define rights in its own way. Rights did not and could not stand outside or above history; they grew out of the historical process. Not surprisingly, then, Harper in his "Memoir on Slavery" viewed the Declaration's truth claims as "palpably false" and "sophistical."[14]

The institution of American slavery was, by contrast, grounded in historical reality, which is why Harper thought it the "principal cause of civilization." Without slavery, he continued, "there could be no accumulation of property, no providence for the future, no taste for comforts or elegancies, which are the characteristics and essentials of civilization." Slavery was good for society, Harper claimed, precisely because it was grounded in "convention" rather than in "natural right." Historically speaking, the "progress of knowledge" and all "progress in moral virtue" had been dependent on slavery, which, over time, would lead society (including the enslaved) to ever-higher levels of "civil freedom." For Harper and his proslavery colleagues, history was moving irreversibly forward and upward:

> There have existed in various ages, and we now see existing in the world, people in every stage of civilization, from the most barbarous to the most refined. Man, as I have said, is not born to civilization. He is born rude and ignorant. But it will be, I suppose, admitted that it is the design of his Creator that he should attain to civilization: That religion should be known, that the comforts and elegancies of life should be enjoyed, that letters and arts should be cultivated, in short, that there should be the greatest possible development of moral and intellectual excellence....But as I have said, so far as reason or universal experience instruct us, the institution of slavery is an essential process in emerging from savage life. It must then produce good, and promote the designs of the Creator.

Harper was convinced that slavery was the best possible condition for the enslaved. It brought those held in servitude into the forward stream of history, thereby contributing to their moral and political improvement. Harper thus accepted Hegel's view that history is the unfolding of God's mind on earth, and that slavery was the only institution that would prepare enslaved Africans for freedom: "Thus, if in the adorable providence of God, at a time and in a manner which we can neither foresee nor conjecture, they are to be rendered capable of freedom and to enjoy it, they would be prepared for it in the best and most effectual, because in the most natural and gradual manner."[15]

Following in Harper's footsteps, South Carolina governor James Henry Hammond, in his *Letter to an English Abolitionist*, likewise rejected the idea that there is such a thing as "abstract moral truth," "abstract liberty," "'abstract' notions of right and wrong," or "natural" rights. He could think of no "single moral truth universally acknowledged," and he was confident that the Declaration's view of liberty and justice was "the merest phantasy that ever amused the imagination." True rights "are real" and "not ideal," he argued, which meant they grow out of the "wisdom of ages" and "prescriptive use" and are the by-products of "our relations with one another."[16] The traditional rights of Englishmen, for instance, were just that—rights that grew out of a particular Anglo-American experience.

Governor Hammond summed up the new Southern view of rights in an extraordinary essay, written in 1847 but never published, titled "Laws of Nature—Natural Rights—Slavery."[17] Hammond's purpose in writing the essay was to respond to frequent abolitionist claims that the moral principles of the Declaration of Independence forbade slavery, that slavery was contrary to the "Law of Nature," and that all human beings have a "Natural Right to freedom." The problem with the philosophic and legal tradition associated with the concept of moral laws and rights of nature, according to Hammond, was that its proponents had never really "told us very distinctly what these Laws and Rights are." He conceded that natural philosophers such as Isaac Newton had discovered and demonstrated the scientific laws of nature, but the South Carolinian could not see how those laws had any "bearing on the Rights of Man." If, for instance, man is subject to the scientific laws of procreation, then why should he not have an unbounded right to fulfill all sexual desires whenever he wants? But such a claim, Hammond noted, was absurd. This example proved, he argued, that some "Natural Rights may justly be curtailed," and this was precisely what both free and slave societies do—they curtail the "natural liberty" of their citizens all the time. Hammond's point was this: the differences between how slaveholders and abolitionists viewed man's rights were ultimately one of degree only and not of kind. All societies curtail man's rights and liberties, which meant that it was simply an issue of "expediency" in distinguishing the liberties and laws of the free North and the slave South.

Hammond then asked a simple but important question: "What then are [the moral laws of nature] and how are we to ascertain them?" He began by making a fundamental distinction between what he called "Absolute Rights" and "Relative Rights." He associated the notion of absolute rights with John Locke and the Declaration of Independence. For Hammond, absolute rights were pure abstractions disconnected from reality; they were deduced from Locke's hypothetical state of nature where man is governed by the law of nature, the existence of which is asserted but never demonstrated or proven. The problem with this view, according to Hammond, was that no such state ever existed, which meant the idea of "natural" rights is a fiction deduced from a fiction. In fact, he did not think that man has, "strictly speaking, any [natural] Rights at all." The defenders of the natural-rights tradition failed, Hammond claimed, "to convey a perfect idea" of natural rights as "a possession certain, complete and universal." The idea of individual, natural rights as "absolute," "inherent," and "inalienable" was groundless; it was nothing more than "an affair of words, ideal, incomprehensible, only suited for metaphysical dialecticians." The idea of absolute rights, which Hammond equated with "Natural Liberty" and the "power of doing what one sees fit without any restraint but that imposed by the Laws of Nature," was both a fraud and dangerous. Indeed, he considered the argument for natural rights as built on a *"Super-natural"* foundation. Such rights never existed anywhere, including in those societies that claim to found their political institutions on the moral laws and rights of nature.

What, then, was the true source of rights? Hammond began with what he considered to be empirically observable: true rights are grounded in "the Regulations of Civil Government and human association." They are strictly conventional or man-made. Rights grow out of the actions and interactions of individuals in civil association and are subsequently institutionalized over time by governments. From the moment an individual is born, "he exists as *one among many* of his kind who at once impose upon him Laws from which he has no possible escape." Every political community has its own unique history, and each has defined and granted various rights and liberties differently. The rights of Englishmen, Frenchmen, Italians, Germans, Yankees, and Southerners were all by-products of the unique histories particular to each place. As such, rights are little more than "Privileges," which the government "permits" individuals "to enjoy, limit and withdraw at their good pleasure." The most important of man's politically created rights "is the enjoyment of Civil Liberty," which varies organically "with times, races, and ever-changing circumstances." The sphere of civil liberty has been "gradually and slowly" evolving and expanding over time in the English-speaking world.

Hammond believed that the most advanced understanding of rights and civil liberty (i.e., the one then existing in the American South as applied to free citizens) "consists in permitting each member of Society to act as he sees fit, except so far as he is restrained by Laws [enacted] for the benefit of Society at large." The rights and privileges granted by government to particular individuals or denied to them must be consistent "with the Will of the Community," which is "for the most part expressed through the Government it has instituted." Hammond took the "Will of the Community" and common good, or the public welfare, as the primary unit of moral and political good—which meant that the government must determine who should and should not be extended the privileges of civil liberty. If his view on the origin and nature of rights were correct, then the issue of rights relative to slavery is this: "whether its existence is in conformity with the ascertained will of the community where it is found." The standard is whether slavery is or is not compatible "with the welfare and happiness of such a community." The slave therefore can have no right derived from "Nature" to be free, "unless his freedom would advance the interests of the Society."

At a deeper level, Hammond claimed that rights are, as he put it, "Relative"—by which he meant historically relative. The source of man's "real moral knowledge" about rights, according to Hammond, can be seen only by looking "to facts established by the history of mankind and to the will of God as revealed in the Scriptures." God's unfolding plan for man reveals itself through "the actual history of man in every stage of his existence," and so therefore men "must be content to build, if we would rear a fabric that may stand the test of Time, and prove worthy to receive the improvements which this slow and silent but ceaseless Innovator is ever making under the wise direction of the Ruler of the Universe, in all human institutions." History or time, for Hammond, was moving man forward and upward toward ever-higher levels of progress, civilization, and rationality. By studying the design in events, he concluded that the institution of slavery was the mechanism that had propelled Southern society to the vanguard of civilization. Hammond's "Innovator" here seems remarkably similar to what Hegel referred to as the *"cunning of reason,"* which used unwitting individuals or institutions to advance civilization without their having any rational foreknowledge of those ends. [18] Finally, Hammond rested the "System" of slavery on "the revealed Will of God—on custom—on utility—on the happiness of the greatest number—in one word on Law." This was the foundation—indeed, the only foundation—on which society can "progress" and on which there could be any "improvement in human affairs." For Hammond, the arc of history was synonymous with the revelation and unfolding of God's will through "primæval Time." Hammond accepted Hegel's belief that human history is the unfolding of God's mind on earth.

Another figure who was no fan of the Declaration of Independence and its self-evident truths was John C. Calhoun, the spiritual and political leader of proslavery intellectuals in the South. In his 1848 Senate speech "On the Oregon Bill," the South Carolina senator appealed to those who possess a "philosophical turn of mind" in order to see the "remote and recondite causes" of America's impending political crisis, which he traced back to the core principles of the Declaration of Independence. Calhoun considered the Declaration's claim that "all men are created equal" to be logically, syntactically, and morally false. There is "not a word of truth in it," he argued. In fact, the opposite was closer to the truth. First, the Bible teaches that only Adam and Eve were "created," while the rest of mankind was born, but even this, he held, is a falsehood because only infants and not men are born. Second, man's social reality teaches him that whether children are created or born, they are subject to the rule of their parents and are therefore never free, and they are born into radically different social conditions, which means they are never equal. The world is therefore defined by subjection and inequality. To the extent that equality and liberty are good for man, they are the products of a historical process; they are the "noble and highest reward bestowed on mental and moral development, combined with favorable circumstances." Men are not born with liberty and equality, nor are they "entitled" to them by nature, according to Calhoun. Instead, liberty and equality "are high prizes to be won, and are in their most perfect state, not only the highest reward that can be bestowed on our race, but the most difficult to be won." The arc of history (at least in some places) is evolving toward a higher state of civilization, which Calhoun identified with the South and chattel slavery. In the end, he believed that it was Jefferson's error to have placed in the heart of America's founding document self-evident falsehoods that did not recognize the "subordinate relation of the black to the white race in the South." From there it was a short step to the position that slavery, rather than being "an evil" was actually "a good—a positive good."[19]

Likewise, George Fitzhugh, the antebellum Southern intellectual with the most theoretical bent, believed that since the time of the Revolution America had been in the grips of what he called the "false philosophy of the age," which mistakenly "treats of men only as separate monads or individuals." The symbol of this false philosophy was embodied in the Declaration of Independence, the "truths" of which he described, in a chapter on "Southern Thought," as both "absurd" and "dangerous."[20] He described Thomas Jefferson, in "The Reformation—The Right of Private Judgment," as the "genius of innovation, the architect of ruin, and the inaugurator of anarchy." Writing on the Declaration of Independence, he said that it was based on "abstract principles" that bore no relationship to reality or history and that were therefore at "war with all government, all subordination, all order." The Declaration was written by men whose "minds were heated and blinded" by a "false philosophy" that originated with John Locke. Drunk on Enlightenment ideals, the "human mind" during the eighteenth century "became extremely presumptuous, and undertook to form governments on exact philosophical principles, just as men make clocks, watches or mills." The result was that America's revolutionary founders "confounded the moral with the physical world, and this was not strange, because they had begun to doubt whether there was any other than a physical world. Society seemed to them a thing whose movement and action could be controlled with as much certainty as the motion of a spinning wheel, provided it was organized on proper principles." The most important philosophic abstraction rejected by Fitzhugh was the notion that all men were created equal and free. Nothing, he argued, could be further from the truth: "Men are not 'born entitled to equal rights!'" Mocking Jefferson's famous last letter in 1826 to Roger Weightman, in which the Virginian had written that men were not born "with saddles on their backs, nor a favored few booted and spurred, ready to ride them legitimately, by the grace of God," Fitzhugh declared that it "would be far nearer the truth to say, 'that some *were* born with saddles on their backs, and others booted and spurred to ride them,'—and the riding does them good. They need the reins, the bit and the spur." In his chapter on "Southern Thought," Fitzhugh encouraged Southern intellectuals to "build up an entire new system of ethical philosophy" and a "new political science, whose leading and distinctive principle will be, 'the world is too little governed.'"[21]

Proslavery intellectuals understood that their critique of the Declaration and the natural-rights philosophy had implications for their political philosophy. Albert Taylor Bledsoe, a professor of mathematics at the University of Virginia and one of the South's most influential thinkers, argued in *Liberty and Slavery: or, Slavery in the Light of Moral and Political Philosophy* that in any conflict between the "inalienable rights of men" and the common or general good of society, the decision must not be made with "the aid of abstractions alone." What was needed instead, he claimed, was "a little good sense and *practical sagacity*," or pragmatic reasoning. Of one thing, though, Bledsoe was certain: "that the rights of the individual are subordinate to those of the community." Duties precede rights, he argued, and "it is the *duty*, and consequently, the *right*, of society to make such laws as the general good demands."[22]

One of the most fascinating aspects of antebellum Southern thought—one almost entirely neglected by modern scholars—was its embrace of socialism as not only compatible with plantation slavery but as its ultimate fulfillment. Many proslavery writers in the American South were, in effect, pre-Marxian socialists. Their critique of capitalism was virtually indistinguishable from Marx's, and they saw the plantation system as the only practical way in which to successfully implement the socialist ideal. Proslavery writers opposed the moral philosophy at the heart of capitalism (e.g., self-interest, natural rights, and individualism), the political principles of laissez-faire (e.g., the separation of economy and state), and the economic mechanisms at the heart of a market society (e.g., division of labor and competition), and they supported plantation socialism as the cure to all the ills associated with capitalism and a free society. Competition and free labor in capitalist nations had the intended effect, argued William Harper, of decreasing the worker's wages and increasing the capitalist's profits.[23] Readers of Fitzhugh and Marx would have a difficult time distinguishing the following passage taken from Fitzhugh's 1856 essay on "Centralization and Socialism" with the *Communist Manifesto* published eight years earlier:

The complaint is universal that modern improvements, while they lessen the labor required to create wealth, and are vastly increasing its aggregate amount, beget continually its more unequal distribution. They are, as yet, but engines in the hands of the rich and the skillful to oppress the laboring class....Every day sends forth its new swarms of paupers, whilst every month begets its millionaire. Capital becomes more powerful as it is wielded in larger masses, and as it grows stronger it becomes more oppressive and exacting. The wealthy capitalist soon learns to look on them as mere human machines representing so much physical and industrial power.[24]

Proslavery writers rejected the old liberalism's individualism for a new kind of plantation collectivism. Explicitly comparing men to ants and bees, Southern intellectuals viewed man as inherently collective and deterministic by nature. According to Fitzhugh, by "observing and studying the habitudes of the bees and the ants, of flocking birds and gregarious animals, we must become satisfied that our social habits and sympathetic feelings are involuntary, a part of our nature, and necessary to our healthful and natural existence." In *A Series of Lectures on the Science of Government, Intended to Prepare the Student for the Study of the Constitution of the United States* (1845), the first systematic "study of political science" published in the South, Virginia's Nathaniel Beverley Tucker claimed that "man is emphatically a social animal" and that "water is no more necessary to the fishes of the deep, than society is to man." Tucker assumed, unlike the revolutionary generation, that men naturally live in and identify with "clustering groups" from which they develop "a sort of collective personality."[25] Individuals and their rights were inseparable from and defined by society and government.

Southern antebellum writers such as Fitzhugh and Tucker typically viewed society as a natural organism, and they began with society or the collective (not with individuals) as the primary unit of moral and political value. As Fitzhugh put it in his *Sociology for the South, or the Failure of Free Society*, society trumps the individual: "Society is the being—he one of the members of that being. He has no rights whatever, as opposed to the interests of society; and that society may very properly make any use of him that will redound to the public good. Whatever rights he has are subordinate to the good of the whole; and he has never ceded rights to it, for he was born its slave, and had no rights to cede."[26] No member of the founding generation would have written that rights are "subordinate to the good of the whole," that man was born a slave to society without prior rights defined by his nature as a man. Fitzhugh rejects entirely the founding generation's conception of individual, natural rights.

Anticipating Marx's famous slogan—"From each according to his ability, to each according to his needs"—Fitzhugh claimed that the plantation system holds "all property in common" and divides "the profits, not according to each man's input and labor, but according to each man's wants." Plantation socialism, he continued, provides "for each slave, in old age and in infancy, in sickness and in health, not according to his labor, but according to his wants."[27] The kind of "free society" built into the principles of the Declaration, he wrote, is an unmitigated "failure" and must be replaced by "domestic slavery," which he called "the oldest, the best and the most common form of Socialism." In fact, a "Southern farm," he continued, "is the beau ideal of Communism."[28]

A Virginian, Edmund Ruffin, wrote in his treatise on *The Political Economy of Slavery* that "so far as their facts and reasoning go, and in their main doctrines, the socialists are right." The system of domestic slavery, he wrote, *perfects* the socialist ideal by elevating "one directing mind, and one controlling will"—that is, the mind and will of the master—over each plantation collective. He continued: "Our system of domestic slavery offers in use, and to the greatest profit for all parties in the association, the realization of all that is sound and valuable in the *socialists'* theories and doctrines.... Thus, in the institution of domestic slavery, and in that only, are most completely realized the dreams and sanguine hopes of the socialist school of philanthropists."[29] In sum, proslavery Southerners rejected what they called the "abstract" and "false" freedom philosophy enunciated in the Declaration of Independence, which, as we have seen, meant that they rejected the founders' understanding of truth—truth as absolute, certain, transhistorical, and universal—as well as the particular moral, political, social, and economic principles that issue from the Declaration: equality, freedom, rights, individualism, limited government, laissez-faire, and capitalism. In place of the founders' liberalism, proslavery thinkers substituted a new philosophy grounded in new principles. They accepted the historicist principle that truth is relative to time and place, and they developed a moral and political philosophy based on self-sacrifice, duty, collectivism, paternalism, central planning, and socialism.

* * *

The Union army destroyed the Confederacy, slavery, and plantation socialism, but many of the core ideas held by proslavery intellectuals in the 1840s and 1850s were given a second life (albeit in new forms) by progressive intellectuals in the decades after 1865. It would not, of course, be the first time in history that the loser on the battlefield nonetheless imposed on its conqueror "the yoke of its own thought."[30] How did this philosophic inversion come about?

Between 1865 and 1914, two generations of young Americans (mostly northerners) went off to study in Europe, primarily at German universities, where they were introduced to the ideas of the German Historical School and German philosophy.[31] Within a generation after the Civil War, American intellectuals, particularly in the North, came to reject not only the Declaration's self-evident truths but the very idea of "truth" itself— truth as absolute, certain, universal, and permanent. Richard T. Ely, one of America's best-known postbellum economists, recalled that during his graduate student days in Germany he was first introduced (echoing James Hammond) to the "idea of relativity as opposed to absolutism."[32] The moral and political principles of the old liberalism, or the founders' liberalism, disappeared almost overnight from American universities. Within a generation, the ideas of Kant, Hegel, Marx, and eventually Nietzsche replaced those of Locke, Montesquieu, Hume, and Adam Smith on America's college campuses.[33] From the Germans, young American graduate students gained an increased respect for the role of the state in promoting social, political, and economic reform.

William James and John Dewey, America's two most influential philosophers at the *fin-de-siècle*, took the trendiest European ideas and translated them into an American-style philosophy known as pragmatism. What was most distinctive and consequential about their philosophy was that it not only rejected the moral and political philosophy of the old liberalism but, more fundamentally, it rejected the eighteenth-century Enlightenment understanding of truth as knowable, certain, and absolute. In the pragmatists' world, there are no entities with fixed identities that can be known with certainty by the human mind, no laws of logic, no objectivity, and, ultimately, no truth. James and Dewey rejected the traditional view held by the American revolutionary founders that truth denotes a relationship between an idea or a proposition and the facts of reality.[34]

William James was the first major American philosopher to reject the founders' view of truth. He mocked what he called the "old-fashioned" view that there is a relationship between man's consciousness and reality, that "truth means essentially an inert static relation" between a thinking mind and an object. Instead, he argued, truth is accessed and known when it provides a "cash-value" by satisfying one's needs, urges, and wishes. True beliefs are those that are useful to the believer. Truth is determined by its function, and it is verified when the application of an idea delivers the desired result. Men experiment until they get what they want, and the method of getting what you want provides the standard of truth. James put it this way: "Truth *happens* to an idea. It *becomes* true, is *made* true by events. Its verity *is* in fact an event, a process: the process namely of its verifying itself, its veri-*fication*. Its validity is the process of its valid-*ation*." There is no objective, absolute truth for James that is timeless and placeless; his "account of truth is an account of truths in the plural," of truth as "*made*," "expedient," "temporary," "relative," "mutable," and "provisional." Truth, according to James, is "plastic" and subjective.[35] The founders' truths were true to them—but to no one else.

John Dewey went a step further than James and transformed the latter's view of truth from a form of personal or individual subjectivism into a form of social or group subjectivism. For Dewey, truth is made and determined by groups of people, and, in a democratic country like that of the United States, it should be determined by the will of the majority. The "*prima facie* meaning of truth," he wrote, "is acceptance of the beliefs that are current, that are authoritative, in a given community or organization." Dewey advocated turning the idea of "Truth as a noun singular and absolute" to the idea of a lowercase "truth" understood as a "noun common and distributive." In other words, truth is a "social virtue, meeting a demand growing out of intercourse, not a logical, much less an epistemological, relation." Truth means accepting as valid the consensus opinions of the community; it means "designating things in terms that observe the conventions of proper social intercourse." A falsehood for Dewey is a claim or proposition that is "contrary to social demands." His standard of truth as it applies to individual moral behavior is determined "according to current prescription." To know the truth about a particular matter is "to observe social prescription." Dewey's socially constructivist understanding of truth held up that which is "socially prescribed" as the standard by which to define "the rightful, the authoritative, definition of the object." By contrast, individuals who hold "private" opinions different from "current convention" should be treated as holding "illicit—anti-social" views.[36] Pragmatic truth is that which is developed and adopted by communities of men and women to serve their collective needs.

For the pragmatists, there is no absolute, universal, eternal, certain truth that can be discovered and understood by the human mind. Pragmatic truth is that which is accepted by and works for the group. By Dewey's standard, then, Athens was right to execute Socrates.

The new conception of truth developed in America by James, Dewey, and other postbellum American philosophers was subsequently broadened in the early twentieth century and applied to various academic disciplines such as history, political science, philosophy, literary criticism, psychology, sociology, anthropology, jurisprudence, and economics. This new conception of truth was transfused into the bloodstream of American academic life in the form of *historicism*, which says that all past ideas are embedded within a context—be it a social, political, economic, religious, linguistic, or psychological context—and, in effect, dissolvable into circumstance, and *moral relativism*, which says that moral principles and judgment are relative to time, place, and, ultimately, to each and every person.

Speaking of the Enlightenment political philosophy associated with the Declaration of Independence, Dewey mocked the founders' liberalism because it lacked what he called "historic relativity." According to the new truth of historicism, what was true in the eighteenth century was irrelevant and passé in the twentieth. Dewey summed up the fundamental defect of eighteenth-century philosophy with a not-so-subtle critique of the Declaration of Independence. He rejected the founders'

> conception of the individual as something given, complete in itself, and of liberty as a ready-made possession of the individual, only needing the removal of external restrictions in order to manifest itself. The individual of earlier liberalism was a Newtonian atom having only external time and space relations to other individuals, save in that each social atom was equipped with inherent freedom. These ideas…formed part of a *philosophy*, and of a philosophy

in which the particular ideas of individuality and freedom were
asserted to be absolute and eternal truths; good for all times and all
places.

But for Dewey and his generation, the traditional definition of truth was
no longer tenable. It had been replaced with what he called "historic" or
"temporal relativity" or what soon came to be just relativism—moral and
cultural. This doctrine became a virtual self-evident truth of the modern
world. The idea of absolute and permanent truth was not only a self-evident
lie for Dewey, it was, in his word, "evil."[37] He told early twentieth-century
Americans that the "ideas of Locke embodied in the Declaration of
Independence were congenial to our pioneer conditions that gave individuals the opportunity to carve their own careers."[38] The problem with such
principles, however, is that America's frontier conditions were gone, and
the "truths" that applied to those conditions could no longer be true under
the new social conditions of an urbanized and industrialized society. That
which inhibited or prevented the coming into being of the new twentieth-
century truths must be undermined, denounced, and ultimately held up as
reactionary and as a "false philosophy."

The new liberalism of the late nineteenth and early twentieth centuries
rejected all of the metaphysical, epistemological, moral, and political principles of the Declaration of Independence and the classical liberal tradition.
The proponents of the new liberalism revolted against what they saw as
the "quest for certainty" and the "formalism," "absolutism," and "rigidity"
of the founders' liberalism. They rejected the claim that nature is lawful
and intelligible, that man's reason is capable of discovering and knowing
objective moral laws, that morally sovereign individuals have unalienable
rights (particularly the rights to property and to the pursuit of happiness),
that the sole purpose of government is the protection of man's natural
rights, and that government should be strictly separated from economics
and education.

In particular, the new liberals reserved their greatest contempt for the
moral philosophy that was implicit in the Declaration but that was never
explicitly defended—namely, a moral philosophy of rational self-interest
and individualism. The intellectual leaders of the new liberalism understood
(as did the proslavery intellectuals) that to dismantle individualism, limited government, and capitalism, they first had to destroy the underlying

epistemological and moral principles of the Declaration—principles to which ordinary Americans were dedicated as a symbol of their ancient faith. Specifically, the founders' old-fashioned notions of "truth" and "rights" had to go. Then and only then could progressives reconstruct America on a new philosophic foundation and build entirely new political, social, and economic institutions.[39]

Woodrow Wilson—president of Princeton University, governor of New Jersey, and president of the United States—had quite a bit to say about the Declaration of Independence. Wilson's primary interpretative task was to historicize the Declaration, to denigrate it as little more than a document of its time. In 1907, during his tenure as president of Princeton, he delivered a Fourth of July oration on "The Author and Signers of the Declaration," in which he claimed that the signers of the Declaration "did not attempt to dictate the aims and objects of any generation but their own." Wilson was here suggesting that American revolutionaries did not think their principles were timelessly true, nor did they think, by his account, any generation beyond their own was beholden to them. This is because "each generation must," Wilson argued, "form its own conception of what liberty is." Thus the great question for twentieth-century Americans was, according to Wilson: Do Americans still accept the Declaration's moral and political principles as true—absolutely, universally, and timelessly? "Does the doctrine of the Declaration of Independence still live in our principles of action, in the things we do, in the purposes we applaud, in the measures we approve?" His answer was no. This is why Wilson believed that every July Fourth "should be a time for examining our standards, our purposes, for determining afresh what principles, what forms of power we think most likely to effect our safety and happiness." The fact is, he continued, that Americans "have come to a new age and a new attitude towards questions of government,…to new definitions of constitutional power, new conceptions of legislative object, new schemes of individual corporate regulation."[40]

Most importantly, Wilson and his fellow progressives rejected the founding generation's moral and political principles. Whereas the revolutionary generation treated the individual as an "integer," Wilson assumed the individual to be a mere "fraction" of a collective whole. And whereas the revolutionary generation was "deeply jealous of too much law," Wilson and the progressives were "in love with law" as an "instrument of reconstruction and control." The coercive power of the state must be used to transform men from integers to fractions. For those recalcitrant individuals who resisted this process, imprisonment was the only solution. As Wilson put it: "One really responsible man in jail, one real originator of the schemes and transactions which are contrary to public interest legally lodged in the penitentiary would be worth more than a thousand corporations mulcted in fines, if reform is to be genuine and permanent."[41]

Several years later, in an "Address to the Jefferson Club of Los Angeles," Wilson went further in historicizing the Declaration. He interpreted the Declaration's ringing words "We hold these truths to be self-evident" and the four truths that followed as mere rhetoric meant only to give flash to the historically contingent list of grievances against George III. But such grievances obviously had no relevance to 1911; therefore the Declaration's self-evident truths were also irrelevant. The business of any "true Jeffersonian is to translate the terms of those abstract portions of the Declaration of Independence into the language and the problems of his own day." For Wilson, the purpose of government was to address the socioeconomic problems of the present, which he and his progressive allies took to be the inequality generated by the private-property order and the self-interested behavior generated by the rise of free-market capital-ism. To dismantle America's system of political laissez-faire meant that progressive intellectuals had to undermine the founding generation's view of human nature as fixed. From this perspective, Wilson encouraged his audience to write a new declaration of independence, one that created a "new set of counts in the indictment" and made a "new statement of the things you mean to set right." He meant to declare independence from the core principles of the old liberalism of the Enlightenment—natural rights, individualism, and limited government. The power of government must now be viewed not as a necessary evil, as it was by the founders, but as a positive good.[42]

The political future of the new liberalism found its voice in the thought of Herbert Croly. Croly was, with Dewey, one of the two great intellectual godfathers of the modern liberal project. He was the founding editor of *The New Republic* magazine, but his most enduring legacy was his political treatise *The Promise of American Life*, published in 1909. The book was a systematic attack on the limited-government political philosophy of the old liberalism. Croly held the founders' liberalism responsible for virtually all of the social problems of late nineteenth- and early twentieth-century America. The Declaration's natural-rights philosophy was, according to Croly, the root cause of laissez-faire capitalism, and capitalism was the cause of all inequality, poverty, and social injustice. He thought the principles of the Declaration and Jeffersonian republicanism—natural rights, individualism, decentralization, limited government, strict constitutional construction, and laissez-faire—were outdated, bankrupt, and unjust: "Reform is both meaningless and powerless unless the Jeffersonian principle of non-interference is abandoned."[43]

Like Dewey, Croly argued for a complete reconstruction of America's political system. His political philosophy explicitly extolled both nationalism and socialism, and it sought to unite the two ideologies in one. The road from plantation socialism to national socialism was short. "The national public interest has to be affirmed by positive and aggressive action," which he meant to be "flagrantly socialistic both in its methods and its objects." His call for a form of national socialism demanded that all Americans "shall love and wish to serve their fellow-countrymen, and it will demand specifically that in the service of their fellow-countrymen, they shall reorganize their country's economic, political, and social institutions and ideas." Such a transformation cannot be achieved unless there is "systematic authoritative transformation of the private interest of the individual into a disinterested devotion to a special object," by which he meant the state. Like Wilson, Croly declared that his brand of national socialism was "equivalent to a new Declaration of Independence." And for this new declaration to become the nation's modern faith, Croly argued that a new kind of schooling would be required, one that would employ "severe coercive measures, but what schooling does not?"[44] Clearly, Croly's declaration was not your founding father's Declaration.

Ideas have consequences, and the ideas of James, Dewey, Wilson, and Croly were bound to seep into other academic disciplines in the years that followed.[45] By the early 1920s, America's leading academic scholars believed that the principles of the Declaration of Independence were outdated and irrelevant in the context of the modern world. In 1922, the Progressive historian Carl Becker published his classic *The Declaration of Independence: A Study in the History of Ideas*, a book that summed up the sentiments of his age and ours: "To ask whether the natural rights philosophy of the Declaration of Independence is true or false is essentially a *meaningless* question."[46] That is because Becker's generation no longer believed that the Declaration's self-evident truths were true. Early twentieth-century Progressives no longer accepted the traditional epistemic understanding of "truth." The search by American revolutionaries for transhistorical truths was, according to Becker, nothing more than an attempt to rationalize underlying social, economic, and psychological needs:

> When honest men are impelled to withdraw their allegiance to the established law or custom of the community, still more when they are persuaded that such law or custom is too iniquitous to be longer tolerated, they seek for some principle more generally valid, some "law" of higher authority, than the established law or custom of the community. To this higher law or more generally valid principle they then appeal in justification of actions which the community condemns as immoral or criminal....To them it is "true" because it brings their actions into harmony with a rightly ordered universe, and enable them to think of themselves as having chosen the nobler part.

For Becker's generation, it was an all but established fact that nineteenth-century philosophers such as Hegel, Bentham, Marx, and Nietzsche (never mind the proslavery Southern thinkers) had successfully dismantled the idea of natural rights as a concept founded "upon a superficial knowledge of history"[47]—in Bentham's phrase, "nonsense upon stilts."[48] The triumph in the nineteenth and twentieth centuries of historicism over natural-rights philosophy was predicated, according to Becker, on its having encountered the Enlightenment natural-rights philosophy "on its own ground, and refuted it from its own premises." The new historic-rights philosophy admitted "that rights were founded in nature," but it did so by identifying "nature with history." It then "affirmed that the institutions of any nation were properly but an expression of the life of the people, no more than the crystallization of its tradition, the cumulative deposit of its experience, the résumé of its history."[49]

Becker's view of history as the foundation of rights was viewed as the cutting edge of sophistication throughout much of the twentieth century. Ironically, his twentieth-century students were apparently unaware of the similarities between their teacher's view of the Declaration and that of the proslavery thinkers. Nor did they consider the possibility that the identification of nature with history is logically impossible as it attempts to reconcile the irreconcilable: that is, the permanent with the impermanent. Ultimately, Becker's truth claim collapses on itself.

It should not surprise us to learn, then, that the age in which we now live is said to be self-consciously "post-truth," which means a post-fact, post-reality world. In 2016, Oxford Dictionaries chose "post-truth" as its international word of the year, which it defines as "relating to or denoting circumstances in which objective facts are less influential in shaping public opinion than appeals to emotion and personal belief."[50] Truth is not possible in a post-truth society because reason is said to be impotent to know what is true or false, right or wrong, good or evil, just or unjust, free or unfree. In other words, there is no basis in objective reality or in reason for moral truth claims qua truth. Reason cannot distinguish between the truth and falsity of different moral claims, which of course means that it cannot distinguish between freedom and slavery. This post-truth philosophy holds that moral values and moral judgment are simply social conventions derived from subrational or nonrational forces, whether historical, economic, cultural, or psychological. Ultimately, relativism says that the fundamental law of each system of cultural values is grounded in nothing more than arbitrary human *will*—the will to assert and uphold authority over all other wills. The logical consequence of this teaching is that there can be no meaningful difference between free and slave or just and unjust societies. And if truth is unknowable, then the freedom of thought and speech necessary to pursue truth are irrelevant and meaningless.

We now live in a world wrought by the unidentified, unacknowledged union of proslavery and progressive thought. This union was consummated by their shared contempt for the animating principles of the Declaration of Independence and the Enlightenment. At the most fundamental level, proslavery and progressive intellectuals rejected the Enlightenment understanding of truth as the recognition of the objective relationship between an idea and the facts of reality. They rejected the possibility that there could be transhistorical truths grounded in an unchanging nature. By contrast, as historicists, they assumed that "truth" was relative to time and place, that each generation or community must discover and implement its own truths, and that truth must evolve toward higher levels of consciousness, social organization, and civilization. Proslavery and progressive intellectuals also rejected the moral, political, and economic principles of the old liberalism. Down the line they all opposed individualism, natural rights, limited government, and free-market capitalism. In varying forms, they stood for altruism (defined by Auguste Comte, the founder of positivism and sociology, as the idea that one must sacrifice one's own interests for the sake of others); for the "common good" as the primary unit of moral and political value; for the use of coercive power against those who refuse to submit; and for socialism as the highest form of social organization. In these ways and in many more, proslavery and progressive intellectuals share a common intellectual heritage.

✯ ✯ ✯

Prominent voices throughout American history have defended the Declaration's self-evident truths as true. The most important such voice was that of Abraham Lincoln. Lincoln anticipated and exposed what would become the progressive and postmodern interpretation of the Declaration in his response to the views of the preeminent antebellum relativists Stephen Douglas and Roger Taney. It seems almost certain that he would have seen Woodrow Wilson's and Herbert Croly's interpretation of the Declaration as fundamentally no different from those of Douglas, Taney, Fitzhugh, and Calhoun. Lincoln interpreted the Declaration's meaning as promoting "the progressive improvement in the condition of all men everywhere." By contrast, he attributed to Douglas and Taney (and by logical extension to Wilson and Croly) a historicist view of the Declaration, which held that it was adopted in 1776 merely "'for the purpose of justifying the colonists in the eyes of the civilized world in withdrawing their allegiance from the British crown, and dissolving their connection with the mother country.'" And given that the revolutionaries had been successful in their Revolution, Douglas and Taney (as would Wilson and Croly) viewed the Declaration as having "no practical use now" in the late 1850s. They viewed it (as would Wilson and Croly) as "mere rubbish—old wadding left to rot on the battle-field after the victory is won." Given the Douglas-Taney (Wilson-Croly) interpretation, the Declaration could have "no reference to the present," Lincoln argued.[51]

As Americans prepared to celebrate the Fourth of July in 1857, Lincoln told his audience in Springfield, Illinois, that they could read the Declaration in one of two ways: it could be read the "old-fashioned way," as was intended by Jefferson and the revolutionary generation, or it could be read as Douglas and Taney would have it read, to wit: "We hold these truths to be self-evident that all British subjects who were on this continent eighty-one years ago, were created equal to all British subjects born and then residing in Great Britain." Wilson and Croly could hardly have said it any better.

Lincoln ended his comments on the meaning and objects of the Declaration by leaving the American people with one last challenge: "are you really willing that the Declaration shall be thus frittered away?—thus left no more at most, than an interesting memorial of the dead past? thus shorn of its vitality, and practical value; and left without the *germ* or even the *suggestion* of the individual rights of man in it?"[52] Sadly, there was no twentieth-century Abraham Lincoln to ask that question of Wilson, Croly, and Becker.

In the end, the philosophic differences between nineteenth-century slaveholders and twentieth-century progressives—at least on the most fundamental issues concerning the nature of truth and rights—are really only differences of degree and not of kind. Once again, Lincoln seemed to anticipate the similarities between the proslavery and progressive views of the Declaration: "These expressions, differing in form, are identical in object and effect—the supplanting the principles of free government, and restoring those of classification, caste, and legitimacy. They would delight a convocation of crowned heads, plotting against the people. They are the van-guard—the miners, and sappers—of returning despotism. We must repulse them, or they will subjugate us."[53]

To his dying day, Lincoln believed that the announced moral and political principles of the Declaration were true—absolutely and permanently true—and he believed they were self-evidently true. He believed the Declaration's moral truths were as true as "the simpler propositions of Euclid are true." And this is why he also believed "it is now no child's play to save the principles of Jefferson from total overthrow in this nation." Jefferson, the man on whom Lincoln bestowed "all honor," had, during a moment of grave national crisis, "the coolness, forecast, and capacity to introduce into a merely revolutionary document, an abstract truth, applicable to all men and all times."[54]

For Lincoln, unlike for Carl Becker, the question of the truth status of the Declaration's principles was not a meaningless question. In fact, it was the *only* question that mattered. And on that very question, hundreds of thousands of men had dedicated and ultimately given their lives. This is why Lincoln implored his fellow citizens to reject John Pettit's heresy—that is, the claim that the Declaration's self-evident truths were actually "self-evident lies"—and to return to the secular sacraments of the old republic. At a Chicago speech in 1854, Lincoln asked his audience, "What would have happened if he [Pettit] had said it in old Independence Hall?" Lincoln's folksy answer captures what the Declaration's truths meant to him emotionally: "The door-keeper would have taken him by the throat and stopped his rascally breath awhile, and then have hurled him into the streets."[55]

Interestingly, when Becker wrote a new introduction, in 1941, to his book on the Declaration, in the face of the "incredible cynicism and brutality of Adolph Hitler's ambitions" and an advancing Nazi state, he was forced to rethink and "reappraise the validity of half-forgotten ideas" and to once again "entertain convictions as to the substance of things not evident to the senses." As Hitler's military was attacking and brutalizing the people of Europe, and as his police state at home was committing genocide against its own citizens, Becker and intellectuals like him were forced to reconsider and to ultimately concede—at least for the moment—that there were and must be objective moral truths that are stateless and timeless. During this dark period of human history, Becker gained a new appreciation for the doctrine of "'the inalienable rights of men'"—"phrases, glittering or not, that denote realities—the fundamental realities that men will always fight for rather than surrender."[56] Becker was now willing to suspend the "truth" of relativism for the truth of an objective moral reality, or at least the possibility of one. Invariably, there is always an eternal return from the Gospel of History to the Book of Nature.

✷ ✷ ✷

Every now and then, Americans are called upon to ask whether or not the principles of the Declaration of Independence are true. It is a question, whether we like it or not, of enduring relevance. Twenty-first-century Americans will no doubt be forced to confront it. In anticipation of that day, we might consider these lines from Robert Frost's haunting 1915 poem

"The Black Cottage." A minister, in talking to the speaker of the poem about "the principle / That all men are created free and equal," remarks:

> That's a hard mystery of Jefferson's.
> What did he mean? Of course the easy way
> Is to decide it simply isn't true.
> It may not be. I heard a fellow say so.
> But never mind, the Welshman got it planted
> Where it will trouble us a thousand years.[57]

Frost captures brilliantly the ambiguous philosophic and moral status of the Declaration in the twentieth—and now in the twenty-first—century. Since the 1830s, America's intellectual class has followed the path laid by Harper, Calhoun, Fitzhugh, Hammond, James, Dewey, Wilson, Croly, Becker, and the like in denying the truth status of the Declaration's principles—and yet, the American people still cling in some vague, emotional way to these principles. As Becker learned, there are times in the course of human events when we are forced to confront the possibility that the Declaration's self-evident truths are just that—true.

In 1860, the New England abolitionist Lydia Maria Child declared in a pamphlet that the time had come for the American people "to decide whether our fathers were mistaken in considering Freedom a blessing; whether our Declaration of Independence embodies eternal principles, or is a mere 'rhetorical flourish.'" She noted that "Slavery and Freedom" stood facing each other as "antagonistic elements," and that "one must inevitably destroy the other." Like Abraham Lincoln, Child knew that a house divided against itself cannot stand. She ended her pamphlet with one last question to the American people: "Which do you choose?"[58]

And so it is with us. We, too, have a choice. We can accept the Declaration's freedom principles as true, or we can adopt very different moral principles. I hope that this book will inspire its readers to think anew about this fundamental choice.

NOTES

PREFACE

1 Abraham Lincoln, "Fragment on the Constitution and the Union," in *The Collected Works of Abraham Lincoln*, ed. Roy P. Basler, with Marion D. Pratt and Lloyd A. Dunlap (New Brunswick, NJ: Rutgers University Press, 1953), 4:168–69. Note: In quotations of primary sources throughout this book, I observe original spellings, punctuation, and treatment of words.

INTRODUCTION

1 James Madison, *Federalist* No. 14, in *The Federalist*, ed. Jacob E. Cooke (Cleveland, OH: Meridian Books, 1961), 89. All subsequent references to *The Federalist* are to this edition.

2 John Adams to Thomas Jefferson, August 24, 1815, in *The Adams-Jefferson Letters: The Complete Correspondence Between Thomas Jefferson and Abigail and John Adams*, ed. Lester J. Cappon (New York: Simon and Schuster, 1959), 455; John Adams to H. Niles, February 13, 1818, in *The Works of John Adams, Second President of the United States*, ed. Charles Francis Adams (Boston: Little Brown, 1865), 10:282–83. Adams's dating of the birth of the American Revolution to 1760 is curious given that most scholars typically begin their narratives with the American reaction to either the passage of the Sugar Act in 1764 or the Stamp Act of 1765. Why 1760? There seem to be two likely explanations. First, Adams knew that the American reaction to the Stamp Act in 1765 did not happen randomly. The Stamp Act violated the Americans' most deeply held moral and political principles—principles that began to come into full consciousness in the years before 1765. Second, Adams is also making room in his narrative for the speech delivered by James Otis before the Superior Court of Massachusetts at the writs of assistance case in 1761, which Adams argued was the moment when the Americans' revolutionary mind was given its birth. According to Adams, British imperial officials initiated the case in late 1760 by ordering that American customs officials use a new kind of writ of assistance against American smugglers after they had received word of General James Wolfe's victory over the Marquis de Montcalm at Montreal, thereby effectively ending the Seven Years' War with France. Otis's speech was the first act of American

resistance to the designs of British imperial officials. Decades later, Adams, who was a witness to the courtroom case, argued—figuratively rather than literally—that Otis's speech "produced the American Revolution." He described the impact of Otis's speech this way: "Otis was a flame of fire!...American independence was then and there born; the seeds of patriots and heroes were then and there sown. . . . Every man of a crowded audience appeared to me to go away, as I did, ready to take arms against writs of assistance. Then and there was the first scene of the first act of opposition to the arbitrary claims of Great Britain. Then and there the child Independence was born. In fifteen years, namely in 1776, he grew up to manhood, and declared himself free." See Adams to William Tudor Sr., December 18, 1816, and March 29, 1817, *Works of Adams*, 10:233–34, 247–48.

3 Thomas Paine, *Common Sense*, in *Collected Writings* (New York: Library of America, 1995), 21. (Emphasis added.)

4 Thomas Paine, *Letter to the Abbé Raynal, on the Affairs of North America, in which the Mistakes in the Abbé's Account of the Revolution of America Are Corrected and Cleared Up* (Philadelphia, 1782), in *The Life and Works of Thomas Paine*, ed. William M. Van der Weyde (New Rochelle, NY: Thomas Paine National Historical Association, 1925), 4:171, 174.

5 Thomas Paine, *The Rights of Man, Part the Second: Combining Principle and Practice* (1792), in *Life and Works of Paine*, 6:232, 236.

6 Joel Barlow, *Advice to the Privileged Orders, in the Several States of Europe, Resulting from the Necessity and Propriety of a General Revolution in the Principle of Government* (New York: Childs and Swaine, 1792), 20–21.

7 Barlow, *Advice to the Privileged Orders*, 23.

8 Thomas Jefferson to Henry Lee, May 8, 1825, in *The Writings of Thomas Jefferson*, ed. Andrew A. Lipscomb and Albert Ellery Bergh (Washington, DC: Thomas Jefferson Memorial Association, 1903), 16:117–19.

9 The contours of this new approach to history writing are laid out in C. Bradley Thompson, "The American Revolution and the New Moral History," *American Political Thought* 8, no. 2 (2019): 175–201.

10 Alexander Hamilton, *Federalist* No. 31, 193–94.

11 See Alexis de Tocqueville, *Democracy in America*, ed. and trans. Harvey C. Mansfield and Delba Winthrop (Chicago: University of Chicago Press, 2000).

12 Adams to H. Niles, February 13, 1818, *Works of Adams*, 10:282–83.

13 Jefferson to Richard Henry Lee, November 29, 1825, *Founders Online*, National Archives, http://founders.archives.gov/documents/Jefferson/98-01-02-5693. (Spelling and other irregularities in the original.)

CHAPTER 1

1 Jefferson to Roger Weightman, June 24, 1826, *Writings of Jefferson*, 16:181–82.

2 Jefferson to Roger Weightman, June 24, 1826, *Writings of Jefferson*, 16:181–82.

3 Thomas Reid, *An Inquiry into the Human Mind, on the Principles of Common Sense* (Edinburgh: Anderson and MacDowall, and James Robertson, 1818; repr., London: Forgotten Books, 2012), 31.

4 For general accounts of the revolution initiated by the Enlightenment, see Peter Gay, *The Enlightenment: An Interpretation*, vol. 1, *The Rise of Modern Paganism* (New York: Norton, 1966), and vol. 2, *The Science of Freedom* (New York: Norton, 1969); Jonathan I. Israel, *Radical Enlightenment: Philosophy and the Making*

of Modernity 1650–1750 (Oxford: Oxford University Press, 2001); Jonathan I. Israel, *Enlightenment Contested: Philosophy, Modernity, and the Emancipation of Man 1670–1752* (Oxford: Oxford University Press, 2006); Jonathan I. Israel, *A Revolution of the Mind: Radical Enlightenment and the Intellectual Origins of Modern Democracy* (Princeton, NJ: Princeton University Press, 2010).

5 Thomas Jefferson to John Trumbull, February 15, 1789, in *The Portable Thomas Jefferson*, ed. Merrill Peterson (New York: Penguin, 1975), 434–35.

6 John Adams, diary entry, April 9, 1754, in *The Earliest Diary of John Adams: June 1753–April 1754, September 1758–January 1759*, ed. Lyman H. Butterfield, Marc Friedlaender, and Wendell D. Garrett (Cambridge, MA: Belknap Press of Harvard University Press, 1966), 60, 63; John Adams, *Autobiography* (November 30, 1804), in *Diary and Autobiography of John Adams*, ed. Lyman H. Butterfield, Marc Friedlaender, and Wendell D. Garrett (Cambridge, MA: Belknap Press of Harvard University Press, 1962), 3:262.

7 See Adams, *Diary and Autobiography*, 1:11, 32–33, 38, 40, 43–44, 98–99.

8 Adams to Jonathan Sewell, February 1760, in *Papers of John Adams*, ed. Robert J. Taylor, Mary-Jo Kline, and Gregg L. Lint (Cambridge, MA: Belknap Press of Harvard University Press, 1977), 1:42–43.

9 James Wilson, *Lectures on Law*, in *The Works of James Wilson*, ed. Robert Green McCloskey (Cambridge, MA: Belknap Press of Harvard University Press, 1967), 1:225–26, 213–14.

10 Standard works on the modern revolution in science include E. A. Burtt, *The Metaphysical Foundations of Modern Physical Science* (Garden City, NJ: Doubleday, 1954); Herbert Butterfield, *The Origins of Modern Science, 1300–1800* (Toronto: Clarke, Irwin, 1977); and Frank Durham and Robert D. Purrington, *Frame of the Universe: A History of Physical Cosmology* (New York: Columbia University Press, 1983).

11 Isaac Newton, *The Mathematical Principles of Natural Philosophy*, trans. Andrew Motte (New York: Daniel Adee, 1845), 384.

12 John Locke, *An Essay Concerning Human Understanding*, ed. John W. Yolton (London: Dent, 1961), bk. IV, chap. xii, para. 11. Hereafter cited as *ECHU* followed by book, chapter, and paragraph numbers.

13 Reid, *Inquiry into the Human Mind*, 365–66.

14 *ECHU*, I.iv.25.

15 On the relationship between Locke's epistemology and his moral and political thought, see Richard I. Aaron, *John Locke* (Oxford: Clarendon, 1955); John W. Yolton, *Locke and the Compass of Human Understanding: A Selective Commentary on the "Essay"* (Cambridge: Cambridge University Press, 1970); Ruth W. Grant, *John Locke's Liberalism* (Chicago: University of Chicago Press, 1987); and Peter A. Schouls, *Reasoned Freedom: John Locke and Enlightenment* (Ithaca, NY: Cornell University Press, 1992).

16 *ECHU*, I.i.2, I.i.6, IV.xxi.1, IV.xxi.3.

17 *ECHU*, I.i.6, IV.xxi.3.

18 The Cambridge Platonists were a group of seventeenth-century English philosophers and theologians at Cambridge University, the best known of whom were Ralph Cudworth (1617–1688) and Henry More (1614–1687).

19 *ECHU*, I.iv.2, I.i.2; "Epistle to the Reader," *ECHU*, p. xxxv.

20 See *ECHU*, II.ix.13. In the secondary literature, see Yolton, *Locke and the Compass of Human Understanding*, 17, and Grant, *John Locke's Liberalism*, 38–39.

Also see John Dunn, *The Political Thought of John Locke: An Historical Account of the Argument of the "Two Treatises of Government"* (Cambridge: Cambridge University Press, 1969), 87–88, 95.

21 John Locke, *Two Treatises of Government*, ed. Peter Laslett (Cambridge: Cambridge University Press, 1963), *First Treatise*, para. 58. Hereafter cited as either *First Treatise* or *Second Treatise*, with paragraph number.

22 *ECHU*, IV.xix.14.

23 *ECHU*, IV.xvii.9, I.i.7.

24 See Hugo Grotius, "The Preliminary Discourse Concerning the Certainty of Right in General; and the Design of His Work in Particular" (1625), in *The Rights of War and Peace*, ed. Richard Tuck, from the edition by Jean Barbeyrac (Indianapolis, IN: Liberty Fund, 2005), 1:89; Montesquieu, *Persian Letters*, trans. C. J. Betts (New York: Penguin, 1973), 162.

25 *ECHU*, I.i.2. On Locke's moral-political theory, see Thomas L. Pangle, *The Spirit of Modern Republicanism: The Moral Vision of the American Founders and the Philosophy of Locke* (Chicago: University of Chicago Press, 1988); Michael P. Zuckert, *Natural Rights and the New Republicanism* (Princeton, NJ: Princeton University Press, 1994); and Peter C. Myers, *Our Only Star and Compass: Locke and the Struggle for Political Rationality* (Lanham, MD: Rowman and Littlefield, 1998).

26 John Locke, *The Reasonableness of Christianity*, ed. George W. Ewing (Chicago: Regnery, 1965), 174.

27 *ECHU*, I.iii.13, IV.iii.18, I.iv.26.

28 *ECHU*, III.xi.16. Locke speaks of his project to build a demonstrative science of morality in at least three other places in the *Essay*: IV.iii.18, IV.iv.7, and IV.xii.8.

29 *ECHU*, IV.iii.18, IV.xii.8 (emphasis added), III.xi.16, and IV.iii.18 (emphasis added). See chapter 3 for a discussion of Locke's understanding of self-evident truths. Interestingly, Thomas Reid, the philosopher described by Garry Wills in his *Inventing America: Jefferson's Declaration of Independence* (New York: Vintage Books, 1979) as one of the leading eighteenth-century Scottish opponents of Locke, wrote an entire chapter supporting (with some reservations and corrections) Locke's attempt to establish a morality capable of demonstration. See Reid, "Whether Morality Be Capable of Demonstration," in *Essays on the Intellectual Powers of Man* (Edinburgh: John Bell and G.G.J. & J. Robinson, 1785; repr., New York: Garland, 1971), 678–88.

30 *ECHU*, IV.xii.11, IV.xii.11.

31 *ECHU*, IV.iii.18.

32 *Second Treatise*, para. 135.

33 *Second Treatise*, para. 4–5.

34 *Second Treatise*, para. 27.

35 *Second Treatise*, para. 123, 172, 54.

36 See *ECHU*, II.xxvii.9–25.

37 *ECHU*, II.xxi.29.

38 *Second Treatise*, para. 6.

39 *ECHU*, I.iii.6, I.iv.9, II.xxviii.8, III.ix.23.

40 *ECHU*, I.iii.13; *Second Treatise*, para. 6.

41 *ECHU*, I.iii3, I.xxi.47.

42 *Second Treatise*, para. 63.

43 *Second Treatise*, para. 16, 57.

44 *Second Treatise*, para. 6.

45 *ECHU*, I.iii.4–5; *Second Treatise*, para. 13, 27; *ECHU*, I.iii.12.

46 *Second Treatise*, para. 142, 10, 12.

47 See *Second Treatise*, para. 124.

48 *ECHU*, II.xxviii.6, I.iii.13, II.xxviii.5.

49 *ECHU*, I.iii.3, I.iii.6. (Emphasis added.)

50 *ECHU*, II.xxviii.6.

51 *Second Treatise*, para. 124.

52 *ECHU*, II.xxviii.10, II.xxviii.9.

53 *ECHU*, II.xxviii.10.

54 *ECHU*, II.xxviii.10–11, II.xxviii.12.

55 *Second Treatise*, para. 10, 16, 8, 16.

56 *Second Treatise*, para. 135.

57 In order to gain a "knowledge of virtue" and to be "instructed in the natural rights of men, and the origin and foundations of society, and the duties resulting from thence," Locke recommends that boys and young men study Cicero's *De Officiis* (44 BCE), Samuel von Pufendorf's *On the Duty of Man and Citizen According to Natural Law* (1673) and *Of the Law of Nature and Nations* (1672), and Hugo Grotius's *On the Law of War and Peace* (1625). See John Locke, *Some Thoughts Concerning Education* (1693), in *Some Thoughts Concerning Education; and, Of the Conduct of the Understanding*, ed. Ruth W. Grant and Nathan Tarcov (Indianapolis, IN: Hackett, 1996), 139.

In "Some Thoughts Concerning Reading and Study for a Gentleman," Locke divides the study of politics into two branches, "the one, containing the original of societies, and the rise and extent of political power; the other, the art of governing men in society." With regard to studying the "original of societies, and the rise and extent of political power," beyond what Locke recommends in *Some Thoughts Concerning Education* he adds Richard Hooker's *Of the Lawes of Ecclesiastical Politie* (1594–97), Algernon Sidney's *Discourses Concerning Government* (1698), Peter Paxton's *Civil Polity: A Treatise Concerning the Nature of Government* (1703), and of course his own *Two Treatises of Government* (1690). As for the "art of government," Locke says it "is best to be learned by experience and history, especially that of a man's own country." See John Locke, "Some Thoughts Concerning Reading and Study for a Gentleman," in *The Works of John Locke* (London: C. Baldwin, 1824), 2:408.

Eighty-seven years later, John Adams drew a similar distinction, between what he called "principles of liberty," which he associated with Locke's *Second Treatise*, and the "principles of political architecture," which he associated with Montesquieu's *Spirit of the Laws*. See Adams to Samuel Adams, September 12, 1790, *Works of Adams*, 6:411–12. For a discussion of Adams's distinction between the "principles of liberty" and the "principles of political architecture," see C. Bradley Thompson, *John Adams and the Spirit of Liberty* (Lawrence: University Press of Kansas, 1998), 174.

58 Locke, *Some Thoughts Concerning Education*, 185–87.

59 *Second Treatise*, para. 12, 42.

60 *Second Treatise*, para. 3, 124–26.

61 On Locke's influence in America, see Merle Curti, "The Great Mr. Locke, America's Philosopher, 1783–1861," *Huntington Library Bulletin* (1937), 107–51; John Dunn, "The Politics of Locke in England and America in the Eighteenth

Century," in *Political Obligation in Its Historical Context: Essays in Political History* (Cambridge: Cambridge University Press, 2002), 53–77; Pangle, *The Spirit of Modern Republicanism*; Steven M. Dworetz, *The Unvarnished Doctrine: Locke, Liberalism, and the American Revolution* (Durham, NC: Duke University Press, 1990); Jerome Huyler, *Locke in America: The Moral Philosophy of the Founding Era* (Lawrence: University Press of Kansas, 1995); and Michael P. Zuckert, *The Natural Rights Republic: Studies in the Foundation of the American Political Tradition* (Notre Dame, IN: University of Notre Dame Press, 1996).

62 The term "Whig," as opposed to "Tory," is used here to describe those colonial and revolutionary Americans who were distrustful of political power and who believed that the purpose of government is to expand the sphere of individual freedom by protecting the citizen's natural and civil rights. The term "Patriot," as opposed to "Loyalist," is used here to describe those colonial and revolutionary Americans who opposed efforts by British imperial officials to legislate for the colonies and who supported the American cause during the War of Independence.

63 John Bulkley, preface to *Poetical Meditations*, by Roger Wolcott (New London, CT: T. Green, 1725), xii; A Virginian [pseud.], *Pennsylvania Gazette*, September 29, 1768; Anon., "To the Inhabitants of Queen's County, Long Island," *Constitutional Gazette*, November 29, 1775; John Tucker, *A Sermon Preached at Cambridge, before His Excellency Thomas Hutchinson…and the Honorable House of Representatives, of the Province of the Massachusetts Bay…* (Boston: Richard Draper, 1771), 19.

64 *Boston Gazette*, March 1, 1773.

65 See Massachusettensis [pseud.], *Massachusetts Spy*, December 5, 1771, and August 27, 1772. (This is not the same Massachusettensis who inspired John Adams to write his Novanglus letters.)

66 Samuel Briggs, ed., *The Essays, Humor, and Poems of Nathaniel Ames, Father and Son, of Dedham, Massachusetts, from Their Almanacks, 1726–1775* (Cleveland: Short & Forman, 1891; New York: Johnson Reprint, 1970), 450. For just one example of a newspaper that devoted its pages to quoting long extracts from Locke's *Second Treatise*, see *Massachusetts Spy*, August 22, 1771, which reproduced the entirety of the eighteenth chapter on "Tyranny."

67 Jonathan Boucher, *A View of the Causes and Consequences of the American Revolution* (London: G.G.J. and J. Robinson, 1797; repr., New York: Russell and Russell, 1967), 531. Boucher, like most American Loyalists and British Tories, rejected Locke's core political principals that the origin of government will be found in equality, consent, and contract. Such a dangerous view, Boucher held, would be the end of all government. Interestingly, some Loyalists thought the Americans had misinterpreted Locke's political philosophy and claimed that they were the true Lockeans. On Lockean Loyalists, see Joseph Galloway, *A Candid Examination of the Mutual Claims of Great-Britain, and the Colonies: With a Plan of Accomodation, on Constitutional Principles* (New York: James Rivington, 1775). See also the views of Peter Van Schaack, of New York, in H. C. Van Schaack, *The Life of Peter Van Schaack* (New York: D. Appleton, 1842), 54–60, 73–76, 87, 26–61. Some of the most interesting debates during the Revolutionary period were between American Whigs and Loyalists over the nature and meaning of Locke's philosophy for America. For an example of

such a debate, see the Loyalist Thomas Bradbury Chandler, *A Friendly Address to All Reasonable Americans, on the Subject of Our Political Confusions*... (Boston: Mills and Hicks, 1774) versus the Whig Philip Livingston, *The Other Side of the Question: or, A Defence of the Liberties of North-America* (New York: James Rivington, 1774).

CHAPTER 2

1 Much has been written since the late twentieth century on the Declaration's philosophic sources. In addition to several works already cited, including Zuckert's *Natural Rights Republic*, see Hans Eicholz, *Harmonizing Sentiments: The Declaration of Independence and the Jeffersonian Idea of Self-Government* (New York: P. Lang, 2001); Paul Eidelberg, *On the Silence of the Declaration of Independence* (Amherst: University of Massachusetts Press, 1976); Pauline Maier, *American Scripture: Making the Declaration of Independence* (New York: Knopf, 1997); Allen Jayne, *Jefferson's Declaration of Independence: Origins, Philosophy, and Theology* (Lexington: University Press of Kentucky, 1998); and Morton White, *The Philosophy of American Revolution* (New York: Oxford University Press, 1978).

2 On Newton's influence on the Declaration and the political thought of the American founding period, see Carl L. Becker, *The Declaration of Independence: A Study in the History of Political Ideas* (New York: Harcourt, Brace, 1922), 24–79; Wills, *Inventing America*, 93–110; and I. Bernard Cohen, *Science and the Founding Fathers: Science in the Political Thought of Jefferson, Franklin, Adams and Madison* (New York: Norton, 1995).

3 Nathanael Emmons, "The Dignity of Man," in *Political Sermons of the American Founding Era, 1730–1805*, ed. Ellis Sandoz (Indianapolis, IN: Liberty Press, 1990), 893; Samuel McClintock, "A Sermon on Occasion of the Commencement of the New-Hampshire Constitution," *Political Sermons of the American Founding Era*, 803–804.

4 Jefferson, *Notes on the State of Virginia*, in *Portable Thomas Jefferson*, 211.

5 Jefferson to Peter Carr, August 10, 1787, *Portable Thomas Jefferson*, 425.

6 The revolutionaries' charge that imperial officials were driven by a conspiracy to enslave them is examined in much greater detail in chapter 9.

7 John Adams, "A Dissertation on the Canon and Feudal Law," in *The Revolutionary Writings of John Adams*, ed. C. Bradley Thompson (Indianapolis, IN: Liberty Fund, 2000), 34.

8 John Dickinson, *Letters from a Farmer in Pennsylvania to the Inhabitants of the British Colonies* (1768), in *The Political Writings of John Dickinson, 1764–1774*, ed. Paul Leicester Ford (Philadelphia: Historical Society of Pennsylvania, 1895; repr., New York: Da Capo, 1970), 355–56.

9 Thomas Jefferson, *A Summary View of the Rights of British-America*, in *Colonies to Nation, 1763–1789: A Documentary History of the American Revolution*, ed. Jack P. Greene (New York: Norton, 1975), 231.

10 John Adams quoting Daniel Leonard in the "Massachusettensis Letters," in *The American Crisis: The Daniel Leonard–John Adams Letters to the Press, 1774–1775*, ed. Bernard Mason (New York: Harper and Row, 1972), 33–34, 39.

11 See David N. Mayer, *The Constitutional Thought of Thomas Jefferson* (Charlottesville: University Press of Virginia, 1994), 37–45.

12 See Wills, *Inventing America*, 71.

13 Jefferson to James Maury, June 16, 1815, *Writings of Jefferson*, 14:319.

14 Dickinson, *Letters from a Farmer in Pennsylvania to the Inhabitants of the British Colonies* (1768), in *Political Writings of Dickinson*, 348.

15 Continental Congress, Declaration of the Causes and Necessity of Taking Up Arms (July 6, 1775), *Colonies to Nation*, 255.

16 Jefferson to James Smith, December 8, 1822, *Writings of Jefferson*, 15:409; Richard Bland, *An Inquiry into the Rights of the British Colonies* (1766), in *American Political Writing during the Founding Era, 1760–1805*, ed. Charles S. Hyneman and Donald S. Lutz (Indianapolis, IN: Liberty Press, 1983), 1:69.

17 Jefferson to Lafayette, February 14, 1815, *Writings of Jefferson*, 14:245; Jefferson to Thomas Law, June 13, 1814, *Writings*, 14:139; Jefferson, *Notes on the State of Virginia* (1782), Q:17, *Writings*, 2:223; Jefferson to Nathaniel Macon, January 12, 1819, *Writings*, 15:180; Jefferson to Pierre Samuel Dupont de Nemours, April 24, 1816, *Writings*, 14:490; Jefferson to John Cartwright, June 5, 1824, *Writings*, 16:43; Jefferson to Richard Rush, October 20, 1820, *Writings*, 15:284; Jefferson to David Harding, April 20, 1824, *Writings*, 16:30; Jefferson, First Inaugural Address (1801), *Writings*, 3:321.

18 Jefferson to William Johnson, June 12, 1823, *Writings of Jefferson*, 15:441; Jefferson to Judge John Tyler, June 28, 1804, *Writings*, 11:33; Jefferson to Benjamin Rush, March 6, 1813, *Writings*, 13:225; Jefferson to the Rev. Samuel Miller, January 23, 1808, *Writings*, 11:429; Jefferson to John F. Watson, May 17, 1814, *Writings*, 14:136; Jefferson to William Duane, March 28, 1811, *Writings*, 13:26.

19 Jefferson to James Madison, March 21, 1786, *Writings of Jefferson*, 6:10; Jefferson to Joseph Priestly, June 19, 1810, *Writings*, 10:324; Enos Hitchcock, "An Oration: Delivered July 4, 1788, at the Request of the Inhabitants of the Town of Providence, in Celebration of the Anniversary of American Independence . . ." (Providence, RI: Bennett Wheeler, 1788), 11.

20 Paine, *Rights of Man, Part the Second*, in *Life and Works of Paine*, 6:231; 7:97; 6:226, 225, 231.

21 Paine, *Rights of Man, Part the Second*, in *Life and Works of Paine*, 6:232, 322.

22 Elihu Palmer, *Principles of Nature; or, A Development of the Moral Causes of Happiness among the Human Species* (New York, 1802), 242, 7, 243, 244, 134.

23 *ECHU*, IV.iii.18.

24 See John Locke, "Essays on the Laws of Nature," in *Locke: Political Essays*, ed. Mark Goldie (Cambridge: Cambridge University Press, 1997), 79–133.

25 Adams, "A Dissertation on the Canon and Feudal Law," *Revolutionary Writings of Adams*, 33. The Stamp Act of 1765 imposed a direct tax on Britain's American colonies by requiring the colonists to purchase stamped paper for various legal documents, magazines, newspapers, and many other types of paper used by the colonists. The purpose of the tax was to help offset British war expenses acquired during the recently concluded Seven Years' War.

26 Alexander Hamilton, *The Farmer Refuted* (February 23, 1775), in *The Papers of Alexander Hamilton*, ed. Harold C. Syrett and Jacob E. Cooke (New York: Columbia University Press, 1961), 1:86.

27 James Otis, *The Rights of the British Colonies Asserted and Proved* (1764), in *Pamphlets of the American Revolution, 1750–1776*, ed. Bernard Bailyn (Cambridge, MA: Belknap Press of Harvard University Press, 1965), 441.

28 John Wise, *A Vindication of the Government of New England Churches* (excerpt), in *Puritan Political Ideas, 1558–1794,* ed. Edmund S. Morgan (Indianapolis, IN: Bobbs-Merrill, 1965), 252–67.

29 Abraham Williams, "An Election Sermon" (1762), *American Political Writing during the Founding Era,* 1:8.

30 See, for example, Charles Turner, *A Sermon Preached Before His Excellency Thomas Hutchinson...and the House of Representatives, of the Province of the Massachusetts-Bay* (Boston: Richard Draper, 1773), 31.

31 Quoted from the 1768 "Preface" to Thomas Bradbury, *The Ass: or, The Serpent,* with a Preface by Concionator [pseud.] (London: N. Cliff and D. Jackson, 1712; repr., Boston: Edes and Gill, 1768); An American [pseud.], *Massachusetts Spy,* December 5, 1771.

32 Anon. from the County of Hampshire, "To the Inhabitants of Massachusetts-Bay, No. 1," *Massachusetts Spy,* February 9, 1775; The Monitor [pseud.], *New-York Journal,* November 16, 1775.

33 Adams, diary entries, August 22, 1756, Summer 1759, May 11, 1756, *Diary and Autobiography,* 1:43–44, 117, 26.

34 Adams, draft of a letter to Jonathan Sewell, *Diary and Autobiography,* 1:123. (Emphasis added.) Compare with Locke, *ECHU,* I.i.5–9.

35 Adams, draft of a letter to an unidentified correspondent (1758), *Earliest Diary,* 71–72.

36 Adams, diary entry, March 3, 1756, *Diary and Autobiography,* 1:11.

37 The proposition that the laws of nature were known through inductive reasoning was not uniform, however, among the founding generation. In the years after the Revolution, some founders such as James Wilson argued that certain moral laws of nature were known to man through an innate moral sense. In his *Lectures on Law* (1790–91), Wilson advanced a very different view of how the moral laws of nature are known from the one presented here: "If I am asked ...—how do you know that you ought to do that, of which your conscience enjoins the performance? I can only say, I *feel* that such is my duty. Here investigation must stop; reasoning can go no farther. The science of morals, as well as other sciences, is founded on truths, that cannot be discovered or proved by reasoning....We cannot, therefore, begin to reason, till we are furnished, otherwise than by reason, with some truths, on which we can found our arguments. Even in mathematicks, we must be provided with axioms perceived intuitively to be true, before our demonstrations can commence. Morality, like mathematicks, has its intuitive truths, without which we cannot make a single step in our reasonings upon the subject." Wilson, *Lectures on Law,* in *Works of Wilson,* 1:133.

38 Adams, diary entry, August 14, 1756, *Diary and Autobiography,* 1:41.

39 Adams, diary entry, December 3 or 4, 1758, *Diary and Autobiography,* 1:61; *Earliest Diary,* 77. This paragraph is partly drawn from Thompson, *John Adams and the Spirit of Liberty,* 19–20.

40 Ethan Allen, excerpt from *Reason the Only Oracle of Man* (1785), in Kerry S. Walters, *The American Deists: Voices of Reason and Dissent in the Early Republic* (Lawrence: University Press of Kansas, 1992), 149, 164.

41 Montesquieu, *Persian Letters,* trans. C. J. Betts (Harmondsworth, UK, and Baltimore: Penguin, 1973), 162–63.

42 Benjamin Franklin, *A Dissertation on Liberty and Necessity, Pleasure and Pain*, in *American Deists*, 59.

43 A Philadelphian [pseud.], "To the Freeman of America," *Pennsylvania Gazette* (n.d.); repr., *Massachusetts Spy*, June 2, 1774.

44 Bland, *Inquiry into the Rights of the British Colonies*, in *American Political Writing during the Founding Era*, 1:85, 75.

45 Elihu Palmer, excerpt from *Principles of Nature; or, A Development of the Moral Causes of Happiness and Misery among the Human Species* (1801), in *American Deists*, 266.

46 For a similar application of the conditional imperative to the ideas and actions of the American Revolution, see Randy E. Barnett, *The Structure of Liberty: Justice and the Rule of Law* (Oxford: Oxford University Press, 1998), 4–12, and *Our Republican Constitution: Securing the Liberty and Sovereignty of We the People* (New York: Broadside Books, 2016), 46–51.

47 Jonas Clark, *A Sermon Preached before His Excellency John Hancock… and the Honorable Senate and House of Representatives of the Commonwealth of Massachusetts* (Boston, 1781), 8–9.

48 Abraham Williams, "An Election Sermon," *American Political Writing during the Founding Era*, 1:7; Anon., "On the Perversion of Law from Its Constitutional Course," *Massachusetts Spy*, February 20, 1772; Massachusettensis [pseud.], *Massachusetts Spy*, November 18, 1773; William Whiting, "An Address to the Inhabitants of Berkshire County, Mass." (1778), *American Political Writing during the Founding Era*, 1:466.

49 Anon., *Boston Gazette*, September 28, 1767; Otis, *A Vindication of the British Colonies…* (1765), in *Pamphlets of the American Revolution*, 554; "A Dialogue Between a Ruler and a Subject," *Massachusetts Spy*, June 18, 1772; Richard Wells, *A Few Political Reflections Submitted to the Consideration of the British Colonies*, (Philadelphia, 1774), in *Colonies to Nation*, 393–96; "To the Inhabitants of Massachusetts-Bay, No. V," *Massachusetts Spy*, March 9, 1775.

50 Hamilton, *Farmer Refuted*, in *Papers of Hamilton*, 1:87–88.

51 Elizur Goodrich, "The Principles of Civil Union and Happiness Considered and Recommended" (1787), *Political Sermons of the American Founding Era*, 914. (Emphasis added.)

52 Goodrich, "Principles of Civil Union and Happiness," *Political Sermons of the American Founding Era*, 915, 914. (Emphasis added.)

53 Wilson, *Lectures on Law*, in *Works of Wilson*, 1:145–46. (Emphasis added.)

54 Jefferson, "Opinion on the French Treaties," April 28, 1793, *Writings of Jefferson*, 3:228.

55 Zuckert draws a similar conclusion in *Natural Rights Republic*, 57–66.

56 Jefferson to Peter Carr, August 10, 1787, *Portable Thomas Jefferson*, 425–26.

57 Hamilton, *Farmer Refuted*, in *Papers of Hamilton*, 1:87–88. The William Blackstone quotation is from his *Of the Rights of Persons* (1765), in *Commentaries on the Laws of England* (Chicago: University of Chicago Press, 1979), 1:41.

58 Samuel Cooke, *The True Principles of Government* (Boston: Edes and Gill, 1770), 21–22. (Emphasis added.)

59 Jefferson to Georgetown Republicans, 1809, *Writings of Jefferson*, 16:349; Jefferson to M. Correa de Serra, April 19, 1814, *Writings of Jefferson*, 19:210; Jefferson, "Opinion on the French Treaties," *Writings of Jefferson*, 3:228; Jefferson, *Summary View of the Rights of British-America*, in *Colonies to Nation*, 228.

Zuckert has referred to what I am calling metaphysical law as the "ultimate realities." See Zuckert, *Natural Rights Republic*, 57–58, 61.

60 Hugo Grotius, Prolegomena, in *De jure belli ac pacis libri tres* (1625), trans. Francis W. Kelsey, vol. 2 of *The Classics of International Law*, ed. James Brown Scott (Oxford: Oxford University Press, 1925).

61 Allen, *Reason the Only Oracle of Man*, in *American Deists*, 177.

62 Elihu Palmer, *Principles of Nature*, in *American Deists*, 264. (Emphasis added.)

63 See Wise, *A Vindication of the Government of New England Churches*, in *Puritan Political Ideas*, 251–67; Abraham Williams, "An Election Sermon," *American Political Writing during the Founding Era*, 1:3–18; Goodrich, "Principles of Civil Union and Happiness," *Political Sermons of the American Founding Era*, 909–40.

64 See John Adams, *Discourses on Davila* (1791), in *The Political Writings of John Adams*, ed. George W. Carey (Washington, DC: Regnery, 2000), 310–15.

65 Anon., "To the People of Massachusetts-Bay," *Independent Chronicle*, April 17, 1777.

66 Some customary law is in accord with the law of nature and some is not. For the best discussion of the distinction and relationship between natural, customary, and statutory law and their practice in different countries around the world, see Montesquieu, *The Spirit of the Laws*, ed. and trans. Anne M. Cohler, Basia Carolyn Miller, and Harold Samuel Stone (Cambridge: Cambridge University Press, 1989).

67 Anon., "To the People of Massachusetts-Bay."

68 Cooke, *True Principles of Civil Government*, 7–8; Tucker, *Sermon Preached at Cambridge*, 22.

69 Clark, *Sermon Preached before His Excellency John Hancock*, 20.

70 John Joachim Zubly, *The Law of Liberty* (Philadelphia: Miller, 1775), 3–4, 6–7.

71 Benevolus [pseud.], *Continental Journal* (Boston), April 15, 1779.

72 Otis, *Rights of the British Colonies Asserted and Proved*, in *Pamphlets of the American Revolution*, 449, 454; Samuel Adams, "The Rights of the Colonists: The Report of the Committee of Correspondence to the Boston Town Meeting," November 20, 1772; James Wilson, *Considerations on the Nature and Extent of the Legislative Authority of the British Parliament* (1774), in *Works of Wilson*, 2:723; Declaration and Resolves of the First Continental Congress (1774), *Colonies to Nation*, 244.

73 Hamilton, *Farmer Refuted*, in *Papers of Hamilton*, 1:136.

74 Joseph Warren, *An Oration...to Commemorate the Bloody Tragedy of the Fifth of March, 1770* (Boston, 1772). (Note: This is one of three orations commissioned for this occasion; the others, cited below, are by Benjamin Church and Thomas Dawes.)

75 Anon., "To the Inhabitants of Queen's County, Long Island," *Constitutional Gazette*, November 29, 1775.

CHAPTER 3

1 Jefferson to John Cartwright, June 5, 1824, *Writings of Jefferson*, 16:44.

2 Adams, Preface, *A Defence of the Constitutions of Government of the United States of America*, in *Works of John Adams*, 4:292.

3 Taylor quoted in Yehoshua Arieli, *Individualism and Nationalism in American Ideology* (Baltimore: Penguin, 1964), 167.

4 Enos Hitchcock, "An Oration: Delivered July 4, 1788," 14.

5 Scholars have differed over the number of self-evident truths in the Declaration. Michael Zuckert counts six. See Zuckert, *The Natural Rights Republic*, 17–18. Danielle Allen counts five, but then reduces the number to three. See Allen, *Our Declaration: A Reading of the Declaration of Independence in Defense of Equality* (New York: Liveright, 2014), 151–55.

6 *ECHU*, IV.vii.10.

7 *ECHU*, IV.ii.1. See also I.ii.19–20, I.iii.4, IV.vii.1–20, IV.xviii.5.

8 See Wilbur Samuel Howell, "The Declaration of Independence and Eighteenth-Century Logic," *William and Mary Quarterly* 18, no. 4 (1961): 463–84, and Howell, "The Declaration of Independence: Some Adventures with America's Political Masterpiece," *Quarterly Journal of Speech* 62, no. 3 (1976): 221–33. See also Mayer, *Constitutional Thought of Thomas Jefferson*, 41–42.

9 Quoted in Howell, "The Declaration of Independence and Eighteenth-Century Logic," 474.

10 See *ECHU*, IV.vii.4.

11 Garry Wills argues that Locke's view of self-evidence was limited to the narrow definition. He argues without evidence that Thomas Reid's *Inquiry into the Human Mind, on the Principles of Common Sense* provided the greatest influence on Jefferson's view of self-evidence and other principles. The truth of the matter is that Reid's view is an extension of Locke's more capacious view of self-evident truths. See Wills, *Inventing America*, 182–83. For sharp rebukes of Wills, see Ronald Hamowy, "Jefferson and the Scottish Enlightenment: A Critique of Garry Wills's *Inventing America: Jefferson's Declaration of Independence*," *William and Mary Quarterly*, 36, no. 4 (1979): 503–23; and Harry V. Jaffa, "Inventing the Past: Garry Wills's *Inventing America* and the Pathology of Ideological Scholarship," chap. in *American Conservatism and the American Founding* (Durham, NC: Carolina Academic Press, 1984), 76–109.

12 *ECHU*, IV.ii.14.

13 *ECHU*, IV.ii.1, I.iii.1.

14 *ECHU*, IV.ii.3.

15 *ECHU*, IV.x.1, IV.xii.7 (emphasis added).

16 *ECHU*, IV.ii.1, IV.ii.3, IV.ii.4.

17 *ECHU*, I.iii.1.

18 *ECHU*, I.iii.4.

19 *ECHU*, IV.vii.2–3.

20 *ECHU*, I.iv.26. For Locke's deductive "proof" for the existence of God, see *ECHU*, IV.x.1–6.

21 *ECHU*, I.ii.12.

22 Quoted in Howell, "The Declaration of Independence and Eighteenth-Century Logic," 474.

23 Reid, *Essays on the Intellectual Powers of Man*, 683–84, 688, 685.

24 Samuel Johnson, *A Dictionary of the English Language: In Which the Words Are Deduced from Their Originals, Explained in Their Different Meanings and Authorized by the Names of the Writers in Whose Works They Are Found*, vol. 2 (London: A. Millar, 1766), available at Internet Archive, https://archive.org/details/dictionaryofenglo2johnuoft.

25 *The London Encyclopædia, or Universal Dictionary of Science, Art, Literature, and Practical Mechanics, Comprising a Popular View of the Present State of Knowledge*

(London: Thomas Tegg, 1829), 22:249–50, available on Google Books, https://
tinyurl.com/yd8b2chg.

26 Noah Webster, *American Dictionary of the English Language* (New York: S.
Converse, 1828), 2:809, available at Internet Archive, https://archive.org/stream/
americandictionao2websrich#page/n807/mode/2up.

27 *ECHU*, IV.v.2, IV.v.8.

28 Reid, *Essays on the Intellectual Powers of Man*, 576.

29 Wilson, *Lectures on Law*, in *Works of Wilson*, 1:369; 2:503, 703; 1:374, 371, 374.

30 Quoted in Charles Francis Adams, *Life of John Adams*, in *Works of Adams*, 1:113.

31 Jefferson, "A Bill for Establishing Religious Freedom," *Portable Thomas Jefferson*,
253.

32 Jefferson, "A Bill for Establishing Religious Freedom," *Portable Thomas Jefferson*,
251; Paine, *Rights of Man, Part the Second*, in *Life and Works of Paine*, 6:232;
Jefferson to David Harding, April 20, 1824, *Writings of Jefferson*, 16:30.

33 In the pamphlet, the author claims that it was originally written in 1779.

34 A Moderate Whig [Stephen Case?], "Defensive Arms Vindicated and the
Lawfulness of the American War Made Manifest," in *Political Sermons of the
American Founding Era*, 717, 719.

35 Hamilton, *Federalist* No. 31, 193–94.

36 Hamilton, *Federalist* No. 31, 193–95.

37 Hamilton, *Federalist* No. 31, 146–47.

38 James Madison uses almost identical reasoning in *Federalist* No. 44, where he
argues: "No axiom is more clearly established in law, or in reason, than that
wherever the end is required, the means are authorized; wherever a general
power to do a thing is given, every particular power necessary for doing it, is
included" (304–5).

39 Wilson, *Lectures on Law*, in *Works of Wilson*, 1:136–37.

40 Wilson, *Lectures on Law*, in *Works of Wilson*, 1:137–38.

41 Wilson, *Lectures on Law*, in *Works of Wilson*, 1:210, 395.

42 Wilson, *Lectures on Law*, in *Works of Wilson*, 2:505.

43 Wilson, *Lectures on Law*, in *Works of Wilson*, 1:210. On the connection to Locke's
Essay, see *ECHU*, IV.ii.3.

44 Michael Zuckert is the first scholar to pay attention to the word "hold" in the
phrase "We hold these truths to be self-evident." (See Zuckert, *Natural Rights
Republic*, 41–55.) This is an important insight. For Zuckert, the word "hold"
implies or imparts a near religious and political meaning to the Declaration;
it is synonymous with "believe." Most men can believe in the Declaration's
principles without knowing them. Zuckert's Declaration might be less
ambiguous if it were to read, "We believe these truths to be self-evident." He
is right to emphasize the importance of the word "hold" in the Declaration's
first sentence, but I interpret it in a different way. I interpret "hold"
epistemologically—i.e., to "hold" an idea is to *grasp* its meaning conceptually,
which implies an active process of thought.

45 Adams to Jefferson, August 24, 1815, *Adams-Jefferson Letters*, 455.

46 Adams, "A Dissertation on the Canon and Feudal Law," *Revolutionary Writings
of Adams*, 34.

47 Adams, "A Dissertation on the Canon and Feudal Law," *Revolutionary Writings
of Adams*, 33, 32–33.

48 Adams, "A Dissertation on the Canon and Feudal Law," *Revolutionary Writings of Adams*, 33.

49 Daniel Dulany, *Considerations on the Propriety of Imposing Taxes in the British Colonies for the Purpose of Raising a Revenue*, 1765, in *Pamphlets of the American Revolution*, 610.

50 Jefferson to Thomas Earle, September 24, 1823, *Writings of Jefferson*, 15:470.

51 Locke, *Second Treatise*, para. 4.

52 In his chapter on "Whether Morality Be Capable of Demonstration," Reid deepens but supports Locke's understanding of equality when he writes that men are "endowed with those faculties which make them moral and accountable agents." See *Essays on the Intellectual Powers of Man*, 683. See also Harry V. Jaffa, *A New Birth of Freedom: Abraham Lincoln and the Coming of the Civil War* (Lanham, MD: Rowman and Littlefield, 2000), 112–13.

53 *Second Treatise*, para. 5.

54 Jefferson to Henry Lee, May 8, 1825, *Writings of Jefferson*, 16:117–119.

55 Paine, *Common Sense*, in *Collected Writings*, 20.

56 Samuel Cooper, "A Sermon Preached Before His Excellency John Hancock" (1780), *Political Sermons of the American Founding Era*, 637.

57 Jefferson to Peter Carr, August 10, 1787, *Writings of Jefferson*, 6:257.

58 Jefferson viewed the Declaration's moral and political truths as available to all men with eyes to see regardless of their education. He is well known for having argued that the ploughman is equally if not better equipped to address moral problems than a professor. See Jefferson to Peter Carr, August 10, 1787, *Writings of Jefferson*, 6:256–62.

CHAPTER 4

1 Abraham Lincoln to Henry L. Pierce and others, April 6, 1859, in *Abraham Lincoln: His Speeches and Writings*, ed. Roy P. Basler (New York: DaCapo, 1990), 488–89.

2 Lincoln, "Speech in Reply to Douglas at Chicago, Illinois," July 10, 1858, *Lincoln: His Speeches and Writings*, 402–3, 401.

3 For Harry V. Jaffa and M. E. Bradford, the equality question was the centerpiece of their debate over the nature of modern conservatism. See Harry V. Jaffa, "Equality as a Conservative Principle," *Loyola of Los Angeles Law Review* 8 (June 1775): 471–505; M. E. Bradford, "The Heresy of Equality: Bradford Replies to Jaffa," *Modern Age* 20 (Winter 1976): 62–77; Jaffa, "Equality, Justice, and the American Revolution: In Reply to Bradford's 'The Heresy of Equality,'" *Modern Age* 21 (Spring 1977): 114–24.

4 Democraticus [pseud.], "Loose Thoughts on Government," June 7, 1776, in *American Archives: Documents of the Revolutionary Period, 1774–1776*, ed. Peter Force (Washington, 1837–56), 4th ser., 6:730. The digital version of *American Archives* is at Northern Illinois University Digital Library, https://digital.lib.niu.edu/amarch.

5 David Ramsay, "An Oration on the Advantages of American Independence," in *Principles and Acts of the Revolution in America*, ed. Hezekiah Niles (Baltimore: William Ogden Niles, 1822; Maywood, CA: Kunkin-Turner Publications, 1961), 375.

6 Locke, *Second Treatise*, para. 6, 4

7 Locke, *Second Treatise*, para. 54.

8 See Leo Strauss, *Natural Right and History* (Chicago: University of Chicago Press, 1953).

9 Wise, *A Vindication of the Government of New England Churches*, in *Puritan Political Ideas*, 259–60.

10 Bulkley, preface to *Poetical Meditations*, xii–xiii.

11 Daniel Dulany, *The Right of the Inhabitants of Maryland to the Benefit of English Laws* (Annapolis, MD: W. Parks, 1728). Reprinted in *The English Statutes in Maryland*, by St. George L. Sioussat (Baltimore: Johns Hopkins Press, 1903), appendix 2, available at HathiTrust Digital Library, https://babel.hathitrust. org/cgi/pt?id=hvd.32044019882695;view=1up;seq=7. Dulany's pamphlet is discussed in Craig Yirush, *Settlers, Liberty, and Empire: The Roots of Early American Political Theory, 1675–1775* (Cambridge: Cambridge University Press, 2011), 142–57.

12 Elisha Williams, "The Essential Rights and Liberties of Protestants" (1744), in *Political Sermons of the American Founding Era*, 56–57, 59.

13 Abraham Williams, "An Election Sermon," *American Political Writing during the Founding Era*, 1:6–7, 9.

14 Anon., *Boston Gazette*, August 24, 1767.

15 Gad Hitchcock, "An Election Sermon" (1774), *American Political Writing during the Founding Era*, 1:288.

16 See Gordon S. Wood, *The Radicalism of the American Revolution* (New York: Knopf, 1992), and Brendan McConville, *The King's Three Faces: The Rise and Fall of Royal America, 1688–1776* (Chapel Hill: University of North Carolina Press, 2007).

17 On the role of the equality principle in eighteenth- and nineteenth-century America, see J. R. Pole, *The Pursuit of Equality in American History* (Berkeley: University of California Press, 1978), and Richard D. Brown, *Self-Evident Truths: Contesting Equal Rights from the Revolution to the Civil War* (New Haven, CT: Yale University Press, 2017).

18 Samuel Williams, *The Natural and Civil History of Vermont* (1794), 2nd ed. (Burlington, VT: Samuel Mills, 1809), 2:374–75.

19 Tocqueville, "How Individualism Is Greater at the End of a Democratic Revolution Than in Any Other Period," in *Democracy in America*, 485.

20 In an otherwise excellent overview of the Revolutionary period, Edmund S. Morgan errs in suggesting that the principle of equality was not discovered until 1776 with the publication of Thomas Paine's *Common Sense*, which propelled the Americans, he argues, "into the great discovery of human equality toward which they had been moving unwittingly ever since they first denied Parliament's right to tax." The Americans discovered and developed the principle of equality in the 1760s, and they did so fully conscious of what they were doing. See *The Birth of the Republic, 1763–1789* (Chicago: University of Chicago Press, 1956), 67, 76.

21 The question and status of the colonists' English rights, liberties, and privileges is the principal theme in John Phillip Reid, *Constitutional History of the American Revolution: The Authority of Rights* (Madison: University of Wisconsin Press, 1986–93).

22 Otis, *Rights of the British Colonies Asserted and Proved*, in *Pamphlets of the American Revolution*, 440; The Virginia Resolves (1765), *Colonies to Nation*, 61; The Declaration of the Stamp Act Congress (October 19, 1765), *Colonies*

to Nation, 64; Silas Downer, "A Discourse at the Dedication of the Tree of Liberty" (1768), *American Political Writing during the Founding Era*, 1:98.

23 Stephen Hopkins, *The Rights of Colonies Examined* (1764), in *American Political Writing during the Founding Era*, 1:49–50; Britannus-Americanus [pseud.], *Boston Gazette*, September 24, 1764; Adams, The Earl of Clarendon [pseud.] to William Pym (III, January 27, 1766), in *Revolutionary Writings of Adams*, 54.

24 Bland, *Inquiry into the Rights of the British Colonies*, in *American Political Writing during the Founding Era*, 1:82–83. See also David S. Lovejoy, "Rights Imply Equality: The Case against Admiralty Jurisdiction in America, 1764–1776," *William and Mary Quarterly* 16, no. 4 (1959): 459–84.

25 Camillus [pseud.], "To the Printers of the Pennsylvania Gazette," March 1775, *American Archives*, 4th ser., 2:11.

26 Wilson, *Considerations on the Nature and the Extent of the Legislative Authority of the British Parliament* (1774), in *Works of Wilson*, 2:723, 732, 741; Jefferson, *Summary View of the Rights of British-America*, in *Colonies to Nation*, 231.

27 This is the interpretation of Willmoore Kendall and George W. Carey in *The Basic Symbols of the American Political Tradition* (Baton Rouge: Louisiana State University Press, 1970), 155. The problem with their interpretation is that it stops halfway and does not credit Jefferson's more complete view of equality.

28 Jefferson to Adams, October 28, 2013, *Adams-Jefferson Letters*, 2:387–92.

29 Daniel Leonard, writing as Massachusettensis, December 26, 1774, in *Tracts of the American Revolution, 1763–1776*, ed. Merrill Jensen (Indianapolis, IN: Bobbs-Merrill, 1967), 287; Thomas Hutchinson, "Strictures upon the Declaration of the Congress at Philadelphia in a Letter to a Noble Lord" (1776), available at Online Library of Liberty, Liberty Fund, https://oll.libertyfund.org/pages/1776-hutchinson-strictures-upon-the-declaration-of-independence.

30 Jonathan Boucher, "On Civil Liberty, Passive Obedience, and Nonresistance" (1775), in *A View of the Causes and Consequences of the American Revolution* (London, 1797), available at Constitution Society, http://www.constitution.org/bcp/nonresis.htm.

31 An Englishman [pseud.], "The Uncommon Sense of the Americans: Notes on the Declaration," in *A Casebook on the Declaration of Independence*, ed. Robert Ginsberg (New York: Crowell, 1967), 6–8; John Lind, "An Answer to the Declaration," *A Casebook on the Declaration of Independence*, 9–17.

32 See Harry V. Jaffa, *The Conditions of Freedom: Essays in Political Philosophy* (Baltimore: Johns Hopkins University Press, 1975), 152–56.

33 The Essex Result (April 29, 1788), and Return of Northampton, Massachusetts (May 22, 1780), in *The Popular Sources of Political Authority: Documents on the Massachusetts Constitution of 1780*, ed. Oscar and Mary F. Handlin (Cambridge, MA: Belknap Press of Harvard University Press, 1966), 330, 580.

34 Otis, *Rights of the British Colonies Asserted and Proved*, in *Pamphlets of the American Revolution*, 438, 440; Dickinson, "Instructions from the Committee to the Representatives in Assembly Met," July 21, 1774, in *Political Writings of Dickinson*, 1:309, quoting Jean-Jacques Burlamaqui, *The Principle of Natural and Politic Law*, ed. Petter Korkman, trans. Thomas Nugent (Indianapolis, IN: Liberty Fund, 2006), 301; Adams, *Defence of the Constitutions of Government*, in *Works of Adams*, 4:380.

35 Paine, *Rights of Man*, in *Life and Works of Paine*, 6:67. (Emphasis added.)

36 For a particularly poignant analysis of the role of inequality as a function of the human condition, see the exchange between Thomas Jefferson and John Adams on the naturalness of the natural aristocracy: Adams to Jefferson, September 2, 1813; Jefferson to Adams, October 28, 1813; and Adams to Jefferson, November 15, 1813, in *Adams-Jefferson Letters*, 2:370–72, 387–92, 397–402.

37 Democraticus [pseud.], "Loose Thoughts on Government," *American Archives*, 4th ser., 6:730.

38 Wilson, *Lectures on Law*, in *Works of Wilson*, 1:240–41.

39 Samuel Williams, *Natural and Civil History of Vermont*, 2:374–75.

40 Jefferson, Opinion on Residence Bill, July 15, 1790, in *Writings of Jefferson*, 3:60. Jefferson's view of equality has its root in Thomas Hobbes's *Leviathan*: "Nature hath made men so equal, in the faculties of body and mind as that, though there be found one man sometimes manifestly stronger in body or of quicker mind than another, yet when all is reckoned together the difference between man and man is not so considerable as that one man can thereupon claim to himself any benefit to which another may not pretend as well as he." See Thomas Hobbes, *Leviathan*, ed. Edwin Curley (Indianapolis, IN: Hackett,1994), 74.

41 Jefferson to Henri Grégoire, February 25, 1809, in *Portable Thomas Jefferson*, 517.

CHAPTER 5

1 Abraham Lincoln, "Speech at a Republican Banquet, Chicago, Illinois," December 10, 1856, *Collected Works of Lincoln*, 2:385. Lincoln, "Address Delivered at the Dedication of the Cemetery at Gettysburg," November 19, 1863, *Lincoln: His Speeches and Writings*, 734.

2 See Harry V. Jaffa, *Crisis of the House Divided: An Interpretation of the Lincoln-Douglas Debates* (Seattle: University of Washington Press, 1959), 211; and Jaffa, *A New Birth of Freedom*, 44, 46–48, 112–13.

3 Continental Congress, Declaration of the Causes and Necessities of Taking Up Arms, *Colonies to Nation*, 255–59.

4 Madison, *Federalist* No. 10, 58.

5 This chapter is concerned with the meaning of equality in the light of slavery. For reasons of space, it does not take up the no less interesting and important question of whether the revolutionary generation meant to include women in the truth that "all men are created equal." A quick review of the primary source literature from the period demonstrates conclusively, however, that by "men" the revolutionary generation meant "mankind," that is, humankind. See Thomas G. West, *Vindicating the Founders: Race, Sex, Class, and Justice in the Origins of America* (Lanham, MD: Rowman and Littlefield, 1997), chap. 3. Thomas Jefferson, in his *Notes on the State of Virginia*, criticized various Native American tribes for their treatment of women and for their failure to recognize the fact that women are equal to men in the rights they retain by nature. Jefferson wrote: "The [Native American] women are submitted to unjust drudgery. This I believe is the case with every barbarous people. With such, force is law. The stronger sex therefore imposes on the weaker. It is civilization alone which replaces women in the enjoyment of their natural equality. That first teaches us to subdue the selfish passions, and to respect those rights in others which we value in ourselves." See Jefferson, *Notes on the State of Virginia* (1783), Query 6, in *Portable Thomas Jefferson*, 96–97.

6 On the origins of slavery in America, see Winthrop D. Jordan, *The White Man's Burden: Historical Origins of Racism in the United States* (Oxford: Oxford University Press, 1974); Edmund S. Morgan, *American Slavery, American Freedom: The Ordeal of Colonial Virginia* (New York: Norton, 1975); Donald R. Wright, *African Americans in the Colonial Era: From African Origins Through the American Revolution* (Arlington Heights, IL: Harlan Davidson, 1990); Peter Kolchin, *American Slavery, 1619–1877* (New York: Hill and Wang, 1993); and William M. Wiecek, "The Statutory Law of Slavery and Race in the Thirteen Mainland Colonies of British America," *William and Mary Quarterly* 34, no. 2 (1977): 258–80.

7 Frederick Douglass, "Lecture on Slavery, No. 1," in *Antislavery Political Writings, 1833–1860: A Reader*, ed. C. Bradley Thompson (Armonk, NY: M. E. Sharpe, 2004), 26.

8 On this point, see Philip D. Morgan, *Slave Counterpoint: Black Culture in the Eighteenth-Century Chesapeake and Lowcountry* (Chapel Hill: University of North Carolina Press, 1998).

9 On American slavery during the Revolutionary period, see David Brion Davis, *The Problem of Slavery in the Age of Revolution, 1770–1823* (Ithaca, NY: Cornell University Press, 1975); Edmund S. Morgan, *American Slavery, American Freedom*; Donald Robinson, *Slavery in the Structure of American Politics, 1765–1820* (New York: Harcourt Brace Jovanovich, 1970); Ira Berlin and Ronald Hoffman, eds., *Slavery and Freedom in the Age of the American Revolution* (Charlottesville: University Press of Virginia, 1983); and Jack P. Greene, "'Slavery or Independence': Some Reflections on the Relationship among Liberty, Black Bondage, and Equality in Revolutionary South Carolina," *South Carolina Historical Magazine* 80, no. 3 (1979): 193–214.

10 Benjamin Franklin, "An Address to the Public from the Pennsylvania Society for Promoting the Abolition of Slavery, and the Relief of Free Negroes Unlawfully Held in Bondage" (1789), in *The Complete Works of Benjamin Franklin*, ed. John Bigelow (New York: Putnam, 1904), 12:157–58; George Washington to Robert Morris, April 12, 1786, in *The Writings of George Washington*, ed. Worthington Chauncey Ford (New York: Putnam's, 1891), 11:25; James Madison, speech at Constitutional Convention, June 6, 1787, in *Notes of Debates in the Federal Convention of 1787, Reported by James Madison*, ed. Adrienne Koch (Athens: Ohio University Press, 1966), 77; Adams to Robert Evans, June 18, 1819, *Works of Adams*, 380.

11 Many prominent historians support the view that Jefferson and the signers of the Declaration of Independence meant to apply the equality principle only to whites. See, for instance, Forrest McDonald, *Novus Ordo Seclorum: The Intellectual Origins of the Constitution* (Lawrence: University Press of Kansas, 1985), 53; Paul Finkelman, *Slavery and the Founders: Race and Liberty in the Age of Jefferson* (Armonk, NY: M. E. Sharpe, 1996); and Gordon S. Wood, "Equality and Social Conflict in the American Revolution," *William and Mary Quarterly* 51, no. 4 (1994): 707. Notable exceptions to this view include Bernard Bailyn, *The Ideological Origins of the American Revolution* (Cambridge, MA: Belknap Press of Harvard University Press, 1967), 232–46; West, *Vindicating the Founders*, chap. 1; Herbert J. Storing, "Slavery and the Moral Foundations of the American Republic," in *The Moral Foundations of the American Republic*, 3rd ed., ed. Robert H. Horwitz (Charlottesville: University Press of Virginia, 1986), 313–32; and

Paul A. Rahe, *Republics Ancient and Modern* (Chapel Hill: University of North Carolina Press, 1992), 617–41.

12 For a general overview of the founding fathers' view of slavery, see William W. Freehling, "The Founding Fathers and Slavery," *American Historical Review* 77, no. 1 (1972): 81–93.

13 Otis, *Rights of the British Colonies Asserted and Proved*, in *Pamphlets of the American Revolution*, 439–40, 446, 439.

14 Benjamin Rush, *An Address to the Inhabitants of the British Settlements in America, on the Slavery of the Negroes in America* (Philadelphia, 1773), 1–2, 19–20, 25–26.

15 Wells, *A Few Political Reflections*, in *Colonies to Nation*, 393–96.

16 On the Somerset case in America, see William M. Wiecek, "Somerset: Lord Mansfield and the Legitimacy of Slavery in the Anglo-American World," *University of Chicago Law Review* 42, no. 1 (1974): 86–146. In 1773–74, several slaves in Massachusetts brought suit against their masters for their freedom. The colony's General Court supported the petitions, but the royal governor of the colony eventually overruled them.

17 Patrick Henry, "Give Me Liberty or Give Me Death" (March 23, 1775), available at the *Avalon Project: Documents in Law, History, and Diplomacy*, Yale Law School, https://avalon.law.yale.edu/18th_century/patrick.asp.

18 Patrick Henry to Robert Pleasants, January 18, 1773, in *The Founders' Constitution*, ed. Philip B. Kurland and Ralph Lerner (Chicago: University of Chicago Press, 1987), 1:517.

19 Henry, speaking to the Virginia Ratifying Convention, June 24, 1788, in *Ratification of the Constitution by the States: Virginia (3)*, ed. John P. Kaminski et al., vol. 10 of *The Documentary History of the Ratification of the Constitution*, ed. Merrill Jensen (Madison: State Historical Society of Wisconsin, 1993), 1476–77.

20 For a stinging analysis of Jefferson's views on slavery, see Finkelman, *Slavery and the Founders*, 105–67. The best monograph on Jefferson and slavery remains John Chester Miller, *The Wolf by the Ears: Thomas Jefferson and Slavery* (New York: Free Press, 1977).

21 Jefferson, *Summary View of the Rights of British-America*, in *Colonies to Nation*, 234.

22 On the first draft of the Declaration of Independence and Jefferson's deleted passage on slavery, see Julian Boyd, *The Declaration of Independence: The Evolution of the Text*, rev. ed., ed. Gerard W. Gawalt (Washington, DC: Library of Congress, 1999), 15–37; Becker, *The Declaration of Independence*, 135–93; and Maier, *American Scripture*, 146–47.

23 Jefferson, Sixth Annual Message (1806), in *Writings of Jefferson*, 3:421. Scholarly interpretations since the 1970s of Jefferson and his relationship to slavery can be divided into two categories: those who seek to expose and condemn Jefferson as a slaveholder, and those who emphasize the paradoxical nature of Jefferson's views and actions on the slavery question. For the former, see Conor Cruise O'Brien, *The Long Affair: Thomas Jefferson and the French Revolution, 1785–1800* (Chicago: University of Chicago Press, 1996); Peter S. Onuf, *The Mind of Thomas Jefferson* (Charlottesville: University of Virginia Press, 2007); Lucia C. Stanton, *"Those Who Labor for My Happiness": Slavery at Thomas Jefferson's Monticello* (Charlottesville: University of Virginia Press, 2012); Henry Wiencek, *Master of the Mountain: Thomas Jefferson and His Slaves* (New York: Farrar, Straus,

and Giroux, 2012). For the latter, see Merrill D. Peterson, *Thomas Jefferson and the New Nation: A Biography* (Oxford: Oxford University Press, 1970); Joseph Ellis, *American Sphinx: The Character of Thomas Jefferson* (New York: Vintage, 1998); Robert M. S. McDonald, *Confounding Father: Thomas Jefferson's Image in His Own Time* (Charlottesville: University of Virginia Press, 2016); Kevin R. C. Gutzman, *Thomas Jefferson, Revolutionary: A Radical's Struggle to Remake America* (New York: St. Martin's, 2017); and Gordon S. Wood, *Friends Divided: John Adams and Thomas Jefferson* (New York: Penguin, 2017).

24 Jefferson to John Holmes, April 22, 1820, *Portable Thomas Jefferson*, 568; Jefferson, *Notes on the State of Virginia*, Query 14, in *Writings of Jefferson*, 2:192.

25 Jefferson, *Notes on the State of Virginia*, Query 14, in *Writings of Jefferson*, 2:192.

26 Jefferson, *Notes on the State of Virginia*, Query 18, in *Writings of Jefferson*, 2:225–27.

27 Jefferson to Henri Grégoire, February 25, 1809, *Writings of Jefferson*, 12:255.

28 Samuel Johnson, *Taxation No Tyranny: An Answer to the Resolutions and Address of the American Congress* (London, 1775), http://www.samueljohnson.com/tnt. html; Thomas Hutchinson, *Strictures upon the Declaration of the Congress at Philadelphia in a Letter to a Noble Lord* (London, 1776), in Eicholz, *Harmonizing Sentiments*, 182.

29 Alexander Hamilton, *A Full Vindication of the Measures of the Congress*, December 15, 1774, in *The Political Writings of Alexander Hamilton*, ed. Carson Holloway and Bradford P. Wilson (Cambridge: Cambridge University Press, 2017): 1:8–9.

30 Rush to Jacques Barbeu-Dubourg, quoted in Davis, *Problem of Slavery in the Age of Revolution*, 274.

31 Quoted in Jordan, *White Man's Burden*, 289.

32 A Constant Customer [pseud.], "Extract of a Letter from a Gentleman in the Country to His Friend" (1773), *American Political Writing during the Founding Era*, 1:183.

33 [John Allen], *The Watchman's Alarm to Lord N---H...* (Salem, MA: E. Russell, 1774), 27.

34 Levi Hart, *Liberty Described and Recommended: In a Sermon Preached to the Corporation of Freemen in Farmington* (1775), in *American Political Writing during the Founding Era*, 1:312–15; "Darien Resolutions" (January 12, 1775), *American Archives*, 4th ser., 1:1136; Massachusetts legislature, quoted in Leon F. Litwack, *North of Slavery: The Negro in the Free States, 1790–1860* (Chicago: University of Chicago Press, 1961), 9; John Jay to Richard Price, September 27, 1785, in *Founders' Constitution*, 1:538.

35 Samuel Hopkins, *A Dialogue Concerning the Slavery of Africans* (New York: Judah P. Spooner, 1776), 1, 16, 37–38.

36 [David Cooper], *A Serious Address to the Rulers of America on the Inconsistency of Their Conduct Respecting Slavery: Forming a Contrast Between the Encroachments of England on American Liberty, and American Injustice in Tolerating Slavery* (Trenton, NJ: Isaac Collins, 1783), 4, 6, 12–13, 17–18.

37 "Anti-Slavery Petitions Presented to the Virginia Legislature by Citizens of Various Counties," *Journal of Negro History* 12 (Oct. 1927): 670.

38 Benjamin Franklin, "Petition from the Pennsylvania Society for the Abolition of Slavery" (February 3, 1790), available at UShistory.org, http://www.ushistory. org/documents/antislavery.htm. I thank José Piñera for bringing this petition to my attention.

39 Theodore Dwight, *An Oration, Spoken Before the Connecticut Society, for the Promotion of Freedom and the Relief of Persons Unlawfully Holden in Bondage* (1794), in *American Political Writing during the Founding Era*, 2:884–85; St. George Tucker, *On the State of Slavery in Virginia* (1796), in *View of the Constitution of the United States, with Selected Writings*, ed. Clyde N. Wilson (Indianapolis, IN: Liberty Fund, 1999), 428.

40 The best treatment of the proslavery argument is Elizabeth Fox-Genovese and Eugene D. Genovese, *The Mind of the Master Class: History and Faith in the Southern Slaveholders' Worldview* (Cambridge: Cambridge University Press, 2005). See also Drew Gilpin Faust, *A Sacred Circle: The Dilemma of the Intellectual in the Old South, 1840–1860* (Philadelphia: University of Pennsylvania Press, 1977), and Michael O'Brien, *Intellectual Life and the American South, 1810–1860: An Abridged Edition of Conjectures of Order* (Chapel Hill: University of North Carolina Press, 2010).

41 *Notes of Debates in the Federal Convention of 1787, Reported by James Madison*, 504.

42 On Jefferson's moral failures with regard to slavery, see C. Bradley Thompson, "The Relevance and Irrelevance of Gordon S. Wood," *Law & Liberty*, May 15, 2018, https://www.lawliberty.org/2018/05/15/the-relevance-and-irrelevance-of-gordon-s-wood/.

43 On the steps taken to abolish slavery during and after the Revolution, see David Brion Davis, *The Problem of Slavery in Western Culture* (Ithaca, NY: Cornell University Press, 1966); Allen Nevins, *American States during and after the Revolution, 1775–1789* (New York: Macmillan, 1924); and J. Franklin Jameson, *American Revolution Considered as a Social Movement* (Princeton, NJ: Princeton University Press, 1926).

44 Constitution of Vermont (July 8, 1777), available at the *Avalon Project: Documents in Law, History, and Diplomacy*, Yale Law School, http://avalon.law.yale.edu/18th_century/vt01.asp. (Emphasis added.)

45 See Gordon S. Wood, *The American Revolution: A History* (New York: Modern Library, 2002), 126–29; and Sean Wilentz, *No Property in Man: Slavery and Antislavery at the Nation's Founding* (Cambridge, MA: Harvard University Press, 2018), 26.

46 Arthur Zilversmit, *The First Emancipation: The Abolition of Slavery in the North* (Chicago: University of Chicago Press, 1967).

47 Preamble, "An Act for the Gradual Abolition of Slavery" (March 1, 1780), in *Life and Works of Paine*, 4:47–49; the full text of Chief Justice Cushing's remarks is printed in John D. Cushing, "The Cushing Court and the Abolition of Slavery in Massachusetts: More Notes on the 'Quock Walker Case,'" *American Journal of Legal History* 5, no. 2 (1961): 132–33; "An Act Authorizing the Manumission of Negroes, Mulattoes, and others, and for the Gradual Abolition of Slavery" (1784), in *A Necessary Evil? Slavery and the Debate Over the Constitution*, ed. John P. Kaminski (Madison, WI: Madison House, 1995), 28. On the movement to end slavery in the wake of the American Revolution, see Manisha Sinha, *The Slave's Cause: A History of Abolition* (New Haven, CT: Yale University Press, 2016); and Ira Berlin, *The Long Emancipation: The Demise of Slavery in the United States* (Cambridge, MA: Harvard University Press, 2015).

48 Hamilton to John Jay, March 14, 1779, in *Papers of Hamilton*, 2:17–19.

49 See Wilentz, *No Property in Man*. The efforts of slaves to secure their freedom during the Revolutionary era can be seen in Benjamin Quarles's *The Negro in the American Revolution* (Chapel Hill: University of North Carolina Press,

1961); Sylvia R. Frey, *Water from the Rock: Black Resistance in a Revolutionary Age* (Princeton, NJ: Princeton University Press, 1991); and Douglas R. Egerton's *Death or Liberty: African Americans and Revolutionary America* (New York: Oxford University Press, 2009).

50 Quoted in Davis, *Problem of Slavery in the Age of Revolution*, 276.

51 Quoted in Winthrop D. Jordan, *White Over Black: American Attitudes toward the Negro, 1550–1812*, 2nd ed. (Chapel Hill : University of North Carolina Press, 2012), 291.

52 Roberts Vaux, *Memoirs of the Life of Anthony Benezet* (Philadelphia: James P. Parke, 1817), 26.

53 See James Brewer Stewart, *Holy Warriors: The Abolitionists and American Slavery* (New York: Hill and Wang, 1976), 22–23; and Davis, *Problem of Slavery in the Age of Revolution*, 24.

54 Jay to the President of the [English] Society for Promoting the Manumission of Slaves, June 1788, in *Founders' Constitution*, 1:550.

55 Winthrop Jordan, the distinguished historian of slavery, has argued that the natural-rights philosophy embedded in the Declaration "led inescapably to [the] realization that Americans were indulging in a monstrous inconsistency." See Jordan, *White Over Black*, 289.

56 Lincoln, "Speech at Springfield, Illinois" (June 26, 1857), *Collected Works of Lincoln*, 2:405–6.

CHAPTER 6

1 Jefferson to Henry Lee, May 8, 1825, *Writings of Jefferson*, 16:117–19.

2 The dual nature of the founders' use of the natural-rights philosophy is nicely captured in Pauline Maier's *American Scripture*. See also Robert H. Webking, *The American Revolution and the Politics of Liberty* (Baton Rouge: Louisiana State University Press, 1988).

3 Otis, *Rights of the British Colonies Asserted and Proved*, in *Pamphlets of the American Revolution*, 444; Bland, *Inquiry into the Rights of the British Colonies*, in *American Political Writing during the Founding Era*, 75; Jefferson, *Summary View of the Rights of British-America*, in *Colonies to Nation*, 228–29, 237; Jefferson to Samuel Adams Wells, May 12, 1819, *Writings of Jefferson*, 15:200.

4 Democraticus [pseud.], "Loose Thoughts on Government," *American Archives*, 4th ser., 6:730; Thomas Jefferson to James Sullivan, February 9, 1797, *Writings of Jefferson*, 9:379; Thomas Jefferson to James Monroe, September 7, 1797, *Writings of Jefferson*, 9:422; James Wilson, *Lectures on Law*, in *Works of Wilson*, 2:609.

5 See Bernard Schwartz, "Revolutionary Declarations and Constitutions," in his *The Great Rights of Mankind: A History of the American Bill of Rights* (Madison, WI: Madison House, 1992), 53–91.

6 Thomas Jefferson to Major John Cartwright, June 5, 1824, *Writings of Jefferson*, 16:48. The Virginia Bill of Rights is available at the Constitution Society, http://www.constitution.org/bor/vir_bor.htm; the Massachusetts Constitution of 1780 is available at the National Humanities Institute, http://www.nhinet.org/ccs/docs/ma-1780.htm.

7 Quoted in Reid, *Constitutional History of the American Revolution: The Authority of Rights*, 3.

8 Anon., *Boston Gazette*, March 1, 1773; Wells, *A Few Political Reflections*, in *Colonies to Nation*, 393–96.

9 See John Finnis, *Natural Law and Natural Rights* (Oxford: Clarendon, 1980); Zuckert, *Natural Rights and the New Republicanism*; Knud Haakonssen, *Natural Law and Moral Philosophy: From Grotius to the Scottish Enlightenment* (Cambridge: Cambridge University Press, 1996); Brian Tierney, *The Idea of Natural Rights: Studies on Natural Rights, Natural Law, and Church Law, 1150–1625* (Grand Rapids, MI: Eerdmans, 1997); Richard Tuck, *Natural Rights Theories: Their Origins and Development* (Cambridge: Cambridge University Press, 1979); Lynn Hunt, *Inventing Human Rights: A History* (New York: Norton, 2007); and John Witte Jr., *The Reformation of Rights: Law, Religion, and Human Rights in Early Modern Calvinism* (Cambridge: Cambridge University Press, 2007).

10 See George Lee Haskins, *Law and Authority in Early Massachusetts: A Study in Tradition and Design* (New York: Macmillan, 1960).

11 See Gilman Ostrander, *The Rights of Man in America: 1606–1861* (Columbia: University of Missouri Press, 1960); Michael J. Lacey and Knud Haakonssen, eds., *A Culture of Rights: The Bill of Rights in Philosophy, Politics, and Law—1791 and 1991* (Cambridge: Cambridge University Press, 1991); James R. Stoner Jr., *Common Law and Liberal Theory: Coke, Hobbes, and the Origins of American Constitutionalism* (Lawrence: University Press of Kansas, 1992); Zuckert, *The Natural Rights Republic*; Tibor R. Machan, ed., *Individual Rights Reconsidered: Are the Truths of the U.S. Declaration of Independence Lasting?* (Stanford, CA: Hoover Institution Press, 2001); Barry Alan Shain, ed., *The Nature of Rights at the American Founding and Beyond* (Charlottesville: University of Virginia Press, 2007); and Ellen Frankel Paul, Fred D. Miller Jr., and Jeffrey Paul, eds., *Natural Rights Individualism and Progressivism in American Political Philosophy* (Cambridge: Cambridge University Press, 2012).

12 Benjamin Rush, *A Vindication of the Address to the Inhabitants of the British Settlements, on the Slavery of the Negroes in America* (Philadelphia: John Dunlap, 1773), 24–25.

13 Elisha Williams, "Essential Rights and Liberties," *Political Sermons of the American Founding Era*, 56; Daniel Shute, "An Election Sermon," *American Political Writing during the Founding Era*, 1:111; A Well-Wisher to Mankind [John Perkins], *Theory of Agency: or, An Essay on the Nature, Source and Extent of Moral Freedom*, in *American Political Writing during the Founding Era*, 1:139, 148. (Perkins, a physician, was best known in New England for having authored pamphlets on earthquakes, comets, and various other natural phenomena.)

14 Matthew Robinson-Morris, 2nd Baron Rokeby, *Considerations on the Measures Carrying on with Respect to the British Colonies in North America* (London, 1774), 7; Jefferson to Pierre Samuel Dupont de Nemours, April 24, 1816, *Writings of Jefferson*, 14:490; Jefferson to Georgetown Republicans, 1809, *Writings*, 14: 349.

15 Democraticus [pseud.], *Loose Thoughts on Government*, in *American Archives*, 4th ser., 6:730.

16 Dan Foster, *A Short Essay on Civil Government* (Hartford, CT: Eben. Watson, 1774), 6 (emphasis added); Moses Mather, "America's Appeal to the Impartial World" (1787), *Political Sermons of the American Founding Era*, 444, 446. Born into a famous New England family of divines, Mather was the congregational

minister for Darien, Connecticut, from 1742 to 1806, and was one of America's most vocal religious leaders in support of liberty and independence.

17 Jacob Green, *Observations: On the Reconciliation of Great-Britain, and the Colonies...* (Philadelphia: Bell, 1776), 9.

18 *New York Gazette*, April 4, 1765, quoted in Bernard Friedman, "The Shaping of the Radical Consciousness in Provincial New York," *Journal of American History* 56, no. 4 (1970): 789–90; An American [pseud.], *Pennsylvania Packet* (Philadelphia), March 11, 1780; Americanus [Timothy Ford], *The Constitutionalist: or, An Inquiry How Far It Is Expedient and Proper to Alter the Constitution of South Carolina*, in *American Political Writing during the Founding Era*, 2:924; Tocqueville, *Democracy in America*, 502, 359.

19 Tocqueville, *Democracy in America*, 504; William Findley, *Observations on "The Two Sons of Oil": Containing a Vindication of the American Constitutions*, ed. John Caldwell (Indianapolis, IN: Liberty Fund, 2007), 198; Tocqueville, *Democracy in America*, 501.

20 Jefferson to Francis W. Gilmer, June 7, 1816, *Writings of Jefferson*, 15:24.

21 The Declaratory Act was passed by the British Parliament in 1766. Its purpose was to assert the authority of Parliament over the colonies "in all cases whatsoever" despite its face-saving repeal of the Stamp Act.

22 This is not to say, as Karl Marx suggested, that the eighteenth-century natural rights philosophy turns men into "an isolated monad, withdrawn into himself." (Marx, "On the Jewish Question," in *The Marx-Engels Reader*, ed. Robert C. Tucker [New York: Norton, 1972], 40.) The purpose of rights is to serve as a bridge between individuals and civil society. Rights are the mechanism by which men can live together peacefully and form voluntary associations.

23 Jefferson, Opinion on the Residence Bill, 1790, *Writings of Jefferson*, 3:60; Jefferson to Colonel James Monroe, May 20, 1782, *Writings of Jefferson*, 4:196; Jefferson to Henri Grégoire, February 25, 1809, *Portable Thomas Jefferson*, 517; Alexander McCleod, *Negro Slavery Unjustifiable: A Discourse* (New York, 1802), 8–9, 23.

24 Report of the Commissioners for the University of Virginia, August 4, 1818, in *Portable Thomas Jefferson*, 334.

25 Otis, *A Vindication of the British Colonies...*, in *Pamphlets of the American Revolution*, 559; Adams, "A Dissertation on the Canon and Feudal Law," in *Revolutionary Writings of Adams*, 22; John Mackenzie, "To Freeman" (October 18, 1769), in *The Letters of Freeman, etc.: Essays on the Nonimportation Movement in South Carolina, Collected by William Henry Drayton*, ed. Robert M. Weir (Columbia: University Press of South Carolina, 1977), 53; The Centinel [pseud.], *Massachusetts Spy*, January 23, 1772; Resolutions by Inhabitants of Granville County Concerning Resistance to Parliamentary Taxation and the Provincial Congress of North Carolina, August 15, 1774, in *Colonial and State Records of North Carolina*, eds. Walter Clark, William Laurence Saunders, and Stephen Beauregard Weeks (Raleigh, NC: P. M. Hale, 1886–1914), 9:1034–36; Foster, *Short Essay on Civil Government*, 9; Jefferson to Pierre Samuel Dupont de Nemours, April 24, 1816, *Writings of Jefferson*, 14:490.

26 Dickinson, "Speech on a Petition for a Change of Government of the Colony of Pennsylvania ..." (1764), *Political Writings of Dickinson*, 34; Adams, "A Dissertation on the Canon and Feudal Law," *Revolutionary Writings of Adams*, 33; Livingston, *Other Side of the Question*, 15; Jefferson, Opinion

on the Residence Bill, 1790, *Writings of Jefferson*, 3:60; Jefferson to Pierre Samuel Dupont de Nemours, April 24, 1816, *Writings*, 14:490; Jefferson to the Republicans of Georgetown, March 8, 1809, *Writings*, 14:349 (emphasis added); Jefferson to Major John Cartwright, June 5, 1824 in *Writings*, 16:51; Wilson, *Lectures on Law*, in *Works of Wilson*, 2:609.

27 William Henry Drayton, Charge to the Grand Jury of Charleston (October 15, 1776), *American Archives*, 5th ser., 2:1047; Livingston, *Other Side of the Question*, 15; Jefferson to William Johnson, June 12, 1823, *Writings of Jefferson*, 15: 441.

28 Wilson, *Lectures on Law*, in *Works of Wilson*, 2:596; John Witherspoon, *Lectures on Moral Philosophy*, in *The Selected Writings of John Witherspoon*, ed. Thomas Miller (Carbondale: Southern Illinois University Press, 1990), 181. Witherspoon's Princeton lectures were first published in 1802, eight years after his death.

29 Lee, "Preface to Williamsburg Edition," *Political Writings of John Dickinson*, 289–92; James Madison, "Property," in *The Mind of the Founder: Sources of the Political Thought of James Madison*, ed. Marvin Meyers (Indianapolis: Bobbs-Merrill, 1973), 244.

30 Jefferson to Pierre Samuel Dupont de Nemours, April 24, 1816, *Writings of Jefferson*, 14:490; Witherspoon, *Lectures on Moral Philosophy*, in *Selected Writings of Witherspoon*, 183.

31 Jefferson, Argument in the Case of *Howell vs. Netherland* (April 1770), in *The Works of Thomas Jefferson*, ed. Paul Leicester Ford (New York and London: Putnam, 1904–5), 1:376. (Emphasis added.)

32 Stephen Johnson, *Integrity and Piety the Best Principles of a Good Administration of Government*… (Connecticut, 1770), 51 Jefferson to Noah Webster, December 4, 1790, *Writings of Jefferson*, 8:112–13; Wilson, *Lectures on Law*, in *Works of Wilson*, 2:597, 609.

33 On the idea of rights as licenses and fences, see Jefferson to Isaac H. Tiffany, April 4, 1819, in *Thomas Jefferson: Political Writings*, ed. Joyce Appleby and Terrence Ball (Cambridge: Cambridge University Press, 1999), 224; Jefferson to Noah Webster, December 4, 1790, *Writings of Jefferson*, 8:112–13.

34 Jefferson, *Notes on the State of Virginia*, in *Portable Thomas Jefferson*, 96–97; Jefferson to Samuel Dupont de Nemours, April 24, 1816, *Writings of Jefferson*, 14:490; Witherspoon, *Lectures on Moral Philosophy*, in *Selected Writings of Witherspoon*, 181.

35 Foster, *Short Essay on Civil Government*, 59.

36 Josiah Quincy, *Observations on the Act of Parliament Commonly called the Boston Port-Bill; with thoughts on Civil Society and Standing Armies* (Boston: Edes and Gill, 1774), 30.

37 Dickinson, *An Address to the Committee of Correspondence in Barbados*… (1766), in *Political Writings of Dickinson*, 261–62; Johnson, *Integrity and Piety the Best Principles of a Good Administration of Government*, 5.

38 Abraham Williams, "An Election Sermon," *American Political Writing during the Founding Era*, 1:11, 15; Whiting, "An Address to the Inhabitants of Berkshire County, Mass.," *American Political Writing during the Founding Era*, 1:474 (emphasis added); [Silas Downer], "A Discourse at the Dedication of the Tree of Liberty," *American Political Writing during the Founding Era*, 1:100 (emphasis added); Jefferson to Francis W. Gilmer, June 7, 1816, *Writings of Jefferson*, 15:24 (emphasis added). Though his treatment is brief, Bernard Bailyn glimpsed the

transition in American revolutionary thought from the "rights of Englishmen" to the "rights of man": see *Ideological Origins of the American Revolution*, 184–98.

39 [Samuel Adams], *A State of the Rights of the Colonists*, in *Tracts of the American Revolution*, 235; Dickinson, "An Address to the Committee of Correspondence in Barbados…," *Political Writings of Dickinson*, 262. See also Dickinson's reformulation of this logic in his *Letters from a Farmer*, in *Political Writings of Dickinson*, 400.

40 For claims that the rights doctrine of the Declaration either imposes positive moral obligations on individuals or that the rights of nature may conflict with one another when put into practice, see Gilbert Chinard, *Thomas Jefferson: The Apostle of Americanism* (Boston: Little, Brown, 1929), 75; Charles M. Wiltse, *The Jeffersonian Tradition in American Democracy* (Chapel Hill: University of North Carolina Press, 1935), 70–71; Arthur M. Schlesinger, "The Lost Meaning of 'The Pursuit of Happiness,'" *William and Mary Quarterly* 21, no. 3 (1964): 325–27; Cecilia M. Kenyon, "The Declaration of Independence," in *Fundamental Testaments of the American Revolution* (Washington, DC: Library of Congress, 1973), 37; and Patrick J. Charles, "Restoring 'Life, Liberty, and the Pursuit of Happiness' in Our Constitutional Jurisprudence: An Exercise in Legal History," *William and Mary Bill of Rights Journal* 20, no. 2 (2011): 457–532.

41 The Centinel [pseud.], *Massachusetts Spy*, March 12, 1773; Hamilton, *Farmer Refuted*, in *Papers of Hamilton*, 1:122.

42 For the view that Jefferson's God is "Nature's God," see Daniel Boorstin, *The Lost World of Thomas Jefferson* (New York: Henry Holt, 1948), 29ff.; Jean Yarbrough, *American Virtues: Thomas Jefferson on the Character of a Free People* (Lawrence: University Press of Kansas, 1998), 7; and Zuckert, *The Natural Rights Republic*, 25, 59–60.

43 Jefferson to Maj. John Cartwright, June 5, 1824, *Writings of Jefferson*, 16:43–44; Jefferson to Georgetown Republicans, 1809, *Writings*, 16:349; Jefferson to M. Correa de Serra, April 19, 1814, *Writings*, 19:210; Jefferson, "Opinion on the French Treaties," *Writings*, 3:228; Jefferson, *Summary View of the Rights of British-America*, in *Colonies to Nation*, 228; Samuel Adams, "Answer of the House of Representatives of Massachusetts to the Governor's Speech" (October 23, 1765), in *Writings of Samuel Adams*, 1:18; Anon., "To the Inhabitants of the Massachusetts-Bay," April 13, 1775, in *American Archives*, 4th ser., 2:332; Jefferson, "Opinion on the French Treaties," *Writings*, 3:228–29.

44 Otis, *Rights of the Colonies Asserted and Proved* (1764), in *Pamphlets of the American Revolution*, 426; "The Massachusetts Resolves" (October 29, 1765), in *Prologue to Revolution: Sources and Documents on the Stamp Act Crisis, 1764–1766*, ed. Edmund S. Morgan (Chapel Hill: University of North Carolina Press, 1959), 56; Bland, *Inquiry into the Rights of the British Colonies*, in *American Political Writing during the Founding Era*, 1:75; Jefferson, *Summary View of the Rights of British-America*, in *Colonies to Nation*, 237; "Declaration and Resolves of the First Continental Congress" (October 14, 1774), *Colonies to Nation*, 244; Hamilton, *Farmer Refuted*, in *Papers of Hamilton*, 1:87–88.

45 Adams to William Tudor, March 29, 1817, *Works of Adams*, 10:246–47.

46 James Otis, quoted in Adams, "Abstract of the Argument," Petition of Lechmere, Boston Superior Court, February 1761, in *Legal Papers of John Adams*, ed. L. Kinvin Wroth and Hiller B. Zobel (Cambridge, MA: Belknap Press of Harvard University Press, 1965), 2:141–43; Otis, quoted in Adams, "Minutes

of the Argument," Petition of Lechmere, Suffolk Superior Court, Boston, February 24, 1761, in *Legal Papers of Adams*, 2:127–28.

47 Adams to H. Niles, January 14, 1818, *Works of Adams*, 10:276.

48 Massachusetts Assembly, Instructions to Jasper Mauduit (1762), in Massachusetts Historical Society, *Collections*, 74:39; see Locke, *Second Treatise*, para. 22.

49 William Pierce, "Oration, Delivered at Christ Church, Savannah" (July 4, 1788), in *Commentaries on the Constitution: Public and Private*, vol. 6, *10 May to 13 September 1788*, ed. John P. Kaminski et al., vol. 18 of *The Documentary History of the Ratification of the Constitution*, ed. Merrill Jensen (Madison: State Historical Society of Wisconsin, 1995), 249; Warren, *Oration… to Commemorate the Bloody Tragedy of the Fifth of March, 1770*, 19–20; Samuel Williams, *The Natural and Civil History of Vermont*, 1:7.

50 Martin Howard Jr., *A Letter from a Gentleman of Halifax* (1765), in *Pamphlets of the American Revolution*, 534–36, 538. The English member of Parliament, Anthony Bacon, similarly mocked the Americans for their use of the concept "natural rights," which, he noted, has no meaning "for men are born members of society, and consequently have no rights, but such as are given by the laws of that society to which they belong. To suppose anything else, is to suppose them out of society, in a state of nature." Quoted in John Phillip Reid, "The Authority of Rights at the American Founding," *Nature of Rights at the American Founding and Beyond*, 96.

51 Otis, *A Vindication of the British Colonies…* (1765), in *Pamphlets of the American Revolution*, 554, 558–63. See Stoner, *Common Law and Liberal Theory*.

52 Mercy Otis Warren, *History of the Rise, Progress, and Termination of the American Revolution*, ed. Lester H. Cohen (Indianapolis: Liberty Fund, 1994), 1:154.

53 Lee, quoted in "Notes of Debates in the Continental Congress," September 8, 1774, in Adams, *Diary and Autobiography*, 2:128–30, 3:309. Richard Henry Lee made his point forcefully in his preface to the Virginia edition of John Dickinson's *Letters from a Farmer in Pennsylvania to the Inhabitants of the British Colonies*. There, Lee noted that the Americans' "possession" of property and freedom has its "foundation on the clearest principle of the law of nature, the most evident declarations of the English constitution, the plainest contract made between Crown and our forefathers, and all these sealed and sanctified by the usage of near two hundred years." Lee adds a possible fifth source for their rights: the argument from purchase, i.e., the idea that the colonists' forefathers purchased their property and freedom with sweat and blood and bequeathed the gift to their descendants, who now have a moral obligation to "guard the sacred deposit committed by their fathers to their care, as well to bless posterity as to secure the happiness of the present generation." Lee, "Preface to Williamsburg Edition," *Political Writings of Dickinson*, 289–92.

54 Declaration and Resolves of the First Continental Congress, October 14, 1774, *Colonies to Nation*, 244.

55 For a very different interpretation of the role of rights in the American Revolution, see John Phillip Reid, *Constitutional History of the American Revolution*, and Reid, "The Irrelevance of the Declaration," in *Law in the American Revolution and the Revolution in the Law: A Collection of Review Essays on American Legal History*, ed. Hendrik Hartog (New York: New York University Press, 1981), 46–89. See also Shain, "Rights Natural and Civil in

the Declaration of Independence," in his *The Nature of Rights at the American Founding and Beyond*, 116–62. Reid and Shain downplay the influence of natural-rights theory in the American Revolution and instead see American revolutionaries as being more influenced by the English common-law tradition.

56 Anon., *Boston Gazette*, October 28, 1765; Anon., *Boston Gazette*, September 14, 1767; Wells, *A Few Political Reflections*, in *Colonies to Nation*, 393–96.

57 American rights talk is not, as Mary Ann Glendon has argued, a dialect. It is, instead, metaphorically speaking, a grammar. Rights are principles that organize and order man's social relations. It is the traditional civil or common-law rights of different places and times (e.g., the rights of Englishmen) that provide the dialect of rights. See Glendon, *Rights Talk: The Impoverishment of Political Discourse* (New York: Free Press, 1991), 109.

58 Washington, Circular Letter Addressed to the Governors of All the States on Disbanding the Army, June 8, 1783, in *Writings of Washington*, 10:256.

59 For an examination of the new society created by the American Revolution, see Wood, *The Radicalism of the American Revolution*.

CHAPTER 7

1 For a helpful discussion of the subsidiary natural rights, see Philip A. Hamburger, "Natural Rights, Natural Law, and American Constitutions," *Yale Law Journal* 102, no. 4 (1993): 907–60.

2 Foster, *Short Essay on Civil Government*, 6–7.

3 Jonathan Mayhew, "The Snare Broken," in *Political Sermons of the American Founding Era*, 263; Foster, *Short Essay on Civil Government*, 54; Anon., "To the Inhabitants of the Massachusetts-Bay" (April 13, 1775), *American Archives*, 4th ser., 2:332; Drayton, Address to the Grand Jury at Charleston, South Carolina (April 23, 1776), *American Archives*, 4th ser., 5:1028; Plain Truth [pseud.], "Letter to Justices in Massachusetts Empowered by the Court to Deal with the Tories" (July 11, 1776), *American Archives*, 5th ser., 1:210; Jefferson, "Opinion on the French Treaties" (April 28, 1793), *Writings of Jefferson*, 3:228–29. For revolutionary Whigs who also saw self-preservation as the first law of nature, see Simeon Howard, "A Sermon Preached to the Ancient and Honorable Artillery Company in Boston," *American Political Writing during the Founding Era*, 1:191; Gad Hitchcock, "An Election Sermon," *American Political Writing during the Founding Era*, 1:294; Charles Turner, *A Sermon Preached Before His Excellency Thomas Hutchinson… and the Honorable House of Representatives, of the Province of the Massachusetts-Bay…* (Boston: Richard Draper, 1773), 31; Richard Wells, *A Few Political Reflections Submitted to the Consideration of the British Colonies* (Philadelphia: John Dunlap, 1774), 1, 4–5; A Philadelphian [pseud.], *Every Friend to the Americans…* (Philadelphia, 1774), 2.

4 Jefferson to Colonel Humphreys, March 18, 1789, *Writings of Jefferson*, 7:323.

5 Jefferson, *Summary View of the Rights of British-Americans*, in *Colonies to Nation*, 238; Anon., *Independent Advertiser*, April 10, 1749; Anon., *Boston Gazette*, August 24, 1767; Tucker, *Sermon Preached at Cambridge*, 6; Thomas Dawes, *Oration… to Commemorate the Bloody Tragedy of the Fifth of March, 1770* (Boston: Fleets, 1781), 8. On the Americans' recognition of the importance of liberty, see John Allen, *An Oration, upon the Beauties of Liberty, or the Essential Rights of the Americans* (New London, CT: T. Green, 1773); and Nathaniel Niles, *Two Discourses on Liberty*, in *American Political Writing during the Founding Era*, 1:257–76.

6 Niles, *Two Discourses on Liberty*, in *American Political Writing during the Founding Era*, 1:259. (Emphasis added.)

7 Anon., *Independent Advertiser*, April 10, 1749.

8 A Well-Wisher to Mankind [John Perkins], *Theory of Agency: Or, An Essay on the Nature, Source and Extent of Moral Freedom* (1771), in *American Political Writing during the Founding Era*, 1:138–140, 142–143.

9 Hart, *Liberty Described and Recommended*, in *American Political Writing during the Founding Era*, 1:308.

10 Adams to John Taylor of Caroline, April 15, 1814, in *Political Writings of Adams*, 369.

11 Freeborn American [pseud.], *Boston Gazette*, March 9, 1767; Simeon Howard, *A Sermon Preached to the Ancient and Honorable Artillery Company in Boston*, in *American Political Writing during the Founding Era*, 1:187; Hart, *Liberty Described and Recommended*, in *American Political Writing during the Founding Era*, 1:310.

12 Anon., *Independent Advertiser*, April 10, 1749.

13 Nathaniel Niles, *Two Discourses on Liberty* (1774), in *American Political Writing during the Founding Era*, 1:270; Zubly, *Law of Liberty*, 6–7; Jefferson to Isaac Tiffany, April 4, 1819, in *Thomas Jefferson: Political Writings*, 224 (emphasis added). For one of the most philosophically sophisticated treatments of liberty written during the Revolutionary period, see [John Perkins], *Theory of Agency*, in *American Political Writing during the Founding Era*, 1:137–57.

14 Tucker, *Sermon Preached at Cambridge*, 5–6.

15 Anon., *Independent Advertiser*, April 10, 1749.

16 Anon., *Independent Advertiser*, April 10, 1749.

17 Poplicola [pseud.], *Rivington's New York Gazetteer*, December 2, 1773.

18 The notion that Jefferson and other revolutionary founders did not regard property to be a natural right seems to date to Vernon L. Parrington's 1927 claim that the "substitution of 'pursuit of happiness' for 'property' marks a complete break with the Whiggish doctrine of property rights that Locke had bequeathed....It was this substitution that gave to the document the note of idealism which was to make its appeal so perennially human and vital." (*Main Currents in American Thought* [New York: Harcourt, Brace, 1927; repr., 1954], 1:350.) Others have followed in Parrington's wake. For instance, see Wills, *Inventing America*, 250–51, 255; and Richard Matthews, *The Radical Politics of Thomas Jefferson* (Lawrence: University Press of Kansas, 1985), 27.

19 Wilson, *On the History of Property* (n.d.), in *Works of Wilson*, 2:712; Madison, "Property," *Mind of the Founder*, 243. (See Blackstone, *Commentaries on the Laws of England*, 2:2.)

20 Jefferson to Samuel Dupont de Nemours, April 24, 1816, *Writings of Jefferson*, 14:490.

21 Madison, "Property," *Mind of the Founder*, 243–44.

22 Locke, *Second Treatise*, para. 27, 44, 87.

23 Foster, *Short Essay on Civil Government*, 7–8.

24 Foster, *Short Essay on Civil Government*, 8–9.

25 Samuel Adams, "The House of Representatives of Massachusetts to Henry Seymour Conway" (February 13, 1768), and "The House of Representatives of Massachusetts to Dennys de Berdt" (January 12, 1768), in *Writings of Samuel Adams*, 1:190, 137.

26 Massachusettensis [pseud.], *Massachusetts Spy*, November 18, 1773.

27 Jefferson, *Summary View of the Rights of British-America*, in *Colonies to Nation*, 237; Anon., *Boston Gazette*, February 2, 1768; Warren, *Oration...to Commemorate the Bloody Tragedy of the Fifth of March, 1770*, 6.

28 Nathaniel Chipman, *Sketches of the Principles of Government* (Rutland, VT: J. Lyon, 1793), 178.

29 Lee, quoted in James W. Ely Jr., *The Guardian of Every Other Right: A Constitutional History of Property Rights*, 2nd ed. (Oxford: Oxford University Press, 1998), 26.

30 Warren, *Oration...to Commemorate the Bloody Tragedy of the Fifth of March, 1770*, 6; Tucker, *Sermon Preached at Cambridge*, 16.

31 Hampden [pseud.], "The Alarm, Number 1," New York, October 6, 1773.

32 The phrase "sacred and undeniable" as it applies to the concept "rights" comes from Jefferson's first draft of the Declaration of Independence. The phrase was later revised to "self-evident." Jefferson, "Instructions for the Deputies Appointed to Meet in General Congress on the Part of This Colony" (August 1774), *Writings of Jefferson*, 1:213; Jefferson, First Inaugural, 1801, *Writings*, 3:320; Jefferson to Samuel Kercheval, July 12, 1816, in *Writings*, 15:36.

33 Madison, "Note to His Speech on the Right of Suffrage," in *Records of the Federal Convention of 1787*, ed. Max Farrand (New Haven, CT: Yale University Press, 1937), 3:450.

34 Jefferson, *The Commonplace Book of Thomas Jefferson: A Repertory of His Ideas on Government*, ed. Gilbert Chinard (Baltimore: Johns Hopkins Press, 1926), 107–8.

35 Jefferson, *Autobiography* (1821), in *Writings of Jefferson*, 1:122.

36 Wilson, *On the History of Property*, in *Works of Wilson*, 2:718–19.

37 Madison, *Federalist* No. 10, 58; Madison, "Property," in *Mind of the Founder*, 244; Adams, diary entry, June 30, 1772, *Diary and Autobiography*, 2:61.

38 Adams, *Defence of the Constitutions of Government*, in *Works of Adams*, 6:8–9; Adams, *Defence of the Constitutions of Government*, in *Works*, 5:453–54.

39 Adams, *Defence of the Constitutions of Government*, in *Works of Adams*, 6:8–9, 65.

40 Jefferson to Joseph Milligan, April 6, 1816, *Writings of Jefferson*, 14: 466; Jefferson, Second Inaugural Address, March 4, 1805, *Writings*, 3:382.

41 Chipman, *Sketches of the Principles of Government*, 180.

42 General analyses of the historical meaning of happiness include: Howard Mumford Jones, *The Pursuit of Happiness* (Cambridge, MA: Harvard University Press, 1953; repr., Ithaca, NY: Cornell University Press, 1966); Ursula M. von Eckardt, *The Pursuit of Happiness in the Democratic Creed: An Analysis of Political Ethics* (New York: Praeger, 1959); and Darrin M. McMahon, *Happiness: A History* (New York: Grove Press, 2006). On the intellectual sources of the phrase "pursuit of happiness" in the Declaration, see McDonald, *Novus Ordo Seclorum*, ix–x.

43 Paine, "Common Sense," *Life and Works*, 2:147; Adams, "Thoughts on Government," *Revolutionary Writings of Adams*, 287; Jefferson to General Thaddeus Kosciusko, February 26, 1810, *Writings of Jefferson*, 12:369–70.

44 The one notable exception to this trend is a series of articles published in 1773–1774 in the *Virginia Gazette* (ed. Alexander Purdie and John Dixon). See, e.g., from that newspaper: "On the Motives to Virtue From Personal Happiness," January 28, 1773; "The Pursuit After Happiness," November 18, 1773; "The Character of a Happy Life," December 3, 1773; "Happiness," January 20, 1774; and "Essay on Happiness," February 10, 1774. These essays are available in digital

form in the collection of Early American Newspapers (a website maintained by Readex, a division of NewsBank, Inc.). Unfortunately, however, the quality of these electronic versions is poor.

45 George Mason, Virginia Bill of Rights, *Colonies to Nation*, 333.

46 Locke, *ECHU*, II.xxi.51. (Emphasis added.)

47 Locke, *ECHU*, II.xxi.43–44.

48 Locke, *ECHU*, II.xxi.47.

49 Locke, *ECHU*, II.xxi.54–55, 60, 47.

50 Locke, *ECHU*, II.xxi.51.

51 Locke, *ECHU*, II.xxi.51.(Emphasis added.)

52 Samuel Adams to Joseph Allen, November 7, 1771, and Samuel Adams to Andrew Elton Wells, October 21, 1772, in *Writings of Samuel Adams*, 2:268, 337–38.

53 Jefferson to John Manners, June 12, 1817, *Writings of Jefferson*, 15:124–25.

54 Jefferson to Francisco Chiappe, September 9, 1789, in *The Papers of Thomas Jefferson*, ed. Julian Boyd (Princeton, NJ: Princeton University Press, 1958), 15:405; Franklin, "Proposals and Queries for Consideration of the Junto," in *Works of Franklin*, 1:338; Jefferson to John Page, July 15, 1763, *Writings of Jefferson*, 4:10.

55 Jefferson to Maria Cosway, October 12, 1786, *Writings of Jefferson*, 5:430–48.

56 Jefferson to Maria Cosway, October 12, 1786, *Writings of Jefferson*, 5:430–48.

57 Adams, *Defence of the Constitutions of Government*, in *Works of Adams*, 6:219.

58 Jefferson to Peter Carr, August 19, 1785, *Writings of Jefferson*, 5:82–87.

59 Jefferson to Peter Carr, August 19, 1785, *Writings of Jefferson*, 5:82–87.

60 Jefferson to Peter Carr, August 10, 1787, *Writings of Jefferson*, 6:256–62; Jefferson to Thomas Jefferson Randolph, November 24, 1808, *Writings*, 12:196–202.

61 Abigail Adams to John Quincy Adams, March 20, 1780, in *Adams Family Correspondence*, vol. 3–4, *April 1778–September 1782*, ed. L. H. Butterfield and Marc Friedlaender (Cambridge, MA: Belknap Press of Harvard University Press, 1973), 3:310–13. (Emphasis added.)

62 See Franklin, *The Autobiography of Benjamin Franklin*, in *Works of Franklin*, 1:189–92; Jefferson to Peter Carr, August 19, 1785, *Writings of Jefferson*, 5:82–87.

63 John Adams to John Quincy Adams, May 18, 1781, *Adams Family Correspondence*, 3:117; John Adams to John Quincy Adams, May 19, 1783, *Adams Family Correspondence*, vol. 5–6, *October 1782–December 1785*, ed. Richard A. Ryerson et al. (Cambridge, MA: Belknap Press of Harvard University Press, 1992), 5:162–63; John Adams to John Quincy Adams, January 23, 1788, *Adams Family Correspondence*, vol. 8, *March 1787–December 1789*, ed. Margaret A. Hogan et al. (Cambridge, MA: Belknap Press of Harvard University Press, 2007), 8:219–20.

64 Jefferson to Maria Cosway, October 12, 1786, *Writings of Jefferson*, 5:443; Jefferson to J. Correa de Serra, April 19, 1814, *Writings*, 19: 210; Jefferson to Amos J. Cook, January 21, 1816, *Writings*, 4: 405; Jefferson to William Short, October 31, 1819, *Writings*, 15: 223–24.

65 Jefferson, *Notes on the State of Virginia*, in *Portable Thomas Jefferson*, 196–97; Jefferson to Amos J. Cook, January 21, 1816, *Writings of Jefferson*, 4:405; Jefferson, *Notes on the State of Virginia*, in *Portable Thomas Jefferson*, 196–97; Jefferson to Miles King, September 26, 1814, *Writings*, 19:197–98. See also Jefferson to John Adams, October 14, 1816, *Writings*, 15:76–77.

66 Franklin, "Articles of Belief and Acts of Religion," *Works of Franklin*, 1:322; Franklin, *Wit and Wisdom from Poor Richard's Almanack* (Mineola, NY: Dover, 1999), 17; Adams, *Thoughts on Government*, in *Revolutionary Writings of John Adams*, 287–88; George Washington, First Inaugural Speech, and Washington to Marquis de Lafayette, January 29, 1789, in *George Washington: A Collection*, ed. W. B. Allen (Indianapolis, IN: Liberty Fund, 1988), 462, 428; Washington to the Bishops, Clergy, and Laity of the Protestant Episcopal Church, August 19, 1789, *Writings of Washington*, 12:162.

67 Jefferson to Destutt de Tracy, January 26, 1811, *Writings of Jefferson*, 13:18; Scipio [pseud.], *Massachusetts Spy*, April 25, 1771.

68 Jefferson to Ellen W. Coolidge, August 27, 1825, *Writings of Jefferson*, 18:341; Jefferson to David Howell, December 15, 1810, *Writings*, 12:436; Jefferson to Thomas Cooper, November 19, 1802, *Writings*, 10:342.

CHAPTER 8

1 John Montague, *Arguments Offer'd to the Right Honourable Lords Commissioners for Trade & Plantation*, in *Exploring the Bounds of Liberty: Political Writings of Colonial British America from the Glorious Revolution to the American Revolution*, ed. Jack P. Greene and Craig B. Yirush (Carmel, IN: Liberty Fund, 2018), 1:210–11, 207.

2 Elisha Williams, *The Essential Rights and Liberties of Protestants*, in *Political Sermons of the American Founding Era*, 59, 56.

3 Elisha Williams, *Essential Rights and Liberties*, in *Political Sermons of the American Founding Era*, 56–57.

4 Elisha Williams, *Essential Rights and Liberties*, in *Political Sermons of the American Founding Era*, 57–58.

5 Elisha Williams, *Essential Rights and Liberties*, in *Political Sermons of the American Founding Era*, 59, 58. (Emphasis added.)

6 Mayhew, *The Snare Broken*, in *Political Sermons of the American Founding Era*, 239–40, 245.

7 Adams to James Sullivan, May 26, 1776, *Works of Adams*, 9:375; Benjamin Church, *An Oration... to Commemorate the Bloody Tragedy of the Fifth of March, 1770* (Boston, 1773), 14.

8 See *Boston Gazette*, August 17 and 24, 1767; *New-York Journal*, September 3, 1767.

9 See *Boston Gazette*, August 17 and 24, 1767; *New-York Journal*, September 3, 1767.

10 A Virginian [pseud.], *Pennsylvania Gazette*, September 29, 1768; Hampden [pseud.], "The Alarm, Number 1," New York, October 6, 1773. For similar American views on property and consent, see also "A View of the British Constitution," *Essex Gazette*, October 11, 1768; Anon., "To the Inhabitants of Queen's County, Long Island," *Constitutional Gazette*, November 29, 1775.

11 Warren, *Oration... to Commemorate the Bloody Tragedy of the Fifth of March, 1770*, 10.

12 Moses Mather, *America's Appeal to the Impartial World* (1775), in *Political Sermons of the American Founding Era*, 443–44, 446.

13 Mather, *America's Appeal to the Impartial World*, in *Political Sermons of the American Founding Era*, 473–74.

14 Boston's Instructions to Its Representatives, May 30, 1776, in *Popular Sources of Political Authority: Documents on the Massachusetts Constitution of 1780*, 95.

15 Mather, *America's Appeal to the Impartial World*, in *Political Sermons of the American Founding Era*, 490.

16 Anon., "To the Inhabitants of Queen's County, Long Island," *Constitutional Gazette*, November 29, 1775, and December 2, 1775; New York Petition to the House of Commons, October 18, 1764, *Prologue to Revolution: Sources and Documents*, 9–10.

17 "The New York Petition to the House of Commons" (October 18, 1764), *Prologue to Revolution: Sources and Documents*, 9–10, 13–14.

18 "The Virginia Resolves: The Resolutions as Recalled by Patrick Henry," *Prologue to Revolution: Sources and Documents*, 48.

19 Quoted in Murray N. Rothbard, *Conceived in Liberty* (New Rochelle, NY: Arlington House, 1976), 3:100. The story of Henry's daring speech was dramatized, promulgated, glorified, and made into legend in William Wirt's famous biography of the Virginian, *Sketches of the Life and Character of Patrick Henry* (Philadelphia, 1817). The only contemporary account of Henry's speech was recorded by a visiting Frenchman, who stood with Thomas Jefferson in the lobby of the Virginia House of Burgesses listening to it. See "The Virginia Resolves: The French Traveller's Account," *Prologue to Revolution: Sources and Documents*, 46.

20 Jefferson, *Autobiography*, in *The Life and Selected Writings of Thomas Jefferson*, ed. Adrienne Koch and William Peden (New York: Modern Library, 1944), 6; Stan V. Henkels, "Jefferson's Recollections of Patrick Henry," *Pennsylvania Magazine of History and Biography* 34, no. 4 (1910): 389.

21 An excellent account of Henry's speech can be found in Webking, *The American Revolution and the Politics of Liberty*, 30–40. Also see Merrill Jensen, "Commentary," in Randolph G. Adams, *Political Ideas of the American Revolution* (New York: Barnes and Noble, 1958), 12. The best accounts of the American response to the Stamp Act are Rothbard, *Conceived in Liberty*, 3:96–137, and Edmund S. Morgan and Helen M. Morgan, *The Stamp Act Crisis: Prologue to Revolution* (New York: Collier, 1962), 120–54.

22 "The Pennsylvania Resolves" (September 21, 1765), and "The Massachusetts Resolves" (October 29, 1765), *Prologue to Revolution: Sources and Documents*, 51, 56.

23 "The Massachusetts Resolves" and "The Maryland Resolves" (September 28, 1765), *Prologue to Revolution: Sources and Documents*, 56, 52; "The Declaration of the Stamp Act Congress" (October 19, 1765), *Colonies to Nation*, 64.

24 Hamilton, *Farmer Refuted*, in *Papers of Hamilton*, 1:105.

25 On Whately's argument, see Morgan and Morgan, *Stamp Act Crisis: Prologue to Revolution*, 104–9.

26 Robert Whately, *The Regulations Lately Made*... (1765), in *Colonies to Nation*, 47–50.

27 Edmund Burke, *Speech to the Electors of Bristol*, in *Select Works of Edmund Burke*, ed. Francis Canavan (Indianapolis, IN: Liberty Fund, 1999), 4:11.

28 Whately, *Regulations Lately Made*, in *Colonies to Nation*, 47–50.

29 Daniel Dulany, *Considerations on the Propriety of Imposing Taxes in the British Colonies, for the Purpose of Raising a Revenue* (New York, 1765), in *Colonies to Nation*, 52.

30 Dulany, *Considerations on the Propriety of Imposing Taxes*, in *Colonies to Nation*, 52–53.

31 Dulany, *Considerations on the Propriety of Imposing Taxes*, in *Colonies to Nation*, 55–56.

32 Quoted in Gordon S. Wood, *The Creation of the American Republic, 1776–1787*

(New York: Norton, 1972), 181, 183. On the American development of actual representation, see J. R. Pole, *Political Representation in England and the Origins of the American Republic* (Berkeley: University of California Press, 1971).

33 On the medieval origins of the American view of representation, see H. Trevor Colbourn, *The Lamp of Experience: Whig History and the Intellectual Origins of the American Revolution* (Chapel Hill: University of North Carolina Press, 1965), and Bailyn, *Ideological Origins of the American Revolution*, 161–75.

34 Anon., "A Dialogue between a Ruler and a Subject," *Massachusetts Spy*, June 18, 1772; Church, *Oration…to Commemorate the Bloody Tragedy of the Fifth of March, 1770*, 14–15. See also A Virginian [pseud.], *Pennsylvania Gazette*, September 29, 1768, arguing that the most "celebrated *English* writers" on parliamentary power "meant the *English representatives of Englishmen*, the *actual*, not the *virtual* representative only, of the people."

35 Granville Sharp, *A Declaration of the People's Natural Right to Share in the Legislature, Which Is the Fundamental Principle of the British Constitution of State* (London, 1774; repr., Philadelphia: John Dunlap, 1774), 7–10.

36 Mutius Scaevola [pseud.], *Boston Gazette*, March 4, 1771.

37 A Son of Liberty [Silas Downer], *A Discourse at the Dedication of the Tree of Liberty* (1768), in *American Political Writing during the Founding Era*, 1:100.

38 John Joachim Zubly, *An Humble Inquiry into the Nature of the Dependency of the American Colonies upon the Parliament of Great-Britain and the Right of Parliament to Lay Taxes on the Said Colonies* (1769), in *Political Sermons of the American Founding Era*, 285, 290.

39 On Bland's argument, see Colbourn, *The Lamp of Experience*, 143–48, and Clinton Rossiter, *Seedtime of the Republic: The Origin of the American Tradition of Political Liberty* (New York: Harcourt, Brace, 1953), 248–80.

40 Bland, *Inquiry into the Rights of the British Colonies*, in *American Political Writing during the Founding Era*, 74–75.

41 Bland, *Inquiry into the Rights of the British Colonies*, in *American Political Writing during the Founding Era*, 75–76; Bland, *The Colonel Dismounted*, in *Pamphlets of the American Revolution*, 323.

42 On Adams's argument, see Thompson, *John Adams and the Spirit of Liberty*, 66–87.

43 Novanglus [John Adams], VIII, March 13, 1775, *Papers of Adams*, 2:328.

44 Locke, *Second Treatise*, para. 115.

45 Novanglus [Adams], VIII, March 13, 1775, *Papers of Adams*, 2:328, 330.

46 Novanglus [Adams], VII, March 6, 1775, *Papers of Adams*, 2:317. (Emphasis added.)

47 Edward Coke, "Prologue" to *The Second Part of the Institutes*, in *The Selected Writings and Speeches of Sir Edward Coke*, ed. Steve Sheppard (Indianapolis, IN: Liberty Fund, 2003), 2:748; see Otis, *Rights of the British Colonies Asserted and Proved*, in *Pamphlets of the American Revolution*, 454.

48 Novanglus [Adams], VIII, March 13, 1775, *Papers of Adams*, 2:353, 328. Here I dissent from Charles McIlwain's otherwise superb history of the Revolution (*The American Revolution: A Constitutional Interpretation* [1923; New York: Da Capo, 1973]). McIlwain argues that the most important colonial constitutional argument against Parliament was contained within an imperial context. His point here is to downplay colonial arguments based on the charters and fundamental law. From Adams's perspective, the imperial, charter, and fundamental law arguments were inextricably intertwined.

49 On this distinction in Hamilton's thought, see Gerald Stourzh, *Alexander Hamilton and the Idea of Republican Government* (Stanford, CA: Stanford University Press, 1970), 26.

50 Novanglus [Adams], XII, April 17, 1775, *Papers of Adams*, 2:373–74. (Emphasis added.)

51 Paine, *Common Sense*, in *Collected Writings*, 6.

52 Paine, *Common Sense*, in *Collected Writings*, 6, 8, 7.

CHAPTER 9

1 See Zuckert, *The Natural Rights Republic*, 18.

2 Locke, *Second Treatise*, para. 6, 124, 34.

3 Clark, *Sermon Preached Before His Excellency John Hancock*, 8–9.

4 Democraticus [pseud.], "Loose Thoughts on Government," *American Archives*, 4th ser., 6:730; Church, *Oration...to Commemorate the Bloody Tragedy of the Fifth of March, 1770*, 5–6.

5 Dawes, *Oration...to Commemorate the Bloody Tragedy of the Fifth of March, 1770*, 7–8.

6 Spartanus [pseud.], "The Interest of America," *New-Hampshire Gazette*, June 15, 1776. For another American view of the state of nature that seeks to reconcile the Hobbesean-Lockean account with the biblical account, see Levi Hart, *Liberty Described and Recommended*, in *American Political Writing during the Founding Era* 1:305–17.

7 Foster, *Short Essay on Civil Government*, 11.

8 "An Address of the Inhabitants of the Towns...," July 31, 1776, in *State Papers of New Hampshire*, ed. Nathaniel Bouton et al. (Concord, NH: Edward A. Jenks, state printer, 1877), 10:234; "A Public Defence of the Right of the New-Hampshire Grants (So Called) on Both Sides Connecticut-River, to Associate Together, and Form Themselves into an Independent State," 1779, in *State Papers of New Hampshire*, 10:299; The Republican [pseud.], January 30, 1777, in Frederick Chase, *A History of Dartmouth College and the Town of Hanover New Hampshire* (Cambridge, MA: John Wilson and Son, University Press, 1891), 431–32.

9 "Address of the Town of the New Hampshire Grants to the Assembly," June 11, 1777, *State Papers of New Hampshire*, 10:455–56; Republican [pseud.], "Observations on the Right of Jurisdiction Claimed by the States of New York and New Hampshire, Over the New Hampshire Grants," 1778, *State Papers of New Hampshire*, 10:264; "A Public Defence of the Right of the New-Hampshire Grants," *State Papers of New Hampshire*, 10:312–13. For a fuller discussion of the controversy over the New Hampshire Grant towns and their battle for recognition, see Wood, *Creation of the American Republic*, 287–89.

10 Samuel Williams, *The Natural and Civil History of Vermont*, 2:164.

11 Jefferson, *Summary View of the Rights of British-America*, in *Colonies to Nation*, 231; Henry, "Notes of Debates in the Continental Congress" (September 6, 1774), quoted in *Diary and Autobiography of John Adams*, 2:124; Gage, quoted in Theodore Draper, *A Struggle for Power: The American Revolution* (New York: Random House, 1996), 425; Warren to John Adams, October 16, 1774, *Papers of Adams*, 2:190–92. For an excellent discussion of the various ways in which Americans used Locke's state of nature metaphor to justify a range of activities from starting new governments to claiming large tracts of royal land, see McDonald, *Novus Ordo Seclorum*, 144–59.

12 Adams to James Burgh, December 28, 1774, *Papers of Adams*, 2:205–8; Adams to
   A Friend in London, January 21, 1775, *Papers*, 2:214–16.

13 Petition of Pittsfield, December 26, 1775, and Petition of Pittsfield, May 1776,
   in *Massachusetts, Colony to Commonwealth: Documents on the Formation of Its
   Constitution, 1775–1780*, ed. Robert J. Taylor (New York: Norton, 1961), 17–19. See
   Robert J. Taylor, *Western Massachusetts in the Revolution* (Providence, RI: Brown
   University Press, 1954).

14 Whiting, "An Address to the Inhabitants of Berkshire County, Mass.," in
   American Political Writing during the Founding Era, 1:466–69.

15 Republican [pseud.], "Observations on the Right of Jurisdiction Claimed by
   the States of New York and New Hampshire, *State Papers of New Hampshire*,
   10:263–66.

16 Pacificus [Timothy Walker], "An Address to the Inhabitants of the New
   Hampshire Grants (So Called) Lying Westward of the Connecticut River," July
   18, 1778, *State Papers of New Hampshire*, 10:270–71.

17 Samuel Lockwood, *Civil Rulers an Ordinance of God, for Good to Mankind*
   (New London, CT: Timothy Green, 1774), 6; Quincy, *Observations on the
   Act of Parliament Commonly Called the Boston Port-Bill*, 32; Thomas Hobbes,
   Leviathan, ed. Edwin Curley (Indianapolis, IN: Hackett, 1994), 76.

18 Foster, *Short Essay on Civil Government*, 13; Zubly, *The Law of Liberty*, 4; Clark,
   Sermon Preached Before His Excellency John Hancock, 8; John Hurt, *The Love
   of Our Country: A Sermon, Preached Before the Virginia Troops in New-Jersey*
   (Philadelphia: Styner and Cist, 1777), 8.

19 See Locke, *Second Treatise*, para. 124.

20 Warren, *Oration…to Commemorate the Bloody Tragedy of the Fifth of March, 1770*,
   5; Church, *Oration…to Commemorate the Bloody Tragedy of the Fifth of March,
   1770*, 5–6 (emphasis added).

21 Locke, *Second Treatise*, para. 220.

22 "Return of Lexington" (June 15, 1778), in *Massachusetts, Colony to Commonwealth:
   Documents on the Formation of Its Constitution, 1775–1780*, 66.

23 On Locke's doctrine of consent, see Peter Josephson, *The Great Art of
   Government: Locke's Use of Consent* (Lawrence: University Press of Kansas,
   2002). See also Dunn, *The Political Thought of John Locke*.

24 Clark, *Sermon Preached Before His Excellency John Hancock*, 9; Church,
   Oration…to Commemorate the Bloody Tragedy of the Fifth of March, 1770, 6–7.

25 Oliver Wolcott to Samuel Lyman, May 16, 1776, in *Letters of Members of the
   Continental Congress*, ed. Edmund C. Burnett (Washington, DC: Carnegie
   Institution, 1921), 1:449; Hart, *Liberty Described and Recommended*, in *American
   Political Writing during the Founding Era*, 1:308; Anon., "Some Thoughts on the
   Constitution of the British Empire, and the Controversy between Great Britain
   and the American Colonies" (June 12, 1775), *American Archives*, 4th ser., 2:962.

26 John Locke [pseud.], *Boston Gazette*, November 18, 1765; "At a Legal Town-
   Meeting of the Freeholders and Other Inhabitants of the Town of Mendon,"
   Boston Gazette, June 7, 1773; [Theophilus Parsons], *The Essex Result*, in *American
   Political Writing during the Founding Era*, 1:488; "The Report of a Constitution,
   or Form of Government, for the Commonwealth of Massachusetts," in
   Revolutionary Writings of Adams, 297–98.

27 *Boston Gazette*, August 24, 1767.

28 On social contract theory in revolutionary America, see Thad W. Tate, "The Social Contract in America, 1774–1787: Revolutionary Theory as a Conservative Instrument," *William and Mary Quarterly* 22, no. 3 (1965): 375–91. In what is otherwise a competent article, Tate errs in arguing that the contribution of American revolutionaries to social contract theory was minimal to nonexistent.

29 Thomas Dawes, *An Oration…in Celebration of the Anniversary of American Independence* (Boston: Samuel Hall, 1787), 10–11; Jefferson, *Notes on the State of Virginia*, Query 13, in *Portable Thomas Jefferson*, 164; Jefferson to Roger C. Weightman, June 24, 1826, *Writings of Jefferson*, 16:181–82.

30 Foster, *Short Essay on Civil Government*, 53; Archibald Kennedy, *An Essay on the Government of the Colonies* (New York: J. Parker, 1752), 13.

31 Tucker, *Sermon Preached at Cambridge*, 13–14.

32 Clark, *Sermon Preached Before His Excellency John Hancock*, 8–10; Anon. from Hampshire County, "To the Inhabitants of Massachusetts-Bay, Number II," *Massachusetts Spy*, February 16, 1775.

33 Spartanus [pseud.], *New-Hampshire Gazette*, June 15, 1776.

34 "The American Whig" [pseud.], "To the Inhabitants of the State of Rhode-Island on the Subject of Altering the Constitution, Number III," *Providence Gazette*, April 3, 1779.

35 Jefferson, *Notes on the State of Virginia*, Query 17, in *Portable Thomas Jefferson*, 210.

36 Drayton, Charge to the Grand Jury of Charleston (October 15, 1776), *American Archives*, 5th ser., 2:1047.

37 Anon., *Massachusetts Spy*, February 16, 1775. This Massachusetts writer, in contrast to the "American Whig" in Rhode Island, reduced the social-contract process from three to two steps.

38 Lockwood, *Civil Rulers an Ordinance of God*, 7.

39 Anon. from Hampshire County, "To the Inhabitants of Massachusetts-Bay, Number II," *Massachusetts Spy*, February 16, 1775.

40 Tucker, *Sermon Preached at Cambridge*, 16; Thomas Paine, "The Forester's Letters to Cato" (1776), in *Life and Works of Paine*, 2:230.

41 Jefferson to John Taylor, May 28, 1816, *Writings of Jefferson*, 15:19, 22.

42 Paine, *Rights of Man*, in *Life and Works of Paine*, 6:268; Samuel Williams, "A Discourse on the Love of Our Country" (1774), available at *Teaching American History*, http://teachingamericanhistory.org/library/document/a-discourse-on-the-love-of-our-country/.

43 The view of American revolutionary republicanism described in these pages is very different from the influential view presented in Wood's *The Creation of the American Republic*, 46–90.

44 Adams, *Defence of the Constitutions of Government*, in *Works of Adams*, 4:370–71; 403–5; 370–71; 5:453–54.

45 Madison, *Federalist* No. 10, pp. 57, 61, 60–61.

46 Madison, *Federalist* No. 10, pp. 62, 64 (emphasis added).

47 Madison, *Federalist* Nos. 48 and 51, 334, 348–50.

48 Madison, *Federalist* No. 51, 351.

49 Madison, *Federalist* No. 55, 374.

50 For an examination of the new society created by the American Revolution, see Wood, *The Radicalism of the American Revolution*.

51 Jefferson to Joseph Priestley, June 19, 1802, *Writings of Jefferson*, 10:324–25. The best discussion of Jefferson's republicanism can be found in Mayer, *Constitutional Thought of Thomas Jefferson*.

52 Jefferson to Francis W. Gilmer, June 7, 1816, *Writings of Jefferson*, 15:24.

53 Jefferson to Samuel Kercheval, July 12, 1816, *Writings of Jefferson*, 15:36.

54 Quoted in Mayer, *Constitutional Thought of Thomas Jefferson*, 76.

55 Jefferson, "Report of the Commissioners for the University of Virginia" (August 4, 1818), *Portable Thomas Jefferson*, 334.

56 Lockwood, *Civil Rulers an Ordinance of Good*, 7.

57 Kennedy, *Essay on the Government of the Colonies*, 11–12; Jefferson, "Bill for Proportioning Crimes and Punishments in Cases Heretofore Capital" (June 18, 1779), in *Papers of Thomas Jefferson*, 2:492.

58 Cooke, *True Principles of Civil Government*, 8–9; Foster, *Short Essay on Civil Government*, 27–28, 35, 36.

59 Turner, *Sermon Preached Before His Excellency Thomas Hutchinson*, 17; Jefferson to Spencer Roane, September 6, 1819, *Writings of Jefferson*, 15:213.

60 An American [pseud.], "Addresses to the People of Maryland" (n.d.), *American Archives*, 4th ser., 6:1095; Massachusettensis [pseud.], *Massachusetts Spy*, December 12, 1771.

61 Jefferson to Ursuline Nuns of New Orleans, July 13, 1804, *Founders Online*, National Archives, http://founders.archives.gov/documents/Jefferson/99-01-02-0068. (This is an early access document from *The Papers of Thomas Jefferson*. It is not an authoritative final version.)

62 Madison, *Federalist* No. 51, 349.

63 Madison, *Federalist* No. 51, 349; Stephen Johnson, *Integrity and Piety the Best Principles of a Good Administration of Government...* (New London, CT: Timothy Green, 1770), 8–9; *Boston Gazette*, November 11, 1765.

64 *Massachusetts Spy*, May 2, 1771; Tucker, *Sermon Preached at Cambridge*, 30.

65 Jefferson to Joseph Priestley, June 19, 1802, *Writings of Jefferson*, 10:325.

CHAPTER 10

1 In *The Anas*, Jefferson called this the "catholic principle of republicanism" (*Writings of Jefferson*, 1:330), which he defined elsewhere as follows: "We certainly cannot deny to other nations that principle whereon our government is founded, that every nation has a right to govern itself internally under whatever form it pleases, and to change those forms at its own will" (Jefferson to Thomas Pinckney, December 30, 1792, *Writings of Jefferson*, 9:7). See also Jefferson to M. Staël-Holstein, July 16, 1807, 11:282.

2 Zubly, *Law of Liberty*, 18.

3 The Prohibitory Act of 1775, which declared and enforced a blockade on American commerce, was an effectual declaration of war, and thereby declared the king's American subjects to be outside his protection. Putting the colonists outside the king's protection effectively made them independent.

4 On the Radical Whig tradition, see Caroline Robbins, *The Eighteenth-Century Commonwealthman* (Cambridge, MA: Harvard University Press, 1959); Bailyn, *The Ideological Origins of the American Revolution*; Maier, *From Resistance to Revolution*, 27–48.

5 Locke, *Second Treatise*, para. 199, 201–2.

6 Locke, *Second Treatise*, para. 202.

7 Locke, *Second Treatise,* para. 207.

8 Locke, *Second Treatise,* para. 208, 209, 210.

9 It is important to note that the particular government Locke describes in this chapter is a thinly veiled version of the mixed and balanced English government, and Locke's particular focus is on the tyranny of the king. American revolutionaries took Locke's argument against monarchical tyranny and applied it to the actions first of Parliament and then of the king.

10 Locke, *Second Treatise,* para. 212, 214, 215, 216, 217.

11 Locke, *Second Treatise,* para. 221, 222.

12 Locke, *Second Treatise,* para. 223.

13 Locke, *Second Treatise,* para. 225.

14 Locke, *Second Treatise,* para. 226.

15 The best treatment of Mayhew's thought is J. Patrick Mullins, *Father of Liberty: Jonathan Mayhew and the Principles of the American Revolution* (Lawrence: University Press of Kansas, 2017).

16 Adams to Jefferson, July 18, 1818, *Adams-Jefferson Letters,* 527; Adams to H. Niles, February 13, 1818, *Works of Adams,* 10:288.

17 Mayhew, *A Discourse Concerning Unlimited Submission and Nonresistance to the Higher Powers,* in *Pamphlets of the American Revolution,* 215, 222, 226, 228, 231.

18 Mayhew, *Discourse Concerning Unlimited Submission,* in *Pamphlets of the American Revolution,* 237, 236, 231.

19 Mayhew, *Discourse Concerning Unlimited Submission,* in *Pamphlets of the American Revolution,* 237n, 231, 241, 232.

20 Mayhew, *Discourse Concerning Unlimited Submission,* in *Pamphlets of the American Revolution,* 235, 237.

21 Mayhew, *Discourse Concerning Unlimited Submission,* in *Pamphlets of the American Revolution,* 237n, 237–38.

22 Bland, *Inquiry into the Rights of the British Colonies,* in *American Political Writing during the Founding Era,* 1:69, 82; Novanglus [Adams], II, January 30, 1775, *Papers of Adams,* 2:242; Dickinson, *Two Letters on the Tea Tax* (1773), in *Political Writings of Dickinson,* 461.

23 Mercy Otis Warren, *History of the Rise, Progress, and Termination of the American Revolution,* 1:3.

24 Jefferson, First Inaugural Address (1801), *Portable Thomas Jefferson,* 292.

25 Zubly, "An Humble Inquiry," *Political Sermons of the American Founding Era,* 298; Adams, notes for an oration at Braintree, *Diary and Autobiography,* 2:58–59; Jefferson to Edward Carrington, January 16, 1787, *Writings of Jefferson,* 6:55–59.

26 Dickinson, *Letters from a Farmer in Pennsylvania,* in *Political Writings of Dickinson,* 356; Zubly, "An Humble Inquiry," *Political Sermons of the American Founding Era,* 298.

27 Jefferson, "The Kentucky Resolutions," *Portable Thomas Jefferson,* 287–88.

28 Bland, *Inquiry into the Rights of the British Colonies,* in *American Political Writing during the Founding Era,* 1:82; Adams, diary entry, February 1765, *Diary and Autobiography,* 1:255–56; Adams, "Dissertation on the Canon and Feudal Law," *Revolutionary Writings of Adams,* 22, 21.

29 Adams, diary entry, December 1765, *Diary and Autobiography,* 1:282.

30 This line of interpretation was first presented in Bailyn's *Ideological Origins of the American Revolution,* 94–159. The implications of Bailyn's original insights were subsequently worked out by Gordon S. Wood in two essays (first published

in 1966 and 1982, respectively), "Rhetoric and Reality in the American Revolution" and "Conspiracy and the Paranoid Style: Causality and Deceit in the Eighteenth Century," in his *The Idea of America: Reflections on the Birth of the United States* (New York: Penguin, 2011), 25–55, 81–123.

31 Dickinson, *Letters to the Inhabitants of the British Colonies* (1774), in *Political Writings of Dickinson*, 491; Mather, "America's Appeal to the Impartial World," *Political Sermons of the American Founding Era*, 481.

32 See Wood, "Rhetoric and Reality in the American Revolution" and "Conspiracy and the Paranoid Style," *The Idea of America*. For a contrary position, see John P. Diggins, "The Problem of Motivation and Causation," in *The Lost Soul of American Politics: Virtue, Self-Interest, and the Foundations of Liberalism* (New York: Basic Books, 1984); and Ralph Lerner, "Prologue: Recovering the Revolution," in *The Thinking Revolutionary: Principle and Practice in the New Republic* (Ithaca, NY: Cornell University Press, 1987), 1–38.

33 Adams, "Dissertation on the Canon and Feudal Law," *Revolutionary Writings of John Adams*, 20.

34 We do a disservice to Adams and to the revolutionary generation if we do not attempt to understand the kind of moral reasoning that might have propelled them to this kind of reaction. We should be open to the possibility that the problem rests not with them but with us. Perhaps *we* lack the kind of moral knowledge and the historical imagination that are required to understand their perspective.

35 Adams, "Instructions of the Town of Braintree to Their Representative" (1765), *Revolutionary Writings of Adams*, 40; John Adams to Abigail Adams, June 17, 1775, *Adams Family Correspondence*, 1:215–17.

36 Dickinson, *The Late Regulations Respecting the British Colonies* (1765), in *Pamphlets of the American Revolution*, 690.

37 Boston Town Meeting to Its Assembly Representatives (1770), in [*Eighteenth*] *Report of the Record Commissioners of the City of Boston Containing the Boston Town Records, 1770 through 1777* (Boston: Rockwell and Churchill, 1887), 26, available at Internet Archive, https://archive.org/details/reportofrecordco18bost/page/26.

38 Novanglus [Adams], I, January 23, 1775, *Papers of Adams*, 228, 233, 231.

39 Dickinson, *Letters to the Inhabitants of the British Colonies*, in *Political Writings of Dickinson*, 473–74.

40 For the Suffolk Resolves, see *America's HomePage* (site maintained by Steven Thomas), http://ahp.gatech.edu/suffolk_resolves_1774.html; quoted in Lawrence H. Gipson, *The British Empire Before the American Revolution*, vol. 12: *The Triumphant Empire: Britain Sails into the Storm: 1770–1776* (New York: Knopf, 1967), 150n.

41 Gipson, *British Empire Before the American Revolution*, 12:173; Ebenezer Baldwin, "An Appendix Stating the Heavy Grievances the Colonies Labor Under . . ." (1774), *Colonies to Nation*, 213; "The Association and Resolves of the New York Sons of Liberty" (1773), *Colonies to Nation*, 198; Alexander Hamilton, *A Full Vindication of the Measures of the Congress . . .* (1774), in *The Works of Alexander Hamilton*, ed. Henry Cabot Lodge (New York: Putnam, 1904), 1:10.

42 Philadelphia merchants' committee, quoted in Maier, *From Resistance to Revolution*, 171–72; Wilson, "Speech Delivered in the Convention for the Province of Pennsylvania" (January 1775), *Works of Wilson*, 2:748–49.

43 Washington to Bryan Fairfax, July 4, July 20, and August 24, 1774, *Writings of Washington*, 2:418, 421–22, 434–35.

44 Richard Henry Lee to John Dickinson, April 4, 1773, in *Letters of Richard Henry Lee*, ed. J. C. Ballagh (New York, 1911), 1:84; Jefferson, *Summary View of the Rights of British America*, in *Portable Thomas Jefferson*, 9.

45 Adams to Horatio Gates, March 23, 1776, *Papers*, IV: 58–60.

46 Jefferson, *Summary View of the Rights of British-America*, in *Colonies to Nation*, 231.

47 Otis, *Rights of the British Colonies Asserted and Proved*, in *Colonies to Nation*, 31–32.

48 Blackstone, *Commentaries on the Laws*, 1:157.

49 Bland, *Inquiry into the Rights of the British Colonies*, in *American Political Writing during the Founding Era*, 1:82–84.

50 Jefferson to M. Staël-Holstein, July 16, 1807, *Writings of Jefferson*, 11:282.

51 Rush to James Cheetham, July 17, 1809, in *The Letters of Benjamin Rush*, ed. Lyman H. Butterfield (Princeton, NJ: Princeton University Press, 1951), 2:1008; Charles Lee and George Washington (letter to Joseph Reed, January 31, 1776), quoted in William H. Nelson, *The American Tory* (Boston: Beacon Press, 1964), 120.

52 Paine, *Common Sense*, in *Collected Writings*, 9, 11, 12.

53 On the ancient English or Cokean constitution, see Colbourn, *Lamp of Experience*, and Mayer, *Constitutional Thought of Thomas Jefferson*.

54 Paine, *Common Sense*, in *Collected Writings*, 16, 17, 19, 16.

55 Paine, *Common Sense*, in *Collected Writings*, 47–48.

56 Paine, *Common Sense*, in *Collected Writings*, 21, 27, 43.

57 Paine, *Common Sense*, in *Collected Writings*, 21, 27, 43, 52 (emphasis added).

58 See John Adams to Abigail Adams, March 19, 1776, in *Adams Family Correspondence*, 1:363.

CHAPTER 11

1 Adams to Mary Palmer, July 5, 1776, *Adams Family Correspondence*, 2:34.

2 William Whipple to John Langdon, July 16, 1776, *American Archives*, 5th ser., 1:368.

3 Paine, *Letter to the Abbé Raynal*, in *Life and Works of Paine*, 4:134.

4 See, e.g., Joseph Galloway to Richard Jackson, August 10, 1774, or John Dickinson, *Arguments Against the Independence of the Colonies…*, in *Colonies to Nation*, 239–240, 292–296.

5 Adams to H. Niles, February 13, 1818, *Works of Adams*, 10:282–83.

6 The social, political, and economic revolution that followed the moral revolution that occurred in the American colonies during the years of the imperial crisis is best captured in Wood, *The Radicalism of the American Revolution*.

7 Hart, *Liberty Described and Recommended*, in *American Political Writing during the Founding Era*, 1:306; *Boston Gazette*, September 14, 1767.

8 Samuel Williams, *The Natural and Civil History of Vermont*, 1:7.

9 Wells, *A Few Political Reflections Submitted to the Consideration of the British Colonies*, 10, 30; Clark, *Sermon Preached Before His Excellency John Hancock*, 43; John Hurt, *The Love of Country: A Sermon Preached Before the Virginia Troops in New-Jersey* (Philadelphia: Styner and Cist, 1777), 16.

10 Phillips Payson, "A Sermon" (1778), *American Political Writing during the Founding Era*, 1:525.

11 Samuel Williams, *Natural and Civil History of Vermont*, 1:6–7; Petition to the King (October 1774), in *Journals of the Continental Congress, 1774–1789*, ed. Worthington C. Ford (Washington, DC: US Government Printing Office), 1:118; Tucker, *Sermon Preached at Cambridge*, 5–6.

12 Massachusettensis [pseud.], *Massachusetts Spy*, December 12, 1771; Howard, "A Sermon Preached to the Ancient and Honorable Artillery Company in Boston," *American Political Writing during the Founding Era*, 1:197.

13 Quincy, *Observations on the Act of Parliament Commonly Called the Boston Port-Bill*, 31; Clark, *Sermon Preached Before His Excellency John Hancock*, 32.

14 See The Centinel [pseud.], *Massachusetts Spy*, May 2, 1771; May 30, 1771; June 20, 1771; September 12, 1771; March 26, 1772; September 26, 1771.

15 A Freeman [pseud.], untitled, July 23, 1774, *American Archives*, 4th ser., 1:608; Vindex [Samuel Adams], *Boston Gazette*, January 21, 1771, quoted in Maier, *From Resistance to Revolution*, 224.

16 Adams, "Dissertation on the Canon and Feudal Law," *Revolutionary Writings of Adams*, 20; Adams, "Governor Winthrop to Governor Bradford," February 9, 1767, *Papers of Adams*, 1:200–1.

17 Adams, Notes for an Oration at Braintree (1772), *Diary and Autobiography*, 2:56–61; John Adams to Abigail Adams, July 7, 1775, *Adams Family Correspondence*, 1:241; Novanglus [Adams], I, January 23, 1775, *Papers of Adams*, 2:229; Novanglus [Adams], III, February 6, 1775, *Papers of Adams*, 2:245. This analysis of Adams's views on the relationship between virtue and freedom is drawn from Thompson, *John Adams and the Spirit of Liberty*, 44–65.

18 Novanglus [Adams], I, January 23, 1775, *Papers of Adams*, 2:230.

19 Adams, on Independence of the Judges (1773–1774), *Diary and Autobiography*, 3:301.

20 Dickinson, *Letters from a Farmer in Pennsylvania*, in *Political Writings of Dickinson*, 388, 346–48, 402.

21 Dickinson, *Letters from a Farmer in Pennsylvania*, in *Political Writings of Dickinson*, 386–90. Machiavelli's chapter in the *Discourses on Livy* (bk. 3, chap. 1) is titled "To Ensure a Long Existence to Religious Sects or Republics, It Is Necessary Frequently to Bring Them Back to Their Original Principles."

22 Dickinson, *Letters from a Farmer in Pennsylvania*, in *Political Writings of Dickinson*, 355–56, 396–97, 382–83. Alexander Hamilton made a similar kind of argument: "How ridiculous then is it to affirm, that we are quarrelling for the trifling sum of three pence a pound on tea; when it is evidently the principle against which we contend." See Hamilton, "A Full Vindication of the Measures of Congress...," December 15, 1774, in *Papers of Hamilton*, 1:46, 48. Likewise, see the view of James Madison: "The people of the U.S. owe their independence & their liberty, to the wisdom of descrying in the minute tax of 3 pence on tea, the magnitude of the evil comprized in the precedent." Quoted in Elizabeth Fleet, ed., "Madison's 'Detached Memoranda,'" *William and Mary Quarterly* 3, no. 4 (1946): 557.

23 Dickinson, *Letters from a Farmer in Pennsylvania*, in *Political Writings of Dickinson*, 356–57; Madison, "Address of the General Assembly to the People of the Commonwealth of Virginia," in *The Writings of James Madison*, ed. Gaillard Hunt (New York: Putnam, 1906), 6:336.

24 Burke, *Speech on Moving His Resolutions for Conciliation with the Colonies* (March 22, 1775), in *Select Works of Edmund Burke*, 1:237–43.

25 Paine, *The American Crisis*, IV (September 12, 1777), in *Life and Works of Paine*, 2:363; Hurt, *Love of Country*, 15–16 (emphasis added).

26 Abraham Clark to Elias Dayton, July 14, 1776, in *Letters of Members of the Continental Congress*, ed. Edmund C. Burnett (Washington, DC: Carnegie Institution, 1923), 2:10; Jonas Clark, *Sermon Preached Before His Excellency John Hancock*, 43; Washington, quoted in David McCullough, *1776* (New York: Simon and Schuster, 2005), 273.

27 John Hancock to Certain States, July 6, 1776, in *Letters of Delegates to Congress, 1774–1789*, ed. Paul H. Smith et al., vol. 4, *May 16–August 15, 1776* (Washington, DC: Library of Congress, 1979), 396.

28 On the reception of the Declaration around the United States, see John Hazelton, *The Declaration of Independence: Its History* (1906; repr., New York: Da Capo, 1970); Frank Donovan, *Mr. Jefferson's Declaration: The Story Behind the Declaration of Independence* (New York: Dodd, Mead, 1968); David Freeman Hawke, *Honorable Treason: The Declaration of Independence and the Men Who Signed It* (New York: Viking, 1976); and Maier, *American Scripture: Making the Declaration of Independence*.

29 Scholars working on developing a new moral history of the American Revolution must examine not only the moral, constitutional, and political writings of the Revolution's greatest thinkers, such as James Otis, Richard Bland, Daniel Dulany, John Dickinson, James Wilson, Thomas Jefferson, John Adams, and Thomas Paine, but they must also connect ideas to the actions of leaders such as George Washington and the thousands of men who fought with Washington. To that end, they should start with the letters, diaries, and newspaper accounts of the soldiers of the Continental Army. See, e.g.: George F. Scheer and Hugh F. Rankin, eds., *Rebels and Redcoats: The American Revolution Through the Eyes of Those Who Fought and Lived It* (1957; repr., New York: Da Capo, 1987); and Frank Moore, comp., *The Diary of the American Revolution, 1775–1781*, ed. John Anthony Scott (New York: Washington Square Press, 1967).

30 Joseph Barton to Henry Wisner, July 9, 1776, *American Archives*, 5th ser., 1:139; Joseph Elmer, quoted in *Diary of the American Revolution*, 279–80; Tristram Dalton to Elbridge Gerry, July 19, 1776, in *American Archives*, 5th ser., 1:461; Rush to Charles Lee, July 23, 1776, in *Letters of Delegates to Congress*, 4:527–28.

31 Hancock to George Washington, July 6, 1776, in *The Papers of George Washington: The Revolutionary War Series*, ed. Philander D. Chase (Charlottesville: University Press of Virginia, 1988), 5:219–21, available at *Founders Online*, National Archives, https://founders.archives.gov/documents/Washington/03-05-02-0153. (Emphasis added.)

32 Washington, General Orders, July 9, 1776, in *Papers of Washington: Revolutionary War Series*, 5:246, available at *Founders Online*, National Archives, https://founders.archives.gov/?q=Volume%3AWashington-03-05&s=1511311112&r=176.

33 James Thacher, *The American Revolution, from the Commencement to the Disbanding of the American Army, Given in the Form of a Daily Journal* (Cincinnati: Barnitz, 1856), 46–47; Ezra Stiles, *The United States Elevated to Glory and Honor: A Sermon Preached…May 8th, 1783* (New Haven, CT: Thomas and Samuel Green, 1783), 46.

34 Samuel Adams to Richard Henry Lee, July 15, 1776, and Samuel Adams to James Warren, July 16, 1776, in *Writings of Samuel Adams*, 3:297–98, 299; Samuel Adams, "Speech on the Declaration of Independence" (August 1, 1776), Samuel Adams Heritage Society, http://www.samuel-adams-heritage.com/documents/speech-about-declaration-of-independence.html; Thacher, *The American Revolution from the Commencement to the Disbanding of the American Army*, 46–47; David Ramsay, *The History of the American Revolution*, ed. Lester H. Cohen (Philadelphia: R. Aitken, 1789; repr., Indianapolis, IN: Liberty Fund, 1990), 1:322.

35 "Speech of a Farmer to an Assembly of His Neighbours of Philadelphia County," in *American Archives*, 4th ser., 4:1525–26.

36 Samuel Adams, "Candidus," *Boston Gazette*, October 14, 1771, *Writings of Samuel Adams*, 2:251.

37 Nathanael Greene to Samuel Ward, July 14, 1775, in *The Papers of General Nathanael Greene*, ed. Richard K. Showman et al. (Chapel Hill: University of North Carolina Press, 1976), 1:99.

38 Washington, General Orders, August 23, 1776, in *Papers of George Washington: Revolutionary War Series*, 6:109–110, available at *Founders Online*, National Archives, http://founders.archives.gov/documents/Washington/03-06-02-0100.

39 Major General Nathanael Greene to George Washington, November 15, 1776, in *Papers of George Washington: Revolutionary War Series*, 7:162, available at *Founders Online*, National Archives, http://founders.archives.gov/documents/Washington/03-07-02-0117. For Magaw's reply, see n1.

40 Charles Willson Peale, *The Autobiography of Charles Willson Peale*, in *The Selected Papers of Charles Willson Peale and His Family*, ed. Lillian B. Miller et al. (New Haven, CT: Yale University Press, 2000), 5:50; William Heath, *Heath's Memoirs of the American War* (New York: A. Wessels, 1904) 107.

41 Paine, *The American Crisis*, I (December 23, 1776), in *Life and Works of Paine*, 2:263.

42 Drayton, Charge to the Grand Jury of Charleston, *American Archives*, 5th ser., 2:1048.

43 Paine, *Letter to the Abbé Raynal*, in *Life and Works of Paine*, 4:134.

44 Adams to Elbridge Gerry, December 6, 1777, *Papers of Adams*, 5:345–47; Continental Congress, Declaration of the Causes and Necessity of Taking Up Arms, *Colonies to Nation*, 258.

45 Henry Knox to John Adams, May 16, 1776, *Papers of Adams*, 4:190. (Emphasis added.)

46 Joseph Reed to Esther Reed, September 2, 1776, quoted in McCullough, *1776*, 201.

47 John Adams to Moses Gill, June 10, 1775, *Papers of Adams*, 3:21; Adams to Horatio Gates, March 23, 1776, *Papers of Adams*, 4:58–60; Adams to Moses Gill, June 10, 1775, *Papers of Adams*, 3:21; Novanglus [Adams], *Papers of Adams*, 2:293.

48 John Adams to Abigail Adams, May 2, 1775, *Adams Family Correspondence*, 1:192.

49 Henry Knox to Lucy Knox, July 11, 1776, quoted in McCullough, *1776*, 134–35.

50 John Adams to Abigail Adams, July 3, 1776, *Adams Family Correspondence*, 2:31.

CONCLUSION

1 J. Hector St. John de Crèvecoeur, *Letters from an American Farmer, and, Sketches of Eighteenth-Century America* (New York: Penguin, 1981), 70.

2 For an examination of the new society created by the American Revolution, see Wood, *The Radicalism of the American Revolution*.

3 John Taylor, *An Inquiry into the Principles and Policy of the Government of the United States* (1814), Online Library of Liberty, Liberty Fund, http://oll.libertyfund.org/titles/taylor-an-inquiry-into-the-principles-and-policy-of-the-government-of-the-united-states; Tocqueville, *Democracy in America*, 359.

4 Jefferson to Joseph Cabell, February 2, 1816; Tocqueville, *Democracy in America*, 371; Taylor, *An Inquiry into the Principles and Policy of the Government of the United States*.

5 Jefferson to Joseph Cabell, February 2, 1816; Madison, *Federalist* No. 48, 332; Jefferson to Colonel Carrington, May 27, 1788.

6 Jefferson, "The Kentucky Resolutions," *Portable Jefferson*, 288.

7 Hamilton, *Federalist* No. 23, 146–47; Jefferson, First Inaugural Address, *Portable Thomas Jefferson*, 293; Madison, "Property," *Mind of the Founder*, 244.

8 Jefferson, "A Bill for Establishing Religious Freedom" (1777), *Portable Thomas Jefferson*, 252.

9 William Leggett, "True Functions of Government," in *Democratick Editorials: Essays in Jacksonian Political Economy*, ed. Lawrence H. White (Indianapolis, IN: Liberty Press, 1984), 3–4. On Leggett, see Marvin Meyers, *The Jacksonian Persuasion: Politics and Belief* (Stanford, CA: Stanford University Press, 1957), 185–205. On the Locofocos, see Arthur M. Schlesinger Jr., *The Age of Jackson* (Boston: Little, Brown, 1945), 190–209.

10 John L. O'Sullivan, "The Democratic Principle," published in *The United States Magazine and Democratic Review*, quoted in Arieli, *Individualism and Nationalism in American Ideology*, 177–78. (Emphasis added.)

11 Leggett, "The Legislation of Congress," *Democratick Editorials*, 20. On the role of government in nineteenth-century America, see Arthur A. Ekirch Jr., *The Decline of American Liberalism* (New York: Longmans, Green, 1955), esp. chap. 6; Robert H. Wiebe, *Self-Rule: A Cultural History of American Democracy* (Chicago: University of Chicago Press, 1995); and Bernard W. Wishy, *Goodbye, Machiavelli: Government and American Life* (Baton Rouge: Louisiana State University Press, 1995).

12 William Sampson, *Memoirs of William Sampson: An Irish Exile* (London, 1832), 282; Leggett, "The Reserved Rights of the People," *Democratick Editorials*, 8; Warren, quoted in Arieli, *Individualism and Nationalism in American Ideology*, 287.

13 Tocqueville, *Democracy in America*, 288.

14 Tocqueville, *Democracy in America*, 290–91.

15 On the Americans' westward movement, see Malcolm J. Rohrbough, *The Trans-Appalachian Frontier: People, Societies, and Institutions, 1775–1850* (New York: Oxford University Press, 1978).

16 Tocqueville, *Democracy in America*, 387, 512.

17 George Flower, *History of the English Settlement in Edwards County, Illinois* (Chicago: Fergus Printing Co., 1882), 29.

18 For a particularly unimpressive and dogmatic critique of the idea of the self-made man, see Carol Nackenoff, *The Fictional Republic: Horatio Alger and American Political Discourse* (New York: Oxford University Press, 1994).

19 Frederick Douglass, "Self-Made Men," in *Great Speeches by Frederick Douglass*, ed. James Daley (Mineola, NY: Dover, 2013), 128, 134.

20 Charles Nisbet, quoted in Samuel Miller, *Memoir of the Rev. Charles Nisbet, D.D., Late President of Dickinson College, Carlisle* (New York: Carter, 1840), 249, 167.

21 Tocqueville, *Democracy in America*, 489.

EPILOGUE

1 Lincoln, "Speech at Chicago, Illinois" (July 10, 1858), *Collected Works of Lincoln*, 2:499–500.

2 Lincoln, "Speech on the Dred Scott Decision" (June 26, 1857), *Collected Works of Lincoln*, 2:405–6.

3 Douglass, "What to the Slave Is the 4th of July?" (July 5, 1852), *Great Speeches by Frederick Douglass*, 30.

4 Lincoln to Henry L. Pierce, April 6, 1859, *Abraham Lincoln: His Speeches and Writings*, 488–89.

5 Cong. Globe, 33d Cong., 1st Sess., appendix (1854), 310. Pettit's speech was partly responsible for awakening Abraham Lincoln from his political slumbers. See Lincoln, "Speech at Peoria" (1854), "Fragment: Notes for Speeches" (1858), "Seventh and Last Debate with Stephen A. Douglas at Alton, Illinois" (1858), *Collected Works of Lincoln*, 2:275, 3:205, 3:301–2.

6 Rufus Choate to E. W. Farley, August 9, 1856, in *The Works of Rufus Choate, with a Memoir of His Life*, ed. Samuel Gilman Brown (Boston: Little, Brown, 1862), 1:215.

7 Lincoln, "Speech at Peoria, Illinois," *Collected Works of Lincoln*, 2:265–66.

8 On proslavery thought, see Drew Gilpin Faust, *A Sacred Circle: The Dilemma of the Intellectual in the Old South, 1840–1860* (Philadelphia: University of Pennsylvania Press, 1977). On the abolitionist movement, see Thompson, *Antislavery Political Writings, 1833–1860*.

9 For the influence of Hegel's thought on the antebellum Southern thinkers, see Michael O'Brien, *Conjectures of Order: Intellectual Life and the American South, 1810–1860*, 2 vols. (Chapel Hill: University of North Carolina Press, 2004), and *Intellectual Life and the American South, 1810–1860: An Abridged Edition of Conjectures of Order* (Chapel Hill, NC: University of North Carolina Press, 2010); and Elizabeth Fox-Genovese and Eugene D. Genovese, *The Mind of the Master Class: History and Faith in the Southern Slaveholders' Worldview* (Cambridge: Cambridge University Press, 2005).

10 Jesse Burton Harrison, "English Civilization," *Southern Review* 8 (February 1832): 463. See O'Brien, *Intellectual Life and the American South*, 272–73.

11 James Warley Miles, *God in History: A Discourse* (Charleston, SC: Steam-Power Press, 1863), 7, 8, 10, 14, 19, 24.

12 Cong. Globe, 36th Cong., 1st Sess., appendix (1860), 113–17. Lamar was quoting from Georg Wilhelm Friedrich Hegel, *The Philosophy of History*, trans. J. Sibree (New York: Dover, 1956), 98–99.

13 See Francis Fukuyama, *The End of History and the Last Man* (New York: Free Press, 1992).

14 William Harper, "Slavery in the Light of Social Ethics," in *Cotton Is King, and Pro-Slavery Arguments*, ed. E. N. Elliott (Augusta, GA: Pritchard, Abbott and Loomis, 1860), 558–59; Harper, "Memoir on Slavery," in *The Ideology of Slavery: Proslavery Thought in the Antebellum South, 1830–1860*, ed. Drew Gilpin Faust (Baton Rouge: Louisiana State University Press, 1981), 83.

15 Harper, "Memoir on Slavery," 81, 84–85, 91, 134.

16 James Henry Hammond, "Letter to an English Abolitionist," in *The Ideology of Slavery: Proslavery Thought in the Antebellum South, 1830–1860*, ed. Drew Gilpin Faust (Baton Rouge: Louisiana State University Press, 1981), 172–73.

17 James Henry Hammond, "Laws of Nature—Natural Rights—Slavery" (manuscript, January 26, 1847), Tucker-Coleman Papers, Special Collections Research Center, Swem Library, College of William and Mary.

18 On the "cunning of reason," see Hegel, *The Philosophy of History*, 33, and Hegel, *The Science of Logic*, trans. George di Giovanni (Cambridge: Cambridge University Press, 2015), 633.

19 John C. Calhoun, "Speech on the Oregon Bill" and "Speech on the Reception of the Abolition Petitions," in *Union and Liberty: The Political Philosophy of John C. Calhoun*, ed. Ross M. Lence (Indianapolis, IN: Liberty Fund, 1992), 565–70, 474.

20 George Fitzhugh, "False Philosophy of the Age," in *Cannibals All! or, Slaves without Masters*, ed. C. Vann Woodward (Cambridge, MA: Belknap Press of Harvard University Press, 1960), 54; Fitzhugh, "Southern Thought," in *The Ideology of Slavery: Proslavery Thought in the Antebellum South, 1830–1860*, ed. Drew Gilpin Faust (Baton Rouge: Louisiana State University Press, 1981), 279.

21 Fitzhugh, "The Reformation—The Right of Private Judgment," in *Cannibals All!*, 135; Fitzhugh, "Declaration of Independence and Virginia Bill of Rights," in *Sociology for the South, or the Failure of Free Society* (Richmond, VA: A. Morris, 1854), 175, 179; Fitzhugh, "Southern Thought," 292.

22 Albert Taylor Bledsoe, *Liberty and Slavery: or, Slavery in the Light of Moral and Political Philosophy*, in *Cotton Is King, and Pro-Slavery Arguments*, ed. E. N. Elliott (Augusta, GA: Pritchard, Abbott and Loomis, 1860), 286–88.

23 Harper, "Memoir on Slavery," 93.

24 Fitzhugh, "Centralization and Socialism," *De Bow's Review* (June 1856): 692–94.

25 Fitzhugh, "Southern Thought," 294; Nathaniel Beverley Tucker, *A Series of Lectures on the Science of Government, Intended to Prepare the Student for the Study of the Constitution of the United States* (Philadelphia: Carey and Hart, 1845), 79, 32, 36.

26 Fitzhugh, "Free Trade," *Sociology for the South*, 25.

27 Fitzhugh, "Free Trade" and "Slavery Justified," *Sociology for the South*, 25, 245.

28 Fitzhugh, "Free Trade," "Failure of Free Society and Rise of Socialism," and "Slavery Justified," *Sociology for the South*, 25–26, 72, 245.

29 Edmund Ruffin, *The Political Economy of Slavery; or, The Institution Considered in Regard to Its Influence on Public Wealth and the General Welfare* (Washington, DC: Lemuel Towers, 1857), 9.

30 Leo Strauss, *Natural Right and History* (Chicago: University of Chicago Press, 1953), 2.

31 Northern postbellum intellectuals were, like their Southern antebellum counterparts, deeply influenced by Hegel's philosophy of history. See John Kaag and Kipton E. Jensen, "The American Reception of Hegel (1830–1930)," in *The Oxford Handbook of Hegel*, ed. Dean Moyar (Oxford: Oxford University Press, 2017), 670–96. See also William Goetzmann, ed., *The American Hegelians: An Intellectual Episode in the History of Western America* (New York: Knopf, 1973).

32 Richard T. Ely, quoted in Arthur A. Ekirch, Jr., *Progressivism in America: A*

Study of the Era from Theodore Roosevelt to Woodrow Wilson (New York: New Viewpoints, 1974), 25.

33 See Benjamin Rand, "Philosophical Instruction in Harvard University from 1636 to 1906, II," *Harvard Graduates' Magazine* 37 (December 1928), 188–200, and "Philosophical Instruction in Harvard University from 1636 to 1906, III," *Harvard Graduates' Magazine* 37 (March 1929), 296–311.

34 See James T. Kloppenberg, *Uncertain Victory: Social Democracy and Progressivism in European and American Thought, 1870–1920* (Oxford: Oxford University Press, 1986); John Patrick Diggins, *The Promise of Pragmatism: Modernism and the Crisis of Knowledge and Authority* (Chicago: University of Chicago Press, 1994); and Louis Menand, *The Metaphysical Club: A Story of Ideas in America* (New York: Farrar, Straus, and Giroux, 2001).

35 William James, "Pragmatism's Conception of Truth" and "What Pragmatism Means," in *Essays in Pragmatism*, ed. Alburey Castell (New York: Hafner, 1948), 159–76, 147–53. On James's philosophy, see Paul Jerome Croce, *Science and Religion in the Era of William James*, vol. 1, *Eclipse of Certainty, 1820–1880* (Chapel Hill: University of North Carolina Press, 1995).

36 John Dewey, "The Problem of Truth," in *John Dewey: The Political Writings*, ed. Debra Morris and Ian Shapiro (Indianapolis, IN: Hackett, 1993), 10, 12, 14, 16, 17. On Dewey's philosophy, see Robert B. Westbrook, *John Dewey and American Democracy* (Ithaca, NY: Cornell University Press, 1991); and Alan Ryan, *John Dewey and the High Tide of American Liberalism* (New York: Norton, 1997).

37 Dewey, "The Future of Liberalism," in *The Later Works, 1925–1953*, vol. 11: *1935–1937*, ed. Jo Ann Boydston (Carbondale: Southern Illinois University Press, 1987), 290–91.

38 Dewey, *Liberalism and Social Action* (1935; repr., Amherst, NY: Prometheus Books, 2000), 28.

39 On the new liberalism, see John Chamberlain, *Farewell to Reform: The Rise, Life and Decay of the Progressive Mind in America* (Chicago: Quadrangle Books, 1932); Richard Hofstadter, *Social Darwinism in American Thought* (Boston: Beacon Press, 1955); Charles Forcey, *The Crossroads of Liberalism: Croly, Weyl, Lippmann, and the Progressive Era, 1900–1925* (Oxford: Oxford University Press, 1961); and Ekirch, *Progressivism in America.*

40 Woodrow Wilson, "The Author and Signers of the Declaration," *North American Review* 186 (Sept. 1907): 22–33.

41 Wilson, "The Author and Signers of the Declaration," 22–33. On Wilson's political thought, see Ronald J. Pestritto, *Woodrow Wilson and the Roots of Modern Liberalism* (Lanham, MD: Rowman and Littlefield, 2005).

42 Wilson, "Address to the Jefferson Club of Los Angeles," in *The Papers of Woodrow Wilson*, ed. Arthur Link, vol. 23, *1911–1912* (Princeton, NJ: Princeton University Press, 1977), 33–34.

43 Herbert Croly, *The Promise of American Life* (1909; repr., New York: Dutton, 1963), 152.

44 Croly, *Promise of American Life*, 190, 209, 438–39, 418, 282–83.

45 See Morton G. White, *Social Thought in America: The Revolt Against Formalism* (Boston: Beacon Press, 1949).

46 Becker, *Declaration of Independence*, 277 (emphasis added).

47 Becker, *Declaration of Independence*, 277, 278.

48 Jeremy Bentham, *Anarchical Fallacies; Being an Examination of the Declarations*

of Rights Issued During the French Revolution, in *The Works of Jeremy Bentham* (Edinburgh: William Tate, 1843), 2:501.

49 Becker, *Declaration of Independence*, 265. For a similar critique of Becker, see Jaffa, *A New Birth of Freedom*, 83–107.

50 Amy B. Wang, "'Post-Truth' Named 2016 Word of the Year by Oxford Dictionaries," *Washington Post,* November 16, 2016, https://www.washingtonpost.com/news/the-fix/wp/2016/11/16/post-truth-named-2016-word-of-the-year-by-oxford-dictionaries/?utm_term=.d556b4eb9a6c.

51 Lincoln, "Speech on the Dred Scott Decision" (June 26, 1857), *Collected Works of Lincoln*, 2:407, 406.

52 Lincoln, "Speech on the Dred Scott Decision," *Collected Works of Lincoln*, 2:407.

53 Lincoln to Henry L. Pierce, & others, April 6, 1859, *Collected Works of Lincoln*, 3:375.

54 Lincoln to Henry L. Pierce, & others, April 6, 1859, *Collected Works of Lincoln*, 3:375–76.

55 Lincoln, "Speech at Chicago, Illinois" (October 27, 1854), *Collected Works of Lincoln*, 2:283–84.

56 Becker, *The Declaration of Independence* (new ed., New York: Vintage, 1941), xviii–ix.

57 Robert Frost, "The Black Cottage," available at Bartleby.com, https://www.bartleby.com/118/7.html.

58 Lydia Maria Child, *The Patriarchal Institution, as Described by Members of Its Own Family*, in *Antislavery Political Writings, 1833–1860*, 23.

INDEX